光棍危机

亚洲
男性人口过剩的
安全启示

Bare Branches
The Security Implication of
Asia's Surplus Male Population

[美]瓦莱丽·M. 赫德森
（Valerie M. Hudson）
[英]安德莉亚·M. 邓波尔
（Andrea M. den Boer）著

邱彰 译
贾宇琰 刘哲 译校

中央编译出版社
CCTP Central Compilation & Translation Press

目 录

第一章 环境与人类安全的性别维度 ········· 1
    一、方法学 ································· 5
    二、后代性别选择的产生 ··················· 6
    三、后代性别选择的持续 ··················· 12
    四、结论 ································· 20
    五、本书的架构 ··························· 20

第二章 历史上的后代性别选择——从杀婴、堕胎，
      到"消失的女性" ··················· 22
    一、与性别无关的后代选择行为 ············· 22
    二、后代性别选择 ························· 28
    三、如何判断性别比例是否正常 ············· 29
    四、后代性别选择概况 ····················· 31
    五、当代不同文化中的后代性别选择 ········· 46
    六、亚洲人重男轻女 ······················· 49
    七、消失的亚洲女性 ······················· 58
    八、结论 ································· 64

第三章 印度的"消失的女性" ··············· 65
    一、历史背景 ····························· 66
    二、宗教 ································· 68

三、社会制度 …………………………………………… 69
　　四、女性的地位 ………………………………………… 71
　　五、杀女婴的开始 ……………………………………… 74
　　六、公开谴责并试图终止杀女婴 ……………………… 75
　　七、目前的情况 ………………………………………… 88
　　八、过去、现在和未来 ………………………………… 122
　　九、结论 ………………………………………………… 126
第四章　中国的"消失的女性" ……………………………… 128
　　一、中国和它的人民 …………………………………… 129
　　二、中国的女性 ………………………………………… 130
　　三、杀婴的历史及后代性别选择 ……………………… 134
　　四、20世纪的变化 ……………………………………… 142
　　五、独生子女政策及重男轻女 ………………………… 146
　　六、上升的出生人口性别比 …………………………… 149
　　七、性别比例不断上升的原因 ………………………… 159
　　八、政府关注过高的性别比例 ………………………… 165
　　九、婴儿的死亡率 ……………………………………… 166
　　十、"消失的女性"及中国的单身汉 ………………… 170
　　十一、结论 ……………………………………………… 175
第五章　高性别比例社会中的光棍：理论和案例 ………… 177
　　一、光棍的特征 ………………………………………… 178
　　二、光棍的行为倾向 …………………………………… 182
　　三、社会性别比例居高的后果 ………………………… 190
　　四、高性别比例对女性的影响 ………………………… 192
　　五、政府的观点 ………………………………………… 196
　　六、其他历史案例 ……………………………………… 209
　　七、结论 ………………………………………………… 214

第六章　21世纪的光棍——政策建议 ················· 215
　一、现代光棍的特征与行为分析 ····················· 215
　二、政府面对光棍问题的对策 ······················· 227
　三、结论 ······································· 241
第七章　结论：高性别比例社会的安全考虑 ············· 244
　一、大预测 ····································· 246
　二、结论 ······································· 247
附　表 ··· 249
参考文献 ······································· 263

第一章　环境与人类安全的性别维度

生物学家、社会学家以及人类学家们长久以来一致认为稀缺性——无论是自然产生还是人为制造的——是社会竞争与冲突的主要诱因。所谓资源稀缺，可以是具体的，如牛群、水源；也可以是抽象的，如社会地位和族群身份。

几十年来，很少有国际关系方面的研究注意到这种稀缺性，或者说是竞争与冲突的生物学根源，人们更多关注冷战背后的意识形态问题。冷战的结束给了人们重新审视这一问题的机会，学者们开始更为全面地思考稀缺性与不平等性在制造国内、国际冲突中的作用。应运而生的是安全研究领域的新分支：环境安全。

安全研究领域的另一个新兴分支是人类安全，在这当中有更为详尽的关于个人安全如何与国家安全有着千丝万缕联系的讨论。[1] 其中学者认为，安全是从下至上、从内而外、个人到个人、家庭到家庭、群体到群体、社区到社区逐层建立。除了一般意义上的外部威胁评估，国家安全还派生于这些微观层面的安全。因此，国家安全有两个参照指标，即国家整体层面的安全和个人层面的安全。两者其一发生

---

[1] 关于这个分支领域的文献概览，参见 Andrew Mack, "The Security Report Project Background Paper," Human Security Center, University of British Columbia, Vancouver, Canada, 2003, http://www.humansecuritybulletin.info/archive/en_vli2。

变动，势必引起另一方面的深刻变动。我们可以直观感受国家整体安全如何影响个人安全，关于个人安全如何反作用于国家整体安全，学者们的研究才刚刚起步。更进一步而言，环境安全分支与人类安全分支之间可能存在的微妙关系也颇为值得玩味。对人类安全学者而言，稀缺性和不平等性的重要性，仅次于国家安全。

我们渐渐可以在环境安全领域较为近期的文献中发现这种微妙的关系。国际关系专家逐渐增加了对民族主义、身份认定和移民等要素的关注度，他们开始用这些要素来解释后冷战时期的世界纷争。1994年，安全学者、环境安全分支的奠基人托马斯·荷姆-狄克森（Thomas Homer-Dixon）指出："这种资源的稀少，是过去以来发展中国家之间暴力冲突的触媒，也是未来即将爆发的更大冲突的前兆。"① 包括荷姆-狄克森在内的很多学者预测，这种暴力活动的增多不仅会引发国内战争，还会导致国际争端。在环境安全领域还有一个重要的关联性问题，那就是稀缺性和环境压力之间的关系。为了获得这种稀缺资源，大量的人口将在国界间移动，势必引起不同族群之间的纷争。② 自从20世纪90年代开始，环境安全领域的学者们大量

---

① Thomas F. Homer-Dixon, "Environmental Scarcities and Violent Conflict: Evidence from Cases," *International Security*, Vol. 19, No. 1 (Summer 1994), p. 5.

② See, for example, Astri Suhrke, "Pressure Points: Environmental Degradation, Migration, and Conflict," Occasional Paper No. 3 (Toronto: Project on Environmental Change and Acute Conflict, University of Toronto and the American Academy of Arts and Sciences, March 1993); Alex de Sherbinin, "World Population Growth and U. S. National Security," *Environmental Change and Security Project Report*, No. 1 (Spring 1995), pp. 24 – 29. Sanjoy Hazarika, "Bangladesh and Assam: Land Pressures, Migration, and Ethnic Conflict," Occasional Paper No. 3 (Toronto: Project on Environmental Change and Acute Conflict, University of Toronto and the American Academy of Arts and Sciences, March 1993); Thomas F. Homer-Dixon, *Environmental Scarcity and Global Security* (New York: Foreign Policy Association, 1993); and Jeffrey Boutwell and Thomas F. Homer-Dixon, "Environmental Change, Global Security, and U. S. Policy," in Charles F. Hermann, ed., *American Defense Annual* (New York: Lexington, 1994), pp. 201 – 224.

阐述了由于上述原因而产生的国内和国际争端的案例。近来，其他领域的研究也佐证了环境安全专家们的论证。① 因此，环境安全这一新兴分支逐渐被国际安全研究领域所接受。②

我们的研究主要关注环境安全和人类安全的关联性。在本书中，我们认为资源稀缺性和获得这些稀缺资源的不平等性是不同层面各种纷争的最关键的原因。然而，与其他环境安全研究所关注的重点不同，我们不讨论臭氧层空洞和森林退化，我们致力于研究一个对人类安全进程影响更为显著的变量，这个变量至今都没有受到环境安全学者们的重视，

---

① Mark Levy, "Global Environmental Degradation: National Security and U. S. Foreign Policy," Working Paper No. 9 (Cambridge, Mass.: Project on the Changing Security Environment and American National Interests, John M. Olin Institute for Strategic Studies, Harvard University, November 1994); Joan M. Nelson, "Migrants, Urban Poverty, and Instability in Developing Nations," Occasional Papers in International Affairs No. 22 (Cambridge, Mass: Center for International Affairs, Harvard University, September 1969); A. S. Oberai, *Population Growth, Employment, and Poverty in Third World Mega-Cities* (New York: St. Martin's, 1993); John Walton and David Seddon, *Free Markets and Food Riots: The Politics of Global Adjustment* (Cambridge, Mass.: Blackwell, 1994); Hans-Georg Bohle, Thomas E. Downing, and Michael J. Watts, "Climate Change and Social Vulnerability: Towards a Sociology and Geography of Food Security," *Global Environmental Change*, Vol. 4, No. 1 (March 1994), pp. 37 – 48; Mark Duffields, "The Political Economy of Internal War: Asset Transfer, Complex Emergencies, and International Aid," in Joanna Macrae and Anthony Zwi, eds., *War and Hunger: Rethinking International Responses to Complex Emergencies* (London: Zed, 1994), pp. 50 – 69; Peter H. Gleick, "Water and Conflict: Fresh Water Resources and International Security," *International Security*, Vol. 18, No. 1 (Summer 1993), pp. 79 – 112; Ted Rober Gurr, "On the Political Consequences of Scarcity and Economic Decline," *International Studies Quarterly*, Vol. 29, No. 1 (March 1985), pp. 51 – 75; Shaukat Hassan, *Environmental Issues and Security in South Asia*, Adelphi Papers No. 262 (London: Brassey's 1991); Robert D. Kaplan, "The Coming Anarchy," *Atlantic Monthly*, Vol. 272, No. 2 (February 1994), pp. 44 – 81; Michael Renner, *National Security: The Economic and Environmental Dimensions*, Worldwatch Paper No. 89 (Washington, D. C.: Worldwatch Institue, 1989); and Arthur H. Westing, ed., *Global Resources and International Conflict: Environmental Factors in Strategic Policy and Action* (Oxford: Oxford University Press, 1986).

② Steven Greenhouse, "The Greening of U. S. Diplomacy," *New York Times*, October 9, 1995, p. A6.

而其对稀缺性和资源获取的不平等性的贡献是那样显著，这个变量就是，严重的性别不平等。这种严重的性别不平等的标志就是单纯因为性别而对女性实施的暴力。如果避而不谈"针对女性的暴力"和"社会内部乃至社会之间的暴力"之间的关系，环境安全研究就会大为失色。本研究将会揭开环境安全和人类安全研究中交叉领域的冰山一角。

目前几乎每个社会对妇女都有某种程度的歧视，例如她们的地位较低，受的教育较少，营养和医疗较为不足，不能够独自作出重要的决定，等等，她们在政治、法律、社会、经济上的权利都不如男性。然而，不是所有的社会都存在"严重的"性别不平等。本书主要探讨"严重的"性别不平等。何谓"严重的"性别不平等呢？就是一个婴儿能否存活，完全取决于他（她）的性别。一种性别能活，另一种性别必死。为人父母者几乎都想有男孩，但在"严重的"性别不平等的社会里，相比男性而言，女性的生命变得毫无价值。① 父母毫不留情地采取子女性别选择手段，以确保得到男孩。在一个社会中，没有比出生性别选择更能显示性别不平等的证据了。

如果说针对女性的暴力会进一步导致社会内部乃至社会之间的暴力的话，那么针对女性的暴力越严重的社会中这种关系就越为显著。盛行实施后代性别选择的社会，例如中国和印度，是世界上人口最多的两个国家，这两个国家的人口占世界的38%，由于它们都默许子女性别选择，以致两国15—34岁的年轻成年男性人数远大于同龄女性人数，这种差距已经到了仅凭自然力量无法企及的地步。中国人把这群过多的男性称为——"光棍"。在当今的中国和印度，年轻男女数量上的差距超过了历史上的任何一个时期。

所以，亚洲性别比例的男性化，是现代最被忽视的一个大趋势，它将影响21世纪的国家乃至国际局势。在中国（个别落后地区——

---

① "子女性别选择"不应混同于进化生物学家所使用的"性别选择"一词。前者是指基于性别的选择性生育。杀女婴和性别选择性堕胎是子女性别选择的两个例子。

编者注）、印度和亚洲其他地区，人为改变性别比例的规模是空前的。出于对各自国家安全的考虑，各国学者和政策制定者必须慎重对待亚洲大规模人口变化所可能产生的潜在影响。在性别比例失衡的国家，国家安全的涵义要和那些拥有正常性别比例的国家大为不同。虽然"性别"的议题在国家安全的领域中从未获得重视，但我们预测在本世纪它将成为一个重要的聚焦点。

在下面的章节中，我们会讲到本书的研究方法和理论路径。继之综述有关人类后代性别选择起源的文献。之后我们发掘了为什么在最初诱因消失了之后，后代性别选择还能持久存在的真相，那与特定的宗教习惯和择优而嫁的社会结构中个人必须履行的义务息息相关。

一、方法学

本研究采用荷姆-狄克森的"验证过程追溯"方法。① 在极其复杂的系统里，社会变量和物理变量同时存在，实证方法要优于证伪方法。当一个变量不确定是否充分且必要时，只有实证方法才允许其还能作为某一现象的一整套充分条件的一部分，被纳入到研究框架中来。这样的一个变量，可以放大、加强所研究的现象，也可能与其他变量一起引起该现象的发生。

我们的方法学可能不会满足那些希望见到性别比例和国际冲突有线性关系的人。② 我们也不认为这两者之间是简单的线性关系。因为

---

① Thomas F. Homer-Dixon, "Strategies for Studying Causation in Complex Ecological-Political Systems" (Toronto: Environment, Population, and Security Project, University of Toronto, June 1995).

② 威廉·狄瓦勒（William T. Divale）和马文·哈里斯（Marvin Harris）对一个部落人群的案例进行了这样的研究。他们发现在子女性别选择与好战之间有极强的相关性。然而，学者们继而对他们的方法、数据和理论展开了争论。参见 Divale and Harris, "Population, Warfare, and the Male Supremacist Complex," American Anthropologist, Vol. 78, No. 3 (September 1976), pp. 521–538。

我们认为一个简单的线性关系并不能说明这个问题。虽然在实施后代性别选择的社会里，有着很多冲突，但在没有后代性别选择的社会，也会发生重大事故。因为出生性别选择与社会冲突之间的关系非常复杂，并且包含多种充分条件，所以唯有一种包容所有复杂和微小变量的研究方法，才是最适当的。

我们采用"过程追溯"（process-tracing）之后，发现由于性别不平等和环境压力的双重因素，父母被迫选择后代的性别，继之又引发了更大的暴力及冲突。我们通过检验杀女婴和堕女胎的数量来确认性别比例被人为扭曲的程度。为了了解中国和印度年轻人口的性别比例面貌，我们也研究了不同年龄层的性别比例，包括0—4岁的婴儿和5—14岁的青少年分性别的死亡率和自杀率。我们发现处于15—34岁年龄层的年轻男性，与社会内部及社会间冲突的关系最为显著，他们要为近乎全部的犯罪行为负责。

我们接下来回顾后代性别选择的历史根源，特别值得注意的是后代性别选择在亚洲尤为盛行。我们发现，最初，后代性别选择是人们对环境压力的一种无奈之举，而之后，这种做法逐渐被宗教和其他社会规范所允许，以至于当最初的环境压力消失之后，后代性别选择仍持续存在。

二、后代性别选择的产生

为什么人类会作出后代性别的选择？为什么它还会持久不衰？历史文献中对后代性别选择的起源和持续施行的原因作了大量的假设和阐述。我们发现在两种环境下——军事侵略和生存环境不利时——父母会被迫作出后代性别选择。所说后代性别选择盛行，是指在社会各个阶层为数甚多的家庭在相当长的时期内都采取这种手段控制后代性别，而且即使在违反当时法律的情况下，这种行为也没有受到制裁。这两种环境压力只是引发了后代性别选择从偶然的、个别的转为广泛的、典型的这个动态过程,我们的研究称之为"恶毒的抵抗政策"。在不利的环境结束后,既得利益者为了永享资源,与传统宗教互相结合,让后代性别选择成为普遍采用的手段。

(一)军事侵略

军事侵略有两个功能:消灭个体生命和消灭社会。一个特定团体的生命灭绝首先是通过男性人数的损失感受到的,尤其是年轻的男性。因为他们可以作战,冒着生命危险保护族群。赢得战争后,侵略者通常会找出存活的战士和其他的年轻男性,将之处死。

对群体的社会性灭绝,则通过侵略者强掳女性为妾、通婚或为奴。若没有女性繁殖和教育下一代,被侵略的族群会在一代或两代之内绝迹。

因此,防止男性的个体伤亡和女性的社会性流失对于团体的生存极为关键。认清个体生命的损失和社会性流失之间的区别至关重要,因为正如我们稍后将会分析到的,有些观点认为,防止女性流失最好的方法就是杀死她们。

军事侵略会导致食物短缺和疾病,会使死亡的阴影从战场上扩大到难民营,给被侵略的族群带来巨大的环境压力。尽管军事侵略是被侵略的族群实施后代性别选择的原因之一,但这不是主要原因。并不是所有族群在遭受外族军事入侵时都会进行后代性别选择。事实上,对族群身份认同产生的威胁——通常伴生于食物短缺和其他环境压力——才是导致后代性别选择盛行的真正原因。①

至少有三个与军事入侵相关的原因导致了后代性别选择的盛行。第一,为了阻止男性人数减少,族群鼓励生男孩。为了确保男婴的存活,父母通常要投入两年的时间和精力,包括出生和哺乳期或是预计

---

① 参见 Judith Banister, *China's Changing Population* (Stanford, Calif.: Stanford University Press, 1987)。

的停经期。父母不希望把精力浪费在养育女婴之上。杀掉女婴后，能让母亲在一年内再生小孩。性别选择性杀婴能够增加母亲在一年内再次生产的可能性，不用等上两年半时间。

第二，女婴会降低族群的抵抗力，威胁其存活。因为为了保护女孩的名誉，防止她们被侵略者掳掠或强暴，常会使得更多的男性丧失生命。所以女性越多，这个团体就变得越弱。因此在战争和被占领期间，人们认为与其失去一些女性和保护她们的男性，还不如不让这些女性出生。

第三，女性需要适当的婚姻对象。为了族群的延续，她们只能从族群中或可以被接受的族群内找寻婚姻对象。但侵略者也会找被侵略的团体中的女性作为性对象，以强暴来摧毁她的道德观及她的族群身份感。为了防御，族群会把女性集中在一个地区保护，但这样会造成一些男性的死亡，也减少了她们可能的婚姻对象。另外，有些有权有势的家庭，不希望他们的财富因为嫁女儿而被分散，所以严格控制女儿的婚姻，但在军事侵略和被占领时，就会造成找到理想的女婿的困难。因此，在种种的考虑下，杀女婴对于一个正在为她的身份而战的族群，代价可说是最小的。

当然，也不是所有的族群在受到军事侵略时，都会杀女婴。例如犹太血统学就认为，所有犹太女子所生的小孩都是犹太人，所以就算有任何团体成功掳掠犹太女子，她们所生的小孩都算是犹太人。这种情况延续至今。萨格勒布的伊玛目就鼓励波斯尼亚伊斯兰教徒（Bosnian Muslim）去娶在20世纪90年代的波斯尼亚冲突时曾被塞族的军队强暴的女人，也鼓励他们接受因强暴而诞生的小孩，并把小孩抚养成波斯尼亚伊斯兰教徒。①

还有一种防御的办法，是让这些女性变得对侵略者没有吸引力。

---

① 参见 Elaine Lutz, "When the Women Cry, Who Will Listen?" *International Relations Journal* (San Francisco State University), Vol. 14, No. 2 (Spring 1993), pp. 29–32。

中国古代盛行"缠足"，可能就是汉族想阻止女儿被蒙古人掳走；同样的，犹太教让已婚的女性剃光头，也是怕她们被侵略者强暴。当已婚的犹太女性碰到侵略者时，她们会把假发拿开来吓人。更激烈的方式，是把女性生殖器官的外阴唇缝合在一起。

在军事入侵的情况下，与屈服于入侵统治相比，后代性别选择是一种极端压力下的抵抗策略。或者说，这是为了实施抵抗而产生的一种掠夺性社会实践。

（二）长期不利的生存环境

长期处于受到饥饿威胁或遭遇真正饥荒的社会，就会通过后代性别选择对所遭受的风险做出应激反应。自然规律也会对这种脆弱的社会发生作用，让族群的妇女生育能力减低。例如在20世纪初期，澳大利亚土著女性几乎都长期不孕，几年才会排卵一次。妇女要受孕，身体内的黄体素必须维持在一定程度，同时她也需要有相当的体脂肪，若体脂肪长期低于标准，女性就会失去生育力。[①] 其他自然的避孕方式，例如女性哺乳期的增长及在哺乳期间不得性交，也会被这些社会所采用。[②]

在某些类似的社会体系中，女性体重下降的程度不足以避孕。尽管有一些性交禁忌，女性还是可能生出很多孩子，以至于超出该社会体系能够承载的数量。这种情况下就可能出现后代性别选择；与此同时，与性别无关的杀婴现象也会出现。下面就用一个简单的案例对这种情况加以说明。

---

① 参见 Richard B. Lee, "Location, Ovulation, Infanticide, and Woman's Work: A Study of Hunter-Gatherer Population Regulation," in Mark Nathan Cohen, Roy S. Malpass, and Harold G. Klein, eds., *Biosocial Mechanisms of Population Regulation* (New Haven, Conn.: Yale University Press, 1980), pp. 321–348。

② 参见 Herbert Aptekar, *Anjea: Infanticide, Abortion, and Contraception in Savage Society* (New York: William Godwin, 1931)。

北极区的人如因纽特人，住在地球上最不适合人类居住的地方。生存对他们来说，是日以继夜的挣扎，农耕是不可能的，打猎及捕鱼就成为最重要的维生之计。长久以来，这里形成了一种根据性别分工的生活方式。男性专注于打猎和捕鱼，女性照顾小孩、煮菜、做衣服和维护居所。捕鱼打猎在北极是非常危险的，许多男性因此死亡或伤残，但因为没有其他可替代的食物来源，至少在过去是这样的。在两性之间出现的严格的劳动分工，以及男人们在获取食物时体力上的优势，使得男性在族群中更为有用。当家中生男孩时，代表这个家将会有新的猎人或渔人出现，即使家中有男性被杀或伤残，还有人可以取而代之。因此对因纽特人而言，维持猎人和非猎人（女性、小孩或老人）的人数之微妙平衡，攸关生死。非猎人过多，族群就要挨饿，甚至死亡。也因此，北极的因纽特人族群发展出一个控制非猎人人数的方法。老人会被要求离开，母亲会被要求长期哺乳，以降低怀孕几率，他们也采取杀女婴的方式来降低非猎人的人数及未来母亲的人数。虽然他们今天已经享有现代生活的便利，拥有精密的打猎工具，可是在一些因纽特人部落中，男女比例还是失衡的。①

在许多社会中，食物获取方式决定了他们是否会杀女婴。如果以打猎、大型牲畜的畜牧和重型器械农耕为主，儿子会比女儿有价值。②在这样以男性为中心的食物获取体系下，代代实行父居制（patrilocality），妻子不仅在婚后加入丈夫的家庭，而且要和她的亲生父母断绝联系。女性也不被允许继承土地，否则在她们婚后，土地会落入夫家。事实上，女性在婚前即不被视为家庭的成员而是客人，投资在她们身

---

① 参见 Eric Alden Smith and S. Abigail Smith, "Inuit Sex-Ratio Variation: Population Control, Ethnographic Error, or Parental Manipulation?" *Current Anthropology*, Vol. 35, No. 5 (December 1994), pp. 595–624。

② 参见 H. Yuan Tien, *China's Strategic Demographic Initiative* (New York: Praeger, 1991); and Barbara D. Miller, *The Endangered Sex: Neglect of Female Children in Rural North India* (Ithaca, N. Y.: Cornell University Press, 1981)。

上是赔本的,"养女儿就像在别人的花园里浇水"。儿子跟家庭成员生活在一起,照顾他们的起居,并为他们提供生活所需,因此对父母更加有用。①

因此,以男性为中心的食物获取体系和父居制结合起来,使得女儿的价值相当低,需要靠嫁妆才能把她们嫁掉。嫁妆制度让父母对女儿原有的一点亲情消失殆尽,因为她们的出生可能让父母破产②,难怪广东有一句老话:"女儿是贼。"嫁后从夫的习俗、以男性为中心的食物供给体系和嫁妆,这三重威胁使该文化中杀女婴的做法成为一种理性选择。相反,在母系社会中,女性是主要的食物提供者,例如在产米、养蚕造丝及小动物畜养的社会中,女儿不但不会造成经济负担,反而是重要的资产,而且女性也可以继承土地,男性在结婚时需要支付聘金。1948年解放之前,印度南部就保留着这样的文化,在那里,杀女婴几乎闻所未闻。

当种族遭到军事入侵时,女儿们个体生命的消亡较之其社会性消亡更有利于一个身处脆弱生存环境中的族群。女儿嫁后从夫,对于娘家而言就是一种社会性消亡,对娘家的损失是巨大的,娘家如不愿独自承担这种损失就会要求夫家支付聘金。而有些族群更为极端,他们宁愿选择杀女婴,用女儿的个体生命消亡来减小其社会性消亡的损失。更有甚者,有些社会(比如因纽特人)理所当然地把女儿的个体消亡当成零和博弈的理性结果。他们认为,女儿们无论是刚出生还是长大以后,会威胁到食物供给者和非食物供给者之间完美的平衡。此外,如果一个家庭选择拒绝分担损失和风险,不接受聘金等形式的补偿的话,也是造成杀女婴行为存在的原因之一。

有些情况下,由于拒绝分担损失和风险,杀男婴的现象也偶有出

---

① 参见 Fei Hsiao-tung, *Peasant Life in China: A Field Study of Country Life in the Yangtze Valley* (1939; reprint, London: Routledge and Kegan Paul, 1962)。

② 参见 Ho Ping-ti, *Studies on the Population of China, 1368–1953* (Cambridge, Mass.: Harvard University Press, 1956)。

现。在历史上的中国，经过几代人的继承，人地比例越来越紧张，很多农民担心有数个儿子分财产，田地会被分得太小，以至于无法耕种。为了防止这点，父母可能会把其他的儿子杀掉，只留下一个或两个，这样做就可以避免一家人眼睁睁地看着自己的遗产被分割得越来越少，直到最后被卖掉。①

在某些文化中，当饥荒来袭，所有的婴儿，无论男女，都被杀掉。②事实上，在某些案例中，甚至出现易子而食的情况。在其他文化中，风险是被共担的，全家人宁愿忍饥挨饿也不会杀掉婴儿和其他孩子。③ 如前所述，让女儿们参与寻找食物的活动能够降低娘家损失，使女儿和儿子一样有用，也会阻止杀女婴的行为。然而还有一些案例中，即使环境压力和其他各种不利生存的压力都不存在的情况下，杀女婴的行为仍旧不合常理地继续存在，而且作为某种恶毒的抵抗措施被该文化所接纳。

三、后代性别选择的持续

当造成杀女婴的环境已不存在时，为什么这个恶习还会继续存在呢？为什么在最后一次军事入侵和大规模饥荒过去几百年之后，杀女

---

① Fei, *Peasant Life in China*.

② 下列故事来自 World Vision International 的负责人，它表明在饥荒时代各种文化中出现的性别选择传统上与这一惯例无关："我飞往南苏丹的卡波埃塔。这一地区正处于饥荒之中，25 万人已被饿死。当我们降落在满是泥土的跑道上时，周围数十里的家庭都赶来看是谁到了这里，这一举动在非洲很常见。他们知道我们来自公益组织，所以母亲们举起她们干瘦的儿子给我们看她们多需要帮助。我很快注意到孩子们鼓胀的肚子——缺乏营养的表现。但是母亲并不举起女儿。在家族世系中女儿是最后一个被喂食的，最先死掉的。在我们到达之前，她们就死了。" "Females: He Created Them," *World Vision Today*, Spring 1988, p. 2.

③ 例如，Jasper Becker, *Hungry Ghosts: Mao's Secret Famine* (New York: Free Press, 1996)。

婴和后代性别选择的行为仍然顽固地存在于某种文化当中呢？我们发现有两个原因：一是宗教信仰对该行为实施的惩罚在不断地发展和变化；二是社会上逐步确立的僵化的男高女低式婚嫁制度，也就是女性必须嫁给一个条件比她更好的男性。

（一）宗教扮演的角色

在有些文化中，杀女婴是很普遍的，虽然他们的宗教经文禁止并谴责这种行为。但宗教方面的反对声音，随着时间逐渐消失，而当军事侵略和饥荒到来时，宗教领袖的家中也会采用这种手段。到了该行为毫无理性可言的时候，宗教方面理应对其作出惩罚却秘而不宣，使之持续存在找到了借口。而这往往是因为宗教领袖或某些杰出人物在杀女婴行为中得到了好处。宗教领袖也会选择杀女婴来保全其家庭不受环境压力的影响。

在印度教的社会中，这种现象最为明显。印度教的经典——吠陀经文说所有的生命都是神圣的。事实上在吠陀时代以前以及在吠陀时代，女性的社会地位和宗教地位比今天高得多，女人可以成为战士甚至将军。政府中也有女性代表，女性可以选择自己的丈夫，婚嫁时男方需要付聘金。早期的其他印度教经文也提到禁止杀婴，例如圣者的警告，有三个行为可以让一个女人被视为不贞：为非作歹而被社会放逐，谋杀丈夫，谋杀未出生的小孩（Vas. Xxviii. 7）。根据乔达摩的说法，流产是一个让女性被放逐的正当原因（G. xxi. 9）。

吠陀时代结束后蒙古人入侵，新的宗教经文诞生了，其中最有影响的是《摩奴法典》。它的概念是，男人结婚的原因是为了生儿子，儿子才能在自己死后为自己举行仪式，净化亡灵。如果没有儿子来举行这些仪式，灵魂是要下地狱的。另外，印度教认为儿童在2岁前没有灵魂，所以在2岁前死亡，不算是人的死亡，不至于侵渎宗教。印度社会如此重男轻女，除了环境因素外，宗教上的默许让杀女婴的犯罪感消失，也是主因。

中国的佛教文化，对杀女婴的态度也模棱两可。例如纪思道（Nicholas Kristof）和伍洁芳（Sheryl WuDunn）写道，中国16、17世纪有一部很有影响力的道德经典，其中禁止杀婴。可是这些禁止的文字是出现在一堆冗长的文字里，例如：要求人不要跳过放在地板上的食物，不要跨过睡在地毯上的人，面对北方的时候不要哭泣、吐口水和小便；不要对流星吐口水，不要对彩虹指指点点，如果你违反了，命运的主宰就会把你的生命减少三天至三百天。这段文字中并不认为杀婴会比面对北方小便更糟糕。①

另外，根据另一部中国佛教文献，杀婴会阻碍你的灵魂得救②，相当于对写色情小说行为的惩罚力度。与印度一样，在20世纪之前的中国人的观念中，杀女婴是很普遍的。中国的哲学家汪士铎（1802—1889）曾倡导杀女婴，他认为这是控制人口增长的一个好办法。③ 与印度教一样，佛教文化中，女儿不能为祖宗灵魂主持香火仪式——只有儿子才能从事这些重要的宗教仪式。另一个与印度文化惊人的相似之处是，中国文化也认为1岁以下的婴儿，或牙齿长满之前，都不算是完整的人。④ 中国的寓言甚至说天神也赞成杀婴。寓言是这样的：有一对年轻的夫妻，担心婴儿会消耗太多的食品，他们认为食品应该先给丈夫生病的母亲享用，就决定把婴儿活埋。这个孝举

---

① Nicholas D. Kristof and Sheryl WuDunn, *China Wakes: The Struggle for the Soul of a Rising Power* (New York: Vintage, 1994), p. 227. 纪思道（Nicholas Kristof），《纽约时报》专栏作家，曾先后出任过《纽约时报》驻香港、北京和东京的首席记者。1990年，他和同为《纽约时报》记者的他太太伍洁芳（Sheryl WuDunn）合著的《中国觉醒了》（*China Wakes: The Struggle for the Soul of a Rising Power*）一书，获得普利策新闻奖，成为第一对获得普利策新闻奖的夫妇。——译者注

② Ho, *Studies on the Population of China, 1368–1953*, p. 60.

③ Robert Hans van Gulik, *Sexual Life in Ancient China: A Preliminary Survey of Chinese Sex and Society from ca. 1500 B.C. till 1644 A.D.* (Leiden, Netherlands: E. J. Brill, 1974), p. 249.

④ Kristof and WuDunn, *China Wakes*, p. 227; and Lillian M. Li, "Life and Death in a Chinese Famine: Infanticide as a Demographic Consequence of the 1935 Yellow River Flood," *Comparative Studies in Society and History*, Vol. 33, No. 3 (July 1991), p. 503.

感动了天神，所以在他们为婴儿挖坟时，天神让他们找到了一坛金块。①

当然，也不是所有的宗教都默许后代性别选择。在伊斯兰教前期，阿拉伯的游牧民族曾流行杀女婴。但先知穆罕默德谴责这种行为，他要追随者想象在最后大审判时，大家都站在上帝的面前，当那个被活埋的女婴被问到究竟犯了什么罪才被杀，这时，每一个灵魂都必须承担他所造的孽。② 这一段经文否定了宗教包容杀婴。事实上，杀女婴违反了伊斯兰教的道德规范。与印度接壤的伊斯兰社会除外。

历史上，宗教在后代性别选择进程中发挥了多种作用。人们在决定是否实施后代性别选择行为时，宗教发展的动态变化始终在起作用。

(二) 女性择优而嫁的必要性

没有了军事侵略及不利的生存环境后，单凭宗教惩戒的力量，很难让杀女婴的行为，历经几个世纪，甚至上千年，在特定的社会中还能持续地存在。还有更基本的因素让人们认识到女婴生而带来的威胁。

我们认为，这个原因就是——家庭担心女儿的出生，会让他们损失既有的资源。因为社会地位让人与人之间有区别——身份的区别，以及财富、权力、特权、风险、脆弱性和安全性的区别。区别让某些

---

① Kristof and WuDunn, *China Wakes*, p. 277; and Li, "Life and Death in a Chinese Famine," p. 504.

② Avner Giladi, "Some Observations on Infanticide in Medieval Muslim Society," *International Journal of Middle East Studies*, Vol. 22, No. 2 (May 1990), p. 186. 见《古兰经》第81章第8节。此外，《古兰经》第16章第57—59节，也提到了对于因女儿出生而羞耻的父亲的道德谴责："他们以女儿归真主——赞颂真主，超绝万物——而以他们所愿望的归自己。当他们中的一个人听说自己的妻子生女儿的时候，他的脸黯然失色，而且满腹牢骚。他为这个噩耗而不与宗族会面，他多方考虑：究竟是忍辱保留她呢？还是把她活埋在土里呢？真的，他们的判断真恶劣。"Ibid., p. 187.

家庭或群体独享资源，也让他们在资源的累积和享用上拥有优势。在环境压力增加的时期，拥有显赫社会地位的家庭和群体无需为保障其安全做出改变；相反，非家庭或群体成员就要脆弱得多，他们面对环境压力的增加，只能做出牺牲，忍受灾难，并作出其他改变。因此，群体成员抗拒适应环境压力，会导致非群体成员很难改变处境。然而，这种社会地位的体系存在明显的缺陷，因为人们总要在自己的家族之外寻找伴侣，而家族的排他性与此冲突。

家庭是区分人们社会地位最基本的单位，家庭所积累的财产、权力，唯有通过继承才能延续。没有了下一代，所有花在积累财富及资源上的努力就白费了，这也是中国帝制时代太监的困扰。太监们为了争取过继子嗣的权利进行了长达几个世纪的抗争，继子可以让太监们拥有家庭，也能继承他们的财富。

理论上，如果一个家庭能够近亲繁殖，那么所积累的财产就能够完整地维持下去。但近亲繁殖会造成严重的后果，人类都知道必须与外通婚。但这也造成了一个棘手的情况——新一代的产生必须能够维护原有的社会资源，但与外通婚会牺牲一些社会资源，并且减损资源占有的排他性。因此，婚姻不仅重要，而且暗含风险。要如何在与外通婚时，减轻它对自己的威胁呢？理解到这个顾忌，就容易理解家庭对于儿女婚姻及继承所作的抉择，也可以了解血缘、阶级对资源维护的影响。为了摸清家庭和群体如何尽量减少资源的损失和资源占有排他性的减损，我们作了以下三个假设：（1）以家庭为基础的资源积累和资源获取具有恒久价值；（2）保有社会地位的欲望会促成财富积累和财富排他；（3）出于生物学原理，人们需要与外通婚。基于以上三点假设，我们得到以下七个结论：

第一，在传统社会里，家庭严格地为子女选择伴侣，尤其是儿子。理由至少有三：（1）儿子更有能力保护所积累的资源。（2）儿子是打猎、捕猎、农地开垦和作战时最主要的力量。（3）儿子比女儿能繁育更多的下一代。华裔美国人口学家田心源认为："男孩能够增加家庭的生产力，提供父母老年时的保障。进一步而言，人们之所以想要很多孩子（至少一个儿子），还有其他原因。在农村，人们要想生存下去，必须抵御邻里的敌意乃至施威于人，这些都是家庭和亲属圈子大小的决定因素。"①

第二，女儿出嫁后，不能参与娘家财产的分配，这样娘家的社会地位和资源才能维持。女儿不能继承家庭财产，尤其不能继承土地。现在虽有法律来维护女性的继承权，但是许多传统家庭仍然坚决地传子不传女。

第三，为了防止现有的社会地位被侵蚀，女婿必须从社会地位更高的家庭中选出②，女儿不能下嫁到社会地位更低的人家，这种通婚策略可保证女儿家庭的地位如果被改变，也只是越变越好。鲁基·加雅拉曼（Ruki Jayaraman）描述印度社会的最高阶级，为了保护自己的地位，把阶层制度定得密不通风，反而对女性造成迫害。③ 这种观点能够在具有男高女低婚嫁习俗的社会中找到支撑。中国的广东人和福建人认为女儿是"赔钱货"，在她身上的投资最后都会拱手让给夫家。④ 所以只有把女儿嫁给地位更高的家庭，且夫家对娘家的态度良好，这样娘家才能获得较多的保护或协助。男高女低式的联姻会提高新娘娘家的社会地位。把女儿嫁过去相当于将两家的力量结合在一起，这种被延伸了的社会关系让娘家可以保护其现有的社会地位，更好地完成资源积累和资源排他。

---

① Tien, *China' Strategic Demographic Initiative*, p. 202.

② 狄克曼关于女性高嫁（Hypergyny）的经验研究和理论研究极为重要，他多年来是加州大学河滨分校的人类学家。参见 Dickemann, "Paternal Confidence and Dowry Competition: A Biocultural Analysis of Purdah," in Richard D. Alexander and Donald W. Tinkle, eds., *Natural Selection and Social Behavior: Recent Research and New Theory* (New York: Chiron, 1981), pp. 471 – 438。

③ 鲁基·加雅拉曼，1991—1996 年间在杨百翰大学担任政治科学访问教授，他于1996 年 4 月 16 日与作者进行了沟通。

④ Hugh D. R. Baker, *Chinese Family and Kinship* (London: Macmillan, 1979), p. 41.

第四，嫁女儿代表单方面地提供新娘，所以娘家的气势比较低。中国有句谚语："嫁女儿的头低低，娶媳妇的头抬高"①。在受到军事侵略时，有些家庭干脆把女儿献给侵略者，使得嫁女儿的家庭颜面尽失，因此夫家必须支付聘金来补偿。

第五，根据狄克曼（Mildred Dickermann）的婚嫁理论，为了保护既有的资源，女儿的家庭会努力安排一个好婚姻。② 许多婚姻是"门当户对"，也就是地位相同的家庭彼此通婚，其他的则是"男高女低"。在人口学上，这至少导致了三个方面的结果：（1）社会地位最高的家庭很难嫁女儿，而且一不小心，就会危及娘家。（2）中等阶层的家庭，比较容易为几位女儿安排婚姻，也不需要担心自己的地位受损。（3）最低阶层的家庭根本就无法为儿子找到妻子。

第六，如果嫁女儿的费用太昂贵，危及其家庭的社会地位，有些家庭就会选择杀女婴，或是提倡妇女的贞节，让女儿终生不嫁。过去有些非常隐秘的尼姑和修女修道所，专门收容社会高层的女儿，她们的家庭为此会支付一笔相当于嫁妆的钱。家庭的社会地位越高，其女儿被"藏"得越好。日本几位天皇的女儿，最后都被送到修道院。被英国接管之前，印度北部拉其普特人的部族，为了维护自身的社会地位，选择把所有的女婴都杀了；印度东部的孔特人的部落则是为了种族的纯正而杀害女婴。中产家庭可以通过一两个女儿的联姻稳固其社会地位，一旦女儿的数量超过其所能承受的范围，就很可能导致新生女婴的被杀。

---

① Arthur Henderson Smith, *Village Life in China: A Study in Sociology* (New York: F. H. Revell, 1899), p. 286.

② Mildred Dickemann, "The Ecology of Mating Systems in Hypergynous Dowry Societies," *Social Science Information*, Vol. 18, No. 2 (May 1979), pp. 163–195; Mildred Dickemann, "Female Infanticide, Reproductive Strategies, and Social Stratification: A Preliminary Model," in Napoleon A. Chagnon and William Irons, eds., *Evolutionary Biology and Human Social Behavior: An Anthropological Perspective* (North Scituate, Mass: Duxbury, 1979), pp. 321–367.

第七，女性择优而嫁让社会最底层的找不到妻子的男性愈来愈多。被排除在婚嫁市场之外的女儿人数越多，择优而嫁的女儿越多，底层讨不到老婆的男人就越多。最底层的女性通常会被卖给同级的男士，或被卖给地位更低者为妻。婚姻主要的交易模式是"聘金"而非嫁妆。因为可以获利，所以底层的父母不会杀女儿，性别比例在这个阶层也最正常。

（三）反例分析

我们找到至少两个反例。第一，在财富较为平均的社会里，或家族积累的财富和独享的资源无法长期占有，或像现代市场经济中那样，家庭的社会地位可能在短时间内发生巨变。人们可以互相交换女儿为其成婚，父母也没有必要杀女婴，像是中古世纪的德国乡村，杀女婴的现象几乎不存在。这也是英国人推广"婚姻市集"的原因之一，这种做法阻止了殖民时期印度的杀女婴现象。在这些案例中，相互交换女儿成婚很普遍，阶级差异也不那么绝对。

第二，女性如果是经济体系中主要的财富制造者，或至少是平等的财富创造者，食物获取方式是非传统的，则女性可以继承，女儿是宝，女婴也不会被杀。在中国的珠江三角洲及印度南方，属于稻米文化或养丝文化，这些地方的女性可以制造财富，所以很少听到杀女婴的消息，而且当地的性别比例也很正常。另外，大部分东南亚地区的性别比例都近乎正常，这可能因为女性是当地经济的主要生产力之故。

研究这些反例有一个重要的注意事项：当社会政策要求每个家庭只能拥有一个孩子时，即便在现代近乎平等的社会里，大多数人仍然偏好男孩，因为他们认为男孩能够更好地保护父母、创造资源、维护家庭。在有独生子女政策的社会中，一个家庭是否生了儿子，的确会决定这个家庭的幸福与否。因此，虽然妇女地位看上去更平等了，但后代性别选择会变本加厉，这种趋势是逐渐形成的。在现代的中国，即便法律同样要求儿女照顾父母，他们也有同等的继承权，情况却并未改变。

四、结论

历史上，对后代作性别选择，是人类对抗不利环境，例如遭到军事侵略或长期的天灾人祸的正常反应。在某些文化中，后代性别选择是为了保护族群及家庭既有的社会地位和资源。但后代性别选择得以持续，多数情况还是由于长久以来宗教的默许以及男高女低的婚姻制度所造成的。我们将在后面的章节分析，持续这么做，人类社会将要付出极大的代价。

五、本书的架构

本书共有七章，在第二章，我们会探讨历史上的后代性别选择。我们会简单地介绍动物世界的杀婴及故意堕胎，以及人类社会中与性别无关的杀婴。我们也会讨论后代性别选择的相关数据及其优缺点。我们还汇集了一些古罗马、古希腊、历史上欧洲社会及世界其他地方杀婴的文献，最后讨论现今的后代性别选择实践。

在第三、四章，我们检视了印度及中国的后代性别选择的历史，讨论了当前的性别比例并分析了不同的资料来源。我们讨论各种不同的地区、不同的部落、城市/乡下人口的数据，以便评估有多少剩余的年轻成年男性或光棍，并预测2020年时的情况。

在第五章，我们提供了"光棍愈多，社会愈不安"的理论及历史案例。人类学、生物学、犯罪学、心理学、组织行为学和社会学的文献都指出，过多的年轻未婚成年男性会对社会的安定形成威胁。光棍是社会上受教育最少、最没有一技之长、也最容易使用暴力来改善他们低下地位的人群。中国的捻军起义、葡萄牙的"收复失地运动"、印度殖民地前期的奥德（现在的乌塔普拉德汗）及清朝统治时期的台湾，都验证了在当时光棍就是社会动荡的主因。我们还探讨了另类光棍，例如中国及波利尼西亚古代的太监和僧侣。

在第六章，我们研究中国及印度现在的光棍族群，比较他们和古代光棍的相似之处，例如他们的流动性、低下的社会地位、缺乏教育和群聚性。同时，我们也对现代光棍为什么容易吸毒、暴力犯罪和群殴行为，作了行为学分析。通过整体相关性分析我们证明在性别比例和犯罪率之间，有着显著的统计学上的关联。我们也讨论了通过政府干预来消减高性别比例社会中不稳定性的可能性，许多相应的对策是令人不快且无用的，还有些甚至会造成国际社会的更大的冲突。但也有一些正面的手段，可以缓和未来不安的局势。

最后，在第七章，我们说明为什么所有的国家都应该了解，高性别比例的社会和正常性别比例的社会有着截然不同的安全系数。在高性别比例的社会中，女性地位的低落必然影响社会民主及和平进程。既然全世界有近半数的人口住在高性别比例的社会里，他们对于全世界安全的影响非同小可。

第二章 历史上的后代性别选择——从杀婴、堕胎,到"消失的女性"

20世纪80年代末期以来,亚洲的高性别比例引起了举世的瞩目。学者发现,男性人数过多是由于父母采取后代性别选择手段,像是杀女婴、堕女胎的结果。为了了解和解释后代性别选择得以持续的原因,我们回顾历史,找出杀婴、特别是杀女婴的原因及程度。杀女婴是因为人们重男轻女,在很多文化中人们都有这种偏好,然而亚洲社会特别重男轻女,通过分析东南亚人口数据可以发现他们以杀婴、堕胎,以及对女婴疏于照顾等方式,来确保生育男孩。最后,我们回顾了关于亚洲"消失的女性"的讨论,并进一步评估了当今女性消失的程度。

一、与性别无关的后代选择行为

为了给我们讨论人类后代性别选择行为提供一个大背景,一定要弄清楚在自然界和人类社会中,与性别无关的杀婴和堕胎行为是很普遍的，这点很重要。自然界的杀婴和堕胎，其实相当普遍。① 专家们已经发现不仅仅昆虫这样的低等动物会吃掉幼虫和幼崽，小型哺乳动物，如猫和仓鼠，也会如此。猩猩、猴子甚至海豚，为了维护社会等级，也会杀婴。堕胎也有生物学的原因：老鼠在受到不熟悉的公鼠释放的费洛蒙的影响时，会自然堕胎；也有主动引发流产的情况，强占配偶的公马会踢已怀孕的母马肚子，以流掉其他公马的后代。

人类的发展也始终伴随着杀婴现象。人类学家莱拉·威廉姆森（Laila Williamson）说："杀婴发生在每块大陆、各种教育程度的人群中，从游牧民族到享有高等文明的人群，包括现代西方世界人们的祖先。杀婴不是例外，它是常态。"② 下面的分析为我们揭示了杀婴行为的背景，为我们进一步讨论有性别选择的杀婴行为奠定了基础，历史学家威廉·森玛（William Sumner）认为，驱使父母杀婴的心理是："儿童增加生存的负担，父母对子女是单向的牺牲，尽管偶有回报，但改变不了双方利害冲突的立场。如果不是出于对后代的热爱，人类宁可选择不要这个负担。堕胎及杀婴说明了在人类早期，儿童的负担就大到让父母想要逃避的地步。"③ 在避孕药不发达的时期，父母认为怀孕生子可能不可预期、无法避免，但养育孩子的责任却能抛弃。

---

① Glenn Hausfater and Sarah Blaffer Hrdy, eds., *Infanticide: Comparative and Evolutionary Perspectives* (Now York: Aldine de Gruyter, 1984).

② Laila Williamson, "Infanticide: An Anthropological Analysis," in Marvin Kohl, ed., *Infanticide and the Value of Life* (New York: Prometheus, 1978), p. 61.

③ William Graham Sumner, *Folkways* (New York: Dover, 1959), pp. 309–310.

人类会无性别选择地杀婴主要有六点理由①：

其一，从历史文献中我们发现，非洲、美洲、亚洲、欧洲、大洋洲，几乎在所有人类文化中，人们都会抛弃"不完美"的婴儿，某些地方甚至会杀害生出畸形婴儿的母亲，仅仅因为人们怀疑致畸的原因可能是她曾不忠于丈夫。亚里士多德的《政治学》一书和塞涅卡（Seneca）的《论愤怒》（De Ira）也赞成抛弃畸婴。

其二，生产状态异常时，所生的婴儿也会被杀。太平洋列岛及西

---

① 有关世界各地各个时期杀婴的文章，包括：Avner Giladi, "Some Observations on Infanticide in Medieval Muslim Society," *International Journal of Middle East Studies*, Vol. 22, No. 2 (May 1990), pp. 185 - 200; Mildred Dickemann, "Demographic Consequences of Infanticide in Man," *Annual Review of Ecology and Systematics*, Vol. 6 (1975), pp. 107 - 137; William L. Langer, "Infanticide: A Historical Survey," *History of Childhood Quarterly: The Journal of Psychohistory*, Vol. 1, No. 3 (Winter 1974), pp. 353 - 365; Sumner, *Folkways*; Edward Westermarck, *The Origin and Development of the Moral Ideas* (London: Macmillan, 1924); Williamson, "Infanticide: An Anthropological Analysisi"; Kathryn L. Moseley, "The History of Infanticide in Western Society," *Issues in Law and Medicine*, Vol. 1, No. 5 (March 1986), pp. 345 - 362; Kees de Meer, "Morality in Children among the Aymara Indians of Southern Peru," *Social Science and Medicine*, Vol. 26, No. 2 (1988), pp. 253 - 258; "Infanticide," in Maria Leach, ed., *Dictionary of Folklore, Mythology and Legend*, Vol. 1 (New York: Funk and Wagnalls, 1949), pp. 522 - 524; Jack Lindsay, *The Ancient World: Manners and Morals* (New York: G. P. Putnam's Sons, 1968); John M. Riddle, *Contraception and Abortion from the Ancient World to the Renaissance* (Cambridge, Mass.: Harvard Unversity Press, 1992); Lloyd deMause, "The Evolution of Childhood," in deMause, ed., *The History of Childhood* (New York: Psychohistory Press, 1974), pp. 1 - 73; Elise Boulding, *The Underside of History: A View of Women through Time* (Boulder, Colo.: Westview Press, 1976); Ruth Oldenziel, "The Historiography of Infanticide in Antiquity: A Literature Stillborn," in Josine Blok and Peter Mason, eds., *Sexual Asymmetry: Studies in Ancient Society* (Amsterdam: J. C. GIEBEN, 1987), pp. 87 - 107; Asen Balikci, *The Netslik Eskimo* (New York: Natural History Press, 1970); Kuhrt, eds., *Images of Women in Antiquity* (Detroit, Mich.: Wayne State University Press, 1993), pp. 207 - 222; Mary R. Lefkowitz and Maureen B. Fant, *Women's Life in Greece and Rome* (Baltimore, Md.: John Hopkins University Press, 1992); and Herbert Aptekar, *Anjea: infanticide, Abortion, and Contraception in Savage Society* (New York: William Godwin, 1931)。除非另有标注，本书接下来所引述的关于人类非性别选择性杀婴的资料都来自上述文献。

半球的土著认为孪生婴儿是不吉之兆而将其中之一或两者都杀害，有时连母亲也一并杀死。① 赫伯特·埃特卡（Herbert Aptekar）及爱德华·威斯特马克（Edward Westermarck）提到，有些非洲土著会将第十个出生的，或是门牙比下排牙齿先掉落的（西非），或在不祥之日出生的小孩杀掉。② 非洲东南部的土著会杀害寡妇再婚后所生的第一个小孩，认为这个小孩会带来厄运，无论其亲生父亲是谁。③ 道德哲学家威斯特马克在研究 20 世纪早期的伦理学时发现，牺牲改嫁者第一胎的传统遍及非洲、澳洲、中国、欧洲、印度及北美的土著部落。④

其三，于婚外诞生的小孩被杀的风险很高，像是私生子、强暴或乱伦后出生的小孩、混血儿等。有时，怀孕的母亲会试图引产，通过吃草药或按摩腹部，如果这些办法都不成功，她就干脆杀婴。有些婴儿会被淹死或被"压死"（母亲说这是因为她在睡眠中不小心造成的），有的则被丢弃。在基督教社会中，非婚生子造成的后果很严重，包括母亲被乱石砸死、吊死、淹死或烧死。在早期欧洲，私生婴儿普遍遭到杀害，一位退休的船长托马斯·柯南（Thomas Coram）叙述自己："沮丧极了，每天都会看到婴儿的尸体被丢到伦敦的垃圾堆中。"1741 年，他决定成立伦敦第一家弃婴医院。⑤ 只是被收容的弃婴最后仍多死于疾病或营养不良（或是二者兼具）。欧洲有不少被丢弃的婴儿（大约三分之二是私生子），它们被送到"杀手护士"或"天使制造者"的手中去照顾，结果可想而知。⑥

---

① 参见 Gary Granzberg, "Twin Infanticide: A Cross-Cultural Test of a Materialistic Explanation," *Ethos*, Vol. 1, No. 4 (Winter 1973), pp. 405–412; and Ludwik Krzywicki, *Primitive Society and Its Vital Statistics* (London: Macmillan, 1934).

② Aptekar, *Anjea*; and Westermarck, *The Origin and Development of the Moral Ideas*.

③ 参见 Westermarck, *The Origin and Development of the Moral Ideas*, p. 460.

④ Ibid., pp. 458–459.

⑤ Langer, "Infanticide: A Historical Survey," pp. 358–359.

⑥ 更多案例，参见 Lionel Rose, *The Massacre of the Innocents: Infanticide in Britain, 1800–1939* (London: Routledge and Kegan Paul, 1986).

其四，如果家庭觉得负担太重，也会杀婴。在很多文化中，父亲有权杀自己的儿女（有时还包括孙儿女），甚至仆人的儿女。举例来说，在古代的希腊和罗马，如果父亲决定不要一个孩子，这个孩子通常会被活埋。结果造成了古希腊罗马都是小家庭，而且性别比例相当不正常。又如原始的条顿人，如果父亲把刚出生的婴儿从地上提起来，他就可以活下来，受洗、被命名，否则，婴儿就会被抛弃。17世纪时，耶稣会的传教士惊恐地发现，单是在北京，"每天都有几千个婴儿像垃圾一样被抛到街上，第二天一早由清道夫捡起，将他们丢到城市之外的大坑中"。① 一些太平洋的小岛上，婴儿的死活由部落酋长决定，而不是父亲。② 虽然在某些文化中有些弃婴会被其他家庭收养，但在大多数的情况下，被弃只是婴儿死亡的一种托词。在19世纪的英格兰，数以千计的婴儿被扔在河流、沟渠、甚至下水道中，这些孩子被"弃置"在了水里。还有一些案例中，母亲会因担心无法照看她们的婴儿而选择杀婴。③ 如北美游牧部落，母亲如果担心婴儿会让自己跟不上其他人的话，就会杀婴。

其五，在天灾人祸时，父母会杀婴儿及幼童，以免消耗资源。④ 如澳洲的土著民族，直到被英国统治接管之前，始终存在杀婴行为，特别是沙漠地区和食物短缺时期。在部分亚洲地区，杀婴现象也很普遍，尤其以中国和日本为甚。

---

① Langer, "Infanticide: A Historical Survey," p. 354, citing a Dr. John B. Beck writing in 1935.

② William Ellis, *Polynesian Researches, during a Residence of Nearly Eight Years in the Society and Sandwich Islands*, Vol. 1 (London: Henry G. Bohn, 1859).

③ William L. Langer, "Checks on Population Growth, 1750-1850," *Scientific American*, Vol. 226, No. 2 (February 1972), p. 94.

④ 参见 Ronald M. Berndt and Catherine H. Berndt, *The World of the First Australians: An Introduction to the Traditional Life of the Australian Aborigines* (London: Angus and Robertson, 1964)。

其六，杀婴还有一个简单的原因，就是父母不想同时拥有太多的婴儿和过小的孩子，担心会来不及照顾。有些母亲认为她一次只能喂一个小孩，这样她如果还在喂奶，再生出来的婴儿就会被杀。① 这种情况是真实存在的，在历史上的原始部落中，其游牧式的生活让人们非常注重流动性。此时，为了保护正在养育着的孩子，杀掉后出生的婴儿就很平常。

婴儿的生命在过去被认为没什么价值。根据史学家威廉·莱克（William Lecky）的观察，杀死不想要的婴儿"司空见惯，父母根本不当回事"。② 在基督教的教义中，杀死无辜是不道德的，但导致婴儿死亡就不那么严重，一直到18、19世纪杀婴才被定为死罪。约翰·包斯威尔（John Boswell）在跨时代的研究《仁慈的陌生人——从中世纪之前到文艺复兴时代西欧的弃婴》中，证实了虽然在数据收集方面存在很大困难，仍能得出这一事实，即弃婴和杀婴在古代相当普遍。近代的西欧有10%—40%的都市儿童被弃，数字与古代类似。③ 不同时期的学者纷纷指出杀婴行为的持续存在简直就是"屠婴的狂欢"、"对无辜者的大屠杀"、"中古时代遗留下来的普遍且难除的罪恶"。换句话说，后代性别选择这个古代的恶

---

① Susan C. M. Scrimshaw, "Infanticide in Human Populations: Societal and Individual Concerns," in Hausfater and Hrdy, Infanticide: Comparative and Evolutionary Perspectives, pp. 439 – 462. 这被作为南美雅诺玛莫（Yanomamo）部落杀婴的一个正常理由。该部落是在巴西中部发现的一个时有冲突的军事部落。查冈（Napoleon A. Chagnon）在20世纪60—80年代对这一部落人群进行了细致研究。参见 Chagnon, *Yanomamo: The Fierce People*, 2d ed. (New York: Holt, Rinehart, and Winston, 1977), p. 15。

② William Edward Hartpole Lecky, *History of European Morals from Augustus to Charlemagne*, Vol. 2 (London: Longmans, Greens, 1869), p. 27.

③ Keith Thomas, "Fateful Exposure," *Times Literary Supplement*, August 25 – 31, 1989, pp. 913 – 914; and John Boswell, *The Kindness of Strangers: The Abandonment of Children in Western Europe from Late Antiquity to the Renaissance* (Chicago: University of Chicago Press, 1998).

行一直被延续至今。① 我们马上就来说说后代性别选择。

二、后代性别选择

历史上,在所有出生性别选择的案例中,父母几乎都选择男婴。出生性别选择可以在受孕之前就开始,例如现代的精子分离术。也可以在受孕之后、出生之前,以性别选择式堕胎的方式或其他生殖技术为之;或出生以后,通过主动或被动的杀婴行为完成,这包括不给食物、衣物、住所、医疗等方式,放弃不想要的小孩。判断胎儿性别的方法古即有之,中国在4400年前就有这类的文献。② 希腊哲学家阿纳萨格拉斯(Anaxagorous)及亚里士多德认为,性交时男女身体的位置可以控制婴儿的性别。③ 为了确保男孩的出生,很多民间偏方指出受孕时间(不同寻常的日子、有冷风吹的夜晚和满月之夜等)和特定的食物(红肉和咸味的零食等)能起决定作用。在印度《阿育吠陀经》(古代经文,描述药物治疗的方法)中指出,胎儿在受孕六周之内性别是不确定的,该经文还列出在受孕六周之内改变胎儿性别的办法。④ 同样是在印度,怀孕的女人可以在头三个月吃特殊一种名叫 seh palatna 的药物,以确保生男孩。

---

① 参见 Langer, "Infanticide: A Historical Survey"; Lecky, *History of European Morals from Augustus to Charlemagne*; and Edward Gibbon, *The Decline and Fall of the Roman Empire* (Chicago: Encyclopedia Britannica, 1990)。

② Manuel J. Gordon, "The Control of Sex," *Scientific American*, Vol. 199, No. 5 (November 1958), p. 87.

③ 关于民间控制婴儿性别的方法,参见 Alison Dundes Renteln, "Sex selection and Reproductive Freedom," *Women's Studies International Forum*, Vol. 15, No. 3 (May-June 1992), pp. 405 – 426。

④ Forum against Sex Determination and Sex Pre-selection, "Using Technology, Choosing Sex: The Campaign against Sex Determination and the Question of Choice," *Development Dialogue* (Uppsala, Sweden) Nos. 1 – 2 (1992), pp. 91 – 102.

对儿子的偏爱是跨时代及地域性的,一般来说,父系社会的家庭都希望至少有一个儿子,而儿子的人数自然是越多越好。这种偏好取决于三类决定女性价值的因素:(1)经济因素,包括女性工作的价值,女性对家庭收入和劳动力的贡献,以及她们是否有嫁妆。(2)社会因素,特别是亲属关系、婚姻模式和宗教信仰。(3)心理因素。这会影响家庭的组成,造成大家庭及高生育率,当然,如果父母采用适当的后代性别选择手段,或父母不干预后代性别,也可以拥有小家庭。我们特别关注的是那些采取各种手段以实现理想的家庭性别结构的人群。

三、如何判断性别比例是否正常

人类偏爱儿子的历史很长,在古籍中就有关于如何判断胎儿性别方法的描述。但如何检验男孩的出生的确是人为选择的结果呢?或者说,如何证明女孩是因为其性别而被主动或被动地杀死的呢?办法之一是查看当时社会中的性别比例,即男女人数的比例,来确定人口的性别是否平衡。只有当人口性别比例符合正常的生物学规律时,才存在所谓的性别平衡。性别比例有两个重要的指数,一是新生儿性别比例,正常值是105—107(男):100(女),不同人群因父母的生育年龄和饮食营养状况而有所差异。[1] 另一是总人口性别比例,正常值

---

[1] 研究者注意到,一般而言,父亲年龄越大,新生儿性别比越低。素食的父母生下的孩子性别比可能也低于一般水平。非洲后裔生女儿的几率较一般水平要高,因此他们的性别比一般在102.5(男):100(女)与103.5(男):100(女)之间。参见 Stephan Klasen, "'Missing Women' Reconsidered," *World Development*, Vol. 22, No. 7 (July 1994), p. 1062。人口学家承认,世界其他地区人口出生性别比在105(男):100(女)与107(男):100(女)之间。William H. James, "The Sex Ratio of Oriental Births," *Annal of Human Biology*, Vol. 12, No. 5 (September/October 1985), pp. 485–487。除了出生性别比,还有怀孕时的性别比,这一比例大约为160(男):100(女),男性居多。多数流产的或死胎都是107(男):100(女)与107(男):100(女)之间。参见 Klasen, "'Missing Women' reconsidered," *World Development*, Vol. 22, No. 7 (July 1994), pp. 1061–1071。

是100（男）：100（女），因整个社会的年龄结构、死亡结构和跨国流动性等因素而存在差异。①

由于女性普遍长寿，所以在发达地区性别比例为97—98（男）：100（女）。新生儿性别比例超过105—107（男）：100（女），则可以认定性别比例不平衡。在孩童人口基数足够大的前提下，整个社会的总体性别比例若超过100（男）：100（女），则表示存在女性的非正常死亡。0—4岁孩童性别比例超过105（男）：100（女），则可断定存在后代性别选择现象。如果男性是100或更高，就表示女性死亡率过高。

新生儿性别比例才是该社会性别是否平衡的最准确的指标，总人口性别比例容易造成误判，例如中东国家有大量的外国男性劳工，就会造成过高的总性别比例。② 类似，城市性别比例也会因为男性向城市的流动性更强而偏高。总性别比例就算正常，也可能掩盖问题的存在，例如后代性别选择只存在于某部分的人口中，却被全体女性的长寿给抵消了。因此，我们必须把数据分开来剖析，才能决定该社会是否采用子女性别选择的手段。

判断性别是否被人为操纵，在现代社会是很直截了当的，因为有精准的数据。但在工业革命之前或在没有准确记录的社会中，难度就大了。有些国家，如印度，通过人口普查有了总人口的性别比例，却没有新生儿性别比例。

考古学家及人类学家发现，从更新世以来的埋葬场可以找到的证

---

① 一般而言，女性的预期寿命比男性长；因而，在有着庞大老龄人口的国家，如在欧洲和北美的国家，女性比例远远高于男性。战争中失去许多男性人口的国家，其性别比就低。

② 例如，2003年估算的巴林（135.1）、约旦（108.6）、科威特（151.3）、阿曼（135.0）、卡塔尔（173.5）、沙特阿拉伯（115.9）、阿拉伯联合酋长国（185.8）等国极高的人口性别比，主要都是因为这些国家有大量外籍劳工。Http://www.un.org/esa/population/publications/wpp2000/annextables.pdf.

据足以证明杀女婴是个世界范围内普遍存在的现象。① 但这些证据的价值有限，因为不知道当时人口的性别组成如何。学者们只能在有限的历史文献中发掘证据。在西方文化中有详尽的关于性别选择性杀婴的记载，来源可靠。而其他文化中相关记录则寥寥无几。当然，也有例外。中国、印度、古希腊、古罗马早期的法律、宗教文献、地方传说、旅行家及传教士的记录，也有关于当时杀女婴的情形。无论数据来源为何，在作分析及结论时必须很小心，因为这些数据本身可能有偏差或根本就是错的。

下文分述了不同地区的后代性别选择的相关文献，之后是关于后代性别选择为何得以长久持续的讨论。

四、后代性别选择概况

澳大利亚、南太平洋、中东、古希腊、古罗马、欧洲、南美、北美及亚洲都不看重女婴，因为男性在食物的取得及劳动的参与上贡献较大，其他例如：男人可以打仗（尤其是南太平洋的部落、南北美洲的土著）、照顾年老的父母（南太平洋、北美洲）、举行宗教仪式

---

① Vallois, "The Social Life of Early Man: The Evidence of Skeletons," in Sherwood L. Washburn, ed., *Social Life of Early Man* (New York: Wenner-Gren Foundation for Anthropological Research, 1961), pp. 214 – 235; and Mark Nathan Cohen and Sharon Bennett, "Skeletal Evidence for Sex Roles and Gender Hierarchies in Prehistory," in Barbara D. Miller, ed., *Sex and Gender Hierarchies* (Cambridge: Cambridge University Press, 1993), pp. 273 – 296. 一些考古学家和人类学家质疑这样的证据是否存在。如人类学家狄克曼（Midred Dikerman）认为，要断定几千前的性别比是不可能的。根据他的观点，男性头骨比女性的重，因此男性头骨及形状比女性的容易保存。他接着表明，没有检测骨盆，确定性别是相当困难的。Correspondence with Valerie Hudson, April 10, 1998. 对于这些质疑的回应，参见 Richard S. Meindl and Katherine F. Russell, "Recent Advances in Method and Theory in Paleodemogrphy," *Annual Review of Anthropology*, Vol. 27 (1998), pp. 375 – 399; and Jane E. Buikstra and Lyle W. Konigsberg, "Paleodemography: Critiques and Controversies," *American Anthropologist*, vol. 87, No. 2 (June 1985), pp. 316 – 333.

（南太平洋、亚洲）及延续家族香火（欧洲、亚洲）。古希腊、古罗马认为女性在体力、智力及精神上都不如男性，同时在欧洲养育女儿的花费比儿子高，因为需要嫁妆。当然，偏爱儿子不代表女婴非死不可，还要视父母对家庭组成的期待（几男几女），养儿育女的成本（在欧洲、亚洲需要嫁妆），以及社会是否看重婴儿的生命。尽管欧洲及中东的宗教严禁杀婴，但这方面的法律一直到16世纪至19世纪才在欧洲确立。而南美的雅诺玛莫部落根本没有这样的法律。以下关于区域性杀女婴的讨论，也许并不全面，但很有代表性。

（一）澳洲及南太平洋

大洋洲的土著民族很早就开始进行后代性别选择了。一位妇女回忆："当我出生时，母亲仍躺在床上，父亲走过来倚着栏杆，大喊着问是男是女。母亲回答'女孩'，父亲说：'杀了她，丢掉吧。'母亲拒绝了，所以我被正式命名 Letahulozo，代表'杀了她，丢掉吧'。"① 根据兰格尼斯（L. L. Langness）的说法，在新几内亚高原的比纳比纳部落一直都有杀女婴的历史，他说，杀女婴最常发生在母亲还在喂奶时。② 比纳比纳的人认为女孩不会成为战士，而且一旦嫁人就无法照顾年老的父母。③ 历史上大溪地部落杀女婴的原因也类似。④

约瑟夫·伯塞尔（Joseph Birdsell）研究澳洲土著，发现18世纪末

---

① 来自1958年巴布亚新几内亚东部高原的基里诺·阿依诺（Kilino Aino）的叙述。转引自 Mildred Dickemann, "Concepts and Classification in the Study of Human Infanticide: Sectional Introduction and Some Cautionary Notes," p. 427。

② L. L. Langness, "Sexual Antagonism in the New Guinea Highlands: A Bena Bena Example," *Oceania*, Vol. 38, No. 3 (March 1967), pp. 161 – 177.

③ Ibid., p. 166.

④ Sumner, *Folkways*, 317.

期（与欧洲人接触之前）的性别比例约为 150（男）：100（女）。① 土著会用杀女婴来控制人口和性别结构。他们经常迁移，母亲喂奶的时间很长，通常每三年才要一个小孩。②

詹姆斯·派格斯（James Peggs）转述一个传教士在 19 世纪时和新西兰土著接触的经验：

> 我们和土著讨论这个主题，他们以快乐的口吻谈到了好几位当地最受尊敬的女性，她们就曾以 ro-mea（在婴儿出生时把鼻子掐住的方法）杀死自己的女儿，然后用蚌壳将自己割伤，大声哭喊，让别人误以为她在哀悼死去的婴儿。她们这么做，一方面是由于女婴对她们在战争中御敌无用，这是最主要的原因；另一方面，如果孩子人数过多，母亲的负担就会过重。于是她们杀死女婴，留下男孩。③

战时，女性不仅无法御敌，还需要男性的额外保护，以防止被掳掠或强暴。

（二）中东

《古兰经》中也有古代中东地区杀女婴的记录，例如在第 16 章第 58、59 节经文中描述生女儿的"不幸"——"当他们中的一个人听

---

① Joseph B. Birdsell, "On Population Structure in Generalized Hunting and Collecting Populations," *Evolution*, Vol. 12, No. 2 (June 1958), pp. 189–205; and Joseph B. Birdsell, "Some Predictions for the Pleistocene Based in Equilibrium Systems among Recent Hunter-Gatherers," in Richard B. Lee and Irven deVore eds., *Man the Hunter* (Chicago: Aldine de Gruyter, 1968), pp. 229–240.

② Dickemann, "Demographic Consequences of Infanticide in Man," p. 121.

③ James Peggs, *Cries of Agony: An Historical Account of Suttee Infanticide, Ghat Murders, and Slavery in India* (originally published as India's Cries to British Humanity, 1830; reprint, Delhi: Discovery Publishing House, 1984 [page references are to print edition]), p. 27.

说自己的妻子生女儿的时候,他的脸黯然失色,而且满腹牢骚。他为这个噩耗而不与宗族会面,他多方考虑:究竟是忍辱保留她呢?还是把她活埋在土里呢?"第81章第8、9节中提到活埋女婴:"当太阳黯黩的时候,当星宿零落的时候,当山峦崩溃的时候,当孕驼被抛弃的时候,当野兽被集合的时候,当海洋澎湃的时候,当灵魂被配合的时候,当被活埋的女婴被询问的时候:'她为什么罪过而遭杀害呢?'当功过簿被展开的时候,当天皮被揭去的时候,当火狱被燃着的时候,当乐园被送近的时候,每个人都知道他所做过的罪恶。"(译文参考了马坚译《古兰经》中译本。——译者注)先知穆罕默德浇灭了杀女婴的热情,但一些伊斯兰国家中(尤其是孟加拉国及巴基斯坦)的性别比例仍然过高。

(三) 希腊、罗马及欧洲

在西方,身为女性是不利的。古希腊、古罗马的哲学家认为,女性的体温比男人低,所以体力、智力也低,亚里士多德认为体温会影响她们推理的能力,很多人还认为她们的灵魂也比男性软弱。值得一提的是,柏拉图派及斯多葛派并不同意这种说法,他们认为女性在灵魂及美德上都可以与男性并驾齐驱。① 此外,女儿不被重视还因为嫁妆太贵。(当然,儿子太多的家庭还会面临财产分割的问题。)②

多数学者认同古罗马存在杀女婴的行为,但这种行为被实施的程度尚存讨论空间。在古希腊、古罗马的神话和戏剧中常有弃婴的故事。③

---

① Gillian Clark, *Women in Late Antiquity: Pagan and Christian Lifestyles* (Oxford: Clarendon, 1994), pp. 120 – 121.

② Sue Blundell, *Women in Ancient Greece* (London: British Museum Press, 1995), p. 131.

③ Donald Engels, "The Problem of Female Infanticide in the Greco-Roman World," *Classical Philology*, Vol. 75, No. 2 (April 1980), pp. 112 – 120. 恩格尔斯认为杀女婴现象存在,但不算普遍。而威廉姆斯则认为杀女婴更为普遍。见 Williams V. Harris, "The Theoretical Possibility of Extensive Infanticide in the Graeco-Roman World," *Classical Quarterly*, Vol. 32, No. 1 (1982), pp. 114 – 116。

弃婴和杀婴不同，弃婴不一定造成婴儿的死亡。古希腊、古罗马的法律都有养育弃婴的条款，明确他们长大之后是奴隶还是自由人。法老时期的埃及允许弃婴被其他家族成员收养，但古罗马对此是明令禁止的。①

从法律条文中，我们也可窥见历史上的后代性别选择长期存在。公元前 8 世纪的法律揭示了杀女婴在当时很普遍，罗马的开国君王罗慕洛斯（Romulus）（公元前 753—前 716 年）要求罗马的公民"把每个男婴及长女抚养成人"。② 父母不得杀女婴，除非是畸形婴，但他们可以将婴儿给五个近邻看过，并征求他们的同意后，将之抛弃。

在已经发现的古罗马统计文献中，当时的人口是男多于女，但专家们认为该数据是不可靠的。公元前 2 世纪公民的注册记录也显现男多于女。潘慕洛（Sarah Pomeroy）认为，这表示当时就已盛行杀女婴。③ 特尔斐（Delphi）的铭文记载，在有公民身份的 600 个家庭中，只有 1% 有一个以上的女儿。④ 公元前 228—前 220 年美里塔司人记录，在 79 个公民家庭中共有 118 个儿子、28 个女儿。⑤ 罗塞尔（Aline Rousselle）研究古罗马，发现当时弃婴相当普遍，尤其是奥古斯丁的法律规定一家只能有 3 个孩子。⑥ 由于不希望女儿们未来找不到结婚对象，而且男性死于战争的几率很高，女儿嫁不掉的可能性大增。⑦ 为了避

---

① Aline Rousselle, "Body Politics in Ancient Rome," in Pauline Schmitt Pantel, ed., *A History of Women in the West*, Vol. 1: *From Ancient Goddesses to Christian Saints* (Cambridge, Mass.: Belknap, 1992), p. 307.

② Lefkowitz and Fant, *Women's Life in Greece and Rome*, pp. 207 – 222.

③ Pomeroy, "Infanticide in Hellenistic Greece," pp. 207 – 222.

④ Jack Lindsay, *The Ancient World: Manners and Morals* (New York: G. P. Putnam's Sons, 1968), p. 168.

⑤ Ibid.

⑥ Rousselle, "Body Politics in Ancient Rome," p. 307.

⑦ Eve Cantarella, *Pandora's Daughters: The Role and Status of Women in Greek and Roman Antiquity*, trans. Maureen B. Fant with a foreword by Mary R. Lefkowitz (Baltimore, Md.: Johns Hopkins University Press, 1987), p. 44.

免让家庭没面子，被弃的女婴远多于男婴。贫穷的家庭尤其容易弃婴，促使康斯坦丁大帝于公元 315 年时，决定提供贫户儿女的衣服及食物。由于宗教法律约束，基督教的欧洲在公元 4 世纪早期就禁止了杀婴行为。① 而当杀婴造成了公元 374 年罗马人口的大幅减少时，罗马也将杀婴定为谋杀罪。②

古希腊也有杀女婴的现象。一封古希腊公民希拉润（Hilarion）在公元前 1 年写给太太阿丽丝（Alis）的信中说："如果你怀孕，是男孩的话就留下来，女孩就打掉。"③ 公元前 3 世纪的一部希腊喜剧中谈到抛弃女婴："所有人，包括穷人，都养儿子；所有人，包括富人，都杀女儿。"④ 父亲通常把不要的婴儿放在陶罐内，弃置于住宅附近的路边。希腊、罗马的法律赋予父亲很大的权力，杀婴往往不被定罪。⑤ 在某些案例中，女人虽有杀婴嫌疑，只要声称是贫穷导致的，通常也会被宽恕。事实上人们很少提请杀婴诉讼，因为很难证明婴儿的死亡是有意为之还是出于意外。但因弃婴太多，古罗马在公元 787 年成立第一所弃婴收容所，类似的机构随后在欧洲各地纷纷成立。⑥

许多世纪以来，杀婴逐渐被当作一种需要严厉惩罚的罪行。16 世纪法国法律、17 世纪英国及苏格兰法律均要求，非婚怀孕者必

---

① Claudia Opitz, "Life in the Late Middle Ages," in Christiane Klapisch-Zuber, ed., *A History of Women in the West*, Vol. 2: *Silences of the Middle Ages* (Cambridge, Mass.: Belknap, 1992), pp. 267–317.

② Ibid., p. 308.

③ From the Papryi Oxyrhynchus 4.774.1–10, quoted in Elaine Fantham, Helene Peet Foley, Natalie Boymel Kampen, Sarah B. Pomeroy, and H. A. Shapiro, *Women in the Classical World: Image and Text* (New York: Oxford University Press, 1994), p. 162.

④ Poseidippus, *Hermaphroditus*, fragment 12, Kassel-Austin, Fantham, et al., *Women in the Classical World*, p. 162.

⑤ John Boswell, *The Kindness of Strangers: The Abandonment of Children in Western Europe from Late Antiquity to the Renaissance* (London: Penguin, 1989), pp. 58–60.

⑥ Poseidippus, *Hermaphroditus*, fragment 12, Kassel-Austin, Fantham, et al., *Women in the Classical World*, p. 162.

须登记，不登记就被认定是有意杀婴，被处以烧死或绞刑。① 德国及瑞士也通过了类似的法律，妇女如犯此罪会遭"利棒穿身而活埋"。② 到了 18 及 19 世纪早期，整个欧洲都把杀婴定为死罪，俄罗斯除外。③

杀婴及弃婴的两个主要原因是：对嫁妆和社会地位的顾虑。欧洲当时嫁妆的金额十分昂贵，15 世纪早期意大利甚至有嫁妆的保险（女儿的父母可存一笔钱直到她出嫁，只要他们的女儿活着且顺利出嫁，利息就付给丈夫作为嫁妆）。④ 另外，有些富有家庭宁可抛弃女儿，也不愿意冒险把她嫁给地位太低的丈夫。⑤ 有权无钱的家庭，干脆把女儿送进修道院，以免筹不到嫁妆钱或找不到适婚对象。⑥

艾米莉·科尔曼（Emily Coleman）研究了公元 9 世纪巴黎圣日耳曼—德普莱的农村人口，她指出另一个与杀女婴有关的因素是给妇女劳动所赋予的价值。⑦ 她从税收记录中发现，可耕地的面积和性别比例有密切关联，耕地越多产量越高的农场，性别比例越正常；耕地面积和产量若不足，性别比例就会呈现男多女少。⑧ 在面积大于 17 布努阿里亚（bunuaria，1 布努阿里亚相当于 120 平方码）的农场里，成

---

① Nicole Castan, "Criminals," in Natalie Zemon Davis and Arlette Farge, eds., *A History of Women in the West*, Vol. 3: *Renaissance and Enlightenment Paradoxes* (Cambridge, Mass.: Belknap, 1993), pp. 474 – 488.

② Westermarck, *The Origin and Development of the Moral Ideas*, p. 412.

③ Ibid., p. 413.

④ Edith Ennen, *The Medieval Woman*, trans. Edmund Jephcott (Oxford: Basil Blackwell, 1989), p. 230.

⑤ Ibid.

⑥ Eileen Power and Michael Moissey Postan, eds., *Medieval Women* (Cambridge. Cambridge University Press, 1975), pp. 89 – 90.

⑦ Emily R. Coleman, "L'infanticide dans le Haut Moyen Age," *Annales: Economies, Sociétés, Civilizations*, Vol. 29, No. 2 (March-April 1974), pp. 315 – 335.

⑧ Ibid., pp. 322 – 323.

人的性别比例为 97.33（男）∶100（女）；在面积小于 1 布努阿里亚的农场，成人性别比例为 421.05（男）∶100（女）。对应于上述两种农场面积，儿童的性别比例则分别为 107.14（男）∶100（女）和 200（男）∶100（女）。① 然而，性别比并没有因为农场尺寸的增加而上升，因为中型农场的性别比例也高达 169（男）∶100（女）。根据科尔曼的观点，这些高性别比例的出现并非因为女性样本的代表数不足，而是因为存在杀女婴的现象。科尔曼认为税务清单上的数据来源"相对合理，且结构严谨"，不会忽略女性纳税人。② 她得出结论：杀女婴反映了一种认识，即男婴在农场会更有价值。性别比例可能会根据生活在农场的男性数量和特定土地上的劳动类型而发生变动。高性别比例是因为在农场耕作或林地开垦时，都需要男性。③

科尔曼还发现，与其他欧洲地区流行"男高女低"的婚嫁模式不同，在圣日耳曼-德普莱的农业人口中流行"女高男低"的婚嫁模式。女性多嫁给地位不如己的男士，因为她看重的不是社会地位而是他的劳力价值。我们并不能从圣日耳曼-德普莱这一案例中推断历史上的法国流行杀女婴，在一国内的不同地区，性别比例也存在差异。例如莫尼克·泽娜-查达万妮（Monique Zerner-Chardavoine）在研究税务记录时发现，在公元 9 世纪的马赛，女孩的人数多于男孩。④

中古世纪后期欧洲女性的地位日高，性别比例也趋向正常，甚至

---

① Emily R. Coleman, "L'infanticide dans le Haut Moyen Age," *Annales*：*Economies, Sociétés, Civilizations*, Vol. 29, No. 2（March-April 1974），p. 318.

② Emily R. Coleman, "Medieval Marriage Characteristics：A Neglected Factor in the History of Medieval Serfdom," in Theodore K. Rabb and Robert I. Rotberg, eds., *The Family in History：Interdisciplinary Essays*（New York：Harper and Row, 1971），p. 5.

③ Ibid., p. 6.

④ Monique Zerner-Chardavoine, "Enfants et jeunes au IXe siècle：La démographie du polyptypue de Marseille, 813–814," *Provence historique*, No. 126（1981），pp. 335–384.

有女多于男的地方。始于 14 世纪都市的女性劳工渐多，富有人家雇用来自较低阶层的女佣、奴隶及奶妈。①年轻妇女开始从事家庭手工业或农业，也是在这一时期，女性获得了拥有财产的权利。经济机会和权利多了，女婴的存活率也高了。

不过，例外还是有的，文艺复兴时期的历史学家崔斯勒（Richard Trexler）就发现 15 世纪意大利的佛罗伦萨曾杀女婴。②他从弃婴医院及税赋记录中，找到在 1427 年的新生儿性别比例是 114.6（男）：100（女），1 岁是 118.4（男）：100（女）。③这些数据类似于同年 0—4 岁的主要性别比例 119.7（男）：100（女）。戴维·赫尔里奇（David Herlihy）在对于中世纪女性预期寿命的研究中发现，当把佛罗伦萨的城市和乡村混合起来计算，儿童的性别比例比崔斯勒所引述的更高。赫尔里奇指出，0—12 岁的儿童性别比例是 123.59（男）：100（女）。④崔斯勒进而提出，有钱人家重男轻女，0—4 岁的性别比例在缴税多于 400 佛罗林银币（florins）的家庭是 124.56（男）：100（女）。⑤佛罗伦萨的弃婴收养院里有许多女孩，也显示一种对女

---

① 关于过剩女性和工作场所中女性可能得到的工作机会的讨论，参见 Mildred Dickemann, "Female Infanticide, Reproductive Strategies, and Social Stratification: A Preliminary Model," in Napoleon A. Chagnon and William Irons, eds., *Evolutionary Biology and Human Behavior: An Anthropological Perspective* (North Scituate, Mass.: Duxbury, 1979), pp. 321–367。

② Richard C. Trexler, "Infanticide in Florence: New Sources and First Results," *History of Childhood Quarterly: The Journal of Psychohistory*, Vol. 1, No. 1 (Summer 1973), pp. 98–116.

③ Richard C. Trexler, "Infanticide in Florence: New Sources and First Results," *History of Childhood Quarterly: The Journal of Psychohistory*, Vol. 1, No. 1 (Summer 1973), pp. 100–101.

④ David Herlihy, "Life Expectancies for Women in Medieval Society," in Rosemarie Thee Morewedge, ed., *The Role of Women in the Middgle Ages: Papers of the Sixth Annual Conference of the Center for Medieval and Early Renaissance Studies*, State University of New York at Binghamton, 6–8 May 1972 (Albany: State University of New York Press, 1975), p. 22.

⑤ 在有钱人家的高性别比例，据崔斯勒的观点，表明这些家庭更倾向于要一个私生子，而不是私生女。参见 Trexler, "Infanticide in Florence," pp. 101, 112。

孩的排斥①,这一点也得到教会告解记录(父母向教士忏悔以求获得原谅)的确证。弃婴医院及教会的告解记录(父母向教士忏悔杀婴以获得原谅),崔斯勒得出的结论是:"无论在法律中、家庭中还是在收容所里,欧洲社会偏爱男孩,导致不少女婴被杀。"②

凯勒姆(Barbara Kellum)研究中世纪的英国,同时找到非性别选择杀婴和杀女婴的证据。③ 虽然关于英国被杀儿童的性别数据不可获,仍有证据表明至少在部分地区存在杀女婴的现象。她参阅了《尸检后的审查报告》(当时佃农关于其所有物和继承人的公共记录),发现从1250—1348年及1430—1545年,人口性别比例从100(男):100(女)增至133(男):100(女),在农民及农奴的相关报告中,性别比例更高,是170(男):100(女)。④ 杀婴的原因无非是:未婚生子的耻辱、私生子女继承的困难、杀婴后果不严重以及养儿育女负担太重。而杀女婴的原因则并不这么明显,凯勒姆并未指出杀女婴的行为动机,我们推测这仍与中世纪女性的社会地位和社会价值相关。

到了16世纪,几乎每个欧洲都市都有弃婴收容机构,兰格(Lange)说,这些机构中的死亡率很高,弃婴在送进来时通常就已奄奄一息而无法存活。其余存活的就被放在通风不良、食物不足的地方,又因为护士人手缺乏,所以弃婴得被送到护士集中站,而在长途

---

① 参见 Richard C. Trexler, "The Foundlings of Florence, 1395 – 1455," *History of Childhood Quarterly: The Journal of Psychohistory*, Vol.1, No. 2 (Fall 1973), pp. 259 – 284。1404—1413年,在佛罗伦萨弃婴收养院中有61.2%的女婴;15世纪30年代,由于乡村受到较大的压力,女婴比例上升到66.3%。

② Trexler, "Infanticide in Florence," p. 110.

③ Barbara A. Kellum, "Infanticide in England in the Later Middle Ages," *History of Childhood Quarterly: The Journal of Psychohistory*, Vol.1, No. 3 (Winter 1974), pp. 367 – 388.

④ Barbara A. Kellum, "Infanticide in England in the Later Middle Ages," *History of Childhood Quarterly: The Journal of Psychohistory*, Vol.1, No. 3 (Winter 1974), p. 368.

跋涉的途中大多数婴儿都夭折了。① 那些活下来的婴儿不断死于蔓延于医院和济贫院的传染病。根据兰格的统计，在 18、19 世纪法国弃婴收容所中，80%—90%的弃婴在第一年内死亡，许多是在几天内就丧生了。②

（四）北美洲

北美洲是否也有杀女婴的习俗，看法不一，但杀女婴的案例在北极区时有所闻——包括奈茨利克的因纽特人（Netsilik Innit），他们生活在佩利湾的奈茨利克，位于布西亚半岛的哈德逊湾西北部。根据弗里曼（Milton Freeman）的说法，历史文献显示，因纽特人常常杀死女婴是因为他们认为儿子比女儿更有价值。③ 半岛地区的因纽特部落，父亲把儿子视为同伴及合伙猎人，女儿则因为亲近母亲，威胁到父亲的地位，所以不为父亲所爱，并因此遭到杀害。

瑞奇（David Riches）认为，不利的环境也会造成杀婴。他指出，因纽特部落的性别比例在 19、20 两世纪中随着环境的好坏而变动。④ 他认为，杀女婴也和通婚制度有关，奈茨利克人会把尚未命名的女婴许配给近亲，如果没有对象，她极可能被杀害，因为父母不愿意冒险把女儿嫁给存在竞争关系的对手。⑤ 艾里克（Eric）和史密斯（Abigial Smith）认为，埃森巴利克对奈茨利克人的研究发现，母亲与祖母在杀女婴的决定中起着一定的作用，因此，这一习俗不能单纯地由男

---

① Langer, "Checks on Population Growth, 1750 – 1850," p. 98.
② Langer, "Checks on Population Growth, 1750 – 1850," p. 98.
③ Milton M. R. Freeman, "A Social and Ecologic Analysis of Systematic Female Infanticide among the Netsilik Eskimo," *American Anthropologist*, Vol. 73, No. 5 (October 1971), pp. 1011 – 1018.
④ David Riches, "The Netsilik Eskimo: A Special Case of Selective Female Infanticide," *Ethnology: An International Journal of Cultural and Social Anthropology*, Vol. 13. No. 4 (October 1974), pp. 351 – 361.
⑤ Ibid., p. 358.

性统治这一因素来解释。①

根据1880—1930年的人口普查数据,杀女婴发生在从阿拉斯加的斯迈斯海角(Cape Smyth,极区的西北)到巴芬岛(Baffin Island)的整个区域。② 近来尽管学者推论说一些因纽特人的性别比例并没有严重扭曲,如一些数据所显示,在105—224之间变动,基本指标为173(男):100(女),但他们确认,存在杀女婴的情形。③ 艾利克(Eric)和史密斯(Abigail Smith)不认为他们杀女婴是想平衡成年人口的比例(成年男性多于觅食时死亡)或控制人口规模,他们的假设是——杀女婴是因为投资男孩的回报较大。如此假设成立,便可对奈茨利克人之外的因纽特人也杀女婴的行为作出解释。④

美国非土著的族群中也有不正常的儿童性别比例,只是数据并不完整。汉默尔(E. A. Hammel)等人在研究19世纪美国儿童性别比的过程中,发现除了人口迁徙的因素,男女童所受照顾不同、女孩死亡率过高是当时儿童性别比例扭曲的重要原因。⑤(14岁以前女童死亡人数多过男童),因为"在农业经济中,男孩与女孩的经济价值不同"。⑥ 尽管在城市中心,男孩女孩被视为具有同等价值,但乡村家庭仍然愿意要能够承担繁重农活的男孩。

---

① Eric Alden Smith and S. Abigail Smith, "Inuit Sex-Ratio Variation: Population Control, Ethnographic Error, or Parental Manipulation?" *Current Anthropology*, Vol. 35. No. 5 (December 1994), p. 604.

② See Asen Balikci, "Female Infanticide on the Arctic Coast," *Man : The Journal of the Royal Anthropological Institute*, Vol. 2, No. 4 (December 1967), p. 165; and Smith and Smith, "Inuit Sex-Ratio Variation," p. 597.

③ 请注意近来文献中因纽特人(Inuit)已取代爱斯基摩人(Eskimo)的用法,主要依据的是当地人的偏好。Smith and Smith, "Inuit Sex-Ratio Variation."

④ Smith and Smith, "Inuit Sex-Ratio Variation."

⑤ E. A. Hammel, Sheila R. Johansson, and Caren A. Ginsberg, "The Value of Children during Industrialization: Sex Ratios in Childhood in Nineteenth-Century America," *Journal of Family History*, Vol. 8, No. 4 (Winter 1983), pp. 346-366.

⑥ Ibid., pp. 346-347.

(五) 南美

南美有几个部落实施后代性别选择。南美的雅诺玛莫印地安人部落在委内瑞拉南部，靠近巴西北部，共有约 125 个村庄，部落之间至今战争不断。该部落男女婴儿都杀，但杀的女婴更多。在对南美雅诺玛莫人的研究中，人类学家查冈（Napoleon Chagnon）发现成人和儿童人口的高性别比例。1964—1968 年在 7 个村庄所作的人口调查，显示共有 449 位男性及 391 位女性，性别比例为 115（男）：100（女）。① 这个数字其实低估了女婴被杀的数目，因为有许多男性都已死于部落战争。② 根据尼尔（James Neel）和查冈的研究，年轻的雅诺玛莫人的性别比例还要更高：15 岁以下人口的性别比例是 128.6（男）：100（女）。③ 查冈认为，这些数据证实了雅诺玛莫人实施了性别选择性杀女婴，父母把有限的资源投资在儿子身上，因为他有一天会成为战士及猎人。④

他们没有预见到的后果是，杀女婴最后让这些战士都找不到太太，这个问题又被酋长的"一夫多妻"所激化，最后雅诺玛莫的战士只好频频袭击邻近的村庄，强掳女性为妻。⑤

其他南美的部落，包括亚马孙河附近的萨拉纳华（Sharanahua）

---

① 查冈于 1964—1968 年间花了 19 个月的时间生活在雅诺玛莫人中。性别比的数据并不是单纯参考某一特定年份得出的。Chagnon, *Yanomamo: The Fierce People*, p. 74.

② 更多男性死于部落战争的数据主要来自查冈收集来自两个部落的死亡原因数据。在研究阶段，萨马塔里（Shamatari）的人口中，5 名女子死于战争中，而男子则有 52 名。同期，纳莫威-泰利（Namowei-teri）的人口中有 9 名女子死于战争，而男子则有 44 名。Chagnon, *Studying the Yanomamo* (New York: Holt, Rinehart, and Winston, 1974), p. 160.

③ James V. Neel and Napoleon A. Chagnon, "The Demography of Two Tribes of Primitive, Relatively Unacculturated American Indians," *Proceedings of the National Academy of Sciences*, Vol. 59, No. 3 (March 1968), p. 681.

④ Chagnon, *Yanomamo: The Fierce People*, p. 75.

⑤ Chagnon, *Yanomamo: The Fierce People*, p. 125.

部落及沙万提（Xavante）部落也会杀女婴。① 在沙万提部落，0—14 岁人口的性别比例是 124（男）：100（女），秘鲁的卡什纳华（Cashinahua）部落的性别比例曾高达 148（男）：100（女）。② 正如在雅诺玛莫人中发生的情形一样，狄克曼认为："择偶的竞争及一夫多妻制的刺激，使儿童订婚和成人抢婚成为南美部落的常见现象。"③

（六）日本

罗伯特·恩格（Robert Eng）研究日本中原地区 18、19 世纪的历史，发现了当时日本人杀女婴的证据。18、19 世纪的日本中原村，曾通过杀女婴，日语称为 mabiki，意味"家庭瘦身"来操纵家庭的人口及组成。父母根据孩子的性别和已有孩子的性别来选择是否留下新生儿，还是"送回去"。④ 当家中儿子多于女儿时，父母希望下一胎是女儿［下一胎的性别比例为 79（男）：100（女）］。儿女人数相等的，则希望下一胎是儿子［下一胎的性别比例为 168（男）：100（女）］。⑤ 样本数据显示了对男性后代的明显偏好。小家庭对后代的性别选择尤其明显（家中有一到三个儿女），性别比例是 188（男）：100（女），中型家庭（四至五个孩子）的性别比例是 130（男）：100（女），大家庭（六个或更多的小孩）的性别比例是 107（男）：100

---

① Warren M. Tern, "Health and Demography of Native Amazonians: Historical Perspective and Current Status," in Anna Roosevelt, ed., *Amazonian Indians from Prehistory to the Present: Anthropological Perspectives* (Tucson: University of Arizona Press, 1994), pp. 123–149.

② Dickemann, "Demographic Consequences of Infanticide in Man," p. 129.

③ Ibid.

④ Robert Y. Eng, "Fertility and Infanticide," in Thomas C. Smith, ed., *Nakahara: Family Farming and Population in a Japanese Village, 1717–1830* (Stanford, Calif.: Stanford University Press, 1977), p. 66.

⑤ Ibid.

（女）。① 在日本家庭人口较多的时期，杀女婴的现象并不多见。但是18、19世纪时期，日本社会以小家庭居多。

石井良一（Ryoichi Ishii）通过研究日本人口趋势发现，人口压力是不同时期杀婴行为的导因，而且不仅限于杀女婴。②根据石井的观点，日本的社会历史反映出，环境压力（特别是饥荒）和经济困境（大多数人的贫穷及微薄的遗产继承收入）都会导致人们采取杀婴来限制家庭规模和构成。他认为，杀婴在日本人口的各个层面都广泛存在。③

一部19世纪末期的作品《人民恶习之条件》（Minkan Akushu Jojitsu）解释了江户时代杀婴的原因:④ 有三个（二男一女）以上的小孩会对家庭和社会造成负担，而且年纪大了还生孩子会让家族蒙羞。尽管江户时期的调查中没有作人口的年龄组分类，到了19世纪晚期和20世纪早期，这种数据已可获得，学者可用来估算婴儿性别比例。1884—1930年五岁以下的儿童性别比例为：1884年112.5（男）：100（女）、1893年117.5（男）：100（女）、1903年128.1（男）：100（女）、1913年133.4（男）：100（女）、1920年133.3（男）：100（女）、1925年138.3（男）：100（女）、1930年139.8（男）：100（女）。⑤

狄克曼在对日本人口的研究中发现了类似的结论。他认为，随着人口的迅速成长，18世纪初期，日本杀婴行为开始出现。杀婴使得父母能放弃女婴而保留儿子，以继承家族香火。根据1750年日本的人

---

① Robert Y. Eng, "Fertility and Infanticide," in Thomas C. Smith, ed., *Nakahara: Family Farming and Population in a Japanese Village, 1717 – 1830* (Stanford, Calif.: Stanford University Press, 1977), p. 77.

② Ryoichi Ishii, *Population Pressure and Economic Life in Japan* (London: P. S. King and Son, 1937).

③ Ibid., p. 31.

④ Cited in Ryoichi Ishii, *Population Pressure and Economic Life in Japan* (London: P. S. King and Son, 1937), pp. 31 – 32.

⑤ Cited in Ryoichi Ishii, *Population Pressure and Economic Life in Japan* (London: P. S. King and Son, 1937), p. 90.

口普查，总性别比例为 114（男）：100（女），在以后的两个世纪性别比例逐渐降低，直到 1950 年成为正常。① 在那之后，后代性别选择在日本就不是问题了。

五、当代不同文化中的后代性别选择

在世界许多地方，重男轻女的观念至今依然。南希·威廉姆森（Nancy Williamson）于 1976 年所作的调查发现，美国、拉丁美洲、加勒比地区、泰国以及以色列的人，重男轻女的程度较为适中。黎巴嫩郊区的女性、印度的都市人、印度的基督教徒、韩国人、台湾地区的人则是"非常"重男轻女。阿尔及利亚的农村、埃及、突尼斯的女人，印度的安德拉邦、古加拉特邦、扎莫和克什米尔邦、克拉拉邦、中央邦等地区的男人，以及古加拉特邦的女人表现出了极度的重男轻女。② 1983 年《世界生育调查》的作者检视了 27 个国家对后代性别的偏好，发现其中有 6 个国家——孟加拉国、约旦、尼泊尔、巴基斯坦、韩国及叙利亚，"极度"重男轻女，有 8 个国家——多米尼加、斐济、莱索托、马来西亚、墨西哥、斯里兰卡、苏丹及泰国，"相当程度"上重男轻女。③

重男轻女会造成高生育率——女性为了生儿子而大量生育，对女

---

① Dickemann, "Demographic Consequences of Infanticide in Man," p. 129.

② Nancy E. Williamson, *Sons or Daughters: A Cross-Cultural Survey of Parental Preferences* (London: Sage, 1976).

③ 下列国家和地区在调查中具有代表性：非洲/中东——约旦、肯尼亚、莱索托、苏丹、叙利亚；亚洲——孟加拉、斐济、印度尼西亚、韩国、马来西亚、尼泊尔、巴基斯坦、菲律宾、斯里兰卡、泰国；美洲——哥伦比亚、哥斯达黎加、多米尼加共和国、圭亚那、海地、牙买加、墨西哥、巴拿马、巴拉圭、秘鲁、特立尼达、委内瑞拉。John Cleland, Jane Verrall, and Martin Vaessen, "Preferences for the Sex of Children and Their Influence on Reproductive Behaviour," World Fertility Survey Comparative Studies No. 27 (Voorburg, Netherlands: International Statistical Institute, 1983).

孩疏于照顾,以及堕胎。《世界生育调查》发现阿拉伯女性虽然也偏爱男孩,但却不会因此改变生育模式。① 但墨西哥及亚洲国家(如斐济、马来西亚、尼泊尔、巴基斯坦、韩国、斯里兰卡)的生育率,则和母亲是否节育有直接关系。②

威廉姆森的研究表明,重男轻女并不局限于发展中国家。克里斯南(Vijaya Krishnan)认为,在发展中国家,社会变迁如女性参与劳动和获得更多的教育机会比子女性别更能影响对于生育和家庭结构的决定;然而性别可能仍然在女性决定是否避孕中起到作用。她发现加拿大女性在决定是否避孕时,会受到她已有的子女的性别影响——已有两个儿子的会比有两个女儿的,更可能使用避孕药。③ 美国人是否也重男轻女,至今我们还没有定论。1988—1996 年,在 7 个欧洲国家所作的生育率调查指出,特别想要儿子、女儿的人都有,也有人根本不在乎。但捷克、立陶宛及葡萄牙人似乎偏爱女孩。④

最重男轻女的地区是在亚洲。1994 年联合国人口基金及韩国政府支持的研讨会中,众口一致地认为亚洲国家和地区对儿子偏爱。⑤ 研究中注意到孟加拉国、中国大陆、印度、尼泊尔、巴基斯坦、韩国、台湾地区及越南,最重男轻女,尽管与会者也注意到这种偏爱在这些国家或地区之内因地域和种族不同而有所不同。他们补充说:"在存在

---

① John Cleland, Jane Verrall, and Martin Vaessen, "Preferences for the Sex of Children and Their Influence on Reproductive Behaviour," World Fertility Survey Comparative Studies No. 27 (Voorburg, Netherlands: International Statistical Institute, 1983). p. 27.

② See ibid., p. 26, Table 7.

③ Vijaya Krishnan, "Gender of Children and Contraceptive Use," Journal of Biosocial Science, Vol. 25, No. 2 (April 1993), pp. 213 – 221.

④ Karsten Hank and Hans-Peter Kohler, "Gender Preferences for Children in Europe: Empirical Results from 17 FFS Countries," Demographic Research, Vol. 2 (January 2000), http://www.demographic-research.org/Volumes/Vol2/1.

⑤ 这一研讨会名为"亚洲快速变动的人口机制中儿童性别选择问题国家研讨会"(International Symposium on Issues Related to Sex Preference for Children in the Rapidly Changing Demographic Dynamics in Asia),1994 年 11 月 21—24 日在韩国首尔举行。

着高生育率或较高生育率地区，甚至生育率的适度下降可能都会加重对女婴、女童和女胎的歧视。"① 尤其当现代人的怀孕次数减少时，更激化了亚洲家庭对儿子的期待。因此，许多家庭以性别选择的手段来获得他们所期待的家庭组成，造成了亚洲特别扭曲的性别比例。表2-1 及表2-2 显示世界各地区的总人口性别比例与 0—4 岁的儿童性别比例。本章后两部分将讨论亚洲地区的重男轻女。

表 2-1 2000 年世界人口的性别比例，年龄介于 0—4 岁之间

地区	男性	女性	性别比
非洲	64431000	63156000	102.0
亚洲	192121000	179788000	106.9
欧洲	18915000	17924000	105.5
拉丁美洲和加勒比海地区	28520000	27429000	104.0
北美	11371000	10818000	105.1
大洋洲	1404000	1327000	105.8
世界	316763000	300442000	105.4

来源：United Nations, Department of Economic and Social Affairs, Population Division, World Population Prospects The 2002 Revision and World Urbanization Prospects: The 2001 Revision, http://esa.un.org/unpp。

表 2-2 2000 年世界人口的性别比例

地区	男性	女性	性别比
非洲	395573000	400097000	98.9
亚洲	1879417000	1800320000	104.4
欧洲	350900000	377086000	93.1
拉丁美洲和加勒比海地区	257526000	262703000	98.0
北美	155239000	160676000	96.6
大洋洲	15585000	15459000	100.8
世界	3054240000	3016341000	101.3

来源：United Nations, Department of Economic and Social Affairs, Population Division, World Population Prospects The 2002 Revision and World Urbanization Prospects: The 2001 Revision, http://esa.un.org/unpp。

---

① Judith Banister, "Son Preference in Asia—eport of a Symposium," at U.S. Census Bureau, http://www.census.gov/ipc/www/ebspr96a.html.

六、亚洲人重男轻女

亚洲的东部及南部至今仍流行杀女婴，一般是由于对她们疏于照顾而致其死亡。在印度和中国都有关于主动杀女婴的记录，但是由于忽略造成的女婴或女童死亡则更为普遍。卡罗尔·麦克柯南克（Carol MacCornack）研究妇女的健康和社会权利时发现，女性地位的低落，使得社会对她们的投资较少。这一倾向反映到男女儿童的死亡率上。①

男女在不同年龄的死亡率有所不同。② 男孩在出生第一年及幼儿期，比女孩更容易死亡。男婴对遗传疾病较无抵抗力，特别容易受到消化及呼吸系统的感染。③ 这可能因为 X 染色体上有控制免疫力的基因，而男孩只有一个 X 染色体的缘故。④ 在生育期，女性的死亡率较高，因为生小孩很危险。进入老年后，男性较女性早死，女性一般寿命较长。

当然，也不是所有国家的情况都一样，例如在孟加拉、中国、印度、尼泊尔，婴儿死亡率（每 1000 个活胎在第一年的死亡率）及儿童死亡率（1—4 岁，每 1000 人中的死亡率），女性都比男性高。这种对女性的歧视甚至出现在各个年龄段。海伦·威尔（Helen Ware）认为，造成女性在 1—4 岁时的死亡率较高的是社会因素。在这个年

---

① Carol P. MacCormack, "Health and the Social Power of Women," *Social Science and Medicine*, Vol. 26, No. 7 (1988), pp. 677 – 683.

② 下面的讨论代表着一种关于男女生命周期的普遍观点。类似讨论参见 Helen R. Ware, "Differential Mortality Decline and Its Consequences for Status and Roles of Women," in *Consequences of Mortality Trends and Differentials*, Population Studies No. 95 (New York: Department of International Economic and Social Affairs, United Nations, 1986), pp. 113 – 125。

③ Lauris McKee, "Sex Differentials in Survivorship and the Customary Treatment of Infants and Children," *Medical Anthropology: Cross Cultural Studies in Health and Illness*, Vol. 8, No. 2 (Spring 1984), pp. 91 – 108.

④ Ibid., p. 93.

龄段，女性因为性别而处于劣势，这是"重男轻女造成影响最大的时期"。在这个年龄段，父母通常需要对食物、医药等有限的资源在儿女间做分配，这类的决定都对女儿不利。①经济学家阿玛蒂亚·森（Amartya Sen）也认为，在极度歧视女性的贫穷社会里，性别歧视表现在食物及医疗资源的分配上。②

一份1954年联合国人口处对于婴儿及幼童的死亡率研究中，可以看到从1915—1949年，在63个国家和地区里女婴的死亡率比男婴低。③但在锡兰、厄瓜多尔、中国台湾、墨西哥、巴勒斯坦、波多黎各及委内瑞拉，女童（1—4岁）的死亡率却较高。④联合国儿童基金会于1986年发表《世界儿童状况研究》，提供45个发展中国家的资料，其中43国的女童1—4岁的死亡率比男童高。⑤1998年联合国研究成果《年轻的死亡：基因或性别》（*Too Young to Die: Genes or Gender?*）记录了亚洲中南部搜集的82个发展中国家女孩的健康和生存现状，尤其是在孟加拉国、印度、尼泊尔及巴基斯坦，女孩的生存状况最差。⑥联合国人口学家估算，到了2000年，仍有孟加拉国、文莱、中国、印度、伊朗、巴基斯坦、斐济、巴布亚新几内亚、瓦努阿图等9个国家，女婴死亡率高于男婴。⑦根据美国人口统计局国际数据库

---

① Ware, "Differential Mortality Decline and Its Consequences for the Status and Role of Women," p. 114.

② Amartya Sen, *Development as Freedom* (New York: Alfred A. Knopf, 1999), p. 194.

③ United Nations, Department of Social Affairs, Population Division, *Foetal, Infant, and Early Childhood Mortality*, Vol. 1: *The Statistics*, Population Studies No. 13 (New York: United Nations, 1954).

④ Ibid., pp. 64 – 76. Table 1.

⑤ UNICEF (United Nations Children's Fund), *Statistical Review of the Situation of Children in the World* (New York: UNICEF, 1986), p. 5.

⑥ United Nations, Population Division of the Department of Economic and Social Affairs, *Too Young to Die: Genes or Gender?* (New York: United Nations, 1998), p. 13.

⑦ United Nations, *The World's Women, 2000: Trends and Statistics*, http://unstats.un.org/unsd/demographic/ww2000/table3a.htm.

2002年的数据，在227个国家和地区中，有15个国家和地区0—4岁的性别比例大于107（男）：100（女）。①其中，中国大陆是109.8（男）：100（女），中国香港地区110.7（男）：100（女），韩国111.1（男）：100（女）及台湾地区108.7（男）：100（女）。高性别比例代表男孩、女孩得到的待遇不同，女孩的死亡率较高。

因为父母偏爱男孩，所以会利用性别选择的技术（尤其是超音波及羊膜穿刺）来堕掉女胎，这点可以从新生儿性别比以及医院对流产胎儿的性别统计得到印证。性别选择的运用，在中国大陆、印度、韩国及中国台湾地区十分普遍，但在孟加拉国及巴基斯坦，我们却没有什么具体的证据。

以下我们讨论四个亚洲国家和地区的性别选择方式：孟加拉国、巴基斯坦、韩国及中国台湾地区。在孟加拉和巴基斯坦，下降的生育率也伴随着持续的重男轻女倾向，这导致女婴和女童的高死亡率，表现出对女婴出生的歧视，进而会引发杀女婴。然而在中国台湾，没有证据显示对男女后代有区别对待，或是有杀女婴的情况；在这一地区，重男轻女表现在使用性别选择技术来堕女胎。在韩国，过去女婴和女童的高死亡率表明存在杀女婴的情况，最近的数据显示，杀女婴正被性别选择性堕胎所取代：韩国出生性别比例高，但女婴和女童的死亡率低。

（一）孟加拉国

根据1996、1997年的《人口及健康调查》，孟加拉国女孩的死亡率比男孩高了27%，正如在其他亚洲国家一样，在那里人们偏好的家庭结构是两个儿子和一个女儿。②一项对孟加拉国玛特拉布地区（Mat-

---

① See Appendix 1 for the sex ratios for all 227 countries.
② 死亡率是以1996—1997年孟加拉的人口健康调查为依据，引自 World Health Organization,"Woman's Health in South-East Asia", http：//w3. whosea. org/woman/ch1_2. htm。有关重男轻女及其影响，参见 M. Kabir, Ruhul Amin, Ashraf Uddin Ahmen, and Jamir Chowdhury, "Factors Affecting Desired Family Size in Bangladesh," *Journal of Biosocial Science*, Vol. 26, No. 3 (July 1994), pp. 369–375。

lab）儿童的研究显示，5岁以下的女孩的死亡率则比男孩高50%。①女孩所获得的食品及医疗少得可怜。②莫胡里（Pradip Muhuri）及普莱斯顿（Samuel Preston）发现，家庭的组成通常为两个儿子、一个女儿。他们在1981年到1982年调查了14125个出生个案，发现父母期待的子女性别组成，影响儿童死亡率最大，至于社会经济因素、母亲的受教育程度、医疗资源的取得，对死亡率影响并不大。这篇报告指出，女孩比男孩的死亡率高，若已有长女，则次女的死亡率比没有姐姐的女婴高5.8倍。男孩的死亡率则不受家庭性别组成的影响，除非他们有两个以上的哥哥，但这不如有几个姐姐的影响那么大。③

尽管玛特拉布的研究呈现女婴和儿童的高死亡率，但孟加拉国2001年的性别比并未反映出对女性的严重歧视。孟加拉国2001年的总性别比例103.8（男）：100（女），相比1951年的109.7（男）：100（女），呈下降趋势。④ 2001年人口普查公布，0—4岁人口性别比例106.1（男）：100（女），相比1991年人口普查中的102.9（男）：100（女），儿童性别比例有明显增长。⑤ 2001年的总性别比例只反

---

① M. Shahidullah, "Breast-Feeding and Child Survival in Matlab, Bangladesh," *Journal of Biosocial Science*, Vol. 26, No. 2 (April 1994), pp. 143 – 154.

② Alaka M. Basu, "Is Discrimination in Food Really Necessary for Explaining Sex Differentials in Childhood Mortality?" *Population Studies*, Vol. 43, No. 2 (July 1989), pp. 193 – 210; Lincoln C. Chen, Emdadul Huq, and Stan D'souza, "Sex Bias in the Family Allocation of Food and Health-Care in Rural Bangladesh," *Population and Development Review*, Vol. 7, No. 1 (March 1981), pp. 55 – 70.

③ Pradip K. Muhuri and Samuel H. Preston, "Effects of Family Composition on Mortality Differentials by Sex among Children in Matlab, Bangladesh," *Population and Development Review*, Vol. 17. No. 3 (September 1991), pp. 415 – 434.

④ Bangladesh, Bureau of Statistics, "Population Census 2001 Preliminary Report," http://www.bbsgov.org; and Bangladesh Bureau of Statistics, 1999 Demographic Data, http://www.bbsgov.org/data-sheet/DEMO_DATA.htm.

⑤ Bangladesh, Bureau of Statistics, "Population Census, 2001: Preliminary Report"; and Bangladesh Bureau of Statistics, "1991 Population Census," http://www.bbsgov.org/ana_vol1/Projection.htm.

映出较高的女婴和女童死亡率,如果出生性别比例低于106.1（男）：100（女）的话。然而孟加拉国的新生儿性别比数据并不可靠,一份1988—1989年的出生数据,显示新生儿性别比为100.2（男）：100（女）,但另外一份报告却说是113（男）：100（女）。① 可能因为许多出生及死亡未被登记,所以我们需要更多的数据,才能决定孟加拉国重男轻女的观念如何影响其婴儿死亡率。

（二）巴基斯坦

与印度西北部各邦类似,巴基斯坦对儿子偏爱也反映在它非常高的性别比例上［从拉贾斯坦的109.5（男）：100（女）到旁遮普的114.5（男）：100（女）］。② 尽管近年来几乎没有对于巴基斯坦整个人口性别比例的研究,但年轻人的性别比例透露出这个国家杀女童的事实。③ 1961年,在45个地区中有37个地区0—9岁儿童性别比例高于正常值105—107（男）：100（女）,一些比例高达114.6（男）：100（女）。④ 根据巴基斯坦的人口普查,1961年0—9岁的儿童性别比例是109.4（男）：100（女）,1972年是109.2（男）：100（女）,1981年是107.7（男）：100（女）,1998年是

---

① Radheshyam Bairagi, Santosh Chandra Sutradhar, and Nurul Alam, "Levels, Trends, and Determinants of Child Mortality in Matlab, Bangladesh, 1966 – 1994," *Asia-Pacific Population Journal*, Vol. 14, No. 2 (June 1999), pp. 51 – 68.,

② India, Office of the Registrar General, India, Office of the Registrar General, *Census of India, 2001, Series-1: India, Paper 1 of 2001: Provisional Population Totals* (New Delhi: India, Office of the Registrar General, 2001), http://www.censusindia.net/results. (New Delhi: India, Office of the Registrar General, 2001), http://www.censusindia.net/results.

③ 印度历史上的一些邦组成了巴基斯坦,包括18和19世纪盛行杀女婴的地区。

④ Barbara D. Miller, "Daughter Neglect, Women's Work, and Marriage: Pakistan and Bangladesh Compared," *Medical Anthropology: Cross Cultural Studies in Health and Illness*, Vol. 8, No. 2 (Spring 1984), pp. 114 – 115.

106.2∶100（女）。① 1998 年的总性别比例为 108.5（男）∶100（女）；在四个省与两个地区，人口性别比例从西北边境较低的 105（男）∶100（女）到伊斯兰堡（首都地区）的 117（男）∶100（女），差异较大。②阿玛蒂亚·森计算出巴基斯坦 1999 年人口性别比例为 111.1（男）∶100（女），如果准确的话，那么这一数据要比其他国家的都糟糕。③芭芭拉·米勒（Barbara Miller）认为巴基斯坦过高的性别比例，源自该国女性地位的低落。这个国家以小麦为经济基础，遵守男尊女卑的婚姻制度，嫁女儿需要嫁妆（虽然嫁妆的金额不像印度那么高）。④

根据 1990—1991 年《人口及健康调查》（DHS），巴基斯坦男婴和女婴的死亡率分别是 102.1‰和 85.5‰。据联合国评估，在 2002 年女婴实际的死亡率仍比男婴高 8%，巴基斯坦女童的死亡率比男童高 66%（女童死亡率 36.5‰，男童为 22‰）。⑤原因是男童可以获得较好的医疗照护（特别是免疫及治疗）及营养补充。⑥

（三）韩国

重男轻女是韩国的传统，只有儿子可以传宗接代、延续家族姓

---

① 1961、1972 和 1981 年的人口普查数据来自 1998 年美国人口普查局国际数据库中的巴基斯坦的数据。1998 年人口性别比的数据来自 2003 年美国人口普查局国际数据库中所列举的 1998 年巴基斯坦人口普查数据。

② http：//www.statpak.gov.pk/depts/pco/statistics/pop_table1/pop_table1.html.

③ Sen, *Development as Freedom*, p. 104.

④ Miller, "Daughter Neglect, Women's Work, and Marriage," pp. 121–122.

⑤ DHS data recorded in Ian Timoeus, Katie Harris, and Francesca Fairbairn, "Can Use of Health Care Explain Sex Differentials in Child Mortality in the Developing World?" in United Nations, *Too Young to Die*, p. 156.

⑥ DHS data recorded in Ian Timoeus, Katie Harris, and Francesca Fairbairn, "Can Use of Health Care Explain Sex Differentials in Child Mortality in the Developing World?" in United Nations, *Too Young to Die*, p. 156. See also Elisabeth Sommerfelt and Fred Arnold, "Sex Differentials in the Nutritional Status of Young Children," in United Nations, *Too Young to Die*, pp. 133–153.

氏、祭祀祖先、对父母提供经济保障。① 虽然女性的地位算是高的，而且在婚嫁时不需要嫁妆，但对儿子的偏好却仍影响了家庭的规模和性别组成。人口学家朴柴冰（Park Chai Bin）及朴赵文（Cho Nam-hoon）发现韩国的新生儿性别比从1985年开始突然增加。②在1970年之前，出生的性别比例维持在105（男）：100（女）—107（男）：100（女）之间，1980年增至108.3（男）：100（女），1985年为108.6（男）：100（女），1990年为116.9（男）：100（女）。③裴华玉（Bae Wha-oak）断言，性别比例的增加，性别比例的增加，原因不是女婴在出生时未被登记，因为韩国的人口普查及出生统计制度相当可靠。④但由于政府对于反性别选择法律的坚持，所以根据2000年普查的结果，新生儿性别比又降到109.6（男）：100（女）。⑤

性别比例的增加和生育率降低也有关系，1971年的总生育率（每位妇女所生下的孩子之平均人数）是4.7，到了1982年降到2.7，到1990年再降到1.63。⑥1988年韩国国家生育率及健康调查显示，人们满意的家庭结构影响到人们对于儿子的偏爱：有一半的女性认为有一个儿子是必要的，61%的女性表示有一个儿子后就不再生了，但只有39%的女性表示有一个女儿后就不再生了。⑦从1974年以来，孩子出生的顺序愈是排在后面，新生儿性别比就愈高。到了1992年，家

---

① Fred Arnold, "Measuring the Effect of Sex Preference on Fertility: The Case of Korea," *Demography*, Vol. 22, No. 2 (May 1985), pp. 283–284.

② Park Chai Bin and Cho Nam-hoon, "Consequence of Son Preference in a Low-Fertility Society: Imbalance of the Sex Ratio at Birth in Korea," *Population and Development Review*, Vol. 21, No. 1 (March 1995), pp. 59–84.

③ See ibid., pp. 61, 66, Tables 1, 6.

④ Bae Wha-oak, "Sex Ratio at Birth in Korea," *Journal of Population, Health, and Social Welfare*, Vol. 11, No. 2 (December 1991), p. 115.

⑤ South Korea (Republic of Korea), *2001 Report of the National Statistical Office of South Korea* (Seoul: National Statistical Office, July 2001).

⑥ Bae, "Sex Ratio at Birth in Korea," p. 120.

⑦ Cited in ibid., p. 121.

中第四个孩子的性别比例高达228.6（男）：100（女）。①

1991年韩国国家生育率及健康调查显示，第一胎的性别比增长惊人。1991年以前，第一胎的性别比例相当正常，只有第二胎以后才会变高。但1991年的调查发现，第一胎的性别比例就是117.9（男）：100（女）。②我们怀疑韩国女性现在采用性别选择的手段，来保证第一胎的性别。③

韩国人重男轻女也反映在女婴和女童的不同死亡率上。甚至在出生人口性别比例正常的时期，3—4岁儿童的性别比例也不同寻常的高。1955年韩国出生人口性别比例是105.7（男）：100（女），但3—4岁儿童的性别比例却是108.1（男）：100（女）及107.5（男）：100（女）。④1985年出生人口性别比例为108.6（男）：100（女），5年后，这个5岁群体的性别比例却变为111.4（男）：100（女）。⑤这些高性别比例显示父母故意对女婴及女童的照顾较差，致使她们死亡。最新的性别选择技术可以让父母得到他们所期望的儿子或女儿，这意味着女婴和女童不再受到差别对待。2000年的韩国人口普查显示，在婴幼儿死亡率中，男婴高于女婴，韩国的父母现在不需要再杀女婴了。⑥

---

① Park and Cho, "Consequences of Son Preference in a Low-Fertility Society," p. 66, Table 6.

② Cited in ibid., p. 66, Table 6.

③ Ibid., p. 67.

④ Park and Cho, "Consequences of Son Preference in a Low-Fertility Society," p. 61. Table 1.

⑤ Ibid.

⑥ 这次人口普查中所记录的死亡率（每10万人中的死亡人数）如下：0岁女婴和男婴，分别为472.2和491.7；1—4岁女童和男童分别为41.6和49.8。South Korea (Republic of Korea), "Census Population, 2000" (Seoul: National Statistical Office, 2000), http://www.nso.go.kr.

(四) 台湾地区

台湾地区的人相当重男轻女（虽然程度可能不如中国大陆），原因与韩国的类似。①从1985年，台湾地区开始有胎儿的性别检验技术。②同年台湾地区的出生人口性别比也开始增加，从1985年的106.6（男）：100（女）到1990年的110.2（男）：100（女），到了2000年略降为109.5（男）：100（女）。③就1990年的出生人口性别比来看，若把城市和乡村分开来比较，台北市有最高的比例112（男）：100（女），然后是农村110（男）：100（女），及其卫星城市109（男）：100（女）。④或许学者需要解释为什么台北市的出生人口性别比这么高，不过大家都同意性别比例在乡村和相对保守地区较高，因为都市中的女性多数就业，其社会地位较高，在家庭之中也比较不会受到歧视。弗里德曼（Ronald Freedman）等人认为，台湾地区的人重男轻女的倾向影响了他们的生育选择。⑤儿子愈多，父母对避孕药的使用率也愈高。与韩国类似，台湾出生次序较晚的孩子，出生性别比例很高。1991年，第三胎和第四胎的性别比例，分别是118（男）：100（女）及

---

① 例如，1990年中国台湾地区出生人口性别比为110.2（男）：100（女），而同年中国大陆出生人口性别比为114.7（男）：100（女）。参见 Gu Baochang and Krishna Roy, "Sex Ratio at Birth in China, with Reference to Other Areas in Asia: What We Know," *Asia-Pacific Population Journal*, Vol. 10, No. 3 (September 1995), p. 20, Table 1.

② "Where Have All the Daughters Gone?" *Sinorama Magazine*, n. d., http://www.taiwaninfo.org/info/sinorama/8502/502006el.html.

③ Gu and Roy, "Sex Ratio at Birth in China," p. 20, Table 1. http://www.gio.gov.tw/taiwan-website/5-gp/yearbook/chpt02-1.htm#1.

④ Gu and Roy, "Sex Ratio at Birth in China," p. 24, Table 3.

⑤ Ronald Freedman, Ming-cheng Chang, and Te-hsiung Sun, "Taiwan's Transition from High Fertility to Below-Replacement Levels," *Studies in Family Planning*, Vol. 25, No. 6 (1994), pp. 317–331, as cited in ibid., p. 27.

130(男)∶100(女)。根据弗里德曼等人的观点,性别比例增长实际上要归因于父母使用性别选择技术和随后有意识地堕掉女胎。①

台湾地区出生人口性别比例反映出了性别选择技术的使用。但没有任何证据足以显示女婴被疏于照顾,而且2000年婴儿的死亡率也很正常,男婴比女婴死亡率略高。②

七、消失的亚洲女性

长期以来,性别选择技术的采用以及人为的疏失导致女婴死亡,使得亚洲大量的女性人口消失了。"消失的女性"指的是如果不是因为性别歧视,今天应该还活着的女性人数。1990年阿玛蒂亚·森统计,有超过1亿的女性从世界上消失了。③柯尔(Ansley Coale)采用亚洲的生育模式及死亡率,算出消失的人口接近于6000万人。④ 经济学家斯蒂芬·克拉森(Stephan Klasen)及克劳迪娅·文克(Claudia Wink)对以上的方法再修正,得到全球"消失的女性"人口是9300万人。⑤

正如克拉森和文克指出的,阿玛蒂亚·森使用撒哈拉以南非洲的

---

① Freedman, Chang, and Sun, "Taiwan's Transition from High Fertility to Below Replacement Levels," as cited in ibid., p. 29.

② 台湾地区男婴和女婴的死亡率分别是7.51和6.42;1—4岁男童和女童的死亡率分别是0.49和0.45。Ibid., pp. 30 – 33, Table 16.

③ Amartya Sen, "More Than 100 Million Women Are Missing," *New York Review of Books*, December 20, 1990, pp. 61 – 66.

④ Ansley J. Coale, "Excess Female Mortality and the Balance of the Sexes in the Population: An Estimate of the Number of Missing Females," *Population and Development Review*, Vol. 17, No. 3 (September 1991), pp. 517 – 523.

⑤ Stephan Klasen and Claudia Wink, "Missing Women: Revisiting the Debate," *Feminist Economics*, Vol. 9, Nos. 2 – 3 (July-November 2003) Taiwan (Republic of China).

性别比作为指标来评估亚洲的预期性别比,这一方法是有问题的,因为非洲出生人口性别比要比世界其他地区低。撒哈拉以南非洲有更多女性,某种程度上是因为每年女性出生率高。柯尔的计算也进一步通过在亚洲国家和地区观察到的超额死亡率作出。据柯尔的观点,西方国家的性别比应该在97.3(男):100(女)与100.3(男):100(女)之间(在无战争及女性特别死亡的情况下),这意味着由于女性有寿命较长的优势,女性数量应该高于或等于男性数量。① 男性出生率超过女性,但是死亡率比女性高,在某一阶段会出现转折点,整个人口性别比会倾向于女性。柯尔认为,整个性别比是由这个转折点出现的年龄决定的,年轻人口性别比可能会比年长人口的略高。因此,他得出结论:如果没有超额死亡率和杀婴情况,亚洲人口性别比应该是介于101(男):100(女)与103(男):100(女)之间。②

克拉森和文克声称柯尔的方法也是有问题的。首先,他们认为比较亚洲和西方国家的死亡率淡化了亚洲国家(地区)的女性死亡率。其次,他们质疑柯尔的假设,即亚洲国家(地区)的出生人口性别比与西方等同:他们的研究认为事实上西方国家的出生人口性别比要比亚洲高一些。西方国家较好的健康和营养条件降低了流产和死胎的几率,因为怀上男孩的比怀上女孩的多,发达国家的出生人口性别比要比发展中国家高一些。据克拉森和文克的观点,亚洲国家(地区)出生人口性别比在102.4(男):100(女)与105.2(男):100(女)之间变动。自1980年以来,中国大陆、印度、韩国及中国台湾地区的出生人口性别比都比预期值要高很多。印度有高生育率及大量人口,却没有可靠的出生统计数据。学者使用样本调查及其他方法计

---

① Coale, "Excess Female Mortality and the Balance of the Sexes in the Population," p. 518.
② Ibid.

算出总的出生人口性别比（表 2-3 是与预估数据及其与预期数据的比较）。

表 2-3　部分亚洲国家与地区的出生人口性别比

国家/地区	预期值	报告值	年份及信息来源
中国大陆	105.0	117.00	2000，中国人口信息研究中心
		120.00	1999，中国社会科学院
		116.57	1995 年 10 月 1 日，国家统计局（1.04% 的样本）
		118.65	1995 年 4 月 1 日，国家统计局（1.04% 的样本）
		115.62	1994 年 10 月 1 日—1995 年 9 月 30 日，中国，国家统计局（1.04% 的样本）
		121.01	1993 和 1994，中国家庭计划委员会，中国《计划生育年鉴 1996》
		113.8—115.4	1989—1990，Zeng et al.，1993
印度	103.9	111.0	1996—1998，国家统计局关于早产儿的数据报告，2001
		113.7	1993—1995，Jhunjhunwala，2001
		132.0	1993，巴基斯坦旁遮普省的一个医院，Booth et al.，1994
		112.2	1981—1991，印度医院出生率，印度注册总署，1991
		156.0	1990，新德里附近的一个小镇罗塔克的麦当劳，1991
韩国	104.7	109.6	2000，韩国国家统计局，2001
		115.3	1993，韩国国家统计局，2002
		114.0	1992，Park and Cho，1995
		116.9	1990，Park and Cho，1995

续表

国家/地区	预期值	报告值	年份及信息来源
中国台湾地区	105.2	117.9	1990,仅指第一胎,Park and Cho, 1995
		109.5	2000,"内政部"
		110.2	1990, Guand Roy, 1995

来源：预期数据来自 Stephen Klasen and Claudia Wink, "Missing Women: Revisting the Debate," *Feminist Economics*, Vol. 9, Nos. 2 – 3 (July-November 2003)。报告数据来自：China Population Information and Research Council (CPIRC), "China Sees a High Gender Ratio of Newborns," May 14, 2002, http://www.cpirc.org.cn/enews20020514.htm; Chinese Academy of Social Sciences-email communication with the director concerning an article in *Nando Times* entitled China Reportedly Has 20 Percent More Males Than Females," January 7, 1999, http://www.nandotimes.com/global/story/body/0, 1025, 5301 – 9190 – 64468 – 0, 00.html; China, State Statistical Bureau (SSB), *China Population Statistics Yearbook*, *1996* (Beijing: China Statistics Prss, 1996), 1.04 percent samples for October 1994, April 1995, and October 1995; China, State Family Planning Commission of China, *China Birth Planning Year-book* (Beijing: 1996); Zeng Yi, Gu Baochang, Xu yi, Li Bohua, and Li Yongping, "causes and Implications of the Recent Increase in the Reported Sex Ration at Birth in China," *Population and Development Review*, Vol. 19, No. 2 (June 1993), pp. 283 – 302; Mahendra K. Premi, "The Missing Girl Child," *Economic and Political Weekly*, May 26-June 2, 2001, pp. 1875 – 1880; Bharat Jhunjhunwala, "Sex Ratio Riddles," Statesman (India), June 2, 2001; India, Office of the Registrar General, *Compendium of India's Fertility and Mortality Indicators Based on the SRS* (Delhi: Controllor of Publications, 1991); Beverley E. Booth, Manorama Verma, and Rajbir Singh Beri, "Fetal Sex Determination in Infants in Punjab, India: Corralations and Implications," *British Medical Journal*, November 12, 1994, pp. 1259 – 1261; Hamish McDonald, "Unwelcome Sex," *Far Eastern Economic Review*, December 26, 1991-January 2, 1992, pp. 18 – 19; South Korea (Republic of Korea), *2001 Report of the National Statistical Office of South Korea* (Seoul: National Statistical Office, July 2001); Park Chai Bin and Cho Nam-Hoon, "Consequences of Son Preference in a Low Fertility Society: Imbalance of the Sex Ratio at Birth in Korea," *Population and Development Review*, Vol. 21, No. 1 (March 1995), pp. 59 – 84; Taiwan, *The Republic of China Yearbook-taiwan*, 2002 (Taiwan: Ministry of the Interior, 2002), http://www.gio.gov.tw/taiwan-website/5-gp/yeabook/chpt02-1.htm#1; and Gu Baogchang and Krishna Roy, "Sex Ratio at Birth in China, with Reference to Other Areas in Asia: What We Know," *Asia-Pacific Population Journal*, Vol. 10, No. 3 (Semptember 1995), pp. 17 – 42.

为了确定性别选择的手段造成多少女性人口的消失,柯尔、克拉森及文克调查了西亚及次撒哈拉地区有大量人口及女性高死亡率的国家。克拉森及文克研究西亚及撒哈拉以南非洲的国家。我们的研究重点则集中在有着较高性别比和较高死亡率的亚洲中南部和东部,因为90%"消失的女性"原诞生于此。尽管其他国家如埃及和伊朗的性别比也显示出可能有性别歧视,但还是需要进一步调查以查明原因。当下它们的青少年性别比并未显示出广泛施行了杀女婴和性别选择性堕胎。根据柯尔、克拉森及文克评估,西方的总性别比例正常值应在96.4(男):100(女)—100.3(男):100(女)之间。结合这个预期值及最新的人口普查数据,我们在表2-4中计算出这些地方有超过9000万的女性消失了(见表2-4)。其中中国大陆占45%,印度占43%,剩下的5个国家和地区则占了12%。"消失的女性"人数占这些国家和地区的全部女性人口的比例很高,例如阿富汗拥有全世界1%的消失女性人口,但她们占该国全部女性的9.5%。评估阿富汗的人口数字要很小心,因为阿富汗的人口数字是由联合国调查的,阿富汗从1979年就没有进行人口普查了。不过,这个数据与学者们对于这个国家的性别歧视水平所作的评估是一致的,特别是在过去十年。中国大陆、印度、巴基斯坦,各自丧失了它们女性人口的6.2%、7.3%及8.6%。孟加拉国、尼泊尔及中国台湾地区失去了它们女性人口的4%,韩国"消失的女性"人数最少,对全部的女性人口来说,比例只有0.7%。

韩国和中国台湾地区的新生儿性别比比预期的要高,但这两者占总消失女性的比例却很少,可能因为这两地的人口本来就少,所以对整体的影响不大。在2000年,台湾地区共有307200个婴儿出生,其中146670个是女性[性别比例为109.45(男):100(女)]。① 台湾地区预期的性别比例是105.2(男):100(女),也就是说有3037

---

① Taiwan (Republic of China), *The Republic of China Yearbook-Taiwan*, 2002.

个女性在那一年消失了。韩国的低出生性别比数据事实上有些误导。韩国人口在55岁以后女性成为多数,24岁以前男性占多数,两者互相抵消,造成了总人口性别比例平衡的假象。事实上,24岁以下的性别比例为110.8(男):100(女),代表在这个年龄层有475561个"消失的女性"人口。① 这个数字占全国女性人口的2.1%,这算是低的。

表2-4 在选定的亚洲国家与地区根据普查数据得到的消失的妇女数量

国家/地区	年份	男性实际数量	女性实际数量	实际性别比	预期性别比	妇女数预期	消失的妇女数
阿富汗	2000	11227000	10538000	106.5	96.4	11646266	1108266
孟加拉国	2001	65841419	63405814	103.8	99.6	66105842	2700028
中国	2000	653550000	612280000	106.7	100.1	652897103	40617103
印度	2001	531277078	495738169	107.2	99.3	535022234	39284065
巴基斯坦	1998	68873686	63445593	108.6	99.2	69429119	5983526
韩国	2000	23068181	22917108	100.7	100.0	23068181	151073
中国台湾	2000	11386084	10914845	104.3	100.2	11363357	448512
总数							90292573

来源:阿富汗——联合国人口司:《世界人口展望(2002年版)》,http://www.un.org./esa/population/publications/wpp2000/annex-tables.pdf;孟加拉国——孟加拉国国家统计局,《人口普查,2001年:初步报告》,http://www.bbsgov.org;中国——中华人民共和国国家统计局:《2000年人口普查数据的重要图表》,2002年4月23日,第1号,http://www.stats.gov.cn/english/newrelease/statisticalreportts/200204230084.htm;印度——印度注册总署:《印度人口普查2001年,系列1,第1篇:印度各邦的人口总数》(新德里:印度,2001),http://www.cesusindia.net/results;巴基斯坦——巴基斯坦政府统计局人口普查处,《1998年的巴基斯坦人口普查》,http://www.pap.org.pk/population/sec2.htm;韩国——国家统计局:《韩国人口普查(2000年)》,http://www.nso.go.kr;中国台湾——台湾统计局:《对普查结果的历史比较(2000)年》,http://www.stat.gov.tw。

---

① South Korea (Republic of Korea), "Census Population, 2000."

八、结论

在对性别选择行为的调查中,我们发现对女性的歧视,自古至今,全世界皆然。重男轻女的原因通常是经济上的考虑:男性劳力较有价值,能够照顾年迈的父母,增加家庭的收入,能够祭祀祖宗。相比之下,女性的就业机会少,受的教育少,她们出嫁时父母需要支付嫁妆。世界各地都有重男轻女的现象,然而亚洲的重男轻女观念相当明显,父母都会采用各种手段来得到他们想要的儿子数量。

重男轻女的社会会有偏高的新生儿性别比例、儿童性别比例、总性别比例及不同的男女死亡率。出生人口高性别比是因为堕女胎,女婴女童的高死亡率则代表她们获得的医药和营养较差,这也是某种程度上的杀婴。不同的国家和地区所用的子女性别选择方法也不同,在孟加拉国及巴基斯坦,女性死亡率高是杀女婴所造成的,韩国及中国台湾地区的高性别比则来自于堕女胎。把南亚及东亚综合起来——包括阿富汗、孟加拉国、中国大陆、印度、巴基斯坦、韩国及中国台湾地区,总共"消失的女性"人口超过9000万人,其中又以印度和中国大陆最多。

我们也以这两个国家作为研究的重点,我们想问的是:印度和中国的性别比例一直都这么高吗?为什么会这么高呢?在各国不同的年龄层中,性别比例也是这么扭曲吗?这种不正常的比例是全国皆然,还是有地区的差异性?这两国未来的性别比例是会降低还是升高?两国的政府和人民关心这个问题吗?当前现实显示,这两个高性别比例的人口大国对世界的影响是什么?我们将在第三章和第四章中一一讨论。

第三章 印度的"消失的女性"

印度的人口在2001年已超过10亿,其中男性5.31亿人,女性4.96亿人,是世界人口第二多的国家。它的人口增长的速度最快,每年为全世界增加1800万人,它的人口总有一天会超过目前排名第一的中国。① 印度人口一直是人口学家、社会学家最感兴趣的议题,尤其是男女的不平等,造成印度女性愈来愈少,这一问题更是近来学者关注的重点。在1991年的人口普查后,它的新生儿性别比在110.2(男):100(女)—113.8(男):100(女)之间徘徊,实际数字可能更高。到了2001年,性别比例降为107.2(男):100(女)。本章主要探讨印度与性别选择相关的性别不平衡的程度、原因及其含义。

印度性别选择的历史与这个国家的历史、宗教、社会结构及其女性角色紧密相关。女性地位在整个历史或国家中不是始终如一的;女性的地位随着宗教、社会等级、地域、经济,以及在家庭中出生次序

---

① 1991—2001年,印度人口增长了1.806亿。India, Office of the Registrar General, *Census of India*, 2001, Series-1: *India*, Paper 1 of 2001: *Provisional Population Totals* (New Delhi: India, Office of The Registrar General, 2001), http://www.censusindia.net/results. 1998年,联合国人口司出版了《世界人口前景(1998年修订版)》,其中提到印度超越中国和其他所有国家,成为人口增长最快的国家。印度人口以20.6%的速度增长,而中国则是14%。参见 United Nations, Population Division of the Department of Economic and Social Affairs, "The 1998 Revision of the United Nations Population Projections," *Population and Development Review*, Vol. 24, No. 4 (December 1998), pp. 891–895.

的不同而不同。要了解印度如何歧视女性，就需要先了解它独特的历史、宗教及社会结构。印度女性的地位随着时代、地区，甚至她的出生顺序的不同而不同。

一、历史背景

"印度"之名来自于梵文词 Sindu，用来形容从里海和黑海之间高地一路迁徙并在印度次大陆定居的讲雅利安语的移民所说的印度河（Indus River）。① 他们于公元前 1500 年定居达罗毗荼原住民的地域，几个族群之间不断地分合，最后产生了部落体系内部的治理。随着印度文明的诞生，也产生了一个复杂的社会结构，遵循瓦尔纳—人生阶段—佛法（varna-ashrama-dharma）的准则——包括阶级、人生阶段（它决定了地位、目标、责任和义务），以及正义和神圣法律——这些在印度经文和传统中有描述。社会和谐与稳定据信是依赖于社会所有成员的正义，以及他们根据自己年龄和身份履行责任。

在印度的历史上，除了部落之间的战争，还有来自阿富汗及巴基斯坦侵略者的攻城略地。公元前 184 年，孔雀王朝结束，新的战国时代开始了。

在随后的百年间，几个王朝（主要为拉其普特人的战士）企图建立版图，但终为伊斯兰教的侵略者所击败。伊斯兰教教徒于公元 997 年进入印度，在公元 1175 年统治了次大陆的大部分地区。② 伊斯兰王国及印度王国之间的纷争，严重骚扰了北部及西北部的地区，间接鼓励莫卧尔王国于 1556 年入侵。莫卧尔王国到 1707 年开始式微，1858 年彻底瓦解，以马拉塔族和锡克族为主的小国之间不断进行战争，19 世纪中期英国控管了印度，直到 1947 年印度才独立。

---

① Richard F. Nyrop, ed., *India: A Country Study*, Foreign Area Studies, the American University (Washington, D. C.: Superintendent of Documents, U. S. Government Printing Office, 1985).

② Stanley Wolpert, *A New History of India*, 4th ed. (New York: Oxford University Press, 1993), pp. 106 - 109.

印度现在有 28 个邦、7 个联邦属地①，人口从 6 万到 16600 万不等（其中 19 个邦的人口都超过 1000 万）；讲 15 种国语（包括英文），还有一些被承认的方言，它们是从至少 1652 种口语和方言中选出的。印度 15200 公里的边界把它和 6 个邻国分开：孟加拉国、不丹、缅甸、中国、尼泊尔和巴基斯坦。喜马拉雅山成为印度与其北边邻国的分野，印度境内的高山、丛林和沙漠则把一块块肥沃的地区隔离起来，阻止内部文化统一，并把印度区分成五块：北部、西北、东/东北、西部、南部。

如图 3-1 及图 3-2 显示，印度的各邦边界在 1990 年后期发生了变化，我们在此讨论这个时期前后的历史，这样便可了解边界是如何变化的。

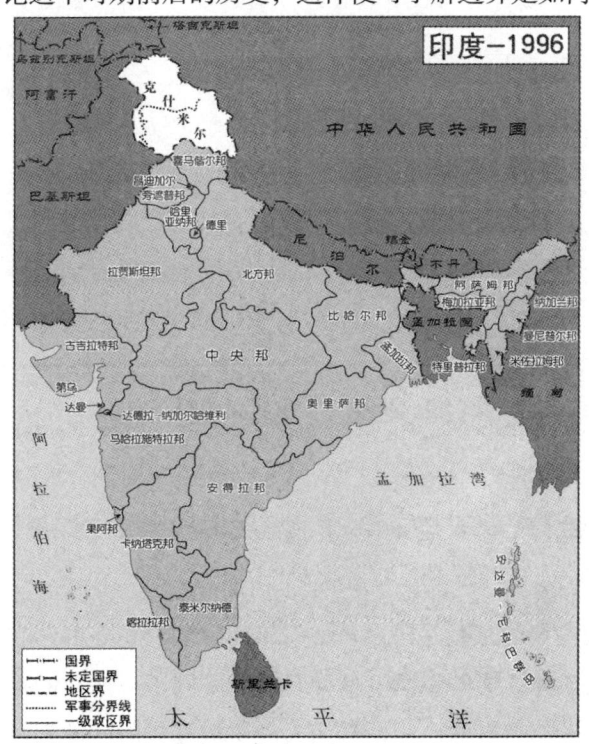

图 3-1　1996 年印度所辖的邦和地区

---

① 其中"查谟和克什米尔"为争议区，包括了我国阿克赛钦地区；"阿鲁那恰尔邦"系强占中国山南的门隅、洛隅、察隅等地区；"锡金邦"为 1975 年强并锡金国设置，2005 年中国国家测绘局正式下发《关于地图上锡金表示方法变更的通知》，从此，锡金不再为主权国家，表示为印度的一个邦。——编者注

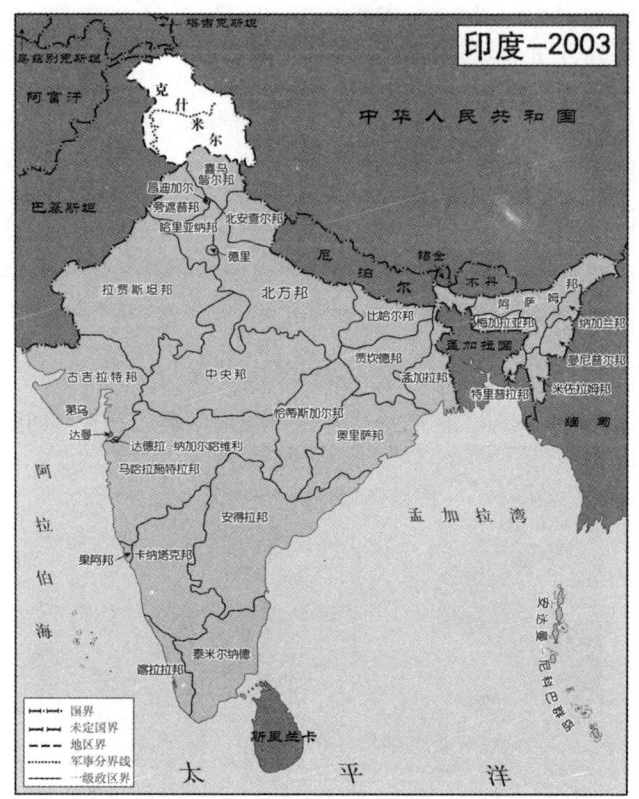

图 3-2　2003 年印度所辖的邦和地区

二、宗教

印度最主要的宗教是印度教，82% 的印度人口信仰，它没有统一的教义，承认多神，接纳不同的信仰，因此不同于一神教的基督教和伊斯兰教。印度教崇尚自然秩序，认为人应该依其年龄、性别与身份各尽其责，奉《吠陀经》（写于公元前 1400—前 1000 年之间）为圣经。① 大多

---

① 斯坦利·沃尔波特（Stanley Wolpert）认为，《梨俱吠陀》写于大约公元前 1400 年，其他部分写于公元前 1000 年。Stanley Wolpert, *A New History of India*, 4th ed. (New York: Oxford University Press, 1993) See ibid. , pp. 26 – 27.

数印度人更感兴趣的是《梵书》、《奥义书》和神秘的《往世书》,以及史书《罗摩衍那》和《摩诃婆罗多》(包括印度最多人在读的印度教经典《薄伽梵歌》)。

伊斯兰教是印度的第二大教,总人口的12%是它的信徒,剩下有6%的人信奉基督教、锡克教、佛教、耆那教等。①

三、社会制度

印度的种姓制度源于印度教,它认为每个人都与生俱来且终其一生地隶属一个迦提(jati,梵文,又称亚种姓)——上万个家族集团之一,迦提又从属于四个瓦尔那(varnas,梵文,又称种姓)之一。一个人的迦提和瓦尔那决定了他的社会地位、职业和婚姻。迦提和瓦尔那都是世袭,婆罗门是这个制度中的最高种姓,而贱民则是最低种姓。《摩奴法典》(公元前5世纪)被公认是印度教的法条,详述种姓的戒律。②虽然佛教、基督教、耆那教、伊斯兰教、锡克教不讲求种姓制度,但它们的教徒都受到印度教的势力影响。在按种姓划分的人群以外,还有8%的人住在喜马拉雅山边,他们各有不同的宗教、语言、经济模式和地理位置,各部落之间完全平等。领导者的产生不靠世袭传承而是靠个人的魅力,部落之间可以自由通婚。为了维护迦提的纯度,所有和较低种姓的接触,包括通婚和交际,都受到严格的控制。在乡村,亲族是迦提的基础。每个乡村中通常都有2—30个迦提,每个迦提至少须和35—40个其他的迦提联络,以便通商或

---

① India, Office of the Registrar General, *Census of India*, 1991, *Census Data Online*, Table 23, http://www.censusindia.net/cendat/datatable23.html.

② William Crooke, *The North-Western Provinces of India: Their History, Ethnology, and Administration* (London: Methuen, 1897), p. 61.

交流。①

通婚对确认迦提的社会地位十分重要，父母为子女安排适当的婚姻，是责无旁贷的。而大多数的婚嫁对象都在同等的迦提中找寻，唯一的例外就是女性可以嫁给种姓更高的男性，但她绝不能嫁给低阶层男性，以免破坏本身迦提的纯度。因此，印度的婚姻模式是一夫多妻制；女性必须嫁给同等身份或者更高身份的男性。狄克曼如此形容："种姓制度犹如金字塔，等级愈高，女儿婚配的对象就愈少，形成了对稀有资源——'高阶层男性'的竞争。"② 印度女性在结婚时，必须提供嫁妆给新郎的家庭，阶级愈高，嫁妆就需要愈多。

人类学家努尔·雅门（Nur Yulman）描述了女性、婚姻、种姓、一夫多妻制与种姓纯正的关系：

> 根据印度男尊女卑的婚配制度和种姓纯正的戒律，男性占尽性别的优势，女性则处处受限：（a）她可以和更高阶层和"种姓纯正"的男子发生性关系。这对种姓纯度没有伤害。（b）她可以和"种姓纯正"或相同种姓的男士生小孩。……但是如果她和低阶层男子发生性关系的话，她便从内部"被污染"，因此所怀的小孩也是"被污染"的。……很显然，一夫多妻制是与这样的体系直接联系，即群体成员身份是来自父母双方，而群体纯度则由女性维护……因此，尽管种姓身份来自父母双方，这些体系仍存在内在的不对称性。③

---

① David G. Mandelbaum, "Family, Jati, Village," in Milton Singer and Bernard S. Cohn, eds., *Structure and Change in Indian Society* (Chicago: Aldine de Gruyter, 1968), p. 41.

② Mildred Dickemann, "Female Infanticide, Reproductive Strategies, and Social Stratification: A Preliminary Model," in Napoleon A. Chagnon and William Irons, eds., *Evolutionary Biology and Human Social Behavior: An Anthropological Perspective* (North Scituate, Mass.: Duxbury, 1979), pp. 321–367, at p. 326.

③ Nur Yulman, "on the Purity of Women in the Castes of Castes of Ceylon and Malabar," *Journal of the Royal Anthropological Society*, Vol. 93, Pt. 1 (January-June 1963), pp. 42–43.

在世袭的社会，身属某个种姓靠父母，但种姓的纯正则要靠女性来维护。因此女性的交往，尤其是她的婚姻，受到严格的控制。印度有几种通婚模式：在北部，女性只能在同种姓内通婚及相应的亚种姓内异族通婚内通婚，血亲之间禁止通婚。对于来自他们曾把女儿嫁过去的村庄的新娘，很多迦提会拒绝接受迦提，南部则是两个村庄之间相互通婚，家族之间常会亲上加亲。中部的婚姻则是以上两种方式都有。

在印度人的生活中，家庭和亲族占很重的分量。个人在家中的地位，取决于年龄、性别和他与领导阶层的关系。例如在喀拉拉邦中的纳雅人，家中最年长的男性权威最大，虽然他不是唯一的财产继承者。根据印度的法律，家中每一个男性都可以参与财产分配，最年长的可能分到最多；女性唯有通过婚姻才能参与分配，尽管目前的法律赋予她们同等的继承权。

四、女性的地位

在印度，儿子的出生受到盛大的欢迎，包括敲锣打鼓、唱歌跳舞、公开宣告。生女儿时就安静多了，但并非一向如此。在印度早期历史中，女性和男性享有同等地位，她可以成为传教士，选择自己的婚姻对象，管理家庭；是否存在萨提（sati，指女人坐在丈夫葬礼的火堆上陪伴丈夫一起死）并不清楚，但在前吠陀时代寡妇可以再嫁。①那时（公元前1500—前800年）的民间传说都褒扬女性的美丽、价值和力量。其中一个故事讲述道，有位名叫莎特巴纳（Satyabhama）的女子，她勇敢无惧。当她见到正在作战的丈夫不敌对手时，奋不顾身

---

① Richard Lannoy, *The Speaking Tree: A Study of Indian Culture and Society* (Oxford: Oxford University Press, 1971), p. 102; and R. Mathulakshmi, *Female Infanticide: Its Causes and Solution* (New Delhi: Discovery Publishing House, 1997), p. 2.

地拿起武器,将敌人的手臂砍断,救了丈夫的性命。女人可以陪男人到任何地方,她们的活动和贡献被认为对未来世代的生存不可或缺。①

公元前 900 年写的《梨俱吠陀》(Rig Veda)是吠陀里最古老最重要的文献,其中提到嫁妆、一夫多妻、新娘的价格等,女性的地位应该是从那时开始改变的。② 吠陀晚期的作品《罗摩衍那》及《摩诃婆罗多》,一再强化女性次等公民的角色。③ 到了公元前 600 年之后,女人的地位开始恶化;她们已不能成为传教士,她们的教育被忽视,她们的适婚年龄也降低了。④ 从公元 6 世纪以来,印度的经典文献中都出现男人必须控制女人的说法,最典型的代表就是《摩奴法典》,其中说道:"女人不该独立,在孩童时代她必须听从父亲,婚后受控于丈夫,夫死从子。"男人还被警告:"女人热情、易变,却也无情,她们倾向于对丈夫不忠。"⑤ 所以,《摩奴法典》宣称:"女孩必须在 8 岁至 12 岁结婚,否则她的父母及长兄就有罪,将来会下地狱。"⑥ 上层社会的女性被家庭藏起来,由一位男性亲属监控,只能和近亲见面,这种做法在印度北部最为普遍,那儿也流行一夫多妻、嫁妆和种姓制度。

现在印度女性的地位反映在识字率和工作参与度上。20 世纪以来,印度女性的识字率一直在上升,但和男性比起来差别仍很大。根据 1991 年的普查,有 53% 的男性识字,但只有 32% 的女性识字,在

---

① Har Bilas Sarda, *History of Ancient Hindu Society* (Delhi: Anmol Publications, 1985), p. 101.

② Dickemann, "Paternal Confidence and Dowry Competition," p. 432.

③ Muthulakshmi, *Female Infanticide*, p. 2.

④ Brij Narain Sharma, *Social Life in Northern India* [A. D. 600—1000] (Delhi: Munshiram Manoharlal, 1966), p. 10.

⑤ Muthulakshmi, *Female Infanticide*, pp. 3 - 4.,

⑥ See Sharma, *Social Life in Northern India*, p. 15.

乡村及北部的识字率更低。① 最新的就业数据显示，在乡村的受薪人口中，女性占29%，男性占55%。在城市的受薪人口中，女性占16%，男性占53%。②

重男轻女在印度的情形与亚洲其他国家一样严重。1997年在印度全国所作的一次研究揭示，重男轻女的情形在印度各个年龄层、各个教育水平的人群中都存在。印度人重男轻女的缘由是：宗教信仰、社会风俗（嫁妆、宗族祭祀、亲属关系等）、经济利益（照顾年老的父母）。对17—41岁的人群来说，理想的家庭组成是两个儿子、一个女儿。42—61岁的人群只想要儿子，可能因为他们担心会无法负担女儿的嫁妆，并希望在年老后有儿子照顾。父母教育程度愈高，对儿子愈不会偏心。但大学程度以上的男性，反而特别想要儿子，因为他们多属上层种姓，更需要儿子来传承香火。③

1992—1993年，在印度进行的全国家庭健康调查中发现了对于重男轻女的评估方法。人口学家认为，对儿子的偏爱基于三个原因：经济、社会文化和宗教期待。研究者解释说："无论家庭业农、工或经商，儿子都比女儿更有能力赚钱养家和支持年迈的父母。"在父系社会中，唯独儿子能够延续家族香火，提升家族地位。根据印度教传统，儿子需要在父母的丧礼中点火祭祀，协助他们的灵魂获得永生。④

---

① Leela Visaria and Pravin Visaria, "India's Population in Transition," *Population Bulletin*, Vol. 50, No. 3 (October 1995), p. 24.

② Ibid., p. 31.

③ Rangamuthia Mutharayappa, Minja Kim Choe, Fred Arnold, and T. K. Roy, "Son Preference and Its Effect on Fertility in India," *National Family Health Survey Subject Report* No. 3 (March 1997), p. 5; K. Mahaderan and R. Jayasree, "Value of Children and Differential Fertility Behavior in Kerala, Andra Pradesh, and Uttar Pradesh," in Shri Nath Singh, ed., *Population Transition in India* (Delhi: B. R. Publishing, 1989), pp. 123 – 131. 四个最受支持的重男轻女的理由是："物质支持和陪伴父母"（91.9%）；"父母年老时给予经济支持"（88.5%）；"举行仪式来祭祀父母"（87.4%）；"延续家族血脉"（81.3%）。

④ Mutharayappa et al., "Son Preference and Its Effect on Fertility in India," p. 5.

女儿相对来说是个负担，除了嫁妆和婚礼的花费之外，家庭必须保护她的贞节，为她寻找适婚对象。她一旦结婚，就成为夫家的一员，父母所花的心血都白送给夫家了。当然，她也不是全然无用，除了提供娘家的精神支持外，在父母的葬礼上，还需要她们来哭悼已逝的父母。①

五、杀女婴的开始

究竟印度是什么时候开始杀女婴呢？看法不一，一种看法认为它自古有之，一种看法是它在伊斯兰教侵略信德（现在巴基斯坦的西南方）之后开始的，或认为它始于18世纪蒙兀儿王朝的瓦解。② 一般相信在吠陀早期（公元前1500—前800年）女性的社会地位很高，也没有杀女婴的问题。印度教经文中暗示生女儿不像生儿子——"女儿出生时，把她放在一边，儿子出生时，把他高高举起（骄傲地、高兴地）"，并说"有妻子就有朋友，有女儿就有羞辱，有儿子像上天堂"。③其他的印度经文中也描述各种仪式及符咒，以确保生男孩，但都仍未提及杀女婴。

吠陀的后期（公元前800—前500年）《梨俱吠陀》的经文中，正式提到生女儿不受欢迎。《耶柔吠陀》（*Yajur Veda*）的经文中谈到如何抛弃刚出生的女婴，是最早关于杀婴的文字记载。④

印度社会接受种姓纯度的概念，个人的种姓纯度取决于他是否严

---

① Mutharayappa et al., "Son Preference and Its Effect on Fertility in India," p. 6.
② 不同的观点，参见 Muthulakshmi, *Female Infanticide*, p. 8; Kanti B. Pakrasi, *Female Infanticide in India* (Calcutta: Editions India, 1970), p. 16; Lalita Panigrahi, *British Social Policy and Female Infanticide in India* (New Delhi: Munshiram Manoharlal, 1972), respectively。
③ "Dharmasastra" and "The Mahabharata," as cited in Panigrahi, *British Social Policy and Female Infanticide in India*, p. 2.
④ Herbert Hope Risley, *The People of India*, ed. William Crooke (Delhi: Oriental Books Reprint Corporation, 1969), p. 166.

格遵守男女的分野。女孩因为她们的身体较容易被污染,被视为是污染源,不能参加神圣的宗教仪式,也不受欢迎。① 印度北部和西北部屡有外患。历史学家拉丽塔(Lalita Panigrahi)发现,在受到侵略时,他们会先把女性隔离起来,以防止她们被敌人掳掠。② 古印度文献《政事论》(Arthashastra)(公元前322—前183年)说,女性若被侵略者掳掠,不仅是她们个人的损失,也是有责任保护她们的男性尊严的丧失,族群也会因之灭绝。所以,杀女婴可能就是屡遭侵略的后果之一。③

英国在1789年发现印度人杀女婴,而且以北部和西北部最为普遍。历史学家巴克锡(Kanti Pakrasi)推论,伊斯兰教的入侵造成了印度的杀女婴行为。④ 拉其普特人原住在信德(Sind),公元8世纪时伊斯兰教第一次入侵,并强迫拉其普特人把女儿嫁给他们。将女儿嫁给比自己更低的阶层已够羞耻了,若还被迫嫁给外族,更是颜面尽失,所以拉其普特人的家庭情愿杀女儿,也不愿意接受这种屈辱。

六、公开谴责并试图终止杀女婴

17世纪早期,吉尔皇帝即颁布法令禁止杀女婴。⑤ 1755年,拉贾斯坦邦的统治者拉贾·杰·辛格也曾限制嫁妆的金额,来减少杀女婴行为,但都没有成功。⑥ 影响最大的是邓肯(Jonathan Duncan)在

---

① Wolpert, *A New History of India*, p. 25.
② Panigrahi, *British Social Policy and Female Infanticide in Infanticide in India*, p. 4.
③ Alice Clark, "Limitations on Female Life Chances in Rural Central Gujarat," in J. Krishnamuty ed., *Women in Colonial India: Essays on Survival Work, and the State* (Delhi: Oxford University Press, 1989), p. 41.
④ Pakrasi, *Female Infanticide in India*, pp. 16–17.
⑤ Manmohan Kaur, *Role of Women in the Freedom Movement (1857–1947)* (Delhi: Sterling, 1968), p. 9.
⑥ Kaur, *Role of Women in the Freedom Movement*, pp. 9–10.

1789 年撰文揭露杀女婴现象，以及英国得知后的强烈反应。

邓肯在印度担任文官，他与一群拉其普特人在西北省（今天的北方邦）的奥德附近恒河流域的贝纳勒斯区工作，他发现了拉杰库马尔的拉其普特人杀女婴。① 他于 1789 年写给孟加拉省地方政府的信上说："拉杰库马尔人常会把女儿杀死，这种恐怖的习俗据说存在于许多部落中，尤其是在大臣统治的地方。"② 据信在拉杰库马尔部落，这一做法源于这一部落的男性想要独立的强烈渴望，加之如果允许那些女孩长大，他们就要想法为她们寻找适婚对象，以及这方面的任何疏忽可能招致的耻辱。邓肯在他的第一描述中触及几个关键点：这一习俗也存在于其他部落，正如他和其他人所发现的；这一习俗与拉其普特较高的社会地位和"独立性"有关；它与印度婚姻习俗问题有关系。

虽然英国早在 1600 年就进入印度，却直到 1789 年才发现杀女婴的习俗，难道他们对于某些村庄中缺乏女性的现象视而不见吗？其实，也许是因为印度教徒非常注重隐私，询问私人问题是不礼貌的，何况最可能杀女婴的是被隔离的高阶女性。所以即使发现了这个风俗，英国人还是很难确定到底谁在杀女婴和杀女婴究竟有多普遍。

英国东印度公司于 19 世纪初在西北邦建立据点，发现了卡提阿瓦（Kathiawar）及卡奇（Cutch）（现在都属于古吉拉特邦）都有杀女婴的习俗。那时一位古吉拉特邦的王子告知当时任孟买总督的邓肯，亚勒甲的拉其普特人（the Jahreja Rajputs）在卡奇大规模地杀女婴。③ 同时，英国上校倭克（Alexander Walker）于 1805 年被派到卡提阿瓦，以调解该地政治团体之间的纠纷。他发现了在亚勒甲的拉其

---

① Crooke, *The North-Western Provinces of India（1857 – 1947）*, p. 136；James Peggs, *Cries of Agony*: *An Historical Account of Suttee Infanticide*, *Ghat Murders*, *and Slavery in India*（originally published as *India's Cries to British Humanity*, 1830；reprint, Delhi: Discovery Publishing House, 1984,）p. 133.

② Quoted in Peggs, *Cries of Agony*, p. 133.

③ 有关古吉拉特邦废除这一习俗的详尽历史，参见 Pakrasi, *Female Infanticide in India*。

普特人中几乎找不到女人。事实上,他发现只有五个家庭没有杀掉自己的女儿。①

(一) 杀女婴习俗的起源

倭克很快就被指派去调查杀女婴习俗的状况、原因和起源。他提到了一个流传广泛的传说,当年一位很有权力的首领有个女儿,漂亮而且能干,他的家庭教士(rajgor)设法为她寻找合适的丈夫,但最终没有找到一位足以与她匹配的王子,所以这个教士就耸恿首领,与其让家族为她的不能成婚而蒙羞,不如把她杀了。虽然首领不愿杀他的女儿,但这个教士说他愿意接受这个罪行所带来的一切后果,所以女儿就遇害了,亚勒甲的拉其普特人从那时起开始有杀女婴的恶习。②倭克写道:

> 这个离奇的传说很难让人满意。它类似于儿童故事,而非部分人类命运变迁的重要历史。不过,这包含了所有亚勒甲人异于自然秩序的习俗起源的全部信息。虽然杀女婴的起源讲述令人失望,但历史上有很多荒唐的习俗,并非有明确原因,而是源于当时特殊的情况,经过了年代的洗礼,反而益发有影响力。③

对于侵略者面临的问题,倭克提出了一个更具可能性的解释:

> 据说早期侵略亚勒甲的伊斯兰教徒在面对当地人捍卫自由的顽强抵抗时,想出了要部落首领把女儿嫁给他们,以便将武力和政策结合起来。愤怒的拉其普特人拒绝受辱,假装说他们的女儿

---

① Panigrahi, *British Social Policy and Female Infanticide in India*, p. 40.
② 倭克的完整叙述,参见 Peggs, *Cries of Agony*, pp. 135–138.
③ Cited in ibid., pp. 136–137.

都被杀了。可是他们又害怕谎言被揭穿，也怕对方会用武力来强求，就听从家庭教士的建议，干脆杀女婴来圆谎。杀婴自此起源，以后成为固定习俗。①

在被问到为什么杀女儿时，亚勒甲人回答他们害怕女儿会被俘虏，或是因为其他的理由让家庭受辱。②所以倭克上校的结论是："亚勒甲人会杀女婴，是由于信德被侵略的结果。"③ 社会对女性的道德期待比较高，女性又容易被侵略者俘虏，于是她们遭到严格的控管，成为族人的负担。特别是拉其普特人是个战士族群，对女性一向轻视。④当拉其普特人发现信德沦陷，自己被伊斯兰教徒团团包围，四周找不到可以做女婿的男孩，此时若千里迢迢去找，花费又太大，再加上不能近亲结合，干脆就把女儿杀了以求解脱。⑤尽管印度教经文宣称杀婴是有罪的，但拉其普特人并不觉得有罪，他们甚至以为这样做是印度教所认同的。

（二）更广泛的调查

为了调查古吉拉特的亚勒甲人杀女婴有多普遍，倭克根据当地家庭数量来推算。每年被杀的女婴在5000—30000人⑥，这一估算在当时的数据条件下是最精确的了。1834年，对卡提阿瓦的亚勒甲人进行了第一次人口普查，普查结果大有问题，因为统计表是由地方官吏自行填写的。统计显示，男人占绝大多数，各年龄层的女性加起来只有

---

① Cited in ibid., p. 137.
② Pakrasi, *Female Infanticide in India*, p. 16.
③ Quoted in ibid., p. 16.
④ Panigrahi, *British Social Policy and Female Infanticide in India*.
⑤ Ibid., p. 11.
⑥ Pegge, *Cries of Agony*, pp. 150–151.

696人，而且光是20岁以下的男性就有1422人。① 一份1841年的样本数据展示当地男性有5760人，女性却还只有1370人，其性别比例是420（男）∶100（女）。这个统计数字被人质疑，因为人口普查的官员可能被贿赂去多报女性人数。② 1841年，卡奇省有2625位男性，335位女性，性别比例是784（男）∶100（女）。③

刚开始时，英国人以为只有北部和西北部拉其普特人的两个分支［亚勒甲人（Jahrejas）和拉杰库马尔人（Rajkumars）］杀女婴。拉其普特人是印度在公元7世纪时优秀的武士阶层，他们的血统可追溯到公元前1000年吠陀的武士世家，一直到20世纪初还存在于印度的西北省。他们自认为血统高贵，是武士又是地主，于是发展出一套内规，严禁与外通婚。④拉其普特人努力维护血缘，以获得继承王位的机会。他们还有一套复杂的财产继承体系，进而产生了另一等级体系。因此拉其普特人在为女儿寻找适婚对象时，困难重重。正如帕克拉西（Pakrasi）所指出的，拉其普特人等级意识的提升导致他们声称自己具有较高的社会地位。⑤ 毫无疑问，这一现象是抗拒家庭和地位变化的政策的结果。正如维什瓦纳（L. S. Vishwanath）所解释的："这种武士/统治者的思维意识，使得拉其普特人拒绝他可能的阶层流动方式，而更加严格地遵守他们固有的等级制度。"⑥

英国人发现不止亚勒甲人和拉杰库马尔人这两个部族杀女婴，其

---

① Panigrahi, *British Social Policy and Female Infanticide in India*, p. 41.
② Ibid., pp. 41 – 42.
③ Ibid., p. 42.
④ Robert C. Hallissey, *The Rajput Rebellion against Aurangzeb: A Study of the Mughal Empire in Seventeenth-Century India* (Columbia: University of Missouri Press, 1977), pp. 11 – 12.
⑤ Pakrasi, *Female Infanticide*, p. 12.
⑥ L. S. Vishwanath, "Female Infanticide and the Position of Women in India," in A. M. Shah, B. S. Baviskar, and E. A. Ramaswampy, eds., *Social Structure and Change*, Vol. 2: *Women in Indian Society* (New Delhi: Sage, 1996), p. 186.

他拉其普特人的部族也一样。到了 1818 年，英国的东印度公司已经控制了所有拉其普特人的省份。英国人了解到卡奇及卡提阿瓦地区的拉其普特人对杀女婴负最大的责任，急于知道拉贾斯坦邦的拉其普特人地区杀女婴的情形。1808 年倭克了解了斋浦尔（Jaipur）和焦特浦尔（Jodhpur）杀女婴的情况，但是因为该地区尚未处在英国控制之下，他无法作深入调查。直到 1833 年威尔金森（Lanncelot Wilkinson）到达拉其普特人居住地，这一情况才为更多人了解。威尔金森是一位英国陆军中校的副官，他发现杰哈兹浦尔（Jehazpur）的米纳斯人（Minus）会杀掉他们的女儿。①

从 1835—1854 年，英国发现 Bais、Bhadauri（Bhadawri）、Chauhans、Gautams、Kacchwa、Kalhanas、Monus、Nanwak、Parihar、Sowan 及 Surajbhan 的拉其普特人部落都会杀女婴。②随着英国调查的继续，更多的拉其普特人被发现杀害家庭的女人：1855 年，英国人访问了 62 个村庄，没看到一个 6 岁以下的女孩。1843 年，在库罕（Chauhans）——最傲慢的拉其普特部落中，找不到任何女婴。③ 事实上，杀女婴的行为在整个拉其普特人居住地的全部中上阶层普遍存在，还有马尔瓦（Malwa，现在是中央邦的一部分）的拉其普特人生活地区也存在。④

拉其普特人不是唯一缺乏女儿的种姓，西北省的帕塔克·阿依尔人（Phatak Ahirs）和古贾尔人（Gujars）也一样。帕尼格拉伊（Panigrahi）认为，这些部族是在模仿拉其普特人的做法，来提高自己的社会地位，尽管这一习俗源于一个艰困时代。⑤维什瓦纳也注意到，古吉拉特中部的勒瓦·坎比斯人（Lewa Kanbis）普遍存在杀女婴的情形。

---

① Panigrahi, *British Social Policy and Female Infanticide in India*, pp. 31 – 32.
② Ibid., pp. 23 – 25.
③ Crooke, *The North-Western Provinces of India*, p. 136.
④ Panigrahi, "British Social Policy and Female Infanticide in India," pp. 19 – 32.
⑤ Ibid., pp. 12 – 13.

随着英国控制地区的增多，人们发现其他地区也普遍存在这一现象。①英国控制苏特莱杰（Sutlej）河流域之后，在贝蒂（Bedis）也发现了杀女婴的情形。锡克族在旁遮普省被称为 kuri-mar（kudi-maar）或"杀女儿的人"，常常故意忽略女儿而致她们死亡。②贝蒂（Bedis）是锡克族的最高阶层，据说他们杀女婴完全是为了面子。16 世纪，锡克族创始人的孙子因为把女儿嫁给一位阶层较低的新郎，备受屈辱。这个颜面尽失的爸爸当时就宣布，贝蒂不该让女儿活着，不杀女儿的，就会被逐出族门。③索蒂人（Sodhees）自视比贝蒂人优越，也把杀女婴作为一件值得夸耀的是，正如曼贾和马尔瓦的锡克族一样。④

除锡克族之外，旁遮普地区的伊斯兰教徒等也选择以杀女儿来维护自己的社会地位。⑤ 其他的少数族群（包括 Aroras, Karrs, Kapurs, Khannas, Malhotras, Seths, Suyals）也在 1853 年旁遮普地区杀女婴的名单之列。旁遮普地区较高阶层的拉其普特人都杀女婴，唯一不这么做的，只有拉其普特人的高山部落。⑥

在印度中部的省份（中央邦及奥里萨的一部分），也存在杀女婴的现象。据称杀女婴的现象在下层人群很少出现，但在较高阶层的拉其普特人、贾克人（Jats）、古贾尔人（Gujars）中都存在。⑦ 普遍存在于勒瓦（中央邦）的拉其普特人中的杀女婴现象是在 1841 年发现的。⑧ 当史利曼（W. H. Sleeman）于 1849 年及 1850 年在奥德（北方

---

① Vishwanath, " Female Infancide and the Position of Women in India," pp. 179 – 205.

② Panigrahi, *British Social Policy and Female Infanticide in India*, pp. 25 – 26.

③ John Cave Browne, *Indian Infanticide: Its Origins, Progress, and Suppression* (London: W. H. Allen, 1857), pp. 115 – 118.

④ Ibid., p. 119.

⑤ Panigrahi, *British Social Policy and Female Infanticide in India*, pp. 28 – 29.

⑥ Browne, *Indian Infanticide*, pp. 111 – 112.

⑦ Ibid., p. 37.

⑧ Panigrahi, *British Social Policy and Female Infanticide in India*, pp. 36 – 37.

邦）旅行时，终于了解到杀女婴的普遍性。

（三）杀女婴的原因

根据史利曼的日记，印度的高等种姓常会因婚姻问题造成经济困扰。史利曼遇见勒瓦的首领，他有两个女儿。他把大女儿嫁给一位适当的对象，花了很多钱。他为儿子从较低的阶层找了五六位妻子，虽然也拿到了不少嫁妆，但这些钱还不够他把第二个女儿风光地嫁出去。① 在奥德，正如在西北省，杀女婴的基本上是拉其普特人。史利曼强调，因为一夫多妻制和嫁妆的习俗，几乎所有拉其普特人都会杀女婴，但森杰尔人（Sengers）是一个例外。② 他这样描述了他对于这一习俗所作的探询：

> 我今天问遍所有的乡民，此处杀婴是否盛行。他们的回答是，在奥德，几乎所有的拉其普特人家庭，无论哪个阶层，都会杀婴。只有那些非常穷的家庭才保留女儿，因为可以把她们嫁给较低的阶层而从中获利。但对富有的家庭来说，为了钱把女儿嫁低，或是花巨资把女儿嫁给适当的对象，还不如不让她们出生。③

把女儿嫁给较低阶层的家族意味着丧失种姓身份，因此多数拉其普特人不会这样做。史利曼讲述了一个故事，或许可以帮助了解母亲

---

① P. D. Reeves, ed., *Sleeman in Oudh: An Abridgement of W. H. Sleeman's A Journey through the Kingdom of Oude in 1849–50* (Cambridge: Cambridge University Press, 1971), pp. 132–133.

② P. D. Reeves, ed., *Sleeman in Oudh: An Abridgement of W. H. Sleeman's A Journey through the Kingdom of Oude in 1849–50* (Cambridge: Cambridge University Press, 1971), p. 169.

③ P. D. Reeves, ed., *Sleeman in Oudh: An Abridgement of W. H. Sleeman's A Journey through the Kingdom of Oude in 1849–50* (Cambridge: Cambridge University Press, 1971), pp. 201–202.

的心理:"母亲通常会在第一个女儿出生后即被抱走时,尖叫并哭泣不已。但到了第二胎、第三胎时,她们就安静多了,最后不得不向现实妥协。她会说:'你爱怎么做就怎么做吧!'"① 拉其普特人是奥德的统治阶层,这也是这一地区杀婴如此泛滥的原因。拉其普特人声称,保留女儿会为家庭和整个族群带来灾难,所以必须消灭她。有了这么强烈的理由,连母亲柔软的心都被说服了。

印度最东端通过孟加拉邦接近缅甸西北边界的地区,是那加兰邦。19世纪中期,马库罗上校(Col. W. McCulloch)经过那儿的一个村庄,发现那儿竟然没有女孩。村民回答,所有女孩都被杀了,因为担心"有强敌会来抢夺女性为妻"。②他们担心女儿会被俘,也担心女儿为家庭带来灾难,因为那个掳走女儿的人,可能会砍下父亲的头颅作为纪念品。③

同样的情景也出现在奥里萨地区的孔特人中。孔特人是德拉维甸人后代,他们认为,女性的人数和被恶邻抢夺的危险性成正比。④孔特人既非伊斯兰教徒,也不是印度教徒,他们内部的活动和社会习俗并不统一。外界根据他们举行的仪式,把他们分成三个团体:第一个团体以杀人为祭,不分男女。第二个团体有杀女婴的传统。第三个团体不从事任何以上的行为。⑤ 杀女婴的那个团体往往只留下第一个女儿,其余的就会被杀。他们不认为这么做是有罪的,因为婴儿要到出生后的第七天,才算是家族的成员。他们相信被杀的女孩灵魂不会再投胎,所以也可以减少未来家族中女性的人数。⑥ 杀女婴现象的背后,

---

① P. D. Reeves, ed., *Sleeman in Oudh: An Abridgement of W. H. Sleeman's A Journey through the Kingdom of Oude in 1849 – 50* (Cambridge: Cambridge University Press, 1971), pp. 208 – 209.

② Risiey, *The People of India*, p. 172.

③ Ibid., p. 174.

④ Ibid., p. 172.

⑤ Barbara M. Boal, *The Konds: Human Sacrifice and Religious Change* (Warminster, U. K.: Aris and Phillips, 1982), p. 47.

⑥ Risley, *The People of India*, p. 172; and Boal, *The Konds*, p. 67.

其实还有强烈的经济动机。孔特人的婚姻制度很奇特，男人不忠会被严厉处罚，女人不忠却可以被容忍。女人可以找爱人，遗弃丈夫。如果太太琵琶别抱，丈夫就可以保留当初岳父所给的钱。对于第二个丈夫，岳父也会赠予同额的钱。难怪孔特人有三分之二的纠纷，都是关于婚姻的争议。①

由于不同地区杀女婴的原因各自有别，杀女婴的方式也不尽相同。一般来说，杀女婴是几乎不举行任何仪式的；但在旁遮普地区的乡村里，最后一个出生的女儿会被杀。谋杀还有仪式，他们把糖浆放在她的嘴中，一团棉花放置在她的胸上，并再三地告诉她："吃糖及纺丝吧！我们不要你，只要弟弟。"然后把女婴放入水缸中淹死并埋葬。② 其他的方式如喂她鸦片，或饿死，或把脐带放入她嘴里造成窒息，或在母亲的乳房上涂抹毒药，或在地上挖洞放满牛奶，再把女婴放入。③

（四）终止杀女婴的努力

英国曾设法终止印度杀女婴的陋习，它通过禁止、奖赏和教育的种种办法，结果有好有坏。在英国长期控管的地区，女性人数开始增加，但因为有些女性找不到合适的婚姻对象，杀女婴的行为又开始了。1868年有一个族群被怀疑杀女婴，因为在他们的人口当中，只有22%是女性。人口的总体规模并未提供。④ 1870年的《禁止杀女婴法》因之诞生，详细规定有关出生、结婚及死亡的注册以及调查和惩罚杀女婴行为的方法，它也对结婚的花费作出限制，并授权当局把营养不良的小孩从父母身边带走。⑤

---

① Boal, *The Konds*, p. 67.
② Risley, *The People of India*, p. 174.
③ Kau, *Role of Women in the Freedom Movement*, pp. 8 – 9.
④ 人口的总体规模尚未给出。参见 Crooke, *The North-Western Provinces of India*, p. 137。
⑤ Panigrahi, *British Social Policy and Female Infanticide in India*, pp. 141 – 142.

英国政府曾企图正确统计印度农村和城镇的人口，但在英国统治早期杀婴现象的严重程度都是无法估量的。1872 年的人口普查显示出印度各省的性别比例，我们才可以从中估计杀女婴有多普遍。表 3-1 列出 12 岁以下的儿童性别比例。

表 3-1　1872 年英属印度 12 岁以下的儿童中每 100 名女性所对应的男性数字

省	对应的性别比
孟加拉	120.1
阿萨姆	116.2
迈索尔	103.1
马德拉斯	104.1
中央省	108.6
贝拉尔	112.8
奥德	118.6
孟买	111.8
西北省	120.1
旁遮普	118.6
库格省	108.3

来源：Barbara D. Miller, *The Endangered Sex: Neglect of Female Children in Rural North India* (Inthaca, N.Y.: Cornell University Press, 1981), p.59。

在 1872 年，印度的人口是 1.9 亿，其中男性为 0.98 亿人，女性 0.92 亿人，总体人口性别比例是 106.4（男）：100（女），青少年的性别比例显示出有忽略女婴或杀女婴的现象。青少年性别比例在各地都很高，除了迈索尔和马德拉斯，这两个省都地处南方。在孟加拉、阿萨姆、奥德、旁遮普（包括巴基斯坦和印度西北地区）等地，青少年性别比例表明杀女婴很普遍。尤其是位处西北的地区，包括中央省，被称为女婴终结地。

人口普查让英国政府确定了杀女婴的地区，但因为人口普查的数据，未包括关于种姓或族群等更具体的数据，所以英国只能从其青少年的性别比例中，判断出某些乡村有罪。如果某一乡村的青少年当中女孩的比例小于40%，该乡村就会被罚。《禁止杀女婴法》于1872年在西北省实施后，4959个乡村共有485938人被判有罪，因为当地女孩的人口少于40%。在这些乡村中，有1013个乡村被认为是"特别血腥的"，其中女孩人口少于青少年人口的25%。① 乡村一旦被判有罪，其中的种姓和家族就会被指认并受到监督，经过一段时间，杀女婴的比例就降低了。在1874年，西北省有389697人被列入监督，当时的青少年性别比例是231（男）：100（女）。六年之后，被监督的人数降到285860人，性别比例下降到159（男）：100（女）。到了1882年，性别比例再降到114（男）：100（女）。② 到了1890年，5岁以下男孩和女孩的人数一样，除了少数几个特别偏远的村落，杀女婴的陋习似乎已停止了。③

英国鼓励各地组成埃克达斯（Ekdas），它由数个家庭组成（家庭的数目并没有限制），互相通婚。Ekdas禁止女性择优而嫁，因为他们认为所有的成员都是平等的，婚资金额也被严格控制。不幸的是，Ekdas当中有很多家庭为了提升自己的社会地位，而离开了这个团体。④ 然而，英国采取限制嫁妆金额的做法也帮助了比最高种姓或亚种姓身份低的每一阶层的人。

英国的干预造成了一个意外的结果，有愈来愈多的女性找不到对象。正如维什瓦纳所说，亚勒甲人虽然被迫保留女儿，但却不知要如何为她们找丈夫⑤，因此强迫守节，就成了许多未在婴儿期被杀的女性的结局。

杀女婴的故事并没有就此结束。1901年的人口普查显示，全国的总人口性别比例是102.9（男）：100（女），这似乎表示英国已经有

---

① Panigrahi, *British Social Policy and Female Infanticide in India*, pp. 162–163.
② Panigrahi, *British Social Policy and Female Infanticide in India*, p. 188.
③ Ibid., pp. 189–190.
④ Vishwanath, "Female Infanticide and the Position of Women in India," p. 195.
⑤ Ibid., p. 189.

效制止了印度杀女婴行为。但图3-1指出，到了2001年，总人口性别比例却上升至107.2（男）：100（女）。

除此之外，证据表明杀女婴的现象从未完全停止。在1901年，当全部人口呈现正常的性别比例时，下列各省及地区的性别比例仍然高于预期：阿萨姆（108.8）、德里（116.0）、哈里亚纳（115.3）、喜马偕尔（113.1）、"查谟和克什米尔"（113.3）、旁遮普（120.2）、拉贾斯坦（110.5）、锡金（109.2）、特里普拉（114.4）及北方省（106.7）。① 所以，即便考虑到杀女婴行为的历史时滞性会导致成年人群的高性别比例，我们依然认为杀女婴在印度并没有完全断绝。

维什瓦纳指出，甚至在1901年之后，在有着杀女婴历史的种姓中，性别比例仍然是扭曲的："1911年人口普查也显示有杀女婴传统的种姓（如拉其普特人等）中，5岁以下的儿童性别比例是120.2（男）：100（女），而没有这一传统的种姓中，该比例是99.5（男）：100（女）。1921年和1931年的人口普查报告显示有杀女婴记录的种姓中男女性别比例仍持续不平衡。……这表明19世纪杀女婴的种姓通过故意忽略或杀女人的方式而将这一习俗传至20世纪。"②

对印度北部和西北部许多种姓和群体杀女婴历史的这一讨论指向新生儿性别选择、忽略女婴和隔离女人的传统。这些歧视女性的形式植根于侵略史，以及一个建立在权力和地位世袭、纯净和不纯净的概念区分、特殊的婚姻模式（强调一夫多妻制）及经济动机（关于女人及其嫁妆的价值）的基础上的复杂社会体系。英国人试图终结杀女婴的行为，影响到许多家庭、种族和村庄，但是因为他们无法触及问题根源，杀女婴的行为仍在印度北部大部分地区继续。

---

① India, Office of the Registrar General, *Census of India*, 1991, Series-1: *India*, Paper 2 of 1992: *Final Population Totals*: *Brief Analysis of Primary Census Abstract* (New Delhi: India, Office of the Registrar General, 1992), pp. 102 – 105.

② Vishwanath, "Female Infanticide and the Position of Women in India," p. 200.

七、目前的情况

在本届我们考察当前印度的人口性别比，主要关注出生人口性别比例上升、对男婴女婴的区别对待，以及其他导致性别比例扭曲的性别不平等现象。接下来我们确定可以被称为造成印度"消失的女性"或"过剩的男性"的因素，并且预测 2020 年的印度男性和女性人口。

我们从 1991 年和 2001 年人口普查的数据来分析印度目前的人口。① 尽管 2001 年人口普查的初步结果已经公布，但仅知道人口总数。印度人口普查的结果有多准确呢？根据统计学家及人口学家普拉文·维萨里亚（Pravin Visaria）表示，人口普查低估的情况不大，在 1961 年低估了 0.7%，1971 年是 1.7%，1981 年是 1.8%。低估的比例会这么低，主要是因为印度城市人口（1991 年占 25.7%）的比例很低的缘故。② 人口学家蒂姆·戴森（Tim Dyson）却认为这次人口普查的数据低估率为 4%。③ 1981 年的事后质量抽查（PEC）显示，对男性人口的低估为 1.710%，女性人口为 1.885%。④ 也就是女性的总人口从 329954637 人增至 336174282 人，男性从 353374460 人增至 359417163 人，性别比例从 107.07（男）：100（女），修正为 106.95（男）：100（女），改变不大。1991 年人口普查的事后质量抽查亦表明，在 1000 个男性人口中，只低估了 17.3 人，在 1000 个女性人口中，低估了 17.9 人，总性别比例的改变也很有限。所以，1991 年修

---

① 尽管 2001 年的普查数据在本书写作时已公布，但仅有总人口数字，因此无法详细分析人口普查数据。

② Pravin M. Visaria, "Indian Population Problem: Emerging Perspective after the 1991 Census," *Demography India*, Vol. 20, No. 2 (July-December 1991), pp. 273 – 295.

③ Tim Dyson, "On the Demography of the 1991 Census," *Economic and Political Weekly*, December 17 – 24, 1994, pp. 3235 – 3239.

④ P. N. Mari Bhat, Samuel H. Preston, and Tim Dyson, *Vital Rates in India, 1961 – 1981* (Washington, D. C.: National Academy Press, 1984), p. 18.

正后的男性总人数为 446829145 人（记录为 439230458），女性总人数为 414358823 人（记录为 407072230），总性别比例为 107.84（男）：100（女）[记录为 107.90（男）：100（女）]。至于 2001 年人口普查的准确性，现在要下定论似乎还太早。

（一）日益增高的性别比例

如图 3-1 所示，印度的人口性别比例在过去 100 年来有增无减。1991 年，印度男性为 439230458 人，女性 407072230 人，总性别比例为 107.9（男）：100（女）[或根据 PEC 是 107.8（男）：100（女）]。2001 年的人口普查显示，印度增为男性 531277078 人，女性 495738169 人，总性别比例是 107.2（男）：100（女）。这两个比例都比 1981 年的 107.1（男）：100（女）高。印度注册总署认为，尽管世界其他地区的高性别比例反映了男性劳工的涌入，但外国男性劳工移民的人数不会改变印度的总性别比例。① 尽管人口普查中也出现了对女性人口的低估，但这并不能解释印度人口性别比例的稳定升高。昆都（Amitabh Kundu）及萨胡（Mahesk Sahu）说："人口统计方式对女性的歧视，或许可以解释过去 10 年内性别比例上升的原因，但却无法解释过去 90 年来的趋势。所以我们不同意性别比例不平衡的原因，是因为每次普查都对女性有更低估的说法。"② 我们认为，它是因为印度采取堕胎、杀婴等歧视女性的手段所造成的。查看人口普查数据、生育率调查和一些研究成果，可以帮助我们判断在哪里和在什么人当中性别比例是最高的，也可以帮助确定导致高性别比例的各种习俗，如堕胎、杀婴、有差别的死亡率。

---

① India, Office of the Registrar General, *Census of India*, 1991, Paper 2, p. 10.
② Amitabh Kundu and Mahesk K. Sahu, "Variation in Sex Ratio: Development Implications," *Economic and Political Weekly*, October 12, 1991, p. 2341. 在这篇文章中，昆都和萨胡提到人口性别比例下降，因为他们的分析单元是每 100 名男性对应的女性人数，而我们的分析单元是每 100 名女性对应的男性人数。

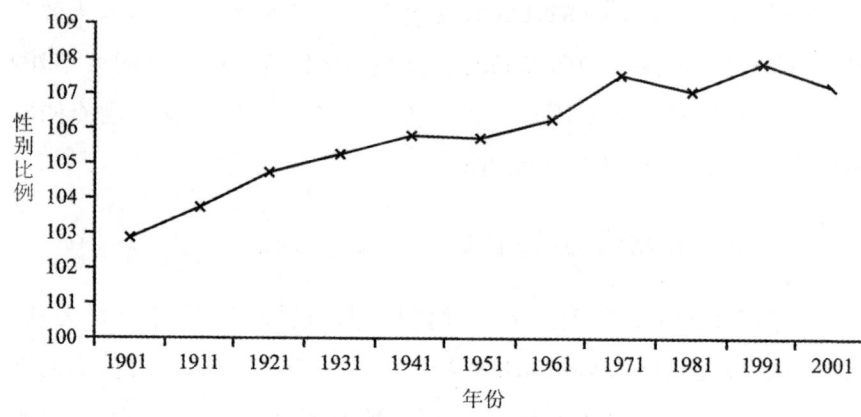

图 3-1　印度的总人口性别比例

来源：India, Office of the Registrar General, *Census of India*, *1991*, *Series-1*: *India*, *Paper 2 of 1992*: *Final Population Totals*: *Brief Analysis of Primary Census Abstract* (New Delhi: India Office of the Registrar General, 1992); and India, *Office of the Registrar General*, *Census of India*, 2001, *Series 1*: *India*, *Paper 1 of 2001*: *Provisional Population Totals* (New Delhi: India, 2001), http://www.censusindia.net/results.

表3-2 是根据2001年的人口普查，列出印度各地区的性别比例，由高至低排列，因此很容易就能看出哪些地区的性别比例较高。表3-3 根据1991年的数据，再把这些地方根据城市、乡村细分，可以看出更多的端倪。

表 3-2　2001年根据邦和中央直辖区划分的印度人口性别比

印度/邦/联邦属地*/地区	性别比
达曼和第乌*	141.01
昌迪加尔*	129.42
纳加尔哈维利*	123.31
德里*	121.87
安达曼和尼科巴群岛*	118.19
哈里亚纳邦	116.12
旁遮普邦	114.46
"锡金"	114.25

续表

印度/邦/联邦属地*/地区	性别比
北方邦	111.30
"查谟和克什米尔"	111.14
"阿鲁纳恰尔邦"	110.98
那加兰邦	110.00
中央邦	108.74
比哈尔邦	108.63
古吉拉特邦	108.62
拉贾斯坦邦	108.45
马哈拉施特拉邦	108.44
阿萨姆邦	107.29
印度	107.17
西孟加拉邦	107.11
米佐拉姆邦	106.61
贾钦德邦	106.23
拉克沙群岛*	105.57
特里普拉邦	105.22
果阿邦	104.14
卡纳塔克邦	103.78
北安查尔邦	103.68
喜马偕尔邦	103.12
奥里萨邦	102.86
梅加拉亚邦	102.60
安得拉邦	102.26
曼尼普尔邦	102.20
泰米尔纳德邦	101.38
恰蒂斯加尔邦	101.05
庞第皆瑞*	99.91
喀拉拉邦	94.49

来源：India, Office of the Registrar General, *Census of India*, *2001*, *Series-1*: *India*, *Paper 1 of 2001*: *Provisional Population Totals*（New Delhi：India Office of the Registrar General, 2001），http：//www.censusindia.net/results。

表 3-3 1991 年根据总数、地区、城市人口区分的印度人口性别比

地区/邦	总数	农村	城市
"阿鲁纳恰尔邦"	116.4	113.6	137.4
哈里亚纳邦	115.6	115.8	115.2
"锡金"	113.9	112.1	133.3
北方邦	113.8	113.2	116.2
旁遮普邦	113.4	112.7	115.2
那加兰邦	112.9	109.1	133.5
拉贾斯坦邦	109.9	108.8	113.7
比哈尔邦	109.8	108.5	118.5
西孟加拉邦	109.1	106.4	116.6
米佐拉姆邦	108.6	109.6	107.3
"查谟和克什米尔"	108.3	107.2	112.0
阿萨姆邦	108.3	107.1	119.4
印度	107.9	106.6	111.9
中央邦	107.4	106.0	112.0
马哈拉施特拉邦	107.1	102.8	114.3
古吉拉特邦	107.1	105.4	110.2
特里普拉邦	105.8	106.2	104.4
梅加拉亚邦	104.7	103.5	109.9
曼尼普尔邦	104.4	105.2	102.6
卡纳塔克邦	104.2	102.7	107.6
果阿邦	103.4	100.7	107.6
奥里萨邦	103.0	101.2	115.4
安得拉邦	102.9	102.3	104.3
泰米尔纳德邦	102.7	101.9	104.1
奥里萨邦	102.5	101.0	120.3
喀拉拉邦	96.5	96.4	96.7

来源：性别比数据根据 1991 年记录的人口总数、农村人口和城市人口数量计算而来。2001 年的普查数据目前还不可得。India, Office of the Registrar General, *Census of India, 1991*, Series-1: Part 2-B (I), Vol.1: *Primary Census Abstract General Population* (New Delhi: India Office of the Registrar General, 1994)。

表3-2、表3-3显示，印度各地及其乡村和城市之间的性别比例并不均衡；性别比例是随着地理位置和乡村、城市人口的不同而发生变动的。印度有75%的人口住在乡村，所以乡村的性别比例对全国影响最大。总的来说，城市的性别比例［111.9（男）：100（女）］要比乡村的［106.6（男）：100（女）］高，但只稍微提升了总性别比例。城市性别比例高虽然有性别选择性堕胎的原因，但主要是由男性人口流动导致的。

表3-2显示性别比例在22个地区特别高［高过106（男）：100（女）］。此外，性别比例只在喀拉拉邦偏低，在安得拉、果阿、奥里萨和泰米尔纳德等几个邦（除了奥里萨，其他都地处南部），性别比例稍高于正常水平。有意思的是，21个性别比例高的邦和地区，也是19世纪杀婴最多的地区——北部和西北部。1872年时，曾有4959个乡村（总人口为485938人）因为性别比例太高而被英国政府监督，今天这些地区的人口更多，约占印度70%的人口（1991年为5.94亿人，在2001年为7.07亿人）。性别比例在南部只比正常值略高一些。

（二）"消失的女性"

今天印度已经没有任何一个乡村完全没有女人了，可是当印度人口快速增加时，"消失的女性"也就越来越多。我们设定在全体人口中，男性和女性的人数大致相等，那么在印度"消失的女性"已从1991年的32158228人增至2001年的35538909人了。克拉森及文克认为"消失的女性"其实更多。如在第二章所述，亚洲国家的生育水平、年龄结构和人口死亡方式也在变动，正如预期出生人口性别比和总人口一样。他们计算出印度预期出生人口性别比在印度是103.9（男）：100（女），总性别比例是99.3（男）：100（女）①，那么在

---

① Stephan Klasen and Claudia Wink, "'Missing Women': Revisiting the Debate," *Feminist Economics*, Vol. 9, Nos. 2–3 (July-November 2003), Table 3.

2001年就有39284065个女性凭空消失了。尽管这个数字可以更准确地代表"消失的女性"数字，但我们还是采取上面所说的保守估计，以便与其他学者的计算作比较。

表3-4列出各个地区的消失女性人数和全国消失女性人数的比例。21个高性别比例的邦和地区，有5个地方的人口少于100万（昌迪加尔、锡金、米佐拉姆、达曼和第乌、安得拉和纳加尔哈维利），在消失女性的全体人口中，比例很小（小于1%）。至于其他16个高性别比例的地区，北方邦一地就占了全国消失女性人数的25%，尽管它的人口只占全国的16%。唯有喀拉拉邦的女性人口比男性多。在2001年，它的女性比男性多90万人。喀拉拉邦的年轻男性移民很多，他们多半前去中东工作。①喀拉拉邦有全国最多的以女性为一家之主的家庭，女性识字率最高，长寿的女性也最多。②

表3-4 2001年印度各邦和地区的"消失的女性"

印度/邦/联邦属地*	总人口	男性总数	女性总数	"消失的女性"	对"消失的女性"贡献	占总人口的比重(%)
印度	1027015247	531277078	495738169	35538909	100.00	100.00
"查谟和克什米尔"	10069917	5300574	4769343	531231	1.49	0.98
喜马偕尔邦	6077248	3085256	2991992	93264	0.26	0.59
旁遮普邦	24289296	12963362	11325934	1637428	4.61	2.37
昌迪加尔*	900914	508224	392690	115534	0.33	0.09
北安查尔邦	8479562	4316401	4163161	153240	0.43	0.83
哈里亚纳邦	21082989	11327658	9755331	1572327	4.42	2.05
德里*	13782976	7570890	6212086	1358804	3.82	1.34
拉贾斯坦邦	56473122	29381657	27091465	2290192	6.44	5.50

---

① S. Irudaya Rajan, "Heading towards a Billion," *Economic and Political Weekly*, December 17, 1994, p. 3205.

② Ibid.

续表

印度/邦/联邦属地*	总人口	男性总数	女性总数	"消失的女性"	对"消失的女性"贡献	占总人口的比重(%)
北方邦	166052859	87466301	78586558	8879743	24.99	16.17
比哈尔邦	82878796	43153964	39724832	3429132	9.65	8.07
"锡金"	540493	288217	252276	35941	0.10	0.05
"阿鲁纳恰尔邦"	1091117	573951	517166	56785	0.16	0.11
那加兰邦	1988636	1041686	946950	94736	0.27	0.19
曼尼普尔邦	2388634	1207338	1181296	26042	0.07	0.23
米佐拉姆	891058	459783	431275	28508	0.08	0.09
特里普拉邦	3191168	1636138	1555030	81108	0.23	0.31
梅加拉亚邦	2306069	1167840	1138229	29611	0.08	0.22
阿萨姆邦	26638407	13787799	12850608	937191	2.64	2.59
西孟加拉邦	80221171	41487694	38733477	2754217	7.75	7.81
贾钦德邦	26909428	13861277	13048151	813126	2.29	2.62
奥里萨邦	36706920	18612340	18094580	517760	1.46	3.57
恰蒂斯加尔邦	20795956	10452426	10343530	108896	0.31	2.02
中央邦	60385118	31456873	28928245	2528628	7.12	5.88
古吉拉特邦	50596992	26344053	24252939	2091114	5.88	4.93
达曼和第乌	158059	92478	65581	26897	0.08	0.02
纳加尔哈维利	220451	212731	98720	23011	0.06	0.02
马哈拉施特拉邦	96752247	50334270	46417977	3916293	11.02	9.42
安得拉邦	75727541	38286811	37440730	846081	2.38	7.37
卡纳塔克邦	52733958	26856343	25877615	978728	2.75	5.13
果阿邦	1343998	685617	658381	27236	0.08	0.13
拉克沙群岛	60595	31118	29477	1641	0.00	0.01
喀拉拉邦	31838619	15468664	16369955	(901291)	(2.54)	3.10

续表

印度/邦/联邦属地*	总人口	男性总数	女性总数	"消失的女性"	对"消失的女性"贡献	占总人口的比重(%)
泰米尔纳德邦	62110839	31268654	30842185	426469	1.20	6.05
庞第皆瑞	973829	486705	487124	(419)	(0.00)	0.09
安达曼-尼科巴群岛	356265	192985	163280	29705	0.08	0.03

资料来源：所计算的人口总数的数据来源于 India, Office of the Registrar General, *Census of India, 2001, Series-1: India, Paper 1 of 2001: Provisional Population Totals*（New Delhi: India Office of the Registrar General, 2001），http://www.censusindia.net/results。

按地理位置划分主要的地区，能够观察到进一步的模式（参见表3-5）。通过把人口最多的邦划分成不同区域，帮助我们进一步了解性别比例变动的模式。根据表3-5，印度北部占总人口的40%，在1991年及2001年，它有为数1700万的"消失的女性"人口（占全体"消失的女性"人口的一半）。西部排名第二，东/东北第三，再次是西北和南部。把各地"消失的女性"人数和当地的总人口相比，北部和西北部"消失的女性"最多，南方最少。北部和西北部占印度总人口的45%，有全国最高的性别比例［109.8（男）：100（女）及115.2（男）：100（女）］，及最多的（57%）"消失的女性"比例。

表3-5　1991年和2001年印度按地区和邦划分的人口性别比

地区/邦	性别比1991	性别比2001	总人口出生率1991	总人口出生率2001	"消失的女性"2001	对"消失的女性"的贡献1991(%)	对"消失的女性"的贡献2001(%)
印度	107.9	107.2	3.7	32158000	35539000	100.00	100.0
北部	111.0	109.8	—	17425000	17128000	54.19	48.2
比哈尔邦	109.8	108.6	4.6	4030000	3429000	12.53	9.7
中央邦	107.4	108.7	4.6	2353000	2529000	7.32	7.1
拉贾斯坦邦	109.9	108.4	4.5	2080000	2290000	6.47	6.4
北方邦	113.8	111.3	5.2	8962000	8880000	27.87	25.0

续表

地区/邦	性别比 1991	性别比 2001	总人口出生率 1991	总人口出生率 2001	消失的女性 2001	对"消失的女性"的贡献 1991(%)	对"消失的女性"的贡献 2001(%)
东部/东北部	107.3	106.0	—	4314000	4209000	13.42	11.8
阿萨姆邦	108.3	107.3	3.4	902000	937000	2.80	2.6
奥里萨邦	103.0	102.9	3.3	469000	518000	1.46	1.5
西孟加拉邦	109.1	107.1	3.2	2943000	2754000	9.15	7.8
南部	102.2	101.2	—	2086000	1350000	6.49	3.8
"阿鲁纳恰尔邦"	102.9	102.3	3.0	941000	846000	2.93	2.4
卡纳塔克邦	104.2	103.8	3.1	927000	979000	2.88	2.8
喀拉拉邦	96.5	94.5	1.8	521000	901000	-1.62	2.5
泰米尔纳德邦	102.7	101.4	2.2	739000	426000	2.30	1.2
西部	107.1	108.5	—	4115000	6007000	12.80	16.9
古吉拉特邦	107.1	108.6	3.2	1401000	2091000	4.36	5.9
马哈拉施特拉邦	107.1	108.4	3.0	2714000	3916000	8.44	11.0
西北部	112.1	115.2	—	2465000	3210000	7.67	9.0
哈里亚纳邦	115.6	116.1	3.9	1191000	1572000	3.70	4.4
旁遮普邦	113.4	114.5	3.1	1274000	1637000	3.96	4.6

来源：计算所需的性别比例和人口总数的数据来自于印度1991年的人口普查，见 India, Office of the Registrar General, *Census of India, 1991, Series-1: Part 2-B (I), Vol. 1: Primary Census Abstract General Population* (New Delhi: India Office of the Registrar General, 1994)；总生育率（一个妇女在其一生中平均拥有的孩子数）来自于 Leela Visaria and Pravin Visaria, "India's Population in Transition," *Population Bulletin*, Vol. 50, No. 3 (October 1995), p. 22。这五个地区所"消失的女性"数据没有加总到印度消失女性的总数里，因为这里只列出了人口最多的邦。2001年的计算数据来自于 India, Office of the Registrar General, *Census of India, 2001, Series: India, Paper 1 of 2001: Provisional Population Totals* (New Delhi: India Office of the Registrar General, 2001), http://www.censusindia.net/results。

结合"消失的女性"人数、总人口数及生育率,我们还可以看到北部和西北部有全国最高的生育率,对印度的高性别比例会有持续的影响。各地以北方邦的生育率最高达5.2%,它也是全国人口最多(1.66亿人)及性别比例最高的地区之一。它的邻居比哈尔拥有全国第三的人口(0.83亿人)及第二高的生育率4.6%。这两个地方加起来,就占了印度绝大部分的消失女性人口。相比之下,南方的性别比例较为正常,生育率也较低。

进一步分析人口普查的数据,我们还可以发现印度"在册"种姓和部落,以及整个人口的其他变化模式(如表3-6)。在册种姓是印度社会经济地位最低的群体,他们以前被称为"贱民",现在受到政府的保护,并享受各项优惠政策。最低阶层的人不信印度教,他们住在印度资源最贫乏的地方。分析这一人群的性别比例,可以了解实施新生儿性别选择的地区和人群存在的问题。

表3-6 1991年印度的种姓和部落中每100个女性所对应的男性数量

地区/邦	整体性别比	在册种姓性别比	在册部落性别比	非在册种姓和非在册部落性别比
印度	107.9	108.5	102.9	108.3
北部	111.0	111.9	103.1	111.8
比哈尔邦	109.8	109.4	103.0	110.5
中央邦	107.4	109.3	101.5	109.2
拉贾斯坦邦	109.9	111.2	107.5	110.0
北方邦	113.8	114.0	109.4	113.8
东部/东北部	107.3	106.4	96.1	109.4
阿萨姆邦	108.3	108.8	103.4	109.2
奥里萨邦	103.0	102.6	99.8	104.3
西孟加拉邦	109.1	107.4	103.7	110.0
南部	102.2	102.5	104.0	102.5
"阿鲁纳恰尔邦"	102.9	103.2	104.2	102.7
卡纳塔克邦	104.2	104.0	104.1	104.3

续表

地区/邦	整体性别比	在册种姓性别比	在册部落性别比	非在册种姓和非在册部落性别比
喀拉拉邦	96.5	97.2	100.4	96.3
泰米尔纳德邦	102.7	102.2	104.2	102.8
西部	107.1	106.5	110.6	107.7
果阿邦	103.4	103.4	112.5	103.4
古吉拉特邦	107.1	108.1	103.4	107.6
马哈拉施特拉邦	107.1	105.9	103.3	107.8
西北部	112.1	113.6	101.9	112.7
哈里亚纳邦	115.6	116.3	—	115.5
喜马偕尔邦	102.5	103.4	101.9	102.2
旁遮普邦	113.4	114.5	—	113.0

来源：每个省份根据在册种姓、在册部落、非在册种姓和非在册部落的性别比数据来自于 India, Office of the Registrar General, *Census of India*, *1991*, Series-1：Part 2-B（I），Vol. 1：*Primary Census Abstract General Population*（New Delhi：India Office of the Registrar General, 1994）。地区性别比的计算数据来自于 S. B. Agnihotri, "Missing Females：A Disaggregated Analysis," *Economic and Political Weekly*, August 19, 1995, p. 2075。

在印度总人口中，有16%的人口属于在册种姓，8%的人口属于在册部落。因为有很小比例的人口属于在册部落，所以这一群体对印度总人口性别比例影响不大，但可能会对地区有影响。在那加兰邦，88%的人口都属于一个在册部落；与此类似，梅加拉亚邦人口的86%属于一个在册部落。在这些地区，部落的性别比例会对地区总人口性别比例有较大影响。在喜马偕尔邦和旁遮普邦，人口的25%以上属于在册种姓，对于整个地区性别比有一定影响。

根据种姓和非在册部落划分，会发现几种性别比例模式。北部、东部/东北部和西北部的在册部落在三种群体（在册种姓、在册部落、非在册种姓和非在册部落）中性别比例最低，也降低了总人口的性别比例。在北部和西北部，在册种姓的性别比例稍高，但仅比非在册种姓和非在册部落高一点。部落和种姓对南部和西部人口有着复杂的影响。历史上,仅有几个部落据称有杀女婴的行为;采取这一行为的人群,例如孔特人,在自己部落的人看来都很奇怪。因为他们没有杀女婴的普遍理由,所以这些部落的预期性别比例比印度的种姓低。在册种姓的高性别比例有些出人意料,因为本来预期这些低等级的种姓不会有杀女婴的行为,杀女婴是和嫁妆及女性择优而嫁的传统有关的。但是在检视在册种姓的性别比例之后,我们发现在那些传统歧视女性的地区这一数据依然较高——北部和西北部,可能因为他们想模仿高阶层的做法吧。尽管在不知道不同群体确切数字的情况下,性别比例是一个反映性别不平衡的较高指标,但很难判断哪里性别不平等最普遍。根据男性女性人数来分析总体人口,有助于断定那些邦以及生活其中的哪类群体存在最多的"消失的女性"人口。

表3-7揭示了印度人口和存在"消失的女性"的不同群体的几个特点。这一表格反映在册种姓在"消失的女性"人口中占最大比例,比来自他们人口规模的估计要高:她们占"消失的女性"人口的17.52%,而只占总人口的16.33%。反之,在册部落所占比例比来自她们人口规模的估计要低:她们占"消失的女性"人口的3.01%,而占总人口的8.01%。在册种姓和部落占印度总人口的24.34%,占全部消失女性人口的20.5%。也就是说,其余的人口占了75.66%,但却有79.5%的消失女性。

在过去30年,在册种姓的性别比例比在册部落和总体人口的增长快。1961年,印度总体人口性别比例是106.3(男):100(女);1991年,上升到107.9(男):100(女)。同一时期,在册部落的性别比例从101.3(男):100(女)上升到102.9(男):100(女);总体人口性别比例从107.1(男):100(女)上升到108.5(男):100(女)。[①]在册种姓人口性别比例的快速上升需要进行深入研究。

---

① S. B. Agnihotri, "Missing Females: A Disaggregated Analysis," *Economic and Political Weekly*, August 19, 1995, p. 2075.

表 3-7 1991 年印度全国在册种姓、在册部落的"消失的女性"

地区/邦	"消失的女性"总数	在册种姓"消失的女性"	在册种姓人口所占比例	在册种姓"消失的女性"所占比例	在册部落"消失的女性"	在册部落人口所占比例	在册部落"消失的女性"所占比例
印度	32158000	5635000	16.33	17.52	968000	8.01	3.01
北部	17425000	3325000	17.60	19.08	427000	8.28	2.45
比哈尔邦	4030000	567000	14.54	14.07	98000	7.66	2.43
中央邦	2353000	429000	14.55	18.23	177000	23.27	4.97
拉贾斯坦邦	2080000	407000	17.29	19.57	199000	12.44	9.57
北方邦	8962000	1922,000	21.04	21.45	13,000	0.21	0.15
东部/东北部	4314000	707000	18.72	16.39	268000	10.92	6.21
阿萨姆邦	902000	70000	7.41	7.76	49000	12.83	5.43
奥里萨邦	469000	64000	16.20	13.65	6000	22.21	1.28
西孟加拉邦	2943000	573000	23.62	19.47	311000	5.04	10.57
南部	2086000	386000	16.07	18.50	137000	3.57	6.57
"阿鲁纳恰尔邦"	941000	167000	15.93	17.75	86000	6.31	9.14
卡纳塔克邦	927000	143000	16.38	15.43	38000	4.26	4.10
喀拉拉邦	521000	41000	9.92	-7.87	1000	1.10	0.19
泰米尔纳德邦	739000	117000	19.18	15.83	12000	1.02	1.62
西部	4135000	372000	9.75	9.00	219000	11.10	5.30
果阿邦	20000	0	2.10	0.00	0	0.00	0.00
古吉拉特邦	1401000	119000	7.41	8.49	102000	14.92	7.28
马哈拉施特拉邦	2714000	253000	11.09	9.32	117000	9.27	4.31
西北部	2529000	656000	24.58	25.94	2000	0.52	0.08
哈里亚纳邦	1191000	245000	19.75	20.57	0	0.00	0.00
喜马偕尔邦	64000	22000	25.33	34.38	2000	4.22	3.13
旁遮普邦	1274000	389000	28.32	30.53	0	0.00	0.00

来源：计算总人口比例的数据来自于 India, Office of the Registrar General, *Census of India, 1991, Series-1: Part 2-B（I）, Vol.*1: *Primary Census Abstract General Population*（New Delhi: India Office of the Registrar General, 1994）。在册部落和在册种姓的总体数据来自于 S. B. Agnihotri, "Missing Females: A Disaggregated Analysis," *Economic and Political Weekly*, August 19, 1995, pp. 2074－2084.

（三）儿童的性别比例

从人口普查的数字，可以找到一些总性别比例虽然正常，但儿童（0—6岁）的性别比例却过高的地区。相反，有些地方总性别比例很高，但儿童的性别比例却很正常，这可能是因为男性大量迁徙或其他原因。表3-8比较了1991年和2001年儿童的性别比例和总人口的性别比例，其中儿童性别比例是由高至低排列的。

表3-8　1991年和2001年印度的儿童性别比比例

印度/邦/联邦属地*	总人口数（1991）	0—6岁（1991）	总人口数（2001）	0—6岁（2001）
印度	107.87	105.82	107.17	107.85
旁遮普邦	113.38	114.29	114.46	126.11
哈里亚纳邦	115.61	113.77	116.12	121.96
查提斯加尔*	126.58	111.23	129.42	118.35
德里*	120.92	109.29	121.87	115.60
古吉拉特邦	107.07	107.76	108.62	113.89
喜马偕尔邦	102.46	105.15	103.12	111.49
北安查尔邦	106.84	105.49	103.68	110.39
拉贾斯坦邦	109.89	109.17	108.45	110.02
北方邦	114.16	107.87	111.30	109.17
马哈拉施特拉邦	107.07	105.71	108.44	109.04
达曼和第乌*	103.20	104.38	141.01	108.07
中央邦	109.65	106.27	108.74	107.64
果阿邦	103.41	103.73	104.14	107.20
"查谟和克什米尔"	—	—	111.14	106.72
比哈尔邦	110.25	104.93	108.63	106.57
泰米尔纳德邦	102.67	105.49	101.38	106.46
卡纳塔克邦	104.17	104.17	103.78	105.32
奥里萨邦	102.99	103.41	102.86	105.21

续表

印度/邦/联邦属地*	总人口数（1991）	0—6岁（1991）	总人口数（2001）	0—6岁（2001）
庞第皆瑞*	102.15	103.84	99.91	104.40
曼尼普尔邦	104.38	102.67	102.20	104.05
"阿鲁纳恰尔邦"	116.41	101.83	110.98	104.04
喀拉拉邦	96.53	104.38	94.49	103.89
西孟加拉邦	109.05	103.41	107.11	103.84
安得拉邦	102.88	102.56	102.26	103.77
阿萨姆邦	108.34	102.56	107.29	103.74
安达曼和尼科巴群岛*	122.25	102.77	118.19	103.61
贾钦德邦	108.46	102.15	106.23	103.56
米佐拉姆邦	108.58	103.20	106.61	103.01
纳加尔哈维利*	105.04	98.72	123.31	102.79
拉克沙群岛*	106.04	106.27	105.57	102.65
特里普拉邦	105.82	103.41	105.22	102.60
那加兰邦	112.87	100.70	110.00	102.55
梅加拉亚邦	104.71	101.42	102.60	102.52
恰蒂斯加尔邦	101.52	101.63	101.05	102.52
"锡金"	113.90	103.63	114.25	101.41

来源：India, Office of the Registrar General, *Census of India, 2001, Series-1: India, Paper 1 of 2001: Provisional Population Totals* (New Delhi: India Office of the Registrar General, 2001), http://www.censusindia.net/results。

采用儿童性别比例，可以推测性别比反映性别不平等的地区所在，以及由于男性移民或其他原因导致性别比例高的地方。例如达曼和第乌有非常高的总性别比例［141（男）：100（女）］，可是儿童性别比例却不高［108（男）：100（女）］。另一方面，北安查尔邦及喜马偕尔邦的总性别比例较低［103.7（男）：100（女），103.1（男）：100（女）］，其儿童的性别比例却相对较高［110.4（男）：100（女），111.5（男）：100（女）］，应该是因为他们对后代的性别选择行为所导致。共有16个地区的儿童性别比例高于106(男)：100(女)，比起1991年只有8个地区有过高的儿童性别比例，其成长率高达百分之百。当年的8个地区是旁遮普、哈里亚纳、昌迪加尔、德里、古吉拉特、喜马偕尔、北安查尔、拉贾斯坦这些地区的儿童性别比超过了110(男)：100(女)。印度的总性别比例在2001年略呈下降，但儿童的性别比例却不断地增加，从1981年的103.95(男)：100(女)到2001年的107.85(男)：100(女)，值得我们关注。

在印度的一个邦内不同的地区和村庄，也可能有不同的儿童性别比例。例如中央邦的儿童性别比例是107.64(男)：100(女)[1991年为106.27(男)：100(女)]。1991年在中央邦的2170个村庄中，研究人员发现有53个村庄的儿童性别比例高于156(男)：100(女)；在131个村庄中的儿童性别比例在139(男)：100(女)—156(男)：100(女)之间；271个村庄在125(男)：100(女)—138(男)：100(女)之间。这个地区的总新生儿性别比例是119(男)：100(女)，其中存活的性别比例为129(男)：100(女)。[1]我们需要进一步研究有较高性别比例的地区，便可以判断印度各邦或地区发生的性别选择的严重程度。

排斥女性的性别选择方式随着时间的推移发生了变化。尽管性别选择性杀婴依然可以造成扭曲性别比例，但性别选择性堕胎和忽略女婴成为印度性别选择的主要方式。现在我们来探讨性别比例如何上升到现在的水平。

（四）出生人口性别比例的上升

如第二章所讨论的，全世界出生人口性别比例的标准是105—107

---

[1] Mahendra K. Premi and Saraswati Raju, "Born to Die: Female Infanticide in Madhya Pradesh," *Search Bulletin*, Vol. 13, No. 3 (July-September 1998), pp. 94–105.

（男）：100（女）。1964年印度全国医院的出生数字，确认了这个标准也适用于印度。① 虽然印度的人口普查没有出生人口性别比例的数据，但其他三个来源有。这三个来源是：公民注册系统（CRS），来自小孩出生时父母的报告；医院注册系统（MRS），它是医院和其他医疗机构对于出生的记录；样本注册系统（SRS），它在全国进行自己的调查。只是，这三个系统对于新生儿性别比例的记录相差极大。

从1978—1980年，CRS记录的出生人口性别比（每100个女性对应的男性数字）是89.4、95.9和85.1。这和MRS在某些邦所记录的107、111.2和106.7不同，这两套数据之间为什么会有这么大的差别呢？CRS的评估涵盖了印度70%的人口，但在比哈尔邦、拉贾斯坦邦、北方邦等地的乡村，涵盖面却严重不足，在安得拉邦、卡纳塔克邦、西孟加拉邦也只包括了少数乡村，而这些地方都是传统上高性别比例的地区。与SRS的数据相对照，我们发现全国有40%—50%的出生人口未被注册②，未注册的男婴人数比女婴多，造成了有记录的性别比例比预期的低。据说父母较不愿意注册男婴，以免他们被恶魔侵犯③，狄克曼则认为，不注册男婴是为了要掩饰杀女婴的事实。④ 无论真相为何，由父母自动注册的数据很难取信于人。

SRS从1960年中期启用双重记录系统，成为印度人口数据最重

---

① Study cited in R. K. Sachar, J. Verma, V. Prakash, A. Chopra, R. Adlaka, and R. Sofat, "Sex-Selective Fertility Control—An Outrage," *Journal of Family Welfare*, Vol. 36. No. 2（June 1991）, pp. 30 – 35. 印度注册总署也表明，印度遵循105（男）：100（女）的出生人口性别比标准。应该注意到：印度人口性别比是以每1000名男性对应的女性数字来公布的。尽管人口普查和其他官方数据都以这种模式提供，但采用这种独特的方式，很难比较印度和其他国家的数据。为了方便比较，所有印度的人口性别比数据都转为每100名女性对应的男性数字。

② 关于公民注册系统的详细讨论，参见Bhat, Preston, and Dyson, *Vital Rates in India*, pp. 28 – 29。

③ 关于亚洲其他地区男性不在册原因的讨论，参见Swapan Seth, "Two-Way Movement of Sex Ratio," *Economic and Political Weekly*, October 5, 1996, pp. 2730 – 2733。

④ Midred Dickemann, correspondence with Valerie Hudson, April 10, 1998.

要的来源。① 如表 3-9 显示，SRS 在 1981—1988 年所记录的性别比例是 108.1（男）：100（女）—112.2（男）：100（女）。② SRS 的数据都经过核查，以防止收集数据方法本身产生的误差。除 SRS 数据，印度注册总署也收集了全国城市医院出生的活婴数字。从 1981 年至 1991 年，全印度共有 600 万名活婴，平均性别比例为 112.2（男）：100（女）。③高性别比例在各个数据收集区都作了公布。这比 1981—1998 年 SRS 收集的数据要高得多，其中性别比例 109.7（男）：100（女）。据印度注册总署的说法，从城市医院所得到的出生人口性别比[112.2（男）：100（女）]，更正确地反映了印度的情况，反映出 SRS 由于缺乏医院数据出现公布数据的偏差。④ 2001 年的人口普查数据，包括了从 SRS 资料取得的新生儿性别比的三年平均值，表 3-10 记载的也是由同一系统取得的新生儿性别比。

表3-9　1981—1988 年印度总体人口、农村和城市人口的出生性别比

年份	总体	农村	城市
1981—1983	108.9	108.9	108.8
1982—1984	109.8	110.0	109.1
1983—1985	110.4	110.0	112.2
1984—1986	109.6	109.1	111.5
1985—1987	109.6	109.4	110.9
1986—1988	109.6	110.1	108.1

来源：India, Office of the Registrar General, *Census of India, 2001, Series-1: India, Paper 2 of 1992: Final Population Totals: Brief Analysis of Primary Census Abtract* (New Delhi: India Office of the Registrar General, 1992), http://www.censusindia.net/results。

---

① 有关 SRS 运作方式的研究，参见 Bhat, Preston, and Dyson, *Vital Rates in India*, pp. 29-34。
② India, Office of the Registrar General, *Census of India 1991*, Paper 2, p. 12.
③ India, Office of the Registrar General, *Census of India 1991*, Paper 2.
④ Ibid., p. 11.

表 3-10 1987—1998 年印度（三年平均）的出生人口性别比

年份	性别比
1987—1989	109.9
1988—1990	109.8
1989—1991	110.2
1990—1992	111.1
1991—1993	111.9
1992—1994	113.0
1993—1995	113.8
1994—1996	113.3
1995—1997	112.2
1996—1998	111.0

来源：India, Office of the Registrar General, *Census of India, 2001, Series: India, Paper 1 of 2001: Provisional Population Totals* (New Delhi: India Office of the Registrar General, 2001), http://www.censusindia.net/results。

遗憾的是，印度人口普查的数据不包括出生人口的数据，又因为 SRS 的数据未根据地区来提供，我们只好假设出生人口性别比在总性别比高的地方也高，在婴儿死亡率较高的地方也高。因此，我们有关性别选择手段的讨论，也局限在全国的层面。

（五）性别选择性堕胎

1971 年印度政府通过了《医疗中止怀孕法》，其中内容包括：若怀孕可能危及母亲的生命或精神健康，或出生小孩可能残废，或因为遭到强暴、避孕失败而怀孕时，准许医生中止怀孕。[1]印度人相信胎儿在怀孕前三个月是没有生命的，中止怀孕也不会造成道德上的问题，因此造成了大量的堕胎。在怀孕的前三个月，称为"延续的日子"

---

[1] Odesa Gorman-Stapleton, "Prohibiting Amniocentesis in India: A Solution to the Problem of Female Infanticide or a Problem to the Solution of Prenatal Diagnosis?" *ILSA Journal of International Law*, Vol. 14, No. 23 (1990), p. 30.

（charhna），是最后一次月经的延续。三个月后，称为"婴儿掉了"（bucha givna），形容流产。①

我们最想知道的是因为性别而被堕掉的胎儿的数字。有证明表明罗吉尔（Roger）和杰弗利（Patricia Jeffery）所说的"文化上的阻力"对印度人做产前胎儿性别检查及堕掉女胎"不是太大"吗？② 证据其实相当多。1975年属于政府的全印度医学研究院开始做羊膜穿刺术，以便测知胎儿正常与否。有50位怀孕妇女自愿接受了这项测验，48位在获知怀的是女胎后决定堕胎。③ 1976年由于妇女团体的关注，印度政府终于发布了禁止性别检查的局部禁令，因为要求堕女胎的妇女实在太多了。④ 政府后来取消了所有的产前性别检查，但私营企业诞生了，来应付这项庞大的要求。在1982—1987年间，做性别检测的诊所数字，以几何倍数增长，单单在孟买，它就从10家增加到248家。⑤ 1985年，一份孟买妇产科医生的研究报告指出，84%的诊所提供羊膜穿刺服务，以便决定胎儿性别。其中有些诊所这么做已经有10—12年了，大部分平均开业5年。⑥ 性别检验的诊所全印度都有，通常以三种方式来决定胎儿的性别：羊膜穿刺、超音波（又称B超）和绒毛膜促性腺素检测。孟买和德里是性别测试的重心，连小城镇的

---

① Roger Jeffery and Patricia Jeffery, "Female Infanticide and Amniocentesis," *Economic and Political Weekly*, April 16, 1983, pp. 1207 – 1212.

② Roger Jeffery, Patricia Jeffery, and Andrew Lyon, "Research Note: Female Infanticide and Amniocentesis," *Social Science and Medicine*, Vol. 19, No. 11 (1984), pp. 655 – 656.

③ Manju Parikh, "Sex-Selective Abortions in India: Parental Choice or Sexist Discrimination?" *Feminist Issues*, Vol. 10, No. 2 (Fall 1990), pp. 19 – 32.

④ Forum against Sex Determination and Sex Pre-election, "Using Technology, Choosing Sex: The Campaign against Sex Determination and the Question of Choice," *Development Dialogue* (Uppsala, Sweden), Nos. 1 – 2 (1992), p. 93.

⑤ Dolly Arora, "The Victimising Discourse: Sex Determination Technologies and Policy," *Economic and Political Weekly*, February 17, 1996, p. 420.

⑥ Forum against Sex Determination and Sex Per-selection, "Using Technology, Choosing Sex," p. 95.

诊所里也都有羊膜穿刺设备，一些移动的诊所甚至把超音波的技术带到更小的乡镇去。① 住在偏远地区的农民，如果愿意走到村里的话，就可以获得这项服务。

性别检测的费用从20世纪80年代以来降低很多。例如羊膜穿刺的费用在1980年是1500—2000卢比（88—117美元），现在只要200—500卢比（12—30美元）。② 有个恐吓的广告词说："今天花500卢比，总比日后花50万卢比好吧！"它的用意在于警告父母，未来养女儿及嫁妆的开销太大，还不如趁现在花点小钱堕胎省事。③ 并不是只有都市中富裕的家庭才会做胎儿性别检查，一位作者就写道："连没有水电的地方都有胎儿性别检验诊所。乡下的健康中心可能没有测肺结核仪器，没有小儿麻痹疫苗，却有办法把羊水用冰块储存，送到最近的都市去做性别检查。连赤贫的农民和苦力，都愿意以25%的复利贷款去做测试。"④

检测胎儿性别的技术，造成了以下的结果：罗赫塔克（Rohtak）是离新德里50公里的一个小镇，根据《远东经济评论》，罗赫塔克在过去十年的性别比例从879降到866。最近新德里模式研究所给联合国人口基金的一份报告上说，新德里的新生儿性别比是156（男）：100（女），此数据并未包括死亡率，但已指出当地男女的比例非常不平衡。还有比罗赫塔克更糟的城市，哈里亚纳邦的4个城市的新生儿性别比例数据看上去更糟。连罗赫塔克医学院的研究员都看不下去

---

① See Hamish McDonald, "Unwelcome Sex," *Far Eastern Economic Review*, December 26, 1991-January 2, 1992, pp. 18 - 19; and Vibhuti Patel, "Sex Determination and Sex Preselection Tests in India: Modern Techniques for Femicide," *Bulletin of Concerned Asian Scholars*, Vol. 21 No. 1 (January-March 1989), pp. 2 - 11.

② Parikh, "Sex-Selective Abortions in India," pp. 21 - 22.

③ Srikanta Ghosh, *Indian Women through the Ages* (New Delhi: Ashish Publishing House, 1989), p. 121.

④ Nivedita Menon, "Abortion and the Law: Questions for Feminism," *Canadian Journal of Women and Law*, Vol. 6, No. 1 (1993), p. 108.

了，他们说:"母亲的子宫不该成为女儿的坟墓。"①

1982年,阿姆利则的医院发生一件意外堕掉男胎的案子,引起了公愤,但由此引发的进一步调查也让大众震惊:发现在1984年的8000件堕胎案例中,有7999个是女胎。孟买的另一份研究指出,1000个堕胎案子中有97%堕的是女胎。②

1988年,马哈拉施特拉邦首先通过了法律禁止做胎儿性别检查后的堕胎,但是想做测试的人,可以到邻邦或是找到愿意非法做这项测试的医生。1996年,印度政府签署了禁止堕掉健康的女胎法案,可是只有哈里亚纳、旁遮普、拉贾斯坦三个邦通过这条法律。测试成为非法后,父母都不愿让研究人员知道他们曾做过这项测试,我们现在更无法知道印度人做胎儿性别测试有多普遍了。一项研究表明,旁遮普邦一所医院1990年5月至1991年12月间新生儿性别比越来越高,据该院医生提供的数据可知,它从1982年的107(男):100(女),增加到1993年的132(男):100(女)。③ 为了了解真相,从1990年5月到1991年12月,他们访问了所有到医院求诊的女性。虽然医生在问问题时略有阻碍,但有13.6%的男孩母亲和2.1%的女孩母

---

① 这些性别比例与罗赫塔克镇人口性别比从113.8(男):100(女)上升到115.5(男):100(女)相对应。参见 McDonald, "Unwelcome Sex," p.18。

② 关于20世纪80年代女性堕胎的统计案例,参见 Patel, "Sex Determination and Sex Preselection Tests in India"; Parikh, "Sex-Selective Abortions in India," pp. 22 – 24; Ghosh, *Indian Women through the Ages*, p. 121; Radhika Balakrishnan, "The Social Context of Sex Selection and the Politics of Abortion in India," in Gita Sen and Rachel C. Snow, eds., *Power and Decision: The Social Control of Reproduction* (Cambridge, Mass.: Harvard University Press, 1994); and K. P. Srikumar, "Amniocentesis and the Future of the Girl Child," in Leelamma Devasia and V. V. Devasia, eds., *Girl Child in India* (New Delhi: Ashish Publishing House, 1989), pp. 51 – 65.

③ Beverley E. Booth, Manorama Verma, and Rajbir Singh Beri, "Fetal Sex Determination in Infants in Punjab, India," pp. 1259 – 1261.

亲,承认她们做过产前性别检查。① 据说在做了胎儿性别检测之后生下女婴的母亲要么是有一位兄弟,要么是被错误的检测为怀上男孩。虽然肯承认的只是少数,但医生的结论是做胎儿性别检查是很普遍的,而且是否会做检查,与家庭的月收入成正比,所有做过检查的女性都受过教育。其中有约24%的女性受过6—10年的教育;约20%的女性受过10年以上的教育。没有子女的只有2%会做产前性别检查。有女儿但没有儿子的,做检查的几率增加到18%,有一个女儿以上但没有儿子的,比率高达63%。但已生有一个儿子者,做性别检查的几率就大大降低,生过一个儿子以上者,没人做检查。②

并非所有学者都认可性别选择式堕胎是导致印度性别比例下降的主要原因这一判断。在《经济和政治周报》上,印度的人口学家和社会学家们就堕胎和高性别比例之间的关系展开辩论。③ 拉扬(Irudaya Rajan)认为,堕胎只在大城市如孟买、加尔各答、德里和马德拉斯较为普遍。他还说,性别比例要增加1%,例如从106%增加到107%,就有60000个女胎需要被堕掉。④从较早引用的统计数字来看,这并非绝无可能。而拉扬却认为只有高估男性人数才能得到那样的比例。事实上,通过人口统计调查可知,当时并未高估男性人数。恰恰相反的是,当时的男性人口和女性人口都是被低估了的。在《经济和

---

① 接受产前性别检测后生下女婴的母亲,要么是被告知怀了龙凤胎,要么是被错误地判断为怀上了男孩。

② Booth, Verma, and Beri, "Fetal Sex Determination in Infants in Punjab, India," pp. 1259 – 1261.

③ See, for example, S. Irudaya Rajan, "Decline in Sex Ratio: An Alternative Explanation?" *Economic and Political Weekly*, December 21, 1991, pp. 2963 – 2964; Saraswati Raju and Mahendra K. Premi, "Decline in Sex Ratio: An Alternative Explanation Re-examined," *Economic and Political Weekly*, April 25, 1992, pp. 911 – 912; S. Irudaya Rajan, U. S. Mishra, and K. Navaneetham, "Decline in Sex Ratio: Alternative Exlplanation Revisted," *Economic and Political Weekly*, November 14, 1992, pp. 2505 – 2508; and Padma Prakash, "Deline in Sex Ratio," *Economic and Political Weekly*, December 19 – 26, 1992, p. 2670.

④ Rajan, "Heading towards a Billion," pp. 3201 – 3205.

政治周报》的另一篇文章里，印度的注册总署承认于1993年到1994年，有36万个女胎被堕掉。① SRS和印度注册总署在1990—1995年收集的数据显示，新生儿性别比在111.1（男）：100（女）—113.8（男）：100（女）之间，这段时期的新生儿性别比平均是112.6（男）：100（女），出生人数为2800万人，其中1320万是女婴。若性别比例正常的话，应该有1410万个女婴出生，换句话说，每年约有953000个女孩消失了，她们都是因为性别而被堕掉的。② 印度每年大约有11000000件堕胎，其中60%是人工流产，所以953000的数字是有可能的。事实上，真正因为性别而堕胎的数字可能更高。③

（六）婴儿死亡率

印度有许多女性没有活过婴儿期。在印度北部，重男轻女的现象依然严重，直接或间接的杀女婴行为仍在发生。女婴的命名就反映出父母的失望之情，例如Akki（受够了）、Kauri（气愤）或Beant（没完没了），都说明了她们的不受欢迎。④ 在正常的情况下，生命的第一年里，男婴的死亡率要比女婴高，尤其是出生后第一个月；印度和中国是仅有的几个女婴死亡率高于男婴的国家。

婴儿的死亡率是婴儿出生后不满周岁死亡人数同出生人数的比率，以千分比表示。1990年，印度男婴的死亡率是79.5‰，女婴是

---

① Arora, "The Victimising Discourse," p. 420.

② 如果采用克拉森和文克的预期出生人口性别比103.9（男）：100（女），那么印度每年"消失的女性"人口就是110万。Klasen and Wink, "'Missing Women': Revisiting the Debate."

③ 关于堕胎的统计数据，参见Visaria and Visaria, "India's Population in Transition," p. 38; and M. E. Khan, Sandya Barge, and George Philip, "Abortion in India: An Overview," *Social Change*, Vol. 26, Nos. 3 – 4 (September-December 1996), pp. 208 – 225。

④ Sachar et al., "Sex-elective Fertility Control-An Outrage," p. 30.

80.4‰。2001年，男婴的死亡率是63.89‰，女婴是62.44‰。① 虽然这比1980年男婴的死亡率113.9‰和女婴的119‰进步很多，但死亡率还是太高。② 基本上，男婴的死亡率在第一年应该比女婴高30%，所以我们推算，印度有175000个女婴在其生命的第一年死亡。③ 从1980年起，女婴和女童的死亡率一直高过男婴，到了孩童期，女孩的死亡率还是太高。所以，男孩女孩不同的死亡率，才是印度新生儿性别比过高的主因。

一项世界卫生组织、世界银行及哈佛大学在1996年进行的研究指出，印度男性和女性有不同的死亡模式。④ 1990年，在0—4岁的幼童中，有1650000个女孩死亡及1600000个男孩死亡，女孩的死亡人数比男孩多了50000人。死亡原因不外是：传染病和寄生虫（包括肺结核、性病、腹泻或婴儿期的疾病如破伤风、麻疹及霍乱）、呼吸系统感染、腹腔疾病、营养不良（蛋白质不足、缺碘、缺维生素A和缺铁性的贫血）、心血管疾病、呼吸道疾病和自残。事实上，30—34岁的女性死亡的人数一直都超过男性。所以在生命的前30年，印度女性的处境十分不利，尤其在生命的头5年里，死亡人数超过后来55年的总和。真正的情况可能更严重，因为许多婴儿的死亡未被登记。

印度婴儿死亡的最主要原因就是传染病和寄生虫（占5岁以下死亡儿童的42%）。不同的疾病死亡率常常源于对男童和女童不同的健

---

① U. S. Bureau of the Census, International Data Base, 1998, http://www.census.gov/ipc/www/idbnew.html.

② 例如，加拿大男婴和女婴死亡率分别是6.08‰和5.06‰；美国分别是7.43‰和5.40‰。Ibid.

③ 人口学家约翰逊（Sten Johannson）和内格伦（Ola Nygren）死亡婴儿的性别比是130（男）：100（女）。Johannson and Nygren, "The Missing Girls of China: A New Demographic Account," *Population and Development Review*, Vol. 17, No. 1 (March 1991), p. 48.

④ Christopher J. L. Murray and Alan D. Lopez, eds., *Summary of the Report: The Global Burden of Disease: A Comprehensive Assessment of Mortality and Disability form Diseases, Injuries, and Risk Factors in 1990 and Projected to 2020* (Geneva: World Health Organization, 1996).

康照顾，这是有历史先例的。在1870年发布禁止杀女婴的禁令后，多数村庄里的女孩数量增长了，但女孩总是得到和男孩一样的照顾。1873年的一份政府报告中显示了在马图拉（Mathura）地区父母对儿女不同的态度："当乡村里谣传天花疫苗对孩童有害时，许多父母赶着把女儿送去注射疫苗，后来证明疫苗让女儿更健康，父母就把女儿带回，让儿子去接受注射。"①

父母非常愿意为儿子的健康投资。《被危害的性别》一书的作者米勒（Barbara Miller）提及她从医院的记录发现，印度男性比女性往往获得更好的医疗照顾（从泰米尔纳德的1.2倍到旁遮普的2.6倍）。② 1992—1993年印度学者在做家庭健康调查时，也获得同样的结论；父母不但较少关注女儿的病情，也难得让女儿接受疫苗注射。③所以女孩容易得急性和慢性营养不良，死于营养不良的比例也比男孩高。"全国家庭健康调查"指出，女婴被喂母乳的很少，哺乳的时间也很短。④ "全国家庭健康调查"指出不是母亲不是故意提早断奶，只是她希望月经能早些来以便再怀孕生男孩。⑤男孩女孩都吃得到谷物及蔬菜，但只有男孩吃得到牛奶制品。父母在分配食物时，会考虑食物是热性还是凉性，他们不给女孩吃热性食品（肉、鱼及蛋），认为它会提高性欲。⑥ 在拉贾斯坦邦和北方邦，女人和女孩只能在男人和男孩吃饭之后用餐，通常吃的也比男性少得多。

印度儿童的死亡率各地不一。根据1992年及1993年的"全国家庭健康调查"，阿萨姆、比哈尔邦、中央邦、奥里萨邦、北方邦，5

---

① Cited in Panigrahi, *British Social Policy and Female Infanticide in India*, p. 166.

② Barbara D. Miller, *The Endangered Sex: Neglect of Female Children in Rural North India* (Ithaca, N. Y.: Cornell University Press, 1981).

③ Mutharayappa et. , "Son Preference and Its Effect on Fertility in India," p. 12.

④ Sachar et al. , "Sex-Selective Fertility Control—An Outrage," pp. 30 – 35.

⑤ Mutharayappa et al. , "Son Preference and Its Effect on Fertility in India," p. 12.

⑥ Malavika Karlekar, "The Girl Child in India: Does She Have Any Rights?" *Canadian Woman Studies*, Vol. 15, Nos. 2 – 3 (Spring/Summer 1995), pp. 55 – 57.

岁以下的死亡率最高。1993年,印度婴儿死亡率(每1000个婴儿中死亡的人数)在喀拉拉邦是13,在旁遮普邦、泰米尔纳德邦、马哈拉施特拉邦是56—59,在北方邦、中央邦及奥里萨邦是98—114。① 在邦的层面的性别数据无法得到,因此我们只能估计女婴的死亡率较高。一般来说,婴儿死亡率在北方比南方高。② 几个研究成功地发现,婴儿死亡率与几个因素有关,包括家庭结构——性别、年龄和出生次序,以及父母偏好、生育率、教育、贫穷、女性工作程度、城市化和部落地位。需要注意的是,高婴儿死亡率,经常代表着父母被动地杀婴或对儿童疏于照顾致死。一项1987年至1989年在印度南方的泰米尔纳德进行的研究表明,杀女婴的行为仍在发生,即使是在传统上婴儿死亡率低的地区。③在印度北方性别比高的地区,婴儿死亡率也高,我们可以推导出性别选择性堕胎、杀婴和忽略女婴导致了女性的缺乏。在马图拉地区,一项1986年在乌斯拉姆帕提政府医院进行的研究提出,有着杀女婴传统的种姓可能仍在实施这一行为:"在乌斯拉姆帕提政府医院中,每年大约有Kallar种姓的近600个女婴出生,其中有570个女婴'和母亲一起失踪'。根据医院的说法,'失踪女婴'大概有80%都被杀了。"④

印度人口高性别比例和父母期待的家庭组成有关:父母的选择主要受到他们希望拥有的孩子数量、孩子出生次序和性别影响。不是每个女孩都会被歧视,父母对长女和对第二、第三个女儿的看法也不同。大多数印度人认为,最理想的家庭组成是一个女儿和一个或两个

---

① Visaria and Visaria, "India's Population in Transition," pp. 18 – 19.

② Tim Dyson and Mick Moore, "On Kinship Structure, Female Autonomy, and Demographic Behavior in India," *Population and Development Review*, Vol. 9, No. 1 (March 1983), pp. 35 – 60. 芭芭拉·米勒注意到印度北部与南部之间同样的地域性变动。参见 Miller, *The Endangered Sex*。

③ Sabu George, Rajaratnam Abel, and Barbara D. Miller, "Female Infanticide in Rural South India," *Economic and Political Weekly*, May 30, 1992, p. 1153.

④ Vishwanath, "Female Infanticide and the Position of Women in India," p. 201.

儿子。在卢迪亚纳（Ludhiana）进行的一项研究中，莫妮卡·达斯·古普塔（Monica Das Gupta）发现，父母对女儿的歧视是有选择性的。① 她发现，女婴的死亡率随着已有的兄弟姐妹人数，尤其是女性人数的增加而增加。如果家中已有一个或两个女儿，那么后来出生的女儿，就会获得较少的照顾，死亡的可能性也比长女高。其他学者从印度1981年人口普查的数据来研究婴儿死亡率时，也得到同样的结论。② 通过把一种经济模型应用到家庭规划中，一群研究者推断，婴儿死亡率取决于父母心中合意家庭的规模、性别构成和预算额度。父母对资源分配的决定，会直接影响到下一代的死亡率。③据研究者的说法："如果'命运'对一对夫妻不够仁慈的话，就会给他们一个不理想的性别组成的下一代，很多父母就会想办法除掉'多余的'女孩，以得到他们想要的家庭构成。"④

生育率也会影响婴儿的死亡率和对男孩女孩的区别对待。在强烈期待儿子的社会里，高生育率会造成扭曲的高性别比例的大家庭，因为父母想要儿子。在印度，后代性别选择方式包括堕胎、杀婴等，在那些生育率最高的地区最严重，如在北部。采用1981年人口普查地区的平均水平数据，一群研究者注意到高生育率与女性死亡率增长之间的关联，显示出女性存活率在生育率高的地区是较低的。⑤因为印度

---

① Monica Das Gupta, "Selective Discrimination against Female Children in Rural Punjab, India," *Population and Development Review*, Vol. 13, No. 1 (March 1987), pp. 77 – 101.

② Katherine L. Bourne and George M. Walker, "The Differential Effect of Mother's Education on Mortality of Boys and Girls in India," *Population Studies*, Vol. 45, No. 2 (July 1991), pp. 203 – 219.

③ George B. Simmons, Celeste Smucker, Stan Bernstein, and Eric Jensen, "Post-Neonatal Mortality in Rural North India: Implications of an Economic Model," *Demography*, Vol. 19, No. 3 (August 1982), pp. 371 – 390.

④ Jeffery, Jeffery, and Lyon, "Research Note: Female Infanticide and Amniocentesis," p. 1210.

⑤ Mamta Murthi, Anne-Catherine Guio, and Jean Dreze, "Mortality, Fertility and Gender Bias in India: A District-Level Analysis," *Population and Development Review*, Vol. 21, No. 4 (December 1995), pp. 745 – 782.

北部和西北省的生育率最高，那儿也有最高的性别比例和最多的人口，可以想象女婴死亡率与高生育率有着很强的关联性，他们采取后代性别选择手段，包括堕胎和杀婴，使得女婴的存活率降低。谢莉·克拉克（Shelley Clark）通过经验分析得出结论："女孩基本上都在大家庭，因为有女孩的家庭是为了生男孩才倾向于成为一个大家庭……生出一群他们并不想要的女孩。似乎可信的是，这些并不被期待的女孩极有可能在很小时就死去。"①

若生育率下降，又会发生什么事呢？近年来，印度大部分地区的生育率都下降了，莫妮卡·达斯·古普塔（Das Gupta）及马里·巴特（P. N. Mari Bhat）的研究发现，当生育率下降时，性别歧视反而增加。在子女人数下降的条件下，因为更想得到儿子，所以父母会想尽办法除去不想要的女儿。② 古普塔与巴特解释说："当生育率下降，想要孩子的家庭数量比想要男孩的家庭数量下降得更多。两种轨迹的速度差异缩小了女儿存活的空间，导致要除去女儿的更大压力。"③ 1980 年印度的生育率降了 20%，可是想要的儿子的数目只降了 7%。如果不考虑家庭人口总数，想要两个男孩的家庭需要生四到五个小孩才会成功。此时家庭性别比例可以维持正常。但如果一个家庭只要三个小孩，并希望其中两个是男孩，那他们就得采用各种可能的方法了。所以当生育率下降时，喜欢儿子的地区更容易采用堕胎、杀婴和对女婴疏于照顾的手段。

---

① Shelley Clark, "Son Preference and Sex Composition of Children: Evidence from India," *Demography*, Vol. 37, No. 1 (February 2000), p. 106.

② Monica Das Gupta and P. N. Mari Bhat, "Fertility Decline and Increased Manifestation of Sex Bias in India," *Population Studies*, Vol. 51, No. 3 (November 1997), pp. 307–315; See also Monica Das Gupta and P. N. Mari Bhat, " Intensified Gender Bias in India: A Consequence of Fertility Decline," Working Paper No. 95.03 (Cambridge Mass.: Harvard Center for Population and Development Studies, May 1995).

③ Das Gupta and Bhat, "Fertility Decline and Increased Manifestation of Sex Bias in India," p. 307.

在 1981 年至 1991 年，古普塔及巴特（Bhat）发现，"当生育率下降时，儿童性别比例在北部急遽上升"，特别是在中央邦、旁遮普邦和贾斯坦邦。① 克拉克分析 1992 至 1993 年的 "全国家庭健康调查"，得到同样的结论。他整理了 140 个完整家庭的性别比例。克拉克发现，家庭愈小，性别比例就愈高。有 8 个以上小孩的家庭，性别比例是 98%，只有两个小孩的家庭的性别比例则为 154%。② 这强烈地证明了印度生育率的下降与印度儿童性别比例上升有着重要联系。

女性识字率、受教育的程度和就业率高，也会降低社会对女性的歧视③，减少女婴的死亡率（它虽然也影响着男婴的死亡率，但是效果不明显）。1991 年，印度女性识字率最低的地方，就是有最多女性消失的地方：比哈尔邦、中央邦、拉贾斯坦邦、北方邦的女性识字率皆少于 30%。④ 然而，识字率与性别比例之间的关系并不清晰。马哈拉施特拉邦、旁遮普邦、西孟加拉邦有着较高的人口性别比例，大量"消失的女性"，但这些邦的识字率高于全国平均的 39%，分别是 52%、50%、47%。事实上，教育可能会造成反效果。古普塔指出，因为控制家庭的组成需要很高的技巧，所以只有受过高等教育的女性，才有能力及欲望来操纵生育率。古普塔通过研究发现，城市化也加剧了女性的劣势，增加了女婴的死亡率。城市较高的性别比例不应单纯归因于男性移民的进入。⑤

贫穷也对女性歧视有影响。在过去，贫穷家庭的女儿比较不会受到歧视，而高收入、高阶层家庭的女儿往往被当成负担。分析 1981

---

① Das Gupta and Bhat, "Fertility Decline and Increased Manifestation of Sex Bias in India," p. 313.

② Clark, "Son Preference and Sex Composition of Children," p. 103, Table 6.

③ Murthi, Guio, and Dreze, "Mortality, Fertility, and Gender Bias in India," pp. 764–765.

④ United Nations Development Programme, *India: The Road to Human Development*, India Development Forum, Paris, France, June 23–25, 1997, document of the United Nations Development Programme, New Delhi, http://www.undp.org.in/REPORT/IDF97/default.htm.

⑤ Das Gupta, "Selective Discrimination against Female Children in Rural Punjab, India."

年地区级的数据，默西（Mamta Murthi）、吉奥（Anne-Catherine Guio）和德勒兹（Jean Dreze）发现家庭愈贫穷，女婴的死亡率愈低。① 地主阶级反而比穷人歧视女性。这一观点也受到克里什纳吉（N. Krishnaji）的支持，他发现对于女婴和成年女性的歧视在地主中比在穷人中严重。正如古普塔一样，克里什纳吉认为富裕阶层可能有更强烈的歧视动机，因为为女儿找到一个适嫁对象要付出很大代价。② 贫穷家庭的女孩因为可以贡献劳力，所以受到重视，但这不意味着在穷人阶层不存在杀女婴的情形。先前对种姓与在册种姓的讨论显示，在册种姓的性别比例高，表明存在杀女婴的行为；然而，这一性别比例并不像非在册种姓的那么高。

只有占人口很高比例的在册部落减少了对女婴的歧视，这和稍早观察到的各部族对印度各邦和地区的总体性别比的积极影响是相对应的。事实是部落群体并没有遵循印度教的婚姻模式，这意味着女儿出嫁后不会消失不见；因而女儿在部落中可以被视为更有价值。部落女性拥有财产权，也逐步减少了对女性的歧视。

最后，我们来讨论一下区域差异。北部和西北部有高性别比例及高婴儿死亡率；南方性别比例较低，死亡率也相对较低。这两个地区主要的不同是：婚姻、财产、宗教、阶级及农耕方式。在北部，农业是大规模的重机械式，南方则属劳力密集型。因此在南方，女性的劳力较有价值。婚姻在北部为族外通婚，新娘通常得离家搬走，父母会觉得"养女儿等于在别人的花园中浇水"。南方的女儿则不远嫁，可以经常拜访娘家，继续照顾年迈的父母，所以也减低了父母对儿子的渴望。③ 此外，历史遗产也大大加剧了

---

① Murthi, Guio, and Dreze, "Mortality, Fertility, and Gender Bias in India," p. 765.

② N. Krishnaji, "Poverty and Sex Ratio: Some Data and Speculation," *Economic and Political Weekly*, June 6, 1987, pp. 892–897.

③ Celia W. Dugger, "Modern Asia's Anomaly: The Girls Who Don't Get Born," *New York Times*, May 6, 2001. sec. 4, p. 4.

当下印度对女性的歧视。历史上，在印度北部各邦具有较高层级的种姓中，杀女婴非常普遍。尽管政府尝试终结这一习俗，但在这一地区，女婴仍在继续死亡。

在印度，不只是女婴的死亡率高，30岁以前女性的死亡人数也比男性高，死亡的原因主要是被烧死。根据世界银行、世界卫生组织和哈佛大学于1996年的研究，发现印度女性"面临着令人发指的被烧死的危机"。单是在1990年，有87000名女子（与37000名男子比较）被烧死，其中53000名是15—44岁的女性。① 虽然在厨房煮饭有遭到火灾的危险，但更可信的原因是她们因为婚姻和嫁妆而死亡。20世纪70年代，妇女团体曾把为嫁妆烧死新娘的新闻公诸于世，引起了举世的公愤。伊丽莎白·布米勒（Elisabeth Bumiller）说："新娘被烧死通常发生在婚后的第一年，亦即当夫家认为娘家无法满足婆家对嫁妆的要求时。新娘被烧死后，夫家会另找能够满足他们要求的新娘。"② 为嫁妆而死是一种极端的性别歧视，这大大降低了印度妇女的预期寿命。1990年至1995年，美国女性的寿命预期值是79岁，高于男性的73岁。贫穷国家如毛里塔尼亚妇女的寿命期待值是50岁，比男性的46岁要高。"③ 只有在孟加拉国、印度、尼泊尔及巴基斯坦，妇女与男子寿命一样长，或比男子短。

在多数国家，女性寿命一般都比男性长，但是表3-11显示印度女性和男性的预期寿命一样，两者都是55.9岁。在比哈尔邦、哈里亚纳邦、奥里萨邦及北方邦，女性的寿命比男性短，也就是说北部对女性的歧视，影响了其中女性的死亡率。

---

① Murray and Lopez, *Summary of the Report: The Global Burden of Disease*.

② Elisabeth Bumiller, *May You Be the Mother of a Hundred Sons: A Journey among the Women of India* (New York: Fawcett Columbine, 1990), p. 49.

③ United Nations, *The World's Women, 1995: Trends and Statistics* (New York: United Nations, 1995), pp. 84–88, Table 6.

表 3-11　印度各邦和地区人口的预期寿命

邦/地区	男性	女性
印度	55.9	55.9
安得拉邦	57.3	60.3
"阿鲁纳恰尔邦"	—	—
阿萨姆邦	52.4	52.5
比哈尔邦	54.9	52.3
果阿邦	—	—
古吉拉特邦	55.9	57.9
哈里亚纳邦	61.5	59.5
喜马偕尔邦	58.5	62.9
"查谟和克什米尔"	60.2	60.7
卡纳塔克邦	59.8	62.4
喀拉拉邦	65.9	72.2
中央邦	50.6	51.8
马哈拉施特拉邦	60.1	62.8
曼尼普尔邦	—	—
梅加拉亚邦	—	—
米佐拉姆	—	—
那加兰邦	—	—
奥里萨邦	53.6	53.1
旁遮普邦	63.0	64.7
拉贾斯坦邦	53.5	54.3
"锡金"	—	—
泰米尔纳德邦	57.4	58.5
特里普拉邦	—	—
北方邦	52.3	49.6
西孟加拉邦	57.9	59.1

来源：India, Office of the Registrar General, *Census of India*, *1991*（New Delhi: Office of the Registrar General, 1991）。

八、过去、现在和未来

印度2001年的人口普查显示，男性比女性要多出3500万人，我们想知道究竟是在哪里、哪个族群和哪个年龄层中男性过多（或女性太少）。我们也想知道在性别比例似乎不断上升的情况下，未来印度男性和女性人口会有什么变化。我们发现15—35岁的族群，是最值得研究的。表3-12显示了1961—1991年的性别比例和人口数。

表3-12 1961—1991年和2006年估算的印度过剩男性人口

年份	年龄介于15—35之间的男性人口总数	年龄介于15—35之间的剩余男性数	剩余男性总人口数
1961	75845000	6566000	18180000
1971	96676000	9201000	24264000
1981	125534886	10500152	25470776
1991	144209649	7267923	32158228
2006	203950520	16509449	—

来源：1961—1981年数据来自于U. S. Bureau of the Census international Data Base, 1998, http://www.census.gov/ipc/www/idbnew.html；1991年数据来自于India, Office of the Registrar General, *Census of India*, 1991, Series-1: India, Part 4 A-C Series: Socio-Cultural Tables, Vol. 2 (New Delhi: Office of the Registrar General, 1998)。2006年的估算数据采用了1991年印度人口普查中年龄介于0—19岁之间的男性和女性人口数字。

1961—1981年之间，15—35岁的人口增加了很多，造成男性过多的情形。[①] 到1991年，人口增长率有所下降。过去15年来，出生

---

① India, Office of the Registrar General, *Census of India*, 1991, Series-1: India, Part 4 A-C Series: Socio-Cultural Tables, Vol. 2 (New Delhi: India, Office of the Registrar General, 1998), pp. 380 – 395, Table C-6. 1991年过剩男性人口下降的原因并不清楚；把1991年和2001年作比较会有用。有意思的是，700多万过剩男性人口都在印度北部具有最高出生性别比例的各邦。这一年龄群中"消失的女性"可以归入以下10个邦：阿萨姆（120421），比哈尔（555094），古吉拉特（404894），哈里亚纳（413358），中央邦（681066），马哈拉施特拉（926154），旁遮普（376620），拉贾斯坦（601047），北部邦（2425329），西孟加拉（857825）。这10个邦的15—35岁过剩男性人口数字为7362108。

人口的性别比例增加很快，所以我们预测未来15岁到35岁的男性和女性人数的差距更大，性别比例会更高，过剩男性人口更多。印度男性和女性的性别比例和相对规模支持这一预测：根据1991年的人口普查，印度15岁以下的人口中，有161727446名男性及150637216名女性，在这个小族群中就有11090230个多出的男性。① 根据1991年0—19岁的过剩男性人口数字，保守地估计，到了2006年，15—35岁的人群中将会多出16500000位男性。未来印度人口将呈现比现在和过去更高的性别比例，将出现更多的过剩男性人口。印度现在已经是男多女少了，如果男人想娶他们同年龄层的女性，将面临问题。很难想象目前的高性别比例及女婴的高死亡率若是持续下去，到了2020年，印度会变成什么样子。

表3-13A和表3-13B采用两种新生儿性别比提供了2个2020年印度人口情景。一是基于保守的新生儿性别比109.65（男）∶100（女），另一是用我们认为更可能的性别比例112.23（男）∶100（女）。我们的估计也相对，因为设定新生儿性别比为常量而非增量。根据表3-13A，到了2020年，在15—35岁的人群中，多出的男性人数为2800万人；根据表3-13B，则是多出3200万人。这些数字并非不可能，因为在1961—1981年间，15—35岁的男性人口增加390万人，增长60%。如果以后的每20年，都以同样的速度增加，直到2021年，多出来的男性人口会达到2690万人。表3-14把我们的预测和世界银行及联合国的预测相对照。

我们所预测的人口总数是介于世界银行和联合国数据之间。因为关于当前和未来人口性别比例的预测有差异，对于2020年15—35岁过剩男性人口的几种预测之间就有较大差异。世界银行采用非常保守

---

① India, Office of the Registrar General, *Census of India, 1991, Series-1: India, Part 4 A-C Series: Socio-Cultural Tables*, Vol. 2 (New Delhi: India, Office of the Registrar General, 1998), pp. 380–395, Table C-6.

的印度人口性别比例104.5（男）：100（女），出生人口性别比例必然比这个数字低很多，因为有差异的人口死亡率会大量减少女性人口。联合国则是采用107.4（男）：100（女），似乎不大可能，因为当前存在高出生人口性别比例及高女性死亡率。研究表明，问题还会继续恶化，甚至我们预测20年后将有0.28亿—0.32亿名过剩男性的人口也属低估。

表3-13A 对2020年印度15—35岁人口的预测：
性别比例为每100个女性对应109.65个男性

年份	出生性别比[a]	总出生数[b]	男性出生数	女性出生数	2020年LTSR男性终生成活率[c]	2020年LTSR女性终生成活率[d]	2020年男性人数	2020年女性人数
1985—1990	109.65	129965000	67972000	61993000	0.80973	0.77931	55039000	48312000
1990—1995	109.65	139695000	73060000	66635000	0.81889	0.79519	59829000	50994000
1995—2000	109.65	139975000	73207000	66768000	0.82485	0.81057	60648000	54120000
2000—2005	109.65	137515000	71920000	65595000	0.83694	0.82258	60193000	53957000
总数							235709000	207383000
消失的女性								28326000

表3-13B 对2020年印度15—35岁人口的预测：
性别比例为每100个女性对应112.23个男性

年份	出生性别比[e]	总出生数	男性出生数	女性出生数	2020年LTSR男性终生成活率	2020年LTSR女性终生成活率	2020年男性人数	2020年女性人数
1985—1990	112.23	129965000	68751000	61214000	0.80973	0.77931	55670000	47704000
1990—1995	112.23	139695000	73899000	65796000	0.81889	0.79519	60515000	52321000
1995—2000	112.23	139975000	74047000	65928000	0.82485	0.81057	61344000	53439000
2000—2005	112.23	137515000	72745000	64770000	0.83694	0.82258	60884000	53278000

续表

年份	出生性别比[e]	总出生数	男性出生数	女性出生数	2020年LTSR男性终生成活率	2020年LTSR女性终生成活率	2020年男性人数	2020年女性人数
总数							238413000	206742000
消失的女性								31671000

来源：India, Office of the Registrar General, *Census of India*, *1991*, *Series-1*: *India*, *Paper 2 of 1992*: *Final Population Totals*: *Brief Analysis of Primary Census Abtract* (New Delhi: India Office of the Registrar General, 1992), http://www.censusindia.net/results。

a. 每100个女性对应109.65个男性的性别比，与1984—1988年在注册系统样本中每912个女性对应1000个男性相同。虽然出生人口性别比一直在上升，但我们用这个保守估计是考虑到长时期的性别比例。India, Office of the Registrar General, *Census of India*, *1991*, *Series-1*: *India*, *Paper 2 of 1992*: *Final Population Totals*: *Brief Analysis of Primary Census Abtract* (New Delhi: India, Office of the Registrar General, 1992).

b. United Naions, Department of International and Economic Social Affair, *World Population Prospects*, *1990*, Population Studies No. 120 (New York: India, United Union, 1991)

c. 终生成活率（LTSRs）是对美国人口普查局1998年国际数据库中的数据加以修订后得到的，见 U. S. Bureau ofthe Census, International Data Base, 1998, http://www.census.gov/ipc/www/idbnew.htm, Life Table Values: India/1980/Total/Male。婴儿（0—1岁）死亡率的nqx值是根据对印度婴儿死亡率数据的变化加以修订的。1980年婴儿死亡率是113.9，1990年男婴死亡率降低到了79.50（根据美国人口普查局数据）。生命表值是根据第一年的死亡率的减少数据进行修订的。目前无法进行进一步的修订，因为印度的人口普查数据无法显示除0—6岁和7岁以后其他年龄段的数据。由印度样本注册系统收集的数据显示，在1979—1991年间0—4岁之间的男婴和女婴死亡率没有显示出任何变化［Monica Das Gupta and P. N. Mari Bhat, "Intensified Gender Bias in India: A Consequence of Fertility Decline," Working Paper No. 95.03 (Cambridge, Mass.: Harvard Center for Population and Development Studies, May 1995)］。终生存活率是由下列公式计算得出：LTSRx = 5Lx/5Lx，其中x是15—20，20—25，25—30，30—35等年龄段。

d. LTSR的计算方法见c。根据美国人口普查局的数据，婴儿死亡率从119.0下降到了80.40，因此相应的0—1岁的nqx的可能值也进行了修订。原始数据来自于 U. S. Bureau of the Census, International Data Base, Life Table Values: India/1980/Total/Female。

e. 表13-3B是根据112.23%的性别比得出的，也就是每1000个男性对应891个女性，性别数据由印度注册总署计算，通过1981—1991年收集的数据，基于该国不同地区的600万新生儿。India, Office of the Registrar General, *Census of India*, *1991*: *Brief Analysis of Primary Census Abtract* (New Delhi: India, Office of the Registrar General, 1992).

表 3-14　比较 2020 年印度的年龄介于 15—35 岁之间的人口估算结果

估算类型	总人口数	男性人口数	女性人口数	性别比例(每1000 个男性对应的女性)	剩余男性数
联合国中变量估算[a]	450069000	233096000	216973000	107.4	16123000
联合国高变量估算	467984000	242360000	225624000	107.4	16736000
联合国低变量估算	432136000	223823000	208313000	107.4	15510000
世界银行估算[b]	442408000	226040000	216368000	104.5	9672000
基于出生性别比估算[a]	443092000	235709000	207383000	113.7	28326000
基于出生性别比估算[b]	445155000	238413000	206742000	115.3	31671000

a. United Naions, Department for Economic and Social Information and Policy Analysis, Population Division, *The Sex and Age Distribution of the World Populations*: *The 1994 Revision* (New York: United Nations, 1994).

b. World Bank, *World Population Projections, 1994 – 95 Edition*: *Estimates and Projections with Related Demographic Statistics* (Washington, D. C.: World Bank, 1994).

九、结论

在对杀婴、堕胎、差异死亡率及其他除掉印度女性的做法进行讨论之后，有必要作一总结。当英国在 19 世纪设法了解杀婴的原因和范围时，他们在家庭和个人的层面上做了调查，并记录每个杀女婴的一家之主的名字。今天印度的人口这么多，这种调查已经不可能了，原因很多，跟印度人口规模无关。但我们还是不应该把印度女性的问题笼统处理，因为并非每个地区的女性都一样地被歧视，北部和南部的妇女地位和待遇就有着显著的不同，城市和农村之间、种姓和部落之间、种姓和族群内部亦如此。其他因素如经济地位、受教育程度、出生次序和父母期待的家庭构成，也都会影响女性的地位。

然而，纵观高性别比例的地区，仍能看出哪里女性死亡率最高，此处所说女性包括女胎、女婴及女孩。北部的比哈尔邦、中央邦、拉贾斯坦邦、北方邦加起来，其中消失女性人口占了印度消失女性人数的一半,若把焦点对准这些地区,就能有效地抑制印度对女性的歧视。研究者不再能开列仍在杀死女儿的种姓名单,但可以这样认为,因为种姓体系严格,并且女性高嫁仍在继续,上层的种姓和部落觉得有必要实施堕女胎或杀女婴,或以其他方式歧视女孩。

这里尚未解决的问题之一是为什么这些做法在印度越来越普遍。有些地方婴儿的死亡率及性别比例在过去的20年来有增无减,尤其是从1991年至2001年,0—6岁的性别比例增加,需要我们更仔细的研究。原因可能是生育率的下降,伴随着重男轻女倾向、环境压力、发展政策带来的社会经济变化(影响到女性劳动的价值及其整体地位)的适当下降。①

对于不断增长的新生儿性别比和总人数性别比,还需要针对国家和区域层面作大量研究。在2001年,至少有0.35亿位女性从印度的人口中消失了,这一数字还在逐年增长。也就是印度有3500万个过剩的男性,其中一半住在北部四个邦。到了2006年,在印度15—35岁的群体中将多出0.165亿个男性。如果这个趋势继续下去,到了2020年,保守估计,印度将有0.28亿—0.32亿个过剩的适龄男性,这个现象值得全世界的人关注。

---

① Susan S. Wadley, "Family Composition Strategies in Rural North India," *Social Science and Medicine*, Vol. 37, No. 11 (December 1993), pp. 1367-1376.

第四章　中国的"消失的女性"

中国是世界上人口最多的国家，它有约13亿的人口，占世界人口五分之一。从20世纪70年代末期的独生子女政策出台到尝试解决人口性别比例高的问题，中国的人口政策一直是举世瞩目的焦点。特别是中国日渐升高的人口性别比例，格外受到媒体的关注。[①] 英国BBC电视台和美国的新闻台曾经播出"死亡之室"，报道中国孤儿院如何对待被抛弃的小孩，尤其是对女孩见死不救。这些新闻也提到中国的单身汉大军——将有0.8亿—1.1亿名男性无法找到妻子。[②] 这些说法到底有多准确呢？

根据中国2000年的人口普查，人口性别比例为106.74（男）：100（女），这和1990年的性别比例105.98（男）：100（女）相比，增加的不多。但总性别比例只是片面的事实，根据官方的统计，5岁以下的

[①] 参见 D. Kristof, "Chinese Turn to Ultrasound, Scorning Baby Girls for Boys," *New York Times*, July 21, 19931, p. Al; Jonathan Mirsky, "Return of the Baby Killers," *New Statesman*, March 21, 1986; Park Chai Bin, " Asia's Female Populations Fall amid Sex-Selection Abortions: Technology Used to Reject Daughters," *Washington Times*, June 30, 1995, p. A149; And Bob Herbert, "China's Missing Girls," *New York Times*, October 30, 1997, p. A31。

[②] 参见 Ren Meng, "Confronting Three Populations of 80 Million," *Inside China Mainland*, Vol. 19, No. 1 (January 1997), pp. 78 - 81; Graham Htchings, "Female Infanticide 'Will Lead to Army of Bchelors,'" *London Daily Telegraph*, April 11, 1997, http://www.telegraph.co.uk/htmlContentjhtml? html =/archiv/1997/04/11/wchill. html; and "China Has 20 Percent Male Surplus," *Agence France-Presse*, January 7, 1999。

孩童性别比例高达118.38（男）：100（女）。①与印度的情况不同，在20世纪里，中国并不是一直都有女性过少的问题。性别比例在1949年共产主义革命胜利之后开始正常化，但在实施独生子女政策后，又再度恶化。我们除了查证有关中国单身汉大军的报道是否正确外，也想了解为什么最近的新生儿性别比会激增。为此，我们研究了影响中国女性社会地位的因素、他们重男轻女的程度、性别选择的历史和现在的性别政策。

一、中国和它的人民

中国人口的组成相当均匀，92%是汉族，94%共同使用一种语言或方言。作为世界的第四大国，中国分成23个省、5个自治区、4个直辖市（北京、重庆、上海、天津）及2个特别行政区（香港、澳门），还包括台湾省，地图4-1是它的省份。纵观中国历史，中国的疆界多为天然的地理屏障，这种地理位置的优势有助于其独特文化的形成和流传。

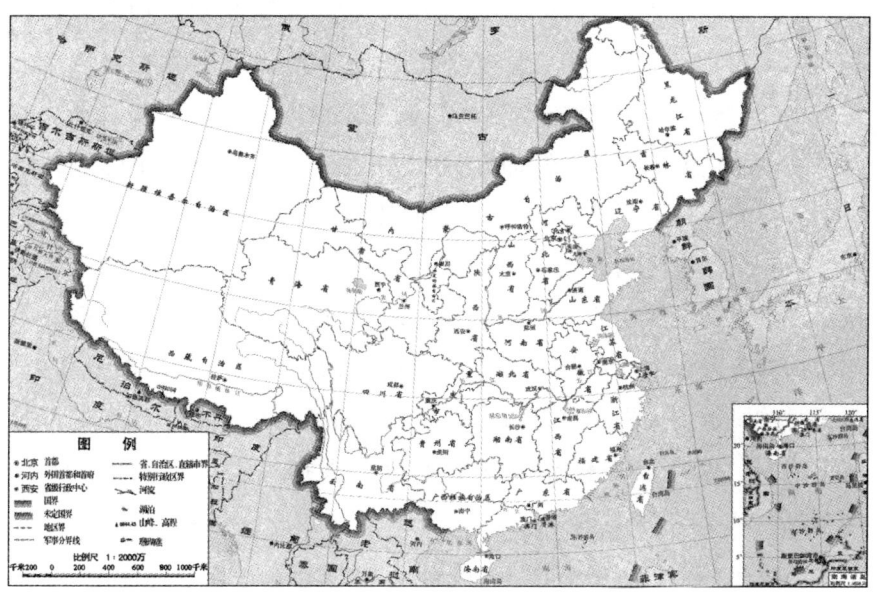

地图4-1　中国的省份（2003）

① China, State Statistical Bureau, *China Population Statistical Yearbook*, *1996* (Beijing: China Statistics Press, 1996).

二、中国的女性

中国女性的历史地位时高时低，与印度的女性相比较要复杂得多。人们能够判断印度社会的女性自主性和权利何时多何时少，以及女性地位在不同社会层级、地区和城乡的差异。但是在中国，除了女性地位的整体趋势之外，还有很多特殊情形。例如慈禧太后（或称"老佛爷"），在1861—1908年间，统治了男尊女卑的清帝国，这就是一个女性掌权的特例。中国女性的地位有异于印度女性，还在于中国的共产主义革命极大地改变了社会中女性的地位。

学者鲍森（Laurel Bossen）认为："传统中国女性的形象是被概而化之的，是被抽象化了的，无视于历史的变迁及区域的差异。"①她们是一个高度相似的群体，具有类似的经历，如杀婴、缠足、地位低下、需要服侍男性等等。但是中国女性的地位，在历史上却会随着族群、阶层和地区而发生不易觉察但富有意义的变化。例如在宋朝（公元960—1279年），女性被严格地控制，杀女婴、缠足及寡妇自杀是司空见惯的，但那时的女性却有财产继承权，可以自己决定嫁妆的用途，甚至能够再婚。以下，我们回顾中国的性别历史。

从新石器时代到商朝（公元前1766—前1122年），考古学的证据显示，当时父系社会的特色并不像后来的时代那么显著。② 大多数人死后都埋在母亲家族的墓园里，也有证据指出那时可能是母系社会。在当时的民俗传说中，英雄冠母姓而非父姓。商朝还有为母亲举行的祭祀仪式，遗产也是根据母姓继承。③男女都可以成为武士，带兵

---

① Laurel Bossen, "Women and Development," in Robert E. Gamer, ed., *Understanding Centemporary China* (Boulder, Colo.: Lynne Rienner, 1999), p. 294.

② Esther S. Lee Yao, *Chinese Women: Past and Present* (Mesquite, Tex.: Ide House, 1983), p. 13.

③ 事实上，"姓"的字根就是"女"和"生"。Ibid., pp. 14–16.

抗敌。

周朝（公元前1122—前221年）尚存母系社会的痕迹：女性的姓氏为家庭的姓氏，男性则是根据出生地和职业命名。① 女性一般并不登记在册。女性与男性平起平坐，除了皇室和贵族的女性吃饭时和男性分开，垂帘听政外，女性还可以自由选择丈夫、离婚和再婚。② 在周朝末期，祖先祭祀成形，流传于后世。孔子（公元前551—前479年）在战国时代（公元前475—前221年）之后重塑了中国的道德体系，他的思想成为中国的主流，永远改变了中国的社会结构及女性地位。

孔子思想与九部作品密切相关，包括《四书》、《五经》，其中包括被归为孔子思想的《论语》，以及其他作者的作品如《易经》。孔子以五常作为道德指标，最重要的一点就是男女有别，两性必须维持分野，以护伦常。③ 孔子的教诲强化了"男尊女卑"的概念，他认为女性的性格不稳定，智慧也比男性低。孔子强调女德，女性应该安静、服从、整洁、贞节、勤于家务，最后造成了她们的足不出户。④ 又因为男女各有所司，女性貌似被给予了与男性平等的地位，而事实上，女性的地位终不及男性。

到了周朝，女性进一步被物化。周朝后期，结婚的方式有三种：俘虏、购买和安排。被俘虏和购买的新娘，没有自由，等同于奴隶，

---

① Lin Yutang, *My Country and My People* (New York: Reynal and Hitchcock, 1935), p. 137.

② Robert Hans van Gulik, *Sexual Life in Ancient China: A Preliminary Survey of Chinese Sex and Society from ca. 1500 B. C. till 1644 A. D.* (Leiden, Netherlands: E. J. Brill, 1974).

③ Richard W. Guisso, "Thunder over the Lake: The Five Classics and the Perception of Women in Early China," in Guisso and Stanley Johannesen, eds., *Women in China: Current Directions in Historical Scholarship* (Youngstown, N. Y.: Philo, 1981), p. 48. 这些说法来自宋代对新儒家学说的阐释。

④ Lin, *My Country and My People*, p. 139.

毫无权利可言，她们主要的功用就是侍候丈夫及生儿子。① 周朝建立"宗族"制度，女性的地位更加从属化，而且女性在宗族中的地位越高，对她的限制就越多。②

秦朝（公元前 221—前 206 年）和汉朝（公元前 202—220 年）曾一度流行女性掩面，女性服从和忠于父亲、丈夫及儿子，成为必须遵守的妇道。在汉朝，女性只能结一次婚，婚前及婚外的性行为，都会被处以死刑。国家为贞节的女性，例如年轻守寡而能从一而终者，树立贞节牌坊。包办婚姻愈发普遍，嫁妆和彩礼的习俗也逐渐形成。杀女婴也开始广泛施行，因为家庭不想花那么多钱来嫁女儿。③《列女传》之类的更加要求女性责任限制女性行动的书籍出版，尽管如此，汉朝还是出现了吕后，她在丈夫死后独掌国家大权。

随后的三国（公元 220—280 年）和晋朝（公元 265—420 年）及南北朝（公元 420—588 年），社会阶级更加僵化，婚姻讲究门当户对，女性不得再婚。到了公元 480 年，为了保护寡妇的贞节，政府在唐州为没有儿女的寡妇兴建道院。④ 那时结婚的花费很高，阻止了许多婚姻，光棍人数大增，杀婴也盛行起来。⑤ 到了唐朝（公元 618—907 年），社会对女性的限制变少，唐朝出现许多女强人，包括武则天，她在公元 684—704 年统治国家，拥有许多男宠。唐朝是中国历史上较为开放的时代，因为佛教的传入降低了儒家学术的影响。

五代（公元 907—960 年）的南唐李后主开创了缠足的传统，他为宠爱的嫔妃设计了特别的小鞋。⑥ 这一习俗在随后的宋朝流行开来。宋朝（公元 960—1279 年）的男尊女卑胜过以后各朝代。上层社会的

---

① Yao, *Chinese Women*, p. 17.
② Ibid., p. 29.
③ Ibid., p. 48.
④ Ibid., p. 46; and Lin, *My Country and My People*, p. 140.
⑤ Yao, *Chinese Women*, p. 52.
⑥ Yao, *Chinese Women*, p. 93.

女性足不出户，她们的身体被宽大的衣服遮住，缠足和杀女婴都很普遍。缠足成为女性地位及美丽的象征，脚越小，女人越美。下层社会的女性就不缠足，因为行动若被局限，她们就无法养家糊口。不过缠足与地区有关系，例如在中国东南方，就没听说过缠足。①

在宋朝，嫁妆变成婚礼的重点，结婚时，女家会把聘金用来准备嫁妆，男女双方的花费相当。夫家对于嫁妆的期待很大，让生女儿的家庭有了经济上的烦恼。② 为了应付这个陋习，政府订立罚则，来确保婚姻不被当作生财工具。③宋朝后期，新儒家思想鼓吹男尊女卑及"三从四德"：在家从父、出嫁从夫、夫死从子。

14—19 世纪的元、明、清时代，中上阶层的女性都被关闭及区隔，甚至连医生都不能看到她们的身体，私闯闺房或碰触女性者，必受重罚。在医学文献中有不少生男孩的秘方。④ 高额嫁妆杀女婴和一夫多妻制很普遍。⑤ 那时的女性对嫁妆无发言权，对自己人生也无法掌控。

19 世纪末期至 20 世纪初，西方思潮进入，改变了中国许多地方妇女的角色及地位。传教士和受过西方教育的中国人纷纷质疑女性的不平等地位，终结了一些伤害女性的传统陋习。女权倡导者如秋瑾，呼吁社会要关注杀女婴、殴妻、贞节牌坊、多妻、纳妾等问题。女性不再掩面，不再缠足。这些变化主要影响到城市富裕人家的女子。新

---

① Yao, *Chinese Women*, p. 94.

② Patricia Buckley Ebrey, *The Inner Quarters: Marriage and the Lives of Chinese Women in the Sung Period* (Berkeley: University of California Press, 1993), p. 101.

③ Idid., pp. 101 – 103.

④ See Charlotte Furth, *A Flourishing Yin: Gender in China's Medical History, 960 – 1665* (Berkeley: University of California Press, 1999), pp. 210 – 216.

⑤ Mildred Dickemann, "Paternal Confidence and Dowry Competition: A Biocultural Analysis of Purdah," in Richard D. Alexander and Donald W. Tinkle, eds., *Natural Selection and Social Behavior: Recent Research and New Theory* (New York: Chiron, 1981), p. 434.

的法律赋予她们选择配偶及财产继承的权利。① 乡村妇女也经历着变革,甚至开始投身政治运动,例如太平天国(1851—1864年)、义和团(1900年)及红枪会(1911—1949年)。② 其中太平天国运动波及中国大江南北,公开挑战男女不平等的传统观念,任命女子担任军中的要职,但这些努力都比不上1949年共产党革命胜利所带来的改变大。

三、杀婴的历史及后代性别选择

中国子女性别选择的历史,一如印度,也需要从支离破碎的史料中拼凑。中国学者从未提起它是何时开始的,中国早期历史中的人口数据也不可靠。某位学者认为中国的后代性别选择行为开始于公元前2000年左右,当时的环境压力大,很多婴儿因此受难。③ 最早关于杀婴的文字记载是《诗经》(公元前800—前600年),其中有一段写到杀男婴的企图,而另一段则写道:"乃生男子,载寝之床,载衣之裳,载弄之璋;乃生女子,载寝之地,载衣之裼,载弄之瓦。"④

公元前5世纪的《左传》曾记录一个女婴被弃于沟渠中。⑤ 当时的家庭为了控制人口数量和结构,男女婴都杀,但仍以杀女婴居多。韩非子(逝世于公元前233年)是周朝后期的法学家,他说:"且父母之于子也,产男则相贺,产女则杀之。此俱出于父母怀衽,然男子

---

① Patricia Buckley Ebrey, *The Cambridge Illustrated History of China* (Cambridge: Cambridge University Press, 1996), pp. 279-281.

② Bossen, "Women and Development," p. 297.

③ Elisabeth J. Croll, *Feminism and Socialism in China* (London: Routledge and Kegan Paul, 1978).

④ Ibid., p. 32.

⑤ Fei Yao, *Chinese Women*, p. 91.

受贺,女子杀之者,虑其后便,计之长利也。"①

然而,另一部文献也提到当食物和必需品匮乏时,男婴女婴都会被父母杀掉。《后汉书》(公元25—220年)写道:"宋度迁长沙太守。人多以乏衣食,产乳不举。度切让三老,禁民杀子。"②父母以杀婴和遗弃小孩来控制家庭人口,可能是穷人的一贯做法,尽管穷人家认为杀婴会遭天谴,他们仍然广泛施行。

一直到12世纪,杀婴才被定为犯罪。许多法律书籍都提到官府认为杀婴,尤其是杀女婴问题十分严重,秦、汉、宋、元及以后的几个朝代都不例外。③ 关于秦汉和以后朝代的杀婴证据很少,但对宋朝的记录较多,主要还是源于宋朝特别歧视女性。家中男孩过多,家产会被严重瓜分,也很让父母头疼,而女孩多就意味着要支付大笔嫁妆钱,因此父母通常只想要小家庭。此外,小孩成年后(16岁),需要支付人头税,这成为父母抛弃婴儿的一个原因。④

公元1110年,中国曾经有过禁止杀婴的赦令,但两年后该赦令的修订部分显示了当时南方的地主和农民杀婴的情况非常普遍。⑤

杀婴的方法以溺死为主,但许多女孩也死于童年时家庭的忽略。

---

① Quoted in Bernice J. Lee, "Female Infanticide in China," in Guisso and Johannesen, *Women in China*, p. 164.

② Quoted in Werner Eichhorn, "Some Notes on Population Control during the Sung Dynasty," in *Etudes d'histoire et de littérature chinoises offertes au Professeur Jaroslav Prusek*, Bibliothèque de l'institut des hautes etudes chinoises, Vol. 24 (Paris: Presses Universitaires de France, 1976), p. 90.

③ 关于犯罪文献的讨论,参见 Sharon K. Hom, "Female Infanticide in China: The Human Rights Specter and Thoughts towards (An) other Vision," *Columbia Human Rights Law Review*, Vol. 23, No. 2 (Summer 1992), pp. 249-314;关于制度文献的讨论,参见 Anne Walter, "Infanticide and Dowry in Ming and Early Qing China," in Anne Behnke Kinney, ed., *Chinese Views of Childhood* (Honolulu: University of Hawaii Press, 1995), pp. 193-217.

④ Eichhorn, "Some Notes on Population Control during the Sung Dynasty," p. 90.

⑤ Ibid., p. 89.

在12世纪初，政府设立了慈幼局，只是被弃的女婴几乎无人收养，男婴则被无子嗣的家庭收养来承传香火。

13世纪的江西赣州也有法令禁止杀女婴，原因出在当时的人"讨厌女孩"①——她们无法承传家族姓氏，无法祭祀祖宗，出嫁时需要嫁妆，长大后要付人头税，还得男性保护。宋朝学者程颐提倡"饿死事小，失节事大"之后，社会对妇女贞节的要求就更严格了。②一位作者就问道："是要养女儿而冒着她未来不贞的危险，还是杀了她以策安全？"③

宋朝强化了宗族制度，大家长会要求父母对子女一视同仁，以免影响家族名声④，杀婴被定为谋杀罪。当时有30个家族的成员因为"溺死女婴"、"虐待童养媳"、"迫女儿为妾"，以及"鬻女为娼"而受到惩罚。⑤

元朝对杀女婴的人的惩罚，是把他们的一半财产充公。⑥当时并没有关于杀男婴的法律，可见杀女婴的问题比较严重。学者田汝康说，尽管有法律及舆论，但杀女婴在明、清两代的人口密集之地仍然十分普遍，然而事实上，杀婴行为在中国历史上一直受到谴责。无数劝诫性的书籍和小册子作为道德戒律和罚则出版，尽管一般成效不显著，但历代都在印行。宋朝，杀婴等同于杀子女，要给予惩罚。元朝的法律体系中，对杀婴者的惩罚就是将其家族的一半财产充公。公元1500—1585年间的明朝统治者会把杀婴者发配千里之外的兵站服劳役。然而，所有这些惩罚与大规模的杀婴劣行不成比例，起不了什么

---

① Lee, "Female Infanticide in China," p. 166.

② Ibid., p. 175.

③ Ibid.

④ Liu Hui-chen Wang, *The Traditional Chinese Clan Rules* (Locust Valley, N.Y.: J. J. Augustin, 1959), pp. 58–59.

⑤ Liu Hui-chen Wang, *The Traditional Chinese Clan Rules* (Locust Valley, N.Y.: J. J. Augustin, 1959), p. 59.

⑥ Lee, "Female Infanticide in China," p. 166.

作用。① 江西抚州城外一个小池边竖立石头，上写"不得在此溺毙女孩"。② 一位16世纪的观察者指出：江西有杀女婴的习俗，造成了适婚年龄的新娘不足。……皇帝还应地方官请求下诏禁止杀婴。③

1583—1610年，一位住在中国的意大利传教士说，父母认为杀女儿没有错，因为可让她转世投胎到较富裕的家庭。④ 清朝学者及官吏也记录了持续的杀女婴情况，导致皇帝于1697年下诏禁止杀婴。18世纪，耶稣会传教士发现北京每天有几千个女婴被丢到街上，清道夫第二天一早把婴尸收起，集中丢到城外。⑤ 这时期，任何养育两个以上女儿的家庭，均可得到皇帝的表彰。

田汝康认为，17、18世纪的杀女婴导致其他后果："性别比例不正常，适婚年龄的女性人数大为减少。福建的情况尤其糟糕。在1649—1659年，建宁县有一半的男性是单身汉。1743年的德化县中，10个男的中有6—7个未婚。虽说'物以稀为贵'，但这对于中国女性并不适用。女性的稀少反而让她们变成被当作财产而占有的对象，无论她是少女、妻子或寡妇。"⑥

19世纪，外国传教士和学者及中国官方数据都记载了当时杀女婴的事实。1838年，广东总督曾下令禁止这个恶习。⑦ 传教士艾比尔（David Abeel）曾尝试统计1843年福建省同安县杀女婴的程度。他发现，依地区而异，少则10%，多则70%—80%，而且杀女婴与父母

---

① T'ien Ju-k'ang, *Male Anxiety and Female Chastity: A Comparative Study of Chinese Ethical Values in Ming-Ch'ing Times* (New York: E. J. Brill, 1988), pp. 28–30.

② Julie Jimmerson, "Female Infanticide in China: An Examination of Cultural and Legal Norms," *Pacific Basin Law Journal*, Vol. 8, No. 1 (Spring 1990), pp. 47–79, at p. 50."

③ Quoted in T'ien, *Male Anxiety and Female Chastity*, p. 24.

④ Lee, "Female Infanticide in China," p. 167.

⑤ William L. Langer, "Infanticide: A Historical Survey," *History of Childhood Quarterly: The Journal of Psychohistory*, Vol. 1, No. 3 (Winter 1974), pp. 353–365.

⑥ T'ien, *Male Anxiety and Female Chastity*, p. 31.

⑦ Lee, "Female Infanticide in China," p. 168.

的经济状况无关。①

有几位学者成功计算出明、清两代人口性别比例,尽管大部分官方统计对女性人数有低估。著名的历史学家与人口学家何炳棣(Ho Ping-ti)提供了1368—1953年间几个时期的数据,显示了男性比例偏高的情况。1381年,湖南地区的比例高达125.9(男):100(女)[儿童性别比例为161.4(男):100(女),成人为109.2(男):100(女)],1368—1953年间,总性别比例为110(男):100(女)。② 这显示了当时广泛杀女婴的情形。明太祖时(1368—1398年)出现首份中国人口的代表性统计,是根据税赋单位,所以不能代表全部人口,还可能低估了女性甚至男性的人数,这个问题一直到1776年才被修正。

明朝没有全国总性别比例的资料,1381—1391年记载了户数、人口数及土地大小,但并未列出人口的性别。少数的省、县史册提供了这方面的数据,可以部分地说明后代性别选择行为,造成了当时的男多于女。1391年人口注册法改了,性别数据被列入,以便征召16岁以上的男性服劳役。但因为注册的重点是男性,所以女性常被忽略,而且为了逃避劳役,男性的人数也会被故意隐瞒。因此,1391年之后的数据并不可靠。

1775年湖北的饥荒,终于让皇帝发现人口被低估的真相,因为需要政府救济的人口,比注册的还要多出10万人。③ 于是新的注册系统诞生了,不再以丁(男性16—60岁,需要以劳力付税)为单位,并严惩造假。然而南方乡村低报的情况仍很普遍。女性人数少,一方面反映出当时杀女婴的事实,另一方面则是有些地方因为耕作需要引进

---

① Lee, "Female Infanticide in China," p. 169.

② Ho Ping-ti, *Studies on the Population of China, 1368 – 1953* (Cambridge, Mass.: Harvard University Press, 1959).

③ Ibid., p. 47.

大量劳工，造成当地的男性比女性多出 2—3 倍。① 女性的死亡，加之当时还有纳妾的做法，使得许多贫穷男性找不到太太。18 世纪的官吏发现，江苏地方上流氓会掳走年轻的寡妇为妻，可见低阶层男性结婚有多困难。(参见表 4-1)②

表 4-1 1773—1833 年中国部分省份的男性与女性人口规模及性别比

省份	年份	总人口数	性别比	男性	女性	地方
直隶	1778	20746519	118.8	11264563	9481956	
直隶	1773	1432031	120.6	782878	649153	永平 P
直隶	1777	196576	108.3	102204	94372	永清 C
山东	1837	4086511	111.5	2154354	1932157	济南 P
山东	1826	400237	115.7	214684	185553	济宁 C
陕西	1083	93990	126.7	52530	41460	洛川 C
陕西	1784	234456	125.0	130253	104203	周至 C
陕西	1783	158310	154.2	96032	62278	澄城 C
陕西	1829	115392	156.4	70387	45005	宁陕厅 C
江苏	1820	5908436	134.4	3387772	2520664	苏州 P
江苏	1793	525617	135.1	302045	223572	常熟
江苏	1816	2472974	128.1	1388812	1084162	松江 P
江苏	1816	261898	131.1	148571	113327	奉贤 C
浙江	1785	513878	118.3	278478	235400	义乌 C
安徽	1826	617111	120.7	337496	279615	歙县 C
广西	1835	877337	109.5	458560	418777	贺州 P
云南	1845	95451	110.9	50192	45259	大姚 C
四川	1843	2071695	112.8	1098154	973541	重庆 P
四川	1814	184679	107.2	95548	89131	三台 C
四川	1795	135788	101.1	68265	67523	崇州
四川	1810	134488	111.5	70900	63588	郫县 C
四川	1815	386397	125.7	215198	171199	成都 C
四川	1833	113963	116.5	61324	52639	西充 C
总数		41763734	120.6	22829204	18934530	

来源：Ho Ping-lti, *Studies on the Population of China*, *1368–1953* (Cambridge, Mass.: Harvard University Press, 1959), pp. 58–59. "P" 代表州，"C" 代表县。

① Ho Ping-ti, *Studies on the Population of China*, *1368–1953*, p. 57.
② Walter, "Infanticide and Dowry in Ming and Early Qing China," pp. 193–217.

想解读1851年以后的人口数据,难度很大。1851年,爆发了太平天国运动,去注册人口等于被征兵。① 所以上海有钱有势的家族都不去注册,只有穷人家的男孩才无法逃避兵役。再加上妇女和儿童也无须注册,所以19世纪后期的性别比例,出现400(男):100(女)的超高记录,有些地方还更高。② 吉尔博特·罗兹曼(Gilbert Rozman)研究19世纪清朝的人口,他的结论是当时的数据正确地反映了直隶省及山东省性别和年龄分布的比例,也代表当时北方的情况。在1837年,山东省某县的成年性别比例为134(男):100(女),儿童性别比例是147(男):100(女),山东省平均的成年性别比例是112(男):100(女),儿童是119(男):100(女)。③ 直隶省的成年性别比例是117(男):100(女),儿童是124(男):100(女)。在随后的1877年,直隶的成年人口性别比例是119(男):100(女),儿童性别比是120(男):100(女)。④ 罗兹曼还研究了河北435个地方,发现其中有21处的成年性别比例是160(男):100(女)或更高;95处或完全没有女孩,或性别比例高于160(男):100(女)。1906年的人口数据只提供了部分的真相,事实上仍有严重低估的情形,而且男女皆然。15岁以下的女性,已婚的才会被登记⑤,一直到20世纪,全国人口才全部被纳入统计范围。

中国封建时代有关婴儿死亡率的数据几乎找不到,我们只能假设过高的儿童性别比例,是由于杀女婴及对她们疏于照顾之故。李中清(James Lee)、康文林(Cameron Campbell)、谭国富在研究1774—1873年辽宁省的人口资料时,发现婴儿死亡率(包括女婴死亡率)及生育

---

① Ho, *Studies on the Population of China, 1368 – 1953*, pp. 67 – 68.
② 例如浙江长兴县儿童性别比例是431.9(男):100(女)。See ibid., p. 68.
③ Gilbert Rozman, *Population and Marketing Settlements in Ch'ing China* (New York: Cambridge University Press, 1982), p. 75.
④ Ibid., pp. 49 – 51.
⑤ Ibid., p. 144.

率皆与经济情况有关。①他们认为："在中国，杀婴被视为产后的堕胎，父母借此选择后代的人数、次序及出生性别，以配合自身的短期经济状况及长期的家庭计划。"② 在这期间的人口资料中显示，男女两性的死亡率及预期寿命不同。通过计算长达 70 年的时间序列数据可知，女性的预期寿命在前 35 年比男性短，以后则相等。例如 5 岁以下的儿童，女孩的预期寿命是 28 岁，男孩是 35.2 岁。③ 在经济萧条时，女性的寿命更明显地缩短了：5 岁以下女孩的预期寿命只有 18.4 岁，男孩则是 28.9 岁。④

这几位学者认为，辽宁省的死亡率显示女儿得到的照顾比儿子少得多。照中国人的算法，一出生就是 1 岁，所以没有 2 岁以下儿童的死亡率数据。在辽宁省人口开始注册的平均年龄是 6 岁。⑤ 在此之前死亡的孩童，尤其是女孩，是没有记录的。因此，他们认为，婴儿出生第一年的死亡率或许要比注册人口所显示的高得多。死亡率的不平衡反映在这一时期的儿童性别比例中。⑥ 在独生子女的家庭中，儿童的性别比例为 576（男）：100（女）。两个小孩的家庭，第一胎的性别比例是 211（男）：100（女），第二胎是 450（男）：100（女）。三个小孩以上的家庭，第一胎的性别比例是 156（男）：100（女），第二胎是 294（男）：100（女），第三胎 324（男）：100（女），只有 5 个以上小孩的大家庭的儿童性别比例是正常的（第一胎是 88%，第五胎是 162%）。⑦ 李中清等人指出："女孩出生时，如果家庭所要

---

① Lee, Campbell, and Tan, "Infanticide and Family Planning in Late Imperial China," p. 146.
② Ibid., p. 147.
③ Ibid., p. 152.
④ Ibid., pp. 153–154.
⑤ Ibid., p. 150.
⑥ 根据出生次序统计性别比例的对象是 1792—1840 年间注册孩子人口的家庭。Ibid., p. 154.
⑦ Lee, Campbell, and Tan, "Infanticide and Family Planning in Late Imperial China," p. 154.

的小孩人数已经够了,那她存活的可能性就很低,活不到注册的时候。这一情形很常见,难以用是否注册来解释。"① 因此,广泛杀女婴和忽略女孩是这个省被观察到的高性别比例的原因。

在辽宁,父母期待的儿女性别组成、家庭经济状况、社会的景气程度等,都会影响女婴的存活。也就是说,该地区的气候影响食物的供应,进而影响价格变动,让父母作出不同的生育决定,而大多数的生育决定,都是在子女出生当下做的,而不是在受孕时。所以,如果物价太高,小孩的存活机会就变少,尤其是女孩,除非家庭富裕,不受价格因素影响。②

李中清、王丰及康文林研究清朝的贵族家庭时发现,连有钱家族的女儿也难免被杀的厄运。根据他们的统计,皇族中有十分之一的女儿被杀,到了18世纪末期情况更糟,有五分之一的贵族女儿被杀。③

地图4-2呈现宋、清两朝已知的杀女婴地区,这些地区颜色较深,颜色较淡的地区不代表那儿没有杀女婴,只是我们的证据不够。

四、20世纪的变化

平等,包括性别的平等,是1949年共产主义革命的主要诉求之一。中国政府说:"国家采取必要措施,逐步完善保障妇女权益的各项制度,清除对妇女的一切形式的歧视。……妇女在政治的、经济的、文化的、社会的及家庭的生活等各方面享有同男子平等的权

---

① Lee, Campbell, and Tan, "Infanticide and Family Planning in Late Imperial China," p. 156.
② Ibid., p. 167.
③ James Lee, Wang Feng, and Cameron Campbell, "Infant and Child Mortality among Qing Nobility: Implications for Two Types of Positive Checks," *Population Studies*, Vol. 48 (1994), pp. 395–411.

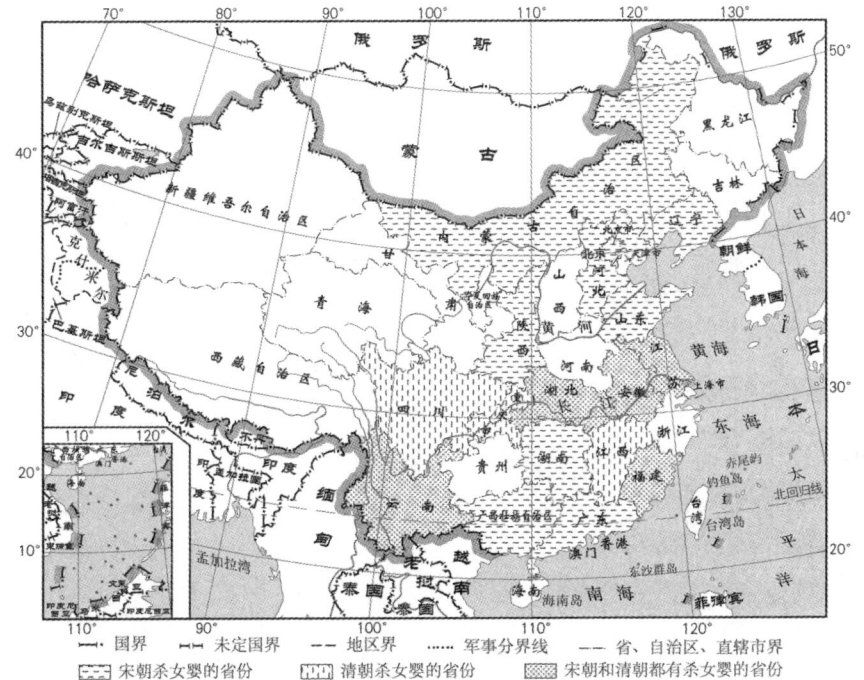

地图 4-2　宋、清两朝杀女婴的地区

利。……国家保障妇女享有与男子平等的婚姻家庭权利。"①

中国共产党人认识到在高性别比例的背景下婚姻问题的政治敏感性。毛泽东在 20 世纪 30 年代早期的江西苏维埃时期宣布,革命将解放所有的小妾,她们此后将可自由婚嫁。史黛西(Judith Stacy)说:"估计有 30% 的贫农和手工艺者、90% 的赤贫无产者、99% 的雇员是单身汉。"② 在 1949 年起草的《婚姻法》中,纳妾、讨嫁妆、杀女婴、卖女儿、娼妓行为及歧视妇女,都被严格禁止。

共产党倡言男女平等,对女性处境也产生了影响。例如,平等入

---

① Information Office of the State Council, *Protection of Chinese Women's Rights and Interests* (Beijing: New Star, zhuyi 1993), pp. 1–2.

② Judith Stacey, *Patriarchy and Socialist Revolution in China* (Berkeley: University of California Press, 1983), p. 161.

学权作为一项法律体现在基础教育中男孩女孩有同等的录取率。《婚姻法》给予女性同等的继承权，但老百姓的法律认知度偏低。① 以前的婚姻模式是两家族间订立固定婚约，而现在则是两人之间签订自由婚约，只是早年间有些难以预料的后果。自由婚嫁改变了媒妁之言，所有在1950年前根据媒妁之言结婚的女子，可以和丈夫离婚，但也冒着被丈夫施暴的危险。也有些女子发现自己被丈夫抛弃了！不肯离婚的妇女会被丈夫提交当地的组织，受到违反新法及反革命罪的处罚。② 在新《婚姻法》实施的第一年，中国南方有超过1万名女性被杀，在1950—1952年，东部有11500名女性丧失生命，全国因婚姻相关议题死亡的女性，每年达7万—8万人。③

女性在工作方面也是好坏参半，农村妇女可以参加集体劳动组织（虽然女性所得还是比男性少），与男人一起挣工分，不过，她们干同样工作却比男人挣的工分少。这类劳动是在她们已有的家务——取水、生火、洗衣——之外的。④ 城市女性则有机会进入工厂，多为轻工厂，工作报酬要比男性少。⑤ 中国对其妇女就业的记录十分自豪，在1999年，女性占全部劳动人口的46.5%，女性收入是男性的80.4%。⑥

女性地位的改变也影响到她们对自己人生的掌控。她们可以在田

---

① Bosen, "Women and Development," pp. 302 – 303; and Rubie S. Watson, "Afterword: Marriage and Gender Inequality," in Watson and Patricia Buckley Ebrey, *Marriage and Inequality in Chinese Society* (Berkeley: University of California Press, 1991), p. 362.

② Bossen, "Women and Development," p. 303.

③ Kazuko Ono, *Chinese Women in a Century of Revolution*, 1850 – 1950 (Stanford, Calif.: Stanford University Press, 1989), p. 181, quoted in ibid.

④ Ibid., p. 304.

⑤ Ibid., p. 305.

⑥ See "China's Population and Development in the 21st Century," Information Office of the State Council of the People's Republic of China, Beijing," December 18, 2000. http://www.china.org.cn/e-white/21st/.

里工作,却很难拥有土地——因为土地是分配给一家之主的,通常都是男性,并不准买卖。① 女性有了经济自主权,可以选择自己的职业;在20世纪70年代末期,在计划生育政策实施的背景下,女性却失去了对于自己身体的主控权。

虽然政府努力提升女性在家庭及社区的地位,但杀女婴行为的延续及女婴死亡率的居高不下仍旧说明女性的价值被大大地低估了。1957年以来,1岁以下的女婴死亡率一直高过男婴。② 1982年1‰人口的生育率及1988年2‰人口的生育率调查显示,只有在20世纪60年代中很短的一段时间里,出生人口性别比例是正常的(见图4-1)。图4-1显示,性别比例一直维持在正常值的105(男):100(女)以上,但当时尚无出生前性别选择的技术,为什么新生儿性别比会这么高呢? 1982年及1988年的生育率调查,询问了许多已婚妇女关于她们自己及其子女出生的情形(1982年,有311000名15—67岁的女性,1988年有459000名15—57岁的女性接受调查)。安斯利·柯尔(Ansley Coale)认为,她们并未提及出生后第一年即死亡的婴儿,所以新生儿性别比的数据可能只反映了存活下来的婴儿而非新生儿出生率。③ 也就是说,高新生儿性别比的原因是许多女婴在出生后的第一年内就死了。特伦斯·荷尔(Terence Hull)则认为,新生儿性别比与预期相符,女婴死亡主要由于父母疏于照顾。④ 从1936年

---

① Bossen, "Women and Development," pp. 307–308.

② Yasuko Hayase and Seiko Kawamata, *Population Policy and Vital Statitics in China* (Tokyo: Institute of Developing Economies, 1991), p. 66.

③ Ansley J. Coale, "Excess Ratio of Males to Females by Birth Cohort in the Census of China 1953 to 1990 and in the Births Reported in the Fertility Surveys, 1982 and 1988," OPR Working Paper No. 93–6 (Princeton, N. J.: Office for Population Research, Princeton University, July 1993).

④ Terence H. Hull, "Recent Trends in Sex Ratios at Birth in China," *Population and Development Review*, Vol. 16, No. 1 (March 1990), p. 72.

到20世纪80年代的高性别比例显示,即使是革命,也未能灭绝杀女婴的陋习(此说并不准确——编者注)。

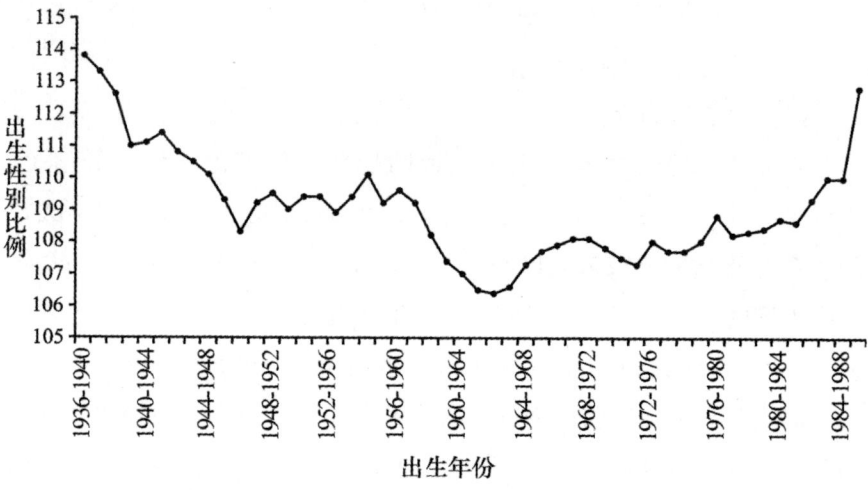

图 4-1 中国出生人口性别比例

五、独生子女政策及重男轻女

1953年,中国进行了第一次全国人口普查,记录的人口是5.83亿人。到了1975年,人口超过9亿。基于以下几个因素,中国政府开始重新检讨毛泽东所说的"人多力量大"的说法:20世纪50年代至70年代初人口快速增长;20世纪60年代早期的饥荒;住房、食物及工作的短缺;全民健康的恶化。① 20世纪70年代,政府提倡"晚、稀、少",鼓励城市的父母生育两个以下的子女,农村三个以下。②

---

① 毛泽东认为:"人不但有一张嘴,还有一双手。"参见 Lisa B. Gregory, "Examining the Economic Component of China's One-Child Family Policy under International Law," *Journal of Chinese Law*, Vol. 6, No. 1 (Spring 1992), p. 48; 1949年新中国成立后,还流行过一个口号"光荣妈妈"(即生得越多,母亲越光荣),参见 Li Xiaorong, "License to Coerce: Violence against Women, State Responsibility, and Legal Failures in China's Family-Planning Program," *Yale Journal of Law and Feminism*, Vol. 8, No. 1 (Summer 1996), p. 148。

② Li, "License to Coerce," p. 148.

1979年,中国采取独生子女政策以控制人口增长。独生子女政策是1980年第五届全国人大所提出的计划生育法的一部分,到了2001年12月全国人大常委会的第25次会议才正式颁布实施。尽管直到2002年9月计划生育政策才成为法律,但自1979年起,中国各级政府都把独生子女政策当作正式的法律来执行。计划生育成为中国的基本国策,它被写入宪法,成为夫妻的义务,而个人的利益不得危害到国家、社会或集体的利益。①

2002年《中华人民共和国人口与计划生育法》(后简称《人口与计划生育法》)明言夫妻只能拥有一个小孩,如果要生第二胎,必须"依法"安排。② 至于在什么情况下才能有第二胎,法律并未明文。在计划生育政策实行之初,有关生育的法规在农村和城市是不同的。在城市,一胎化的政策被严格执行,在农村,一胎是被鼓励的,二胎会受到控制,三胎则被禁止。甚至这一政策也根据新生儿性别而有所不同。生有两个女儿的父母,通常会被允许生第三胎,其他的例外如:第一胎有非遗传的缺陷、父母都是独生子女、配偶双方皆为归国人员、少数民族、或是当地缺乏劳工。③ 女性的合法婚龄是20岁,男性是22岁,农村的男性要满25岁、女性满23岁才准结婚。另外,农村居民婚后即可生第一胎,四年后才可生第二胎。④ 在校大学生被禁止结婚,在读研究生的婚嫁也受到限制,违反者需支付高额罚款,包

---

① Lisa B. Gregory, "Examining the Economic Component of China's One-Child Family Policy under International Law: Your Money or Your Life," *Journal of Chinese Law*, Vol. 6, No. 1 (Spring 1992), pp. 50 – 51.

② 《人口与计划生育法》第十八条有规定。Population and Family Planning Law of the People's Republic of China, http://www.unescap.org/pop/database/law_china/ch_record052.htm.

③ Li, "License to Coerce," p. 154.

④ Sulamith Heins Potter, "Birth Planning in Rural China: A Cultural Account," in Nancy Scheper-Hughes, ed., *Child Survival: Anthropological Perspectives on the Treatment and Maltreatment of Children* (Dordrecht, Netherlands: D. Reidel, 1987), pp. 41 – 42.

括一次性和几年分期的罚款。① 违法生育的父母拿不到政府津贴,例如贫穷补助、农产品的提供、技术培训及子女医疗和教育。②

自从独生子女政策实施之后,出生率降低了,愈来愈多的人使用避孕药、子宫颈结扎手术及堕胎。③ 被杀及被弃的婴儿也增加了,尤其是女婴。为此,2001 年的《婚姻法》及 2002 年的《人口与计划生育法》都列有禁止杀婴的条款。④ 李晓荣认为,地方政府的政策和相关竞争使杀婴、弃婴、强行拆房及胁迫妇女节育等问题被极大地恶化了。⑤ 父母现在无权决定自己的家庭构成,而是由地方计划生育官员拍板定案。事实上,《人口与计划生育法》第二十二条禁止歧视或虐待生女儿及无法生育的妇女,也禁止歧视、虐待及抛弃女婴。

独生子女政策反而强化了重男轻女的传统观念。想了解中国人对独生子女政策的反应,必须先了解儿子在中国家庭中扮演的角色,和父母对生育问题的艰难思考。

在中国文化里,下一代是家庭传承的工具、繁衍的基础及老年时的保障。儿子的主要责任是照顾年迈的父母,女儿不但不能继承家庭姓氏,她的劳力价值也远不如儿子,虽然有时女儿比儿子能干,赚的也更多。

在农村,生儿子的需要更强烈,因为男性被认为是更有价值的劳

---

① 纪思道和吴敦提供了一个案例:一位中学老师 4 年内生了两个孩子,被处以罚款。1983 年超生第二胎违反计划生育政策,政府对教师的罚款是 2456 元。这笔罚金是当年教授年薪的 17 倍。接下来的 10 年间,这名教师每年工资都会被扣掉 80%,以支付罚金。类似情形,参见 Kristof and WuDunn, *China Wakes: The Struggle for the Soul of a Rising Power* (New York: Vintage, 1994), pp. 237–239。

② Li, "License to Coerce," pp. 158–159.

③ 关于堕胎率、绝育、出生控制上升的讨论,参见 H. Yuan Tien, Zhang Tianlu, Ping Yu, Li Jingneng, and Liagn Zhongtang, "China's Demographic Dilemmas," *Population Bulletin*, Vol. 47, No. 1 (June 1992), p. 12。

④ 《人口与计划生育法》第二十一条有规定。Http://www.unescap.org/pop/database/law_china/ch_record052.htm。

⑤ Li, "License to Coerce," pp. 145–191.

动力。儿子能够下田耕作，成为主要的收入来源。虽然自1970年起，农耕方式从集体变成家庭式，但需要体力的工作非儿子不行，儿子也能出面解决土地及资源的纠纷。女儿只能做些轻松的工作，相对来说价值不高。① 因此田心源认为："重男轻女并非只是学者们经常说的封建心态，而是劳力密集的农耕经济之所需，甚至在人民公社、集体农场的时代，家中男性愈多，所得工分也愈多，生活水平也比较好。"②

在农村，儿子还有其他经济上的优势：有90%的农村人没有退休金，必须在老年时依赖儿子供养。③女儿则是嫁到夫家去照顾公婆。人类学家波特（Sulamith Heins Potter）描述，没有儿女的老人，悲惨可怜，必须依赖政府的补助。他们多半住在危楼中，缺少食物，还得靠好心的邻居提供柴水。④

六、上升的出生人口性别比

独生子女政策及其执行情况促进了中国的出生人口性别比的增长。1982年及1988年的生育率调查显示，1936年至1989年的新生儿性别比，一直高于正常值的105—107（男）：100（女），虽然在1970—1980年间，新生儿性别比曾接近于正常，但自那以后性别比例远高于正常值，且不断开始攀升。另外，中国的人口普查数据不是全体人口的数据，而是代表性的样本，所以准确的新生儿性别比难以取

---

① Li, "License to Coerce," p. 173. 在对中国农村的研究中，格林哈尔（Susan Greenhalgh）等发现，因为"农村文化一直把妇女和女孩视为低人一等，限制女性参与重要的农业劳动，把儿子塑造为家庭劳动力的骄傲成员"。参见 Greenhalgh and Li, " Engendering Reproductive Practice in Peasent China: The Political Roots of the Rising Sex Rations at Birth," Working Paper No. 57 (Beijing: Population Council Research Division, 1993), p. 15。

② H. Yuna Tien, *China' Strategic Demographic Initiative* (New York: Praeger, 1991), p. 202.

③ Potter, "Birth Planning in Rural China," p. 35.

④ Ibid.

得。1990年7月1日第四次全国人口普查，取自10%的人口样本，2000年的普查也一样。1995年的数据来自于1.04%的人口样本调查，1994年的数据样本量只有0.63%。这么少的样本是无法代表全中国的，据此得出的计算也很难精确。图4-2是中国人口学家顾宝昌和李涌平计算出的总人口新生儿性别比，可看出从1980年的独生子女政策以来，新生儿性别比一直在增高。在一些地区的比例要比正常值高很多，有些地区的新生儿性别比接近正常值。

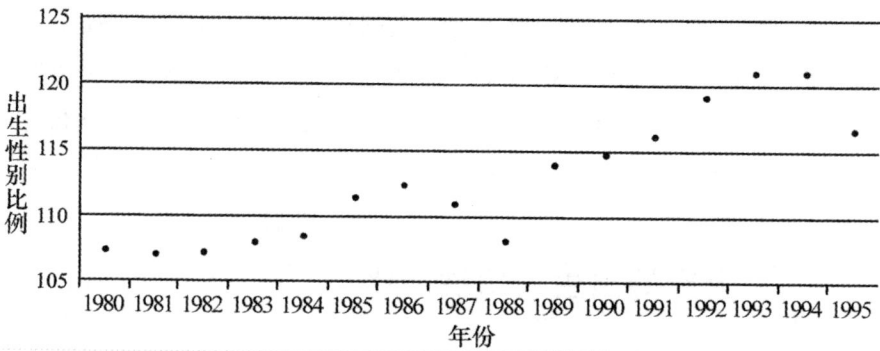

图 4-2　中国总人口新生儿性别比

表4-2展示了1982、1989、1995年的新生儿性别比，根据省、自治区和直辖市来分类。表中显示中国的新生儿性别比从108.5（男）：100（女)增加到115.6（男）：100（女），其中有一省在1995年高达130.3（男）：100（女）。与印度南北方具有明显区别的情形不同的是，我们发现中国大部分地区的新生儿性别比例分布均类似，唯一例外的是在贵州省、西藏、新疆等自治区，那儿的新生儿性别比一直保持在正常值附近。其中原因我们在后文会讨论到。

从新生儿性别比及男女的出生人数，我们可以推算出中国的出生人口中，有多少女性凭空消失了（表4-3）。例如1985年的总新生儿性别比是111.4（男）：100（女），共有1160万名男婴出生，1042万女婴诞生。若采用预期出生比例105（男）：100（女）来算，原本应有1105万名女婴出生，也就是有62.8万个女性在那年消失了。

据此估算，在1985—1995年间，"消失的女性"人数在34.2万—147万人之间，占女性出生率的3%—15%，也就是说在这段期间，共有1068万名"消失的女性"。

表4-2 1982—1995年中国各地区的出生性别比

地区	1982	1989	1995
中国	108.5	111.3	115.6
北京	107.0	107.1	112.4
天津	107.7	110.4	110.5
河北	108.2	110.9	115.2
山西	109.4	110.1	112.0
内蒙古	106.8	108.5	110.0
辽宁	107.1	110.5	111.4
吉林	107.8	107.8	109.6
黑龙江	106.9	107.3	110.0
上海	105.4	104.1	104.8
江苏	107.9	113.8	123.4
浙江	108.8	116.7	115.2
安徽	112.5	111.3	116.4
福建	108.6	109.9	122.3
江西	107.9	110.4	115.4
山东	109.9	115.0	118.8
河南	110.3	116.2	126.7
湖北	107.0	109.5	130.3
湖南	107.6	110.1	116.4
广东	110.5	111.3	123.1
广西	110.7	117.4	119.1
海南	—	116.1	124.5
四川	108.0	112.1	110.1
贵州	106.8	103.4	99.1
云南	106.2	107.3	108.5

续表

地区	1982	1989	1995
西藏	101.3	103.6	100.7
陕西	109.2	110.3	123.1
甘肃	106.3	108.4	108.6
青海	106.2	104.6	107.1
宁夏	106.2	109.7	107.4
新疆	106.1	104.1	102.0

来源：1982 年数据——中国国家统计局人口统计处和国务院共同领导下的人口普查办公室：《1982 年人口普查（主要表格）》（香港：经济信息署，1982 年）；1989 年数据——中国国家统计局：《中华人民共和国 1990 年人口普查中 10% 的样本制表》（北京：中国统计出版社，1991 年）；1995 年中国出生性别比数据来自于中国国家统计局：《中国人口统计年鉴（1996）》（北京：中国统计出版社，1996 年）；地区数据来自于 1995 年 1% 的样本调查，来自于国家统计局：《中国人口统计年鉴（1997）》（北京：中国统计出版社，1997 年），表 2-32。

表 4-3　1985—1995 年中国人口中"消失的女性"人数

年份	出生性别比	出生数	男性	女性	预期女性数	"消失的女性"人数
1985	111.4	22020000	11600000	10420000	11047619	627619
1986	112.3	23840000	12610000	11230000	12009524	779524
1987	111.0	25220000	13270000	11950000	12638095	688095
1988	108.1	24570000	12760000	11810000	12152381	342381
1989	113.9	24070000	12820000	11250000	12209524	959524
1990	114.7	23910000	12770000	11140000	12161905	1021905
1991	116.1	22580000	12130000	10450000	11552381	1102381
1992	119.0	21190000	11510000	9680000	10961905	1281905
1993	121.0	21260000	11640000	9620000	11085714	1465714
1994	121.0	21040000	11520000	9520000	10971429	1451429
1995	115.6	20630000	11060000	9570000	10533333	963333
1985—1995	114.7	250330000	133690000	116640000	127323810	10683810

来源：1985—1990 年的出生性别比来自于 Gu Baochang and Krishna Roy, "Sex Ratio at Birth in China, with Reference to Other Areas in Asia: What We Know," *Asia-Pacific Population Journal*, Vol. 10, No. 3 (September 1995), p. 20; 1991—1994 年的出生性别比来自于 William Lavely, "Unintended Consequences of China's Birth Planning Policy," Unversity of Washington, July 14, 1997; 1985—1995 年的总出生人口数和 1995 年的出生人口性别比来自于中国国家统计局：《中国人口统计年鉴（1996）》（北京：中国统计出版社，1996 年），第 372 页。

中国的出生人口从1981年以来一直维持在每年2000万—2500万人的水平,但因性别比例一直上升,所以"消失的女性"人口也愈来愈多。表4-4及表4-5显示1989年和1995年出生的人口中,"消失的女性"从70万人增至80万人,1995年以来每年约有超过100万名女性不见了。

表4-4 1989年中国各省的出生人口中"消失的女性"人数（10%的人口样本）

地区	男性	女性	性别比	预期女性数	"消失的女性"人数	占"消失的女性"比例（%）	"消失的女性"比例（%）
中国	1299880	1168165	111.28	1238032	69867	100	6.0
北京	8003	7469	107.15	7622	153	0.2	2.0
天津	7682	6959	110.39	7316	357	0.5	5.1
河北	69616	62756	110.93	66300	3544	5.1	5.6
山西	34039	30904	110.14	32417	1513	2.2	4.9
内蒙古	21878	20156	108.54	20836	680	1.0	3.4
辽宁	33261	30140	110.49	31678	1574	2.3	5.2
吉林	25355	23524	107.78	24147	623	0.9	2.6
黑龙江	33055	30797	107.33	31480	683	1.0	2.2
上海	8224	7897	104.14	7832	−65	−0.1	−0.8
江苏	74182	65185	113.80	70648	5463	7.8	8.4
浙江	33623	28805	116.73	32023	3218	4.6	11.2
安徽	73090	65642	111.35	69612	3970	5.7	6.0
福建	38353	34905	109.88	36527	1622	2.3	4.6
江西	48024	43516	110.36	45737	2221	3.2	5.1
山东	90205	78444	114.99	85907	7463	10.7	9.5
河南	121502	104553	116.21	115715	11162	16.0	10.7
湖北	70131	64019	109.55	66793	2774	4.0	4.3
湖南	76482	69490	110.06	72839	3349	4.8	4.8
广东	76047	68352	111.26	72427	4075	5.8	6.0
广西	52194	44447	117.43	49709	5262	7.5	11.8
海南	8608	7417	116.06	8198	781	1.1	10.5

续表

地区	男性	女性	性别比	预期女性数	"消失的女性"人数	占"消失的女性"比例(%)	"消失的女性"比例(%)
四川	102953	91817	112.13	98052	6235	8.9	6.8
贵州	40482	39139	103.43	38554	-585	-0.8	-1.5
云南	45194	42126	107.28	43041	915	1.3	2.2
西藏	3478	3356	103.64	3313	-43	-0.1	-1.3
陕西	42429	38484	110.25	40408	1924	2.8	5.0
甘肃	29461	27183	108.38	28058	875	1.3	3.2
青海	5337	5102	104.61	5083	-19	0.0	-0.4
宁夏	6174	5628	109.70	5880	252	0.4	4.5
新疆	20818	19989	104.15	19827	-162	-0.2	-0.8

来源：数据来源于1990年7月1日中国第四次全国人口普查的10%样本，见中国国家统计局：《中国人口统计年鉴（1991）》（北京：中国统计出版社，1991年）。

表4-5 1995年中国各省的出生人口中"消失的女性"人数
（人口的1.04%的样本）

地区	男性	女性	性别比	预期女性数	"消失的女性"人数	占"消失的女性"比例(%)	"消失的女性"比例(%)
中国	95144	82293	115.62	90616	8323	100.0	10.1
北京	562	459	122.44	535	76	0.9	16.6
天津	496	449	110.47	472	23	0.3	5.2
河北	4249	3687	115.24	4047	360	4.3	9.8
山西	2760	2464	112.01	2629	165	2.0	6.7
内蒙古	1917	1743	109.98	1826	83	1.0	4.7
辽宁	2720	2441	111.43	2590	149	1.8	6.1
吉林	1794	1637	109.59	1709	72	0.9	4.4
黑龙江	2627	2389	109.96	2502	113	1.4	4.7
上海	455	434	104.84	433	-1	0.0	-0.2
江苏	4832	3915	123.42	4602	687	8.3	17.5

续表

地区	男性	女性	性别比	预期女性数	"消失的女性"人数	占"消失的女性"比例（%）	"消失的女性"比例（%）
浙江	3003	2607	115.19	2860	253	3.0	9.7
安徽	5116	4396	116.38	4872	476	5.7	10.8
福建	2485	2032	122.29	2367	335	4.0	16.5
江西	4200	3641	115.35	4000	359	4.3	9.9
山东	4342	3655	118.80	4135	480	5.8	13.1
河南	6230	4918	126.68	5933	1015	12.2	20.6
湖北	5091	3907	130.30	4848	941	11.3	24.1
湖南	4123	3542	116.40	3927	385	4.6	10.9
广东	7033	5714	123.08	6698	984	11.8	17.2
广西	3998	3356	119.13	3808	452	5.4	13.5
海南	768	617	124.47	731	114	1.4	18.5
四川	9881	8979	110.05	9411	432	5.2	4.8
贵州	3901	3938	99.06	3715	-223	-2.7	-5.7
云南	4192	3864	108.49	3992	128	1.5	3.3
西藏	293	291	100.69	279	-12	-0.1	-4.1
陕西	2943	2391	123.09	2803	412	4.9	17.2
甘肃	2565	2362	108.59	2443	81	1.0	3.4
青海	525	490	107.14	500	10	0.1	2.0
宁夏	521	485	107.42	496	11	0.1	2.3
新疆	1521	1491	102.01	1449	-42	-0.5	-2.8

来源：数据来自于1995年对1%的人口样本的调查。中国国家统计局：《中国人口统计年鉴（1997）》（北京：中国统计出版社，1997年），第183页，表2-32。出生日期介于1994年10月1日到1995年9月30日。

高性别比例的地区从北方沿海的辽宁、南方沿海的广西到中南部的四川，在这几省覆盖的范围内，是中国女性消失最多的地方。新生儿性别比也有地区性的差异，而教育及民族也是造成新生儿性别差异的主因。学者顾宝昌和徐毅分析1990年的资料，发现性别比例正常的地区呈现两极式分布：一是经济发达、人民心态开放的地区；一是经济一直很落后的地区。①

中国人口情报研究中心从1990年的人口普查数据看出，民族不同，新生儿性别比也不同；不一样的文化及宗教，会影响其中个人对性别的看法及后代性别选择的手段。汉族占中国90%以上的人口，其新生儿性别比高达111.71（男）：100（女）。少数民族则为107.5（男）：100（女）。这和政府对少数民族宽松的生育政策有很大的关系。（例如，蒙古族的家庭可以有三个小孩，维吾尔族可以生五个，藏族则没有人数限制。）在这些少数民族的部落中，新生儿性别比也各不相同，有些部落强烈地偏好儿子，性别比例更高。超过100万人口的少数民族有18个，其中侗族、哈尼族、满族、壮族的新生儿性别比皆高于110（男）：100（女）。②

如上表所示，新生儿性别比有地区性的差异，也有市、镇、乡村的不同。图4-3显示，城市人口的新生儿性别比最低，镇比乡村高。人口学家顾宝昌和徐毅认为，这是因为镇包含了流动人口，它的高性别比例值得研究。③

性别比例也和出生顺序及家庭组成有关。第二胎以后，性别比例开始攀升，例如，1989年第一胎的性别比例是105.2（男）：100（女），第二胎升至121.0（男）：100（女）。对全国总体性别比例而言，大多数人不只生一胎。一如印度，即使不实行独生子女政策，中国人对第一胎的性别较无偏见，父母多数愿意不做性别选择，但以后几胎就不同了，这便产生了高度扭曲的总体性别比。从扭曲的高性别比例数据可见，性别选择行为仍旧存在。表4-6显示了1981—1993年根据出生顺序得到的性别比例。

---

① Gu Baochang and Xu Yi, "A Comprehensive Discussion of the Birth Gender Ratio in China," *Chinese Journal of Population Science*, Vol. 6, No. 4. (1994), p. 423.

② Gu Baochang and Xu Yi, "A Comprehensive Discussion of the Birth Gender Ratio in China," *Chinese Journal of Population Science*, Vol. 6, No. 4. (1994), p. 423.

③ Ibid., p. 422.

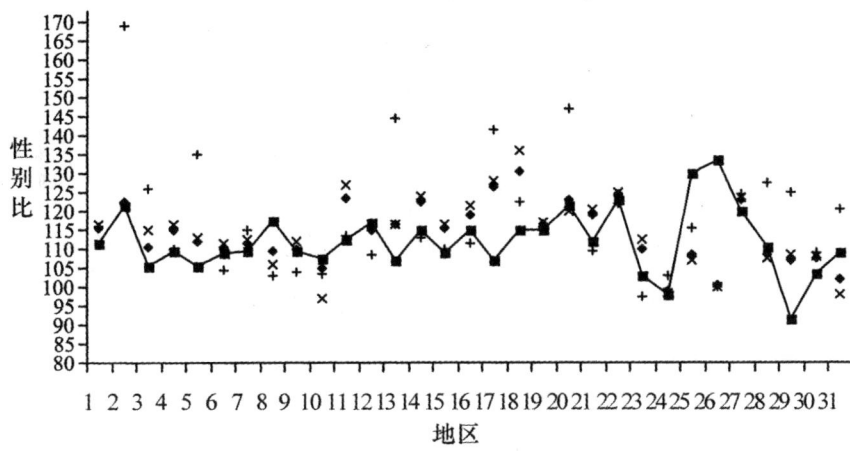

图 4-3　1994—1995 年中国城市、镇、乡村的新生儿性别比

表 4-6　1981—1993 年按出生顺序报告的中国出生人口性别比

（每 100 个女性对应的男性）

年份	第一	第二	第三	第四	第五及以上	总出生
1981	105.1	106.7	111.3	106.5	114.1	107.1
1982	106.6	105.2	109.4	112.9	109.9	107.2
1983	107.8	107.2	109.5	104.7	112.1	107.9
1984	102.5	113.3	113.0	115.3	127.3	108.5
1985	106.6	115.9	114.1	126.9	117.3	111.4
1986	105.4	116.9	123.1	125.3	123.5	112.3
1987	106.8	112.8	118.9	118.6	124.6	110.0
1988	101.5	114.5	117.1	123.1	108.7	108.1
1989	105.2	121.0	124.3	131.7	129.8	113.9
1990	—	—	—	—	—	114.7
1991	110.8	122.6	124.3	—	—	116.1
1992	106.7	125.7	126.7	—	—	114.2
1993	105.6	130.2	126.1	—	—	114.1

来源：Gu Baochang and Krishna Roy, "x Ratio at Birth in China, with Reference to Other Areas in Asia: What We Know," *Asia-Pacific Population Journal*, Vol. 10, No. 3（September1995），p. 24，table 3.

拥护独生子女政策的家庭是少数的。在独生子女政策执行的最初几年，根据生育率的调查，获得独生子女证（决定只要一个小孩的家庭，可以得到教育及工作上的方便）的妇女比例相当低，只占乡村被调查女性的3.8%，占城市被调查女性的14.4%。① 得到独生子女证的母亲，60%有一个儿子，40%有一个女儿。在乡村，得到独生子女证的母亲中，64%有儿子；在城市得到独生子女证的母亲中，55%有儿子。摩尔（Trent Wade Moore）说："虽然不签署独生子女证会受到严格的处罚，例如食物分配变少，子女受教育及工作的机会皆受影响等……但许多乡下人宁可被罚，放弃独生子女的各项优惠，也要多生一个。"② 在1991年，育龄已婚妇女中，只有18%签订计生协议书，其中有三分之二都生了儿子。③ 虽然计划生育政策带来了压力，但很少有人心甘情愿只生一个孩子。值得一提的是，中国生育率开始下降，在1990年是2.25%，在1997年，估计已降至2.0%—2.1%。④

从1989年的普查数据中，学者李涌平和高凌发现，第二胎以后的性别和他们兄姊的人数正相关。在乡村中，如果第一胎是女的，第

---

① Li Jieping and Shao Wei, "Single Childern and Their Mothers," in China Population Information Center, *Analysis on China's National One-per-Thousand Population Fertility Sampling Survey* (Beijing: China Population Information Center, 1984), p. 147.

② Ternt Wade Moore, "Fertility in China, 1982 – 1990: Grnder Equality as a Complement to Wealth Flows Theory," *Population Rsesarch and Policy Review*, Vol. 17, No. 2 (April 1998), pp. 197 – 222, at p. 198.

③ Ibid., p. 198.

④ 关于1990年生育率，参见 Gu Baochang and Krishna Roy, "Sex Ratio at Birth in China, with Reference to Other Areas in Asia: What We Know," *Asia-Pacific Population Journal*, Vol. 10, No. 3 (September 1995), p. 22。尽管中国政府宣称1997年总体人口生育率是1.8%，但中国人口学家并不认可这一数字。1997年10月12日，国际人口科学联盟（IUSSP）大会在北京举行。中国人口情报研究中心的徐毅不断提及2.1%是中国总体人口生育率，南京学者冯九璋以及其他到场的学者都予以支持。北京大学教授曾毅也称2.0%是偏低的。有关会议报告，参见"China's One Child Policy, Two Child Reality", a Report from U. S. Embassy Beijing, October 1997, http://www.usembassy-china.org.cn/english/sandt/fert21.htm。

二胎的性别比例是 138（男）：100（女），第三、四、五胎分别是 188（男）：100（女）、182（男）：100（女）及 204（男）：100（女）。已有一子的家庭中，以后几胎的性别比例依序是 101（男）：100（女）、108（男）：100（女）及 128（男）：100（女）。家中已有两个儿子的，下一胎的性别比例很低。[①] 就像在印度，当生育率下降时，对儿子的偏好加强了，前面几胎的性别比例也增高了。

除了地区和民族差异，母亲的教育程度也影响了新生儿性别比例。中国学者对于 1989 年人口普查数据的研究，揭示出母亲受教育程度与其子女性别比的关联。小学程度以下的母亲，新生儿性别比为 112.5（男）：100（女）；小学程度的母亲，新生儿性别比为 114.2（男）：100（女）；初中程度的母亲，新生儿性别比为 116.2（男）：100（女）；大专程度的母亲，新生儿性别比降到 110.7（男）：100（女）。[②] 与印度不同的是，在中国，教育会减少性别歧视及对女性的伤害。

七、性别比例不断上升的原因

大多数学者对于中国子女性别选择的程度，在认知上有很大的差异。有些学者认为女性的消失，是因为在普查时低估了女性人口以及未列入被收养的女婴人数；其他学者则认为，这是堕胎及杀女婴的结果。

（一）女性人口被低估

北京大学人口研究所及中国人口情报研究中心的学者曾毅、涂

[①] Cited in Gu and Xu, "A Comperhensive Discussion of the Birth Gender Ratio in China," p. 424.

[②] Ibid., p. 422.

平、顾宝昌、徐毅、李伯华和李涌平等人认定,中国性别比例过高是因为女性人口被低估了。他们认为父母比较愿意登记儿子身份以确定法律继承权,无论他的出生顺序为何,或是自己会受到什么样的惩罚。父母会把女婴"藏起来",接受他人领养,在她出生过后一段时间,再以认养身份为其办户口,或是根本不替她办户口。① 有学者研究河北及陕西的生育率,发现绝大多数的母亲是在医院外生产,没有医生、护士或助产士的协助,所以很容易隐瞒女婴的出生。②

顾宝昌和徐毅的说法则是:不但父母会隐瞒女孩的出生,连地方官员也会知情不上报。③ 果真如此吗? 曾毅的报告代表中国官方的立场:他们从1989年人口普查数据中得到的结论是,出生统计的错误(少报了女性人口) 对性别比例歧高的贡献占50%—75%。④

顾宝昌和徐毅注意到,统计上的错误不能解释国内所有地区女性的消失。据浙江及山东省的数据,男女出生人数都有不同程度的被低估情况。⑤ 地方官员比家长们更频繁地低估新生儿人数。地方官员认为男婴被低估的人数实际超过女婴,顾和徐却不以为然。父母害怕被强迫进行输卵管结扎手术,特别对于那些没有儿子的家庭而言,更容易瞒报女婴出生人数。为了反诘那些不承认存在瞒报现象的人,曾毅

---

① Zeng Yi, Tu Ping, Gu Baochang, Xu Yi, Li Bohua, and Li Yongping, "Causes and Implications of the Recent Increase in the Reported Sex Ratio at Birth in China," *Population and Development Review*, Vol. 19, No. 2 (June 1993), p. 290.

② Wen Xingyan, "Effect of Son Preference and Population Policy on Sex Ratios at Birth in Two Provinces of China," *Journal of Biosocial Science*, Vol. 25, No. 4 (October 1993), p. 518.

③ Gu and Xu, "A Comprehensive Discussion of the Birth Gender Ratio in China," p. 424.

④ 北京大学和中国人口情报研究中心组成的学术团队的研究成果在1992年10月19—23日第四届北京人口普查国际讨论会上首度公布,参见 Zeng Yi, Gu Baochang, Tu Ping, Xu Yi, Li Bohua, and Li Yongping, "Analyses on the Origins and Consequences of the Increase in China's Gender Ratio at Birth," *Population and Economy*, Vol. 1 (1993);另一篇包含他们研究成果的文章,见 "Causes and Implications of the Recent Increase in the Reported Sex Ration at Birth in China," *Population and Development Review*, Vol. 19, No. 2 (June 1993)。

⑤ Gu and Xu, "A Comprehensive Discussion of the Birth Gender Ratio in China," p. 424.

的团队用反向存活方法（reverse survival method）来估算，约有2.26%的男婴及5.94%的女婴的出生人数是被低估的。① 西方人口学家柯尔（Ansley Coale）及巴纳斯特（Judith Banister）不同意这种说法。他们指出1990年的人口普查中，男女婴被低估的比例与1982年的普查相同②，而1990年以后出生的数据是准确的。

我们认为父母有低报女婴数字，但地方官员也有高报女婴数字。莱夫利（William Lavely）把1990年中国人口普查的数据与其他公开数据相对照，发现有足够的证据证明地方官员高报女婴的出生率。③如果这一情形反映了国家趋势，那么在一些情形中家庭低报的女婴数字可能少于官方高报的数字。基于这些理由，我们认为低估女婴的人数不能解释为什么中国的性别比例这么高。

（二）领养

斯滕·约翰逊（Sten Johansson）与奥拉·纳根（Ola Nygren）判断，20世纪80年代中国有一半"消失的女性"是被他人领养了，所以亲生父母未报她们的户口。④ 约翰逊等人计算出1987年被领养的小孩约为50万人，其中80%是女婴⑤，这约为那年消失女性人数的一半。在凯伊·乔纳森（Kay Johnson）等人1995—1996年的研究中发现，性别、出生顺序及其他家庭成员的性别构成的性别是婴儿被抛弃

---

① Zeng et al., "Causes and Implications of the Recent Increase in the Reported Sex Ratio at Birth in China," p. 285.
② Ansley J. Coale and Judith Banister, "Five Decades of Missing Females in China," *Demography*, Vol. 31, No. 3 (August 1994), p. 476.
③ William Lavely, communication with Valerie Hudson, September 26, 2000.
④ Sten Johansson and Ola Nygren, "The Missing Girls of China: A New Demographic Account," *Population and Development Review*, Vol. 17, No. 1 (March 1991), pp. 35 – 51.
⑤ Sten Johansson, Zhao Xuan, and Ola Nygren, "On Intriguing Sex Ratios among Live Births in China in the 1980s," *Journal of Official Statistics*, Vol. 7, No. 1 (1991), http://www.jos.nu/Articles/abstract.asp? article = 7125.

的主要原因。根据他们的统计,在 237 个弃婴中,90% 是女性,87% 没有兄弟,95% 是次女、三女或四女。① 所以弃婴的特征都是:刚出生的健康女孩,家里已有姐姐,没有哥哥。她被抛弃是因为父母想要儿子。亲生父母都说其实不想把女儿送人,政府的计划生育政策让他们"别无选择"。②

领养问题很难一下说清。在生育调查中,确实涉及领养的孩子,但并没有涉及领养的时间,因此,人口学家们无法认定领养与瞒报出生人数具有直接关联。根据人口学家的发现,在河北和陕西领养的女婴比男婴多(领养的性别比例在此两省分别为 38.9% 及 73.6%),但被领养的儿童人数很少(在河北是 75 人,陕西是 158 人)③,无法与"消失的女性"人数相比。柯尔及巴纳斯特也同意领养儿童不能作为解释人口普查数据中"消失的女性"的理由,因为"她们是领养家庭的成员,并且家庭大概会给她们上户口以申请有关福利"。④

(三) 性别选择性的堕胎及杀婴

1980 年以来,稳定上升的人口性别比例告诉我们,除了低报及领养女婴之外,一定还有别的原因。柯尔及巴纳斯特认为:"在 20 世纪 80 年代,西方的人口学家无法确定过高的新生儿性别比是否因为堕胎造成的,因为那时鉴定胎儿性别的技术还不存在。但到了 1992 年,中国政府及学者透露,这项技术已被广泛地使用了。"⑤ 20 世纪 70 年代末期,中国开始进口超音波仪器,并于 20 世纪 80 年代大量进口,

---

① Kay Johnson, Huang Banghan, and Wang Liyao, "Infant Abandonment and Adoption in China," *Population and Development Review*, Vol. 24, No. 3 (September 1998), pp. 469 – 481, at p. 475.

② Ibid. , p. 477.

③ Wen, "Effect of Son Preference and Population Policy on Sex Ratios," p. 51.

④ Coale and Banister, "Five Decades of Missing Females in China," p. 475

⑤ Ibid.

据人口学家的说法,当时中国也已开始自己制造相关仪器。① 在1991年底,2227个县有了计划生育中心,乡镇共有29000个计划生育诊所,每县平均有12台超音波仪器。顾宝昌和徐毅评估,到了1994年,中国至少有10万台超音波仪器。就算只有部分的诊所以超音波来侦测胎儿性别及堕胎(两者在中国皆属非法),其后果也十分严重。②

超音波仪器的影响,可以从1989年山东、河南、广东、江苏、福建、江西及山西的性别比例从109.4(男):100(女)上升至115.6(男):100(女)看出。③ 1993年,纪思道(Nicholas Kristof)提出在1992年中国的性别比例达到118.5(男):100(女)。④ 厦门的村民告诉他,由于可以堕胎,"去年我们全村只生了一个女孩,其他的都是男孩"。村民再解释:"只要给医生35—50元的贿赂,医生就会告诉你怀的是男孩还是女孩,是女孩的话,可以马上打掉。"纪思道后来证实,只要送给医生一条烟,他就会告诉你怀的是男孩还是女孩。⑤

有学者指出,通过医院检查可以评估超音波仪器和性别比例的关系。他认为医院检查是瞒报、遗弃或杀婴的前兆,并且发现华西医院报告在29省及945家医院的新生儿性别比,1986—1987年是108.0(男):100(女),至1991年上升至109.7(男):100(女)。⑥ 当然,可以认为女性知道自己怀的是女儿,拒绝在医院生产,以便瞒

---

① Gu and Xu, "A Comprehensive Discussion of the Birth Gender Ratio in China," p. 425.
② Ibid.
③ Ibid., p. 427. 独生子女政策实行前几年,堕胎率猛增。1978年,共实施5391000起堕胎,但1982年数量增长到12412000起。整个20世纪80年代堕胎率都保持每年平均11010000起。1989年之前,全中国每1000个新生儿中就有632个被堕掉。其中,堕胎数最少的辽宁省,181个;堕胎数较多的上海,2022个。
④ Krisof, "Chinese Turn to Ultrasound," p. A4.
⑤ Krisof, "Chinese Turn to Ultrasound," p. A4.
⑥ Xu, "A Quest on the Causes of Gender Imbalance in China."

报、遗弃或杀婴的行为逃过官方的监督。但这并不足以解释这五年中新生儿性别比的上升。

尽管中国每年超音波仪器和堕胎的数量表明通过检测的性别选择和堕胎在发生，但坚实的数据难以取得。根据顾宝昌和徐毅的观点："高性别比例的地区通常也是超音波仪器最多的地区。"① 巴纳斯特估计，从1980年中期至1990年，中国有选择性地堕掉了150万个女胎。这个数字比起20世纪80年代中每年"消失的女性"人口来说是太少了。②

除了堕胎，造成中国高性别比的原因还有杀女婴（直接或间接）。中国人口及信息研究中心承认，尽管法律禁止，许多女婴仍被淹死或被丢弃。遗弃也是造成高性别比的一个原因，因为被遗弃的多为女婴。虽然有些女婴被收容在孤儿院，但这些"死亡之室"的设施太差，只有很少的婴儿能够存活下来。

在1949年解放后的头30年内，杀女婴的状况几乎没有获得重视，但到了1982年，中国的报纸开始报道杀女婴问题，公众开始注意到这个问题了。③ 1983年，中宣部要求："保护女婴及母亲，社会不该排斥她们，父母及公婆、亲属也不该虐待她们。"④ 除了女婴之外，有报道医生主动杀死第三个小孩或任何未被母亲工作单位批准生出的婴儿。⑤ 女人违反政策怀孕后，除了堕胎，几乎没有选择，就算胎儿被保住了，医生也会在其出生时，迅速使之窒息而死，以逃避"违反

---

① Gu and Xu, "Comprehensive Discussion of the Birth Gender Ration in China," p. 426.

② Quoted in Rick Weiss, "Anti-Girl Bias Rises in Asla, Studies Show: Abortion Angmenting Infanticide, Neglect," *Washington Post*, May 11, 1996, p. A1.

③ John S. Aird, *Slaughter of the Innocents: Coercive Birth Control in China* (Washington, D. C.: AEI Press, 1990).

④ H. Yuan Tien, "Provincial Fertility Trends and Patterns," in Elisabeth Croll, Delia Davin, and Penny Kane, eds., *China's One-Child Family Policy* (New York: St. Martin's Press, 1985), p. 131.

⑤ See Aird, *Slaughter of the Innocents*, pp. 91 – 92.

计划生育"的罪名及处罚。① 不杀婴的后果要比杀婴严重得多。对杀女婴的处罚，各省不同，但执行与否，就要看被控违法的母亲的工作单位了。李晓荣说，政府一般无法惩罚杀女婴的行为。②

八、政府关注过高的性别比例

中国政府的人口政策致力于减少人口总数，但较少关注性别比例问题。过去十年内，政府做了五个有关生育的普查，并且注意到了新生儿性别比的增长。政府颁布法令禁止产前胎儿性别检查，并规定："严格禁止通过技术方式鉴定胎儿性别，除非出于和医疗有关；违反规定者将取消其从医执照。"③1991年，时任全国计划生育委员会主任的彭佩云宣布，下一个五年计划要研究新生儿性别比例的问题。1993年3月，党中央就计划生育开了一次工作会，彭佩云提出新生儿性别比上升的问题，并获得《中国人口报》及《人民日报》的报道，这是第一次全国性的报纸报道国家领导人承认新生儿性别比是有问题的。④

中西方在解读中国人口数据时有所不同，中国学者倾向于认为统计错误导致了过高的性别比例，而西方学者认为性别选择性堕胎和杀婴是主要因素。⑤ 目前，性别比例的话题在中国较少公开讨论，而中国官方发言也对性别比例问题关注不足。⑥ 2000年12月18日，国务院信息中心发表了《中国21世纪人口与发展》白皮书，提到中国必须改变对女孩的歧视态度，谴责虐待女孩及禁止杀女婴，但对选择性

---

① Li, "License to Coerce," p. 163.
② Ibid., pp. 167 – 168.
③ Li, "License to Coerce," pp. 169 – 170.
④ Gu and Xu, "A Comprehensive Discussion of the Birth Gender Ration in China," p. 429.
⑤ Ibid., p. 419.
⑥ Tien, *China's Strategic Demographic Intiative*, p. 190.

的堕胎，则只字未提。尽管没有官方讨论，但一些省份已经开始严禁堕女胎了。

中国人口的官方数据质量也许受到影响。赫伯特·史密斯（Herbert Smith）最近在研究中国人口生育率时，提到中国政府所提供的人口及计划生育数据："在中国及其他地方，统计被视为一种中立的观察方式。只是在官方的统计系统中，政治考虑决定了哪些因素可以被测量、应该如何测量以及如何解释它的结果。"①所有的数据都必须上报，经过审核，然后才能发表。

除了要完成国内的人口发展目标，国际舆论的压力也很大，美国尤其关注中国的人口政策。中外媒体也爱夸大人口问题，并迅速予以报道，也许出于无意，它们还会把新生儿性别比报道成总人口的性别比例。

中国的人口学家致力于对人口数字作出正确的评估，以正视听。1997年在北京举行的"人口科学研究国际联盟"会议上，他们断言中国政府公布的生育率数字过低。此外，他们认为，1995年的人口普查数据（人口样本只有1.04%）不够准确，所以他们采用1990年的人口普查数据作为计算的基础。他们还说，中国人口太多，因此生育率及其他相关数据是不可能准确的。②

九、婴儿的死亡率

在正常的情况下，婴儿的死亡率以男婴为高。在第一年中，每100个女婴死亡就有130个男婴死亡，因为男婴的先天疾病较多。③

---

① Herbert L. Smith, Tu Ping, M. Giovanna Merli, and Mark Hereward, "Implementation of a Demographic and Contraceptive Surveillance System in Four Counties in North China," *Population Research and Policy Review*, Vol. 16, No. 4 (August 1997), p. 292.

② "China's One-Child Policy, Tow-Child Reality."

③ 瑞典学者约翰逊和奈根通过计算发展中国家和发达国家的死亡婴儿的性别比得出这一数据。参见 Johansson and Nygren, "The Missing Girls of China," p. 48。

但在中国，一如印度，女婴死亡率反而比较高。目前，对于婴儿死亡率的统计数字并不完整，且中外学者都不认可这一数据。根据顾宝昌和徐毅的观点，最新研究表明1989年女婴死亡率较高——男婴死亡率从1981年的38.84‰降到1990年的35.5‰，女婴死亡率则从36.87‰上升到40.4‰。① 一如新生儿性别比，婴儿死亡率的数据也依其来源而异。例如，根据美国人口普查局国际数据库记录的中国婴儿死亡率，1990年男婴是39.69‰，女婴65.88‰。美国人口学家朱迪思·巴纳斯特（Judith Banister）则认为，婴儿死亡率要低得多。1992年在北京举行的1990年中国人口普查国家论坛上，巴纳斯塔提交了一份论文，指出男婴死亡率为28.2‰，女婴死亡率为32.7‰。② 巴纳斯特的研究结论与顾宝昌和徐毅的一致，男婴死亡率的下降比女婴快得多。1990年中国的人口普查显示，男婴死亡率为32.2‰，女婴死亡率为36.8‰。③ 图4-4是从最近的两次人口普查和巴纳斯特的数据得来的，它显示男婴死亡率的下降及女婴死亡率的上升。

但无论资料来源为何，目前女婴死亡率高于男婴。但中国1岁以下婴儿死亡的性别比例依据表源为61%—88%（男婴死亡数/每100个女婴死亡），而正常值为130%。表4-7给出了1989—1990年间，中国女婴的超额死亡人数。这个数据逐年增高，而且还在持续增高中。

---

① Gu and Xu, "A Comprehensive Discussion of the Birth Gender Ratio in China," pp. 426 – 427.

② Judith Banister, "Implications and Quality of China's 1990 Census Data," paper presented at the International Seminar on China's 1990 Population Census, Beijing, China, Octorber 1992, Cited in Daniel Goodkind, "On Substituting Sex Preference Strategies in East Asia: Does Prenatal Sex Selection Reduce Postnatal Discrimination?" *Population and Development Review*, Vol. 22, No. 1 (March 1996), p. 117.

③ Reported in William Lavely, "Unintended Consequences of China's Birth Planning Policy," University of Washington, July 14, 1997.

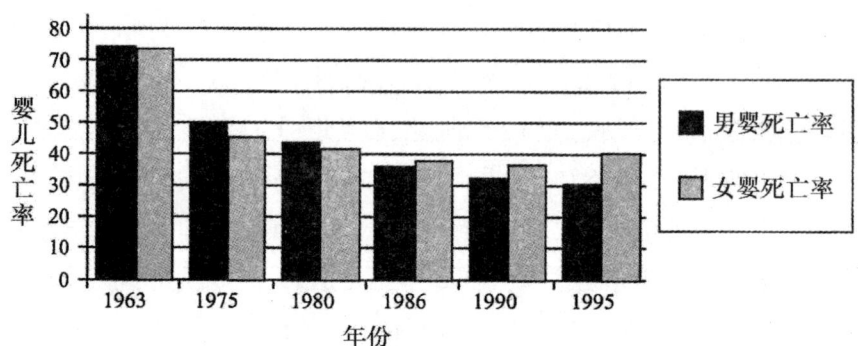

图 4-4　中国男婴与女婴死亡率（1966—1995）

来源：1963 年——Yasuko Hayase, and Seiko Kawamata, *Population Policy and Vital Statistics in China* (Tokyo: Institute of Developing Economies, 1991), Table 8；1975 年、1980 年和 1986 年——中国国家统计局：《中国人口统计年鉴（1989）》（北京：中国统计出版社，1989 年）；1990 年——ajusted rate for1990 census, reported in William Lavely, "Unintended Consequences of China's Birth Planning Policy," University of Washington, July 14, 1997；1995 年——中国国家统计局：《中国人口统计年鉴（1996）》（北京：中国统计出版社，1996 年）。

表 4-7　1989—1990 年中国 1 岁以下女婴的超额死亡数

数据来源	男婴死亡率[a]	女婴死亡率	女婴出生率	预期的婴儿死亡率[b]	估算的死亡数[c]	预期的死亡数[d]	超额的死亡数
巴纳斯特	28.2	32.7	11655803	22.0	318145	256428	124717
国家统计局	32.2	36.8	11655803	24.8	428934	289064	139870
顾宝昌和徐毅	35.5	40.4	11655803	28.0	470894	326362	144532
美国国际数据库	39.7	65.9	11655803	31.0	768117	361330	406787

来源：女婴死亡数来自于 1990 年中国人口普查数据，见顾宝昌、徐毅：《中国婴儿出生性别比综论》，载《中国人口科学》，第 6 卷，1994 年第 3 期，第 417—431 页；Judith Banister, reported in Daniel Goodkind, "On Substituting Sex Preference Strategies in East Asia: Does Prenatal Sex Selection Reduce Postnatal Discrimination?" *Population and Development Review*, Vol. 22, No. 1 (March 1996), p. 111-125；顾宝昌、徐毅：《中国婴儿出生性别比综论》；and U. S. Bureau of the Census, International Data Base, 1998.

a. 婴儿死亡率是指每 1000 个出生婴儿中不满周岁死亡的人数。
b. 预期的婴儿死亡率的计算方法如下：假设的男婴死亡率/每 130 个女婴死亡数。
c. 估算的死亡数是通过出生人口数和有记录的女婴死亡率计算得出的。
d. 预期的死亡数是通过预期的婴儿死亡率计算得出的。

婴儿死亡率与其出生顺序有关。无论男女，出生得越晚，存活率就越低，但男婴的存活率还是高于女婴。史蒂夫·任（Steve Ren）研究中国了三个省份，发现第四胎及以后女婴的存活率只有第一胎的41%，男婴存活率则为第一胎的63%。① 由于父母优先照顾已有孩子，出生顺序越靠后，获得生存资源的机会越小。婴儿的存活率和母亲的教育程度也有关，尤其是女婴。史蒂夫·任的解释是："母亲的教育程度是衡量她社会地位的指标，对女婴的存活也有决定性影响。"② 和印度不同，一个受过教育的中国母亲较为尊重女性和同为女性的女儿。

统计数据显示，在正常的情况下，4岁以下男孩的死亡率是女孩的1.11—1.24倍。但在中国，2岁以下女孩的死亡率较高。中国1995年的数据显示，2岁女孩死亡率为3.123%，男孩为3.081%；到了3岁，女孩死亡率降到1.918%，男孩为2.228%；4岁时，女孩死亡率再降到1.410%，男孩为1.426%；5岁时，女孩死亡率为0.894%，男孩为1.041%。③ 也就是说，3岁和5岁时，两性的存活率才处于正常范围，而1岁、2岁、4岁时，女孩死亡率较高，并受到歧视。拿这些数据与1989年新生儿性别比例相比较，能够观察到在生命前四年，性别比例一直很高，而在正常人口中，性别比例通常会在1岁以后下降，稳定保持在105—107（男）：100（女）之下的正常水平。表4-8显示在1953—1996年间的大多数年份中，1岁儿童的性别比例明显升高，1岁以后性别比例畸形的持续增高至4岁。

---

① Xinhua Steve Ren, "Sex Differences in Infant and Child Mortality in Three Provinces in China," *Social Science and Medicine*, Vol. 40, No. 9 (May 1995), pp. 1263 – 1264.

② Ibid., pp. 1265 – 1266.

③ Data from China, State Statistical Bureau, *China Population Statistical Yearbook*, *1996* (Beijing: China Statistics Press, 1996), p. 77, Table 3 – 9.

表 4-8　1953—1996 年中国 4 岁以下人口性别比

年份	0 岁	1 岁	2 岁	3 岁	4 岁	1—4 岁
1953	104.88	105.58	106.59	108.62	109.38	107.32
1957	105.41	—	—	—	—	106.45
1963	105.59	—	—	—	—	105.44
1964	103.83	105.31	106.38	106.96	108.68	106.47
1975	106.63	—	—	—	—	104.86
1982	107.63	107.82	107.35	106.71	106.19	107.00
1987	112.24	114.74	110.39	95.88	101.13	110.05
1989	112.54	110.26	108.03	110.59	108.75	109.38
1990	111.68	111.68	110.13	109.28	108.36	109.88
1994	116.30	119.43	119.58	115.18	113.07	116.30
1995	116.57	121.08	121.26	119.17	115.01	118.82
1996	116.16	120.89	121.32	120.83	120.94	120.99

来源：1953 年、1964 年和 1982 年——China, Population Census Office under the State Council and the Department of Population Statistics of the State Statistical Bureau, *The 1982 Population Census of China*（*Major Figures*）（Hong Kong: Economic Information Agency, 1982）；1957、1963、1975 和 1987 年——Hasuko Hayase and Seiko Kawamata, Population Policy and Vital Statistics in China（Tokyo: Institue of Developing Economies, 1991）；1989 年——中国国家统计局：《中国人口统计年鉴（1990）》（北京：中国统计出版社，1990 年）；1990 年——中国国家统计局：《中国人口统计年鉴（1991）》（北京：中国统计出版社，1991 年）；1994 年——中国国家统计局：《中国人口统计年鉴（1995）》（北京：中国统计出版社，1995 年）；1995 年——中国国家统计局：《中国人口统计年鉴（1996）》（北京：中国统计出版社，1996 年）；1996 年——中国国家统计局：《中国人口统计年鉴（1997）》（北京：中国统计出版社，1997 年）。

十、"消失的女性"及中国的单身汉

在中国全部的人口中，有多少女性消失了？根据 2000 年的普查，中国共有 6.53 亿个男性以及 6.12 亿个女性，这代表有 4100 万个女性消失了，或是有 4100 万个多出来的男性。在 1990 年，这个数字只有 3500 万人。在这群过剩的男性中，超过半数是属于 15—34 岁的年龄层。表4-9显示，过剩的男性人数还在增加中。①

表4-9 1964—2000年中国过剩的男性人口

年份	15—34岁之间的男性总人数	15—34岁之间的过剩男性数量	所有年龄段的男性总数	过剩的男性总数
1964	110357642	10677546	356517011	18452263
1982	191184794	13193750	519406895	30661653
1990	226020631	14857587	585476497	35877844
2000	—	—	653550000	41270000

来源：1964年和1982年——China, Population Census Office under the State Council and the Department of Population Statistics of the State Statistical Bureau, *The 1982 Population Census of China*（*Major Figures*）（Hong Kong：Economic Information Agency，1982；1990年——中国国家统计局：《中国人口统计年鉴（1991）》（北京：中国统计出版社，1991年）；2000年——根据2000年人口普查初步数据计算得出。

中国存在大量未婚男子的问题吸引了国际媒体的目光。报道说，在1992年，中国有4800万名未婚男子（25岁以上），如果目前新生儿性别比继续下去的话，这一人数很快就会增加到8000万人。② 也有数据称，中国可能已经有9000万个单身汉了。③

① 2000年按年龄划分的人口普查数据还无法获得；因此，我们无法提供任一特定年龄群的过剩人口数字。

② Ren, "Confronting Three Populations of 80 Million."文章作者根据1991年的统计数据计算出8000万的数字，指出那年出生的2300万人口中，1330万是男性，970万是女性，总共有360万过剩男性。推展至未来，作者预测，10年之内（到20世纪末为止），会有3600万过剩男性人口，加上当前的4800万过剩男性人口，不久的将来，中国将有8000万单身汉。这估算一方法有几个问题：1991年数据显示的新生儿性别比例是115（男）：100（女），而不是137（男）：100（女），因此那年大概有160万过剩男性人口出生，而非360万。作者使用137（男）：100（女）是不准确的，而判断以后年份新生儿性别比不同寻常的高，则更不准确。此外，我们注意到，单身男性人数显然不同于实际上的过剩男性人数。尽管中国有4800万单身汉，他们中很多人还是会结婚的。我们认为，计算过剩男性人口，可能保守，但更接近中国单身男性人口的真实数据。

③ Hutchings, "Female Infanticide 'Will Lead to Army of Bachelors.'"哈钦斯引用一位中国记者的说法，该记者引述中国新生儿性别比为131（男）：100（女），每年新生儿出生人数2500万，当前总人口中有4600万未婚单身男性。此外，自1990年以来，出生人口数字一直远远低于2500万，并正在下降。

新生儿性别比持续增高，对20年以后的中国会有什么样的影响呢？目前多出来的男性与多出来的男婴相比，还算少的，因为在15—34岁之间的绝大多数男性都是在1980年至1990年间大力实施独生子女政策以前出生的。我们以1985—1995年的出生人口及性别统计数字为基础来预测2020年的人口数据。1995年以后出生人口数字，采用对1995—2004年减少的出生人口数和新生儿性别的保守估计。最后，利用中国寿命表中生命存活比来预估2020年的人口数据。结果见表4-10及表4-11。我们发现到2020年，在15—34岁的群体中，将有2900万至3300万过剩男性，是目前的两倍。

表4-12将我们的数据与联合国、世界银行的数据作一比较。我们对15—34岁族群整体人数的评估与它们的类似，其中男性的人口也与联合国的类似，略高于世界银行数据。我们之间主要的不同在于计算性别比例以及女性人口。联合国及世界银行计算的性别比例为107（男）：100（女），性别比例这么低，那么新生儿性别比也得低到相应的水平，男婴女婴的死亡率差距也都得相对降低。但这是不可能的，因为到2020年15—43岁的人群已经具有高性别比例和非常高的差异死亡率了。

中国政府对未来人口的预测又是如何呢？在2000年12月的《中国21世纪人口与发展白皮书》上，政府计划，到2010年"普遍实行避孕措施的知情权，出生性别比趋于正常"。但为什么要降低出生性别比呢？白皮书中并未提及，它只是说："动员全社会关心和帮助女童、残疾儿童、离异家庭儿童、特困儿童、流浪儿童，禁止溺婴、弃婴，严厉惩治虐待、残害、拐卖少年儿童的违法犯罪行为。"

表 4-10 2020 年中国 15—34 岁的男性和女性人口预测

年份	出生性别比[a]	总出生数[b]	男性出生数	女性出生数	2020 年的男性 LTSR[c]	2020 年的女性 LTSR[d]	2020 年 15—34 岁的男性数量	2020 年 15—34 岁的女性数量
1985—89	111.3	119720000	63061983	56658017	0.9140	0.88605	57638652	50201836
1990—94	118.2	109980000	59578594	50401406	0.9212	0.89380	54883800	45048777
1995—99	115.4	101900000	54597887	47302113	0.92825	0.90088	50680488	42613528
总数							212585768	179526075
消失的女性数								33059694

a. 1985—1995 年的出生性别比，见本章的表 4-2；1996 年的出生性别比来自于国家统计局，《中国人口统计年鉴 (1997)》(北京：中国统计出版社，1997 年)；1997—2004 的出生人口性别比根据目前的出生人口性别比估算而得。

b. 1985—1996 年的中国出生人口总数，来自于国家统计局：《中国人口统计年鉴 (1997)》，表 4-10；1997—1999 年的出生人口数根据当前的出生人口总数估算而得；2000—2004 年的出生人口估算数来自于 United Nations, Department of International and Economic Social Affairs, *World Population Prospects, 1990*, Population Studies, No. 120 (New York: United Nations, 1991)。

c. LTSR 是对美国普查局 1998 年国际数据库数据加以修正而得到的，见 http://www.census.gov/ipc/www/idbnew.html，修订的 nqx 值是根据 1990 年数据（男婴死亡率是 39.69‰）修正的 1q0 值（以 1990 年数据（女婴死亡率为 65.88‰）为基础，数据来自美国人口普查局 1998 年国际数据库。

d. U.S. Bureau of the Census, *International Data Base*, 1998, Life Table Values; China/1981/Total/Female。LTSR 按上述第三条 (c) 的方法计算，修正 1981/Total/Male。婴儿 (0—1 岁) 死亡率的 nqx 值是根据年龄段 15—20 岁，20—25 岁，25—30 岁，30—35 岁。其中 x 代表年龄段 15—20 岁，20—25 岁，25—30 岁，30—35 岁。

e. LTSR 的计算公式是 LTSRx = 5Lx/5L₀，其中 x 代表年龄段 15—20 岁，20—25 岁，25—30 岁，30—35 岁。

表 4-11 2020 年中国 15—34 岁的男性和女性人口预测

年份	出生性别比	总出生数	男性出生数	女性出生数	2020年的男性LTSR[a]	2020年的女性LTSR[b]	2020年15—34岁的男性数量	2020年15—34岁的女性数量
1985—89	111.3	119720000	63061983	56658017	0.92345	0.91853	57638588	50042088
1990—94	118.2	109980000	59578594	50401406	0.93220	0.92766	55539165	46755369
1995—99	115.4	101900000	54597887	47302113	0.93737	0.92789	51178421	43391158
2000—04	115.0	98895000	52897326	45997674	0.94454	0.93525	49963640	43019325
总数							214915814	185707940
缺失的女性数								29207874

来源：来源于表 4-10 中相同，但生命表的 1q0 和 4q1 的数值不同。

a. 如同表 4-10，数据是对美国人口普查局 1998 年国际数据库数据加以修正而得到的，1990 年数据中的 1q0 被修订为 28.2，4q1 被修订为 9.3，根据巴纳斯特的 1990 年数据，参见 Daniel Goodkind, "On Substituting Sex Preference Strategies in East Asia: Does Prenatal Sex Selection Reduce Postnatal Discrimination?" *Population and Development Review*, Vol. 22, No. 1 (March 1996), p. 117, Table 1。这一生命表又被用于计算 1985—1994 年的 LSTR 值。1995—2004 年的生命表有了变化，因为根据 1995 年中国 1.04% 的抽样数据，1q0 被修订为 30.45。参见国家统计局：《中国人口统计年鉴（1996）》(北京：中国统计出版社，1996年)，第 77 页，表 3-9。

b. 女性的生命表值是对美国人口普查局 1998 年国际数据库数据加以修正而得到的，见 U. S. Bureau of the Census, International Data Base, 1998, Life Table Values: China/1981/Total/Female，同时 1q0 被修订为 32.7，4q1 被修订为 9.8，根据巴纳斯特的 1990 年数据，参见 Daniel Goodkind, "On Substituting Sex Preference Strategies in East Asia: Does Prenatal Sex Selection Reduce Postnatal Discrimination?" *Population and Development Review*, Vol. 22, No. 1 (March 1996), p. 117, Table 1。生命表又被用于计算 1985—1994 年的 LSTR 值。1995—2004 年的生命表有了变化，因为根据 1995 年中国抽样调查，1q0 被修订为 40.84。参见国家统计局：《中国人口统计年鉴（1996）》(北京：中国统计出版社，1996年)，第 77 页，表 3-9。

表 4-12 2020 年中国 15—34 岁的预测人口比较

预测类型	总人口	男性总数	女性总数	性别比	男性剩余
联合国中变量预测	417548000	216130000	201418000	107.3	14712000
联合国高变量预测	456044000	235971000	220073000	107.2	15898000
联合国低变量预测	381699000	197653000	184046000	107.4	13607000
世界银行预测	410030000	211709000	198321000	106.8	13388000
表 4-10 预测	392634000	214916000	179526000	118.4	33060000
表 4-11 预测	400624000	214916000	185708000	115.7	29208000

来源：United Nations, Department for Economic and Social Information and Policy Analysis, Population Division, *The Sex and Age Distribution of the World Populations: The 1994 Revision* (New York: United Nations, 1994); and World Bank, *World Population Projections, 1994 – 1995 Edition: Estimates and Projections with Related Demographic Statistics* (Washington, D.C.: World Bank, 1994)。

美国人口普查局也同意中国官方的预测：出生性别比到了 2020 年将会下降到 106（男）：100（女）。其中研究亚洲人口问题的研究员丹尼尔·古得金（Daniel Goodkind）说："韩国及中国台湾地区的出生性别比（SRBs）已经自峰值下降。"他认为中国大陆也是如此。[1] 但没有任何证据显示中国大陆的性别比例已到峰值，我们也不认为中国大陆的出生人口性别比将会正常化，如果重男轻女的观念还没有改变的话。

十一、结论

在本章中试图说明，中国跟印度一样，在大部分史实中都能够找到证据证明，性别不平等导致的各种形式的后代性别选择现象普遍存在，并将持续存在下去。20 世纪后期，中国经济、政治及社会的改革，与传统重男轻女的观念、生育率的降低及独生子女政策相结合，

---

[1] Daniel Goodkind, correspondence with Andrea den Boer, April 26, 2001.

反而使得杀女婴及堕女胎更为普遍。我们计算出，到了2020年，在中国15—34岁的年龄层中，将有2900万—3300万名过剩男性。在以下的第五、六、七章中，我们将讨论中国及印度人口男性化的影响，并向政策制定者提供对策。

第五章　高性别比例社会中的光棍：理论和案例

人为导致的高性别比例将带来严重的社会问题。[1]这些问题也给政府造成棘手的政策困境。布恩（James Boone）指出："生育政策对一国执政党的发展有着重要影响，个人与家庭的生育计划与国家的生育政策有着本质上的差异。"[2]我们即将讨论这种差异。

中国和印度拥有全世界一半以上的人口，这两国的性别比例都在持续地升高，继而导致无法预计的为数众多的过剩男性。这一结果是由多重因素综合作用形成的，包括杀女婴、性别选择性堕胎、幼女的高死亡率，以及女性自杀率上升等。同时，这些因素的作用下，两国都存在被夸大的性别不平等问题。

在本章中，我们将勾画一个过剩年轻男性行为理论，这一理论将从各学科出发综合理论观点与观察发现。引用19世纪中国的俗语，这群年轻男性被称为"光棍"。光棍很难找到妻子，无法成家。[3]正

---

[1] 本章讨论高性别比例社会的问题，然而低性别比例社会也一样存在负面的后果。

[2] James L. Boone, "Parental Investment and Elite Family Structure in Preindustrial States: A Case Study of Late Medieval-Early Modern Portuguese Genealogies," *American Anthropologist*, Vol. 88, No. 4 (December 1986), p. 859.

[3] 光棍是单身汉的俗称，老光棍是老单身汉的俗称。这一预言解释要感谢杨百翰大学的戴维·莱特（David Wright）的解释。Elizabeth Perry, *Rebels and Revolutionaries in North China, 1845–1945* (Stanford, Calif.: Stanford University Press, 1980).

如一位当代中国公民所描述的：这是一个比喻，说明未婚男性就像树木的光杆一样无依无靠。光棍给人一种凄凉和孤独的印象，没有温暖的家庭支持和安慰他们，也没有小孩在他们年老时孝顺他们。①

一、光棍的特征

高性别比例的社会中，过剩男性拥有很多共同特征。第一，光棍大多数处于社会最底层，他们没有筹码谈论婚嫁，多数孤独终老。这一说法的证据很丰富：从生物演化的角度来看，当雌性稀少时，无法传宗接代的都是些条件不佳的雄性。②正如第一章中所说，女性高嫁的理由是拥有高地位和财富的男性更能够吸引她。"光棍群"的概念是从对哺乳类的研究而来，它形容一群地位低下、无法接近雌性的动物③，他们群集在种群边缘等待机会取代雄性头领。在会唱歌的鸟类中，永远有一群游荡的

---

① Quoted in Ren Feng, "Bare Branches among Rural Migrant Laborers in China: Causes, Social Implications, and Policy Proposal," Foreign Affairs College, Beijing, March 1999, p. 6.

② John H. Crook, "Sexual Selection, Dimorphism, and Social Organization in the Primates," in Bernard Campbell, ed., *Sexual Selection and the Descent of Man* (Chicago: Aldine de Gruyter, 1972), pp. 231 – 281; Irven de Vore, "Male Dominance and Mating Behavior in Baboons," in Frank Ambrose Beach, ed., *Sex and Behavior* (New York: Wiley and Sons, 1965), pp. 266 – 289; Mildred Dickemann, "The Ecology of Mating Systems in Hypergynous Dowry Societies," *Social Science Information*, Vol. 18, No. 2 (May1979), pp. 163 – 195; Mildred Dickemann, "Female Infanticide, Reproductive Strategies, and Social Stratification: A Preliminary Model," in Napoleon A. Chagnon and William Irons, eds., *Evolutionary Biology and Human Social Behavior: An Anthropological Perspective* (North Scituate, Mass.: Duxbury, 1979), pp. 321 – 367.

③ S. M. Mohnot, "Peripheralization of Weaned Male Juveniles in Presbytis entellus," in David John Chivers and J. Herbert, eds., *Recent Advances in Primatology*, Vol. 1: *Behavior* (London: Academic Press, 1979), pp. 87 – 91; J. K. Russell, "Exclusion of Adult Male Coatis from Social Groups: Protection from Predation," *Journal of Mammalogy*, Vol. 62, No. 1 (February 1981), pp. 206 – 208; and Thad Q. Bartlett, Robert W. Sussman, and James M. Cheverud, "Infant Killing in Primates: A Review of Observed Cases with Specific Reference to the Sexual Selection Hypothesis," *American Anthropologist*, Vol. 95, No. 4 (December 1993), pp. 958 – 990.

雄鸟,聚集在幸运的有配偶的雄鸟周遭,随时准备取而代之。在猴子里独居的公猴和公猴群非常渴望闯入正在繁殖的公母混居的猴群。①达利(Martin Daly)和威尔逊(Margo Wilson)发现,雄性的领头者会欺压其他同性,让它们无法成长,无法社交,无法找到交配对象。

第二,在市场经济中,光棍多为失业游民,他们多屈就一些低层次、危险、重劳力、或是季节性的工作。② 1990年中国的调查报告指出,中国94%的未婚者是男性;其中73.8%没有高中学历。③

在非市场经济中,光棍缺乏土地或其他资源来吸引女性。在长子继承制的社会中,次子以降都可能会变成光棍。甚至在非长子继承制的社会如中国,长子的资源也比其他儿子多,次子只好铤而走险以冀出人头地,他们最常采取的方式就是从军。社会底层的光棍也采取这一方式。据柏恩(Boone)的说法:"许多社会底层男性被迫过着独身生活,更多的从事生产、建筑和参军入伍这类职业,试图通过危险职业和险恶条件来提升他们的道德水准。他们可怜的社会经济处境和对后代的期望使得他们长年热衷于侵略扩张和军事叛乱,或许希望能借此取得较高的社会地位。"④

第三,光棍像浮萍,他们与工作地点多无地缘关系。他们频繁地换工作,隐匿性很高。⑤ 这种隐匿性和社区归属感的缺乏一并使得光

---

① Martin Daly and Margo Wilson, *Sex, Evolution, and Behavior*: *Adaptations for Reproduction* (North Scituate, Mass.: Duxbury, 1978), p. 201.

② See David T. Courtwright, *Violent Land*: *Single Men and Social Disorder From the Frontier to the Inner City* (Cambridge, Mass.: Harvard University Press, 1996).

③ 也就是说,他们或者是文盲(17.24%),只接受了基础教育(23.13%),或者仅仅初中毕业(33.36%)。这一数据是在1987年统计的,来源于Zhang Ping, "Issues and Characteristics of the Unmarried Population," *Chinese Journal of Population Science*, Vol. 2, No. 1 (1990), pp. 87–97。

④ Boone, "Parental Investment and Elite Family Structure in Preindustrial States," p. 862.

⑤ Courtwright, Violent Land; Joan M. Nelson, "Migrants, Urban Poverty, and Instability in Developing Nations," *Occasional Papers in International Affairs* No. 22 (Cambridge, Mass.: Center for International Affairs, Harvard University, September 1969); Howard M. Bahr, ed., *Disaffiliated Man*: *Essays and Bibliography on Skid Row*, *Vagrancy and Outsiders* (Toronto: University of Toronto Press, 1970); and Gregory R. Woirol, *In the Floating Army* (Chicago: University of Illinois Press, 1992). 社会地位低下的男性劳动者的流动性是中世纪欧洲的一个公共议题。

棍放松了对自己实施犯罪行为的心理约束。就算犯罪,他们也不容易被捉到。有两位犯罪学家解释了目前的中国情形:

在经济改革以前,中国稳定的社会秩序建立在三个要素相互作用的基础之上,包括对人口流动的严格限制;单位、学校、居委会等非正式管控机制;以及社会中基于意识形态和道德的对人的拘束。但现在这个管理机制被大规模的流动人口破坏了。因为各个居住地区临时雇工的引入,犯罪机会大大增加了。超过8000万的人离乡背井,四处作乱,在一个意识形态和道德规范严重式微的新环境中,作为流动人口,不受管控。所有这些改变不可思议地消减了过去曾经有效运作的控制机制。随着外部控制的减弱,犯罪的增长不可避免。①

第四,光棍们生活在一起,彼此影响,渐渐形成专属光棍的独特亚文化圈。进而,他们被其他人视为异类。② 从历史的角度看,詹姆斯·罗尼(James Rooney)说:"光棍文化的特点在于他们与社会格

---

① Yingyi Situ and Liu Weizheng, "Transient Population, Crime, and Solution: The Chinese Experience," *International Journal of Offender Therapy and Comparative Criminology*, Vol. 40, No. 4 (December 1996), p. 297.

② Lionel Tiger, *Men in Groups* (London: Marion Boyars, 1984); Courtwright, Violent Land; John C. Burnham, *Bad Habits: Drinking, Smoking, Taking Drugs, Gambling, Sexual Misbehavior, and Swearing in American History* (New York: New York University Press, 1993); George Gilder, *Naked Nomads: Unmarried Men in America* (New York: Quadrangle, 1974); Bell I. Wiley, *The Life of Billy Yank: The Common Soldier of the Union* (Baton Rouge: Louisianna State University Press, 1979); J. S. Holliday, *The World Rushed In: The California Gold Rush Experience* (New York: Simon and Schuster, 1981); Joe B. Frantz and Julian Ernest Choate Jr., *The American Cowboy* (Norman: University of Oklahoma Press, 1960); Murray Melbin, "Night as Frontier," *American Sociological Review*, Vol. 43, No. 1 (February 1978), pp. 3 - 22; Murray Melbin, *Night as Frontier: Colonizing the World after Dark* (New York: Free Press, 1987); and Sanyika Shakur, *Monster: The Autobiography of an L. A. Gang Member* (New York: Atlantic Monthly Press, 1993).

格不入，缺乏住家男人的责任感，容易放浪形骸，及时行乐。"①

以上四项特征，是高性别比例社会中过剩男性人口的典型标志。在边疆地区②、劳工聚集地③及游民"社群"中的男性身上都可以找到这些特征。在这些地方，女性通常不会超过总人口的3%—5%。④

总之，大多数生活在高性别比例社会中的光棍，并非自愿当光棍。有些出于宗教信仰的原因而自愿当光棍的男性，如中国的僧侣，其社会地位远高于被迫当光棍的人们。

---

① See James F. Rooney, "Societal Forces and the Unattached Male," in Bahr, *Disaffiliated Man*, p. 18.

② 考特莱特的 *Violent Landkeneng* 可能是有关这一问题的代表作品。另参见 David Dary, *Cowboy Culture: A Saga of Five Centuries* (Lawrence: University Press of Kansas, 1989); Frantz and Choate, *The American Cowboy*; David H. Breen, *The Canadian Prairie West and the Ranching Frontier: 1874 – 1924* (Toronto: University of Toronto Press, 1983); Robert Wooster, *Soldiers, Sutlers, and Settlers: Garrison Life on the Texas Frontier* (College Station: Texas A & M University Press, 1987); and Ray A. Billington, *America's Frontier Culture* (College Station: Texas A & M University Press, 1977). 阿根廷高乔人时代也是一个有意义的例子。

③ 澳大利亚起初是这样的殖民地；其他地方包括美国加州淘金劳工营、从事跨州铁路修建的劳工营，以及加州早期中国城的劳工营。A. Ged Matin, ed., *The Founding of Australia: The Argument about Australia's Origin* (Sydney: Hale and Iremonger, 1978); Holliday, *The World Rushed in*; Charles Ross Parke, *Dreams to Dust: A Diary of the California Gold Rush, 1849 – 1850*, ed. James E. Davis (Lincoln: University of Nebraska Press, 1989); James McCague, *Moguls and Iron Men: The Story of the First Transcontinental Railroad* (New York: Harper and Row, 1964); Gunter Barth, *Bitter Strength: A History of the Chinese in the United States, 1850 – 1870* (Cambridge, Mass.: Harvard University Press, 1964); Lucie Cheng and Edna Bonacich, eds., *Labor Immigration under Capitalism: Asian Workers in the United States before World War II* (Berkeley: University of California Press, 1984); and Sian Rees, *The Floating Brothel: The Extraordinary True Story of an Eighteenth-Century Ship and Its Cargo of Female Convicts* (New York: Theia/ Hyperion, 2002)

④ 男性游民通常是原先的士兵，在欧洲中世纪和文艺复兴时期都很常见。事实上，《安徒生童话》和《格林童话》中的许多重要角色都是光棍。James L. Boone, "Noble Family Structure and Expansionist Warfare in the Late Middle Ages," in Rada Dyson-Hudson and Michael A. Little, ed., *Rethinking Human Aaptation: Biological and Cultural Models* (Boulder, Colo.: Westview, 1983), pp. 79 – 96。到"一战"之前，男性游民在美国也很常见。例如，Eri H. Monkkonen, *Walking to Work: Tramps in America, 1790 – 1935* (Lincoln: University of Nebraska Press, 1984); Roger Bruns, *Knights of the Road: A Hobo History* (New York: Methuen, 1980); and Woirol, *In the Floating Army*。男性游民的群体中，也包括流动的军队。参见 Olive Knight, *Life and Manners in the Frontier Army* (Norman: University of Oklahoma Press, 1978)。

二、光棍的行为倾向

通常，光棍比其他男性更可能投入淫乱和暴力活动。① 这些行为包括身体侵害、吸毒酗酒、抢劫、性犯罪。光棍得不到社会的认同，干脆把微薄的薪水花在赌博、酗酒、吸毒及嫖妓上，他们常在享乐时发生暴力行为②，并对社会产生极坏的影响。以下是关于光棍与暴力的讨论：第一，男性比女性暴力。经过人类学家百年来的观察，男性比女性更具攻击性。这种性别上的差异有生物学的基础，此外，男性荷尔蒙的多寡可以决定其侵略性的强度。③ 虽然有时女性也有一定的攻击性，如当其后代受到威胁时，但男性往往会造成更大的伤害。事实上，男性要为绝大多数的暴力死亡负责。④ 兰汉（Richard Wrang-

---

① 坎伯（Theodore D. Kemper）构建了一套关于这种机制的简要理论。他指出社会地位低下的未婚年轻男性几乎没有机会掌握重要位置或引人关注，因此就去采取一些行为，来取得那些其他方式没法获得的"轰动效应"（T surge）。参见 Kemper, *Social Structure and Testosterone: Explorations of the Socio-Bio-social Chain* (New Brunswick, N. J.: Rutgers University Press, 1990)。这样的行为包括攻击、吸毒、酗酒和滥交。

② Courtwright, *Violent Land*, especially chap. 5.

③ Eleanor Emmons Maccoby and Carol Nagy Jacklin, *The Psychology of Sex Differences* (Stanford, Calif.: Stanford University Press, 1974), pp. 227 - 247.

④ D. Ben-ton. "Do Animal Studies Tell Us Anything about the Relationships between Testosterone and Human Aggression?" in Graham C. L. Davey, ed., *Animal Models of Human Behavior* (Chichester, U. K.: Wiley, 1983), pp. 281 - 298; Marie-France Bouissou, "Androgens, Aggressive Behaviour, and Social Relationships in Higher Mammals," *Hormone Research*, Vol. 18, Nos. 1 - 3 (1983), pp. 43 - 61; John M. W. Bradford and D. McLean, "Sexual Offenders, Violence, and Testosterone: A Clinical Study," *Canadian Journal of Psychiatry*, Vol. 29, No. 4 (June 1984), pp. 335 - 343; Kerrin Christiansen and Rainier Knussmann, "Androgen Levels and Components of Aggressive Behavior in Men," *Hormones and Behavior*, Vol. 21, No. 2 (June 1987), pp. 170 - 180; James M. Dabbs Jr. and Robin Morris, "Testosterone, Social Class, and Antisocial Behavior in a Sample of 4, 462 Men," *Psychological Science*, Vol. 1, No. 3 (May 1990), pp. 209 - 211; Bruce B. Svare, ed., *Hormones and Aggressive Behavior*, New York: Plenum, 1983, pp. 209 - 211; Janet Shibley Hyde, eds., "Gender Difference in Aggression," in Janet Shibley Hyde and Marcia C. Linn, *The Psychology of Gender: Advances through Meta-Analysis* (Baltimore, Md.: Johns Hopkins University Press, 1986); Kenneth E. Moyer, "Sex Differences in Aggression," in Richard C. Friedman, Ralph M. Richart, and Raymond L. Vande Wiele, eds., *Sex Differences in Behavior* (New York: Wiley, 1974), pp. 335 - 372; and Dolf Zillmann, *Connections between Sex and Aggression* (Hillsdale, N. J.: Lawrence Erlbaum, 1984).

ham）及彼得森（Dale Peterson）发现："男性犯罪多为暴力犯罪。在美国，男人犯谋杀罪的几率比女人大 9 倍，犯强暴罪的几率大 78 倍，持械抢劫的几率大 10 倍，暴力攻击的几率大 6.5 倍。总之，美国男性平均暴力犯罪的几率比女性高 8 倍。"①

第二，男性更容易做出反社会行为。

> 美国男性犯"诈欺罪"的几率比女性高 13.5 倍，"携带武器罪"高 13 倍，"偷窃罪"高 10 倍，"偷车罪"高 9 倍，"酗酒"高 8.5 倍，"肇事"高 8 倍，"破坏罪"高 8 倍，"接受赃物"高 7.5 倍，"纵火罪"高 7 倍，"赌博"高 6.5 倍，"酒醉驾车"高 6.5 倍，"性犯罪"（嫖妓及强暴罪除外）高 5.5 倍，"吸毒"高 5 倍，"对小孩及家庭暴力"高 4.5 倍，"伪造罪"高 2 倍，"侵占公款"高 1.5 倍。②

年轻男性的反社会行为又比年长的男性多得多。暴力犯罪最频繁的年龄是 15—35 岁，而在青春期末期达到颠峰，然后在 40 岁左右降到较低的稳定期。③ 年轻男性也要对大部分犯罪所导致的死亡负责。④

---

① Richard Wrangham and Dale Peterson, *Demonic Males: Apes and the Origins of Human Violence* (New York: Houghton Mifflin, 1996), p. 113.

② Ibid., pp. 113 – 114.

③ Travis Hirschi and Michael Gottfredson, "Age and the Explanation of Crime," *American Journal of Sociology* (November 1983), pp. 552 – 584.

④ Dan Olweus, Ake Mattsson, Daisy Schalling, and Hans Loew, "Circulating Testosterone Levels and Aggression in Adolescent Males: A Causal Analysis," *Psychosomatic Medicine*, Vol. 50, No. 3 (May-June 1988), pp. 261 – 272; Margo Wilson and Martin Daly, "Competitiveness, Risk Talking, and Violence: The Young Male Syndrome," *Ethnology and Sociobiology*, Vol. 6, No. 1 (1985), pp. 59 – 73; Derral Cheatwood and Kathleen J. Block, "Youth and Homicide: An Investigation of the Age Factor in Criminal Homicide," *Justice Quarterly*, Vol. 7, No. 2 (June 1990), pp. 265 – 292; and Christian G. Mesquida and Neil I. Wiener, "Human Collective Aggression: A Behavioral Ecology Perpective," *Ethology and Sociobiology*, Vol. 17, No. 4 (July 1996), PP. 247 – 262. 15—35 岁的男性占自杀人群的绝大多数，其中 20—29 岁的男性占绝大多数。参见 Wison and Daly, "Competitiveness, Risk Taking, and Violence"。

在中国，上世纪90年代间被关在监狱里的男性有超过80%是小于30岁的。① 所有社会中暴力行为和犯罪的实施者都是以年轻男性为主。② 他们独自犯案或集体犯案的潜在可能性很高。在对20世纪60年代以来的集体攻击事件的分析中，梅斯奎达（Christian Mesquida）和维纳（Neil Wiener）写道："15—29岁男性与30岁以上男性的比例同由冲突所致死亡数来测定的集体攻击水平存在一种持续性的关联。"③

第三，未婚男性的犯罪比例又高于已婚男性。④ 考特莱特（David Courtwright）写道："当年轻男性无法结婚或没有结婚，他们的社会性破坏活动就会增强。"⑤ 根据罗伯特·赖特（Robert Wright）的说法：

---

① James D. Seymour and Richard Anderson, *New Ghosts, Old Ghosts: Prisons and Labor Reform Camps in China* (London: M. E. Sharpe, 1998), p. 115. 这些数字可能只是类似于代表性案例中的数字。

② Satoshi Kanazawa and March C. Still, "Why Men Commit Crimes (and Why They Desist)," *Sociological Theory*, Vol. 18, No. 3 (2000), pp. 443 – 447.

③ Mesquida and Wiener, "Human Collective Aggression," p. 247.

④ See ibid.; John H. Laub, Daniel S. Nagin, and Robert J. Sampson, "Trajectories of Change in Criminal Offending: Good Marriages and the Desistance Process," *American Sociological Review*, Vol. 63, No. 2 (April 1998), pp. 225 – 238; Robert J. Sampson and John H. Laub, *Crime in the Making: Pathways and Turning Points through Life* (Cambridge, Mass.: Harvard University Press); Daly and Wilson, *Sex, Evolution and Behavior*; Courtwright, *Violent Land*; Kemper, *Social Structure and Testosterone Moral Animal* (New York: Pantheon, 1994); Laura Betzig, "Despotism and Differential Degree of Polygny," *Ethology and Sociobiology*, Vol. 3, No. 4 (1982), pp. 209 – 221; Martin Daly and Margo Wilson, *Homicide* (Hawthorne, N. Y.: Aldine de Gruyter 1988); Martin Daly and Margo Wilson, "Killing the Competition: Female/Female and Male/Male Reproductive Success Equal in Egalitarian Societies?" in Chagnon and Irons, *Evolutionary Biology and Human Social Behavior*, pp. 374 – 401; David Buss, *The Evolution of Desire: Strategies of Human Mating* (New York: Basic Books, 1994); Frank A. Pedersen, "Secular Trends in Human Sex Ratios: Their Influence on Individual and Family Behavior," *Human Nature*, Vol. 2, No. 3 (1991), pp. 271 – 291; and Randy Thornhill and Nancy Thornhill, "Human Rape: An Evolutionary Analysis," *Ethology and Sociobiology*, Vol. 4, No. 3 (1983), pp. 137 – 173.

⑤ Courtwright, *Violent Land*, p. 202.

没有女人的男人……靠特殊的暴行来竞争。24—35岁的未婚男性,谋杀他人的几率是同龄已婚男性的3倍。这一差异毫无疑问反映了已婚与未婚的不同类型……差异可能在于婚姻的"镇定效果"。谋杀并不是"不平静的"男子最有可能做的事。除了谋杀,他还会抢劫、强暴、吸毒及酗酒——以获得吸引女性的资源。他实施强奸的可能性很高。吸毒和酗酒……减少了他以合法手段挣钱吸引女性的机会,使问题愈加混杂。①

马促(Allan Mazur)及麦可利克(Joel Michalek)发现,男性的T浓度(男性荷尔蒙)在婚后会降低。②"T浓度的改变可以解释已婚男性的低犯罪率,他们和妻子过着安定的日子,不太会有杀人的念头。"他们认为,"T值和反社会行为成正比。当T值降低时,犯罪的倾向也降低了。"③ 心理学家卡纳查瓦(Satoshi Kanazawa)认为,男性把结婚看成是停止犯罪的信号:"预测一个人是否会再犯罪,最可靠的指标是婚姻。如果婚姻美满的话,他通常会停止犯罪,与他同龄的未婚同道则会继续其罪恶生涯。"④

马促及麦可利克指出:

---

① Wright, *The Moral Animal*, p. 100.

② Allan Mazur and Joel Michalek, "Marriage, Divorce, and Male Testosterone," *Social Forces*, Vol. 77, No. 1 (September 1998), p. 315.

③ 参见 Allan Mazur and Alan Booth, "Testosterone and Dominance in Men," *Behavioral and Brain Sciences*, Vol. 21, No. 3 (June 1998), pp. 353–397。关于男性荷尔蒙对行为的影响争论是不计其数的。有些人认为男性荷尔蒙转化为雌性激素导致这种影响,有些人认为这种影响根本不存在。See, for example, David France, "Testosterone, the Rogue Hormone, Is Getting a Makeover," *New York Times*, February 17, 1999, p. G3.

④ Satoshi Kanazawa, "Why Productivity Fades with Age: The Crime-Genius Connection," *Journal of Research in Personality*, Vol. 37 (2003), pp. 257–272, at p. 269.

单身男性有较多的时间与其他男性相处，所以容易遇到纷争与挑衅。缺乏妻子的支持，他们容易用暴力来护卫尊严，这时他的 T 浓度就会上升。结婚是渐进式的追求和约定，男性接受了伴侣的支持与安慰，不需要与别人争取性伴侣，他的 T 值就会下降。①

所以，据马促和麦可利克分析，社会上无法结婚的男人愈多，乱窜的 T 值就愈高，暴力及反社会行为也就愈多。卡纳查瓦认可如下观点："在结婚和孩子出生后，男性睾丸素（男性荷尔蒙的一种）的突然下降可能为解释男性犯罪的心理机制提供了生化证据。……结婚或孩子出生后就'停下来'，也同时解释了男性未婚时为何同样的心理机制无法'停下来'。"② 葛得（George Gilder）这样表述："在一夫一妻的婚姻中，个人的价值比单身时要高。"③ 这并不是一个新的现象，犹太的经文中描述："葡萄园若是没有围墙，必遭毁坏；人若没有妻子，也就成了没有家室的人。谁会相信这种男人呢？"④

第四，与上流社会的男性相比，生活在底层的男性犯罪手段通常更残暴。这种经验主义的发现在人类社会得到了广泛的确认。⑤ 正如坎伯（Theodore Kemper）所言："经过对社会文献的仔细分析，一种观点得到了有力支持，即底层阶级生理上比中产阶级在社会关系上更加

---

① Mazur and Michalek, "Marriage, Divorce, and Male Testosterone," p. 327.

② Kanazawa, "Why Productivity Fades with Age," p. 270.

③ Gilder, *Naked Nomads*, p. 152.

④ 在此要感谢坎伯引起我们对此的关注。《便西拉智训》，又名《传道经》。詹姆斯（King James）版本的语言没有准确反映第 36 章这段希伯来语言的细微差别。

⑤ Wilson and Daly, "Competitiveness, Risk Taking, and Violence"; Mesquida and Wiener, "Human Collective Aggression"; Kemper, *Social Structure and Testosterone*; Courtwright, *Violent Land*; Betzig, "Despotism and Differential Reproduction"; Laura Betzig, *Despotism and Differential Reproduction: A Darwinian View of History* (New York: Aldien de Gruyter, 1986); Daly and Wilson, *Sex, Evolution, and Behavior*; and William H. Durham, "Resource Competition and Human Aggression," *Quarterly Review of Biology*, Vol. 51, No. 3 (September 1976), pp. 385 – 415.

具有侵略性和暴力性，无论这个人是在抚养子女，青春期，年轻人，同龄群体，街头邂逅，家庭关系，解决冲突，或犯罪。"① 威尔逊和达利的研究结果显示，失业男性犯蓄意谋杀罪的比例比就业的要高4倍。② 考特莱特发现，失业与暴力致死之间的相关性为0.73，与蓄意谋杀罪的相关性为0.65，两个数据都具有统计意义。③ 马促和布斯引用了一项研究成果，其中失业男性在所有的男性中，有最高的T值。④

第五，在酒精和药物的影响下，男性会变得更残暴，而年轻未婚男性使用的酒精及药物最多，其用量超过已婚男性、老年男性和女性。⑤ 他们还会吸食可卡因、麻黄碱、天使粉等毒品，这些经常与犯罪的较高水平相关。⑥ 一份报告称1996年，美国有80%的人在被捕时

---

① Kemper, *Social Structure and Testosterone*, p. 73.
② Wilson and Daly, "Competitiveness, Risk Taking, and Violence."
③ Courtwright, *Violent Land*.
④ Mazur and Booth, "Testosterone and Dominance in Men," p. 361.
⑤ Wilson and Daly, "Competitiveness, Risk Taking, and Violence."
⑥ Judith Roizen, "Issues in the Epidemiology of Alcohol and Violence"; Kai Pernanen, "Alcohol-Related Violence: Conceptual Models"; Klaus A. Miczek, Elise M. Weerts, and Joseph F. DeBold, "Alcohol, Aggression, and Violence: Psychological Perspectives"; and Alan R. Lang, "Alcohol-Related Violence: Psychological Perspectives," all in Susan E. Martin, ed., *Alcohol and Interpersonal Violence: Fostering Multidisciplinary Perspectives*, NIAAA Research Monograph No. 24 (Rockville, Md.: National Institues of Health, 1993), pp. 30 – 36, 37 – 69, 83 – 119, and 121 – 147. See also James J. Collins, "Alcohol Use and Expressive Interpersonal Violence"; David Levinson, "Social Setting, Cultural Factors, and Alcohol-related Aggression"; Richard E. Boyatzis, "Who Should Drink What, When, and Where If Looking for a Fight," all in Edward Gottheil et al., ed., *Alcohol, Drug Abuse, and Aggression* (Springfield: Charles C. Thomas, 1983), pp. 5 – 25, 1 – 58, and 314 – 329; as well as A. James Giannini, Robert H. Loiselle, and Brian H. Graham, "Violence and Relationship to Route of Administration," *Journal of Substance Abuse Treatment*, Vol. 10, No. 1 (January-February 1993), pp. 67 – 69; Norman S. Miller, Mark S. Gold, and John C. Mahler, "Violent Behaviors Associated with Cocaine Use: Possible Pharmacological Mechanisms," *International Journal of the Addictions*, Vol. 26, No. 10 (1991), pp. 1077 – 1088; and P. M. Marzuk, K. Tardiff, D. Smyth, M. Stajic, and A. C. Leon, "Cocaine Use, Risk Taking, and Fatal Russian Roulette," *JAMA*, May 20, 1992, pp. 2635 – 2637.

都正在酗酒或嗑药。

另一方面，毒品如鸦片会降低服用者的暴力倾向，但为了得到买鸦片的钱，他们还是不免使用暴力。① 考特莱特说，对19世纪加州的中国移民，"鸦片是个强力的镇静剂。吸鸦片上瘾的人，不会无端地攻击他人，但他们会偷窃，尤其当鸦片的买卖成为非法之后。鸦片也让犯罪组织为了争夺它们的控制权，彼此展开血腥的恶斗"。②

第六，男性的流动人口是最暴力的，他们也多受害于暴力。任孟（Ren Meng，音译）说："在1990年，上海浦东金桥地区的流动人口犯罪占当时该地区犯罪总数的30%，到了1997年这一数字上升至90%以上。"此外，绝大多数流动人口可能是穷人，这与光棍亚文化的特征相符。③

马促和布斯提供了对于暴力行为迅速发生与暴力行为趋向之间协同作用的一种心理学阐释：

> 在任何亚文化中的年轻男子身上都可能普遍存在对于侮辱的无法容忍，他们并不受传统社会的控制机制所限，而这往往发生在社会组织松散的地方如边疆地区、流氓组织、游民群体，或是在天灾人祸后社会秩序崩盘时。那些年轻男子重视维护自身名誉，并且不止于此，寻求控制的竞争无处不在，成为男人之间关系的标志。……T水平（男性荷尔蒙）会升高。④

第七，倾向于冒险的男性（如年轻的、未婚的、社会地位低下

---

① Christopher Wren, "Drugs Alcohol Linked to 80% of Inmates," *New York Times*, January 9, 1998, p. A14.

② Courtwright, *Violent Land*, pp. 165–166. See also David T. Courtwright, *Dark Para dise: Opiute Addiction in America before 1940* (Cambridye, Mass.: Harvard Vnirersity Press, 1982).

③ Ren Meng, "Confronting Three Populations of 80 Million," *Inside China Mainland*, Vol. 19, No. 1 (January 1997), pp. 78–81.

④ Mazur and Booth, "Testosterone and Dominance," p. 360.

的、吸毒酗酒的）在人愈多的场合，表现得愈夸张愈暴力。① 实验证明，男性群体中的这种"人来疯"现象比女性群体中明显。② 考特莱特指出："当许多男子聚在一起时，对地位和名誉非常在意。即使没有喝醉或被侮辱激怒，他们也会互相探试，互相挑衅。他们以为自己愈是凶狠，别人就愈让步。……不受尊重的、社会地位低下的男性……在单身汉社区如工棚、矿工营地等施加影响。他们被诱惑也被惩罚，因为不做出些惊世骇俗的坏事来，否则用他们自己的话说，就不算是男人了。"③

因此，男性，特别是年轻的、未婚的、社会地位低下的男性群体行为无外乎个体最糟的行为。总体而言，他们独自一人时会冒更大险，犯更重的罪。兰汉及皮德森阐释了男性群体中的冒险行为与他们的暴力倾向之间的联系：

> 男性有传宗接代的压力，因此在进化时，冒险犯难的性格会得到钟爱。这种性格表现在个人身上，影响较小。男性有时比女性更爱开快车、赌博及从事危险的运动。但是那种可以打折扣的疯狂感，拉高了青少年的汽车保险理赔率，也使他们产生一种要赌上自己和他人生命的强烈意愿；当他们拥有武器或加入帮会后，这种冒险的吸引力会变得有意义。一旦男人进入群体如帮会、村庄或部落等，这种有驱动力的、冒险的伦理很快就会变得具有攻击性及致命性。④

---

① See Irving Lester Janis, *Groupthink*: *Psychological Studies of Policy Decisions and Fiascoes* (Boston: Houghton Mifflin, 1982); Nathan Kogan and Michael Wallach, *Risk Taking*: *A Study in Cognition and Personality* (New York: Holt, Rinehart, and Winston, 1964); and Norris R. Johnson, Joanne G. Stemler, and Deborah Hunter, "Crowd Behavior as 'Risky Shift': A Laboratory Experiment," *Sociometry*, Vol. 40, No. 2 (June 1977), pp. 183 – 187.

② Johnson, Stemler, and Hunter, "Crowd Behavior as 'Risky Shift'."

③ Courtwright, *Violent Land*, pp. 42 – 43.

④ Wrangham and Peterson, *Demonic Males*, p. 235.

总之，群聚的男性多为单身的（本身就提高了 T 值）；他们也多有着较高的 T 值，因为他们倾向于竞争群体之内的身份地位。在未婚男性群体中所宣称的冒险的转变因而并不令人惊奇。如果这些群体经历了冒险的转变，可能结果会是集体努力通过侵略和暴力来获取资源。

三、社会性别比例居高的后果

如以上分析是可靠的，一个社会在经历了各种性别选择手段之后，男性比例呈快速的、不成比例的增长，其结局将会如何？在一个存在大量光棍的社会中会发生什么？我们认为社会将会面临更多的暴力与冲突。① 一夫多妻的社会犯罪率较高，高性别比例的社会在这点上类似一夫多妻的社会。② 此外，暴力增长将表现在个体与集体两个层面。梅士奎达（Mesquida）及维纳（Wiener）认为：

> 未婚的年轻男人，聚众生事，掠取资源，主要的目的就是要找女人，可以想见军中多数人都是来自贫穷的人群。……统治阶

---

① 在对美国本土人口的研究中，梅斯纳（Steven F. Messner）和桑普森（Robert J. Sampson）发现，高性别比引发较低水平的家庭破裂（如离婚和非法婚姻）。较低水平的家庭破裂进而导致较低的犯罪率。这些发现与印度和中国的情况并不吻合，因为作者是在一个社会内部比较，而不是在不同社会之间比较。在美国内部，女性从一个地区向另一个地区迁移并不受边界所限。另一方面，两人分析了一个有着各种家庭破裂类型的社会，并与那些社会习俗缩减了破裂类型的社会作比较。我们认为，各种社会之间，包括那些有着强烈反家庭分裂传统的社会，高度扭曲的性别比是与社会内分裂的增长水平相关的。这并不是反驳梅斯纳与桑普森的发现，但也表明文化背景是要考虑在内的。Messner and Sampson, "The Sex Ratio, Family Disruption, and Rates of Violent Crime: The Paradox of Demographic Structure," *Social Forces*, Vol. 69, No. 3 (March 1991), pp. 693–713.

② Margaret K. Bacon, Irvin L. Child, and Herbert Barry, "A Cross-Cultural Study of Correlates of Crime," *Journal of Abnormal and Social Psychology*, Vol. 66, No. 4 (1963), pp. 291–300; and Betzig, "Despotism and Differential Reproduction."

级很有可能不乐见这群贫无立锥之地的人，为了争夺资源而对他们进行集体攻击，所以干脆采取扩张主义或殖民主义来把他们送走。我们姑且相信，这种世代内对资源的争夺，被大量贫穷的年轻男性强化时，可能会导致男性集体攻击行为，有时表现形式就是侵略战争。①

柏恩指出中世纪的葡萄牙有大量的光棍（他们多为幼子），使得殖民地政策成为必需。"过多的幼子像颗定时炸弹，造成社会不安，统治阶级要么面临社会失序、政权被推翻的危险，要么选择分散个体。"② 他进而写道，"向外扩充领土，不一定是当政者想霸占资源，或是要解决国内生产不足的问题，很多时候，战争只是统治阶级把来自下属的纷争转向邻国，以免对着自己。从总体人口的视角看，这些战略……可以在大量资源缺乏时保持住。"③

赖特甚至说出："对统治精英来说没有什么比有点政治权力但又无妻小的男人帮更让人焦虑的了。……极端的一夫多妻制是与极端的政治等级制相伴生的，并在最专制的体系下达到顶点。……让许多男子没有妻子不只是不平等，而是危险。……一个国家，如果有许多低收入的男子未婚，那我们许多人都不会想要生活在这里。"④ 卢拉·贝兹克（Leura Betzig）对186个社会作了实证研究之后，得出结论：一夫多妻制与专制统治在统计上高度相关。⑤

至此，我们可以得出如下两个结论：第一，唯有靠威权体制才能治理性别比例那么高的社会。它可以压制国内的暴乱，通过殖民或是

---

① Mesquida and Wiener, "Human Collective Aggression," pp. 256–260.
② Boone, "Parental Investment and Elite Family Structure in Preindustrial States," p. 868.
③ Boone, "Noble Family Structure and Expansionist Warfare in the Late Middle Ages," p. 81.
④ Wright, *The Moral Animal*, pp. 98–101.
⑤ Betzig, *Despotism and Differential Reproduction*, p. 94.

战争将内乱输出国外。① 第二，在高性别比例的社会中如存在多元的民族，政府则倾向于鼓励针对少数民族的民族冲突。在我们的研究中，前者如中国，后者如印度。

四、高性别比例对女性的影响

女性在高性别比例的社会中是处于不利地位的，首先，她们原本已经很低的社会地位会变得更低。这看上去有些违反常识，根据市场供需定律，女性会因人数少而变得尊贵及更有权力。② 可惜这在高性别比例的社会中不会发生。因为男性尤其是有权力的男性，会把她们看成商品进行买卖，对她们的监控反而更严。③绍斯（Scott South）及尊特（Katherine Trent）描述了这一机制：

> 在高性别比例的社会中，女性的"增值"反而使她的生活选择更局限。这看似矛盾，但我们的研究结果发现，在女性缺乏时，男性则拥有强大的权力，这一切造成高结婚率、高生育率、低婚外生育率及低离婚率。而高生育率也有助于匡定和约束女性所起的作用。在女性短缺的社会中，相比男性，她们的识字率和就业率低，自杀率高。因此在当今的社会权力架构下，女性人数

---

① 参见 Divale and Harris, "Population, Warfare, and the Male Supremacist Complex," *American Anthropologist* Vol. 78, No. 3 (September 1976), pp. 531, 528。

② 我们不同意下列著作所代表的分析：Marcia Guttentag and Paul L. Secord, *Too Many Women? The Sex Ratio Question* (Beverly Hills, Calif.: Sage, 1983); and Mary Anne Warren, *Gendercide: The Implication of Sex Selection* (Totowa, N. J.: Rowman and Allanheld, 1985)。

③ Scott J. South and Katherine Trent, "Sex Ratios and Women's Roles: A Cross-National Analysis," *American Journal of Sociology*, Vol. 93, No. 5 (March 1988), pp. 1096 – 1115; And Ashok Mitra, *Implications of the Declining Sex Ration in India's Population* (Bombay Allied Publishers, 1979)。

的缺乏对女性反而不利。①

其次，当女性稀少时，她们被绑架及买卖的可能性大增。中国已出现拐卖妇女儿童的市场。有来源显示，"从 1991 年到 1996 年，警察救出了 88000 个被绑架的女性及小孩；逮捕了 143000 个参与贩卖人口的警察"。② 1993 年中国官方的报告说，有 15000 名女性在那年被绑架。1997—1998 年，警察共救出 23000 名女性及 4260 名小孩，并破获了 8000 个绑架集团。③在 20 世纪 90 年代末期，买一个绑架来的女性的价格是 240—480 美元，但聘金则需要 1200 美元以上。④

中国官方认为被贩卖的女性人数，实际上还要更多。李济（Li Ji，音译）解释说："警察抱怨，当他们企图救出这些女子时，地方上的一些人认为买媳妇是合情合理的，常常设法阻止救援行动。所以官方公布的被绑架的女子数字，应该是保守的。"⑤ 典型情况是，成年女子在城市中被拐卖且被卖到乡村。即使一个被拐卖的女人怎样尝试去逃离监禁限制，她的家庭可能都不会再接受她了。人类学家认为在对女性的控制普遍流行的社会，一种反馈回路以这样的行为方式形成了：控制女性的欲望增强了对男性后代的性别选择。⑥

第三，当年龄层较高的男性都想娶年纪轻的女性为妻时，新娘的

---

① South and Trent, "Sex Ratios and Women's Roles," p. 1112.

② Dorinda Elliot, "Trying to Stand on Two Feet," *Newsweek*, June 29, 1998, pp. 48–49.

③ "China Arrests Thousands for Trading Women and Children," Associated Press, June 8, 1999.

④ Li Ji, "Discussions on the Gender Imbalance in China and the Entailed Social Problems," Foreign Affairs College, Beijing, 1999, p. 23.

⑤ Li Ji, "Discussions on the Gender Imbalance in China and the Entailed Social Problems," Foreign Affairs College, Beijing, 1999, p. 23.

⑥ 这明显是南美雅诺马莫人（南美印第安人）的情况。那里出生性别比例 129（男）：100（女）是部落捕获新娘的结果。Napoleon A. Chagnon, Mark V. Flinn, and Thomas F. Melancon, "Sex-Ratio Variation among the Yanomamo Indians," in Chagnon and Irons, *Evolutionary Biology and Human Social Behavior*, pp. 290–320.

年龄降低了。① 她的家庭可能在她还没成为被绑的对象时，就尽早把她"转送"到夫家去。新娘的年龄越小，父母需要为她准备的嫁妆就越少，这也成了父母将幼女早嫁的诱因。在过去，中国及印度的家庭经常会把未成年的女孩甚至女婴，交给夫家，她们在未成年时就成婚了。② 1993 年，一项在印度拉贾斯坦邦的调查发现，有 56% 的女子在 15 岁前结婚，19% 在 10 岁以前就结婚了。③ 在中国，"童养媳"现象也很普遍。中国也有贩卖女婴的地下市场，客户有两种：买不起黑市男婴的，想为儿子找媳妇的。成年女子通常是由城市被绑架到乡村，女婴则是从乡村被绑，然后转卖到都市。④

第四，同样违背常理的是，在高性别比例的社会中，人口生育率不一定会低。因为男性对女性的控制变严，强迫每个女性所生的胎数更多。⑤ 这直接导致了女性自杀人数的增多。在低性别比例的社会中，情况正好相反。⑥ 在高性别比例的社会中，有更多的年轻女性（比起年长女性）自杀。全世界有 56% 的自杀女性来自中国，她们的年龄绝

---

① South and Trent, "Sex Ratios and Women's Roles"; and Courtwright, *Violent Land*. 考特莱特注意到："年幼的新娘在男性人口过剩的地区特别常见。……在切萨皮克（Chesapeake）殖民地，听说过有 12 岁、13 岁女孩结婚的，这种事在加州'淘金潮'时代很出名。在密歇根的边远地区，女性法定的性交年龄是 8 岁。"

② 参见 James Hayes, "San Po Tsai (Little Daughters-in-Law) and Child Betrothals in the New Territories of Hong Kong from the 1890s to the 1960s," in Maria Jaschok and Suzanne Miers, eds., *Women and Chinese Patriarchy: Submission, Servitude, and Escape* (London: Zed, 1994), pp. 45 – 76。另一部不错的参考书是 Arthur P. Wolf and Chieh-shan Huang, *Marriage and Adoption in China, 1845 – 1945* (Stanford, Calif.: Stanford University Press, 1980)。

③ John F. Burns, "Though Illegal, Child Marriage Is Popular in Part of India," *New York Times*, May 11, 1998, p. A1.

④ Damien McElroy, "Chinese Buy Baby Girls on the Black Market," *London Daily Telegraph*, August 1, 1999, http://www.telegraph.co.uk/htmlContent.jhtml? html = %2Farchive%2F1998%2F04%2F02%2Fnlot02.html.

⑤ South and Trent, "Sex Ratios and Women's Roles"; and Mitra, *Implications of the Declining Sex Ratio in India's Population*.

⑥ South and Trent, "Sex Ratios and Women's Roles."

大多数是在生育年龄。在中国45岁以下的自杀人口中，女性是男性的2倍。①（相比而言，美国男性自杀率是女性的4倍。）在印度，年轻女性的自杀率也高于年轻男性。②观察家认为在父系社会中，女性地位低，负担重，尊严少，无法掌握自己的命运，因此选择自杀的女性较多。③

第五，在高性别比例的社会中，女性做娼妓者众。有证据表明，同性恋和共妻现象的比例也较高。④基于此，政府有时也会鼓励红灯区的成立。19世纪的澳大利亚政府公开承认男性太多是危险的："第一批流放犯的船上占主要比重的男子从一开始就被意识到是一个社会和政治问题：那些权威人士认为：'如果女性不够，殖民地会变得无法无天。'"⑤若想减少性犯罪，保护上流社会的女性不受侵犯，社会

---

① Christopher J. L. Murray and Alan D. Lopez, eds., *The Global Burden of Disease: A Comprehensive Assessment of Mortality and Disability from Diseases, Injuries, and Risk Factors in 1990 and Projected to 2020* (Cambridge, Mass.: Harvard University Press, 1996), p. 448; and Elisabeth Rosenthal, "Women's Suicides Reveal Rural China's Bitter Roots," *New York Times*, January 24, 1999, sec. 1, p. 1.

② Murray and Lopez, *The Global Burden of Disease*, p. 444.

③ Ling Li, "China's Suicide Rate," *New York Times*, January 28, 1999, p. A26.

④ Courtwright, *Violent Land*; Wright, *The Moral Animal*; and Nels Anderson, *The Hobo: The Sociology of the Homeless Man* (Chicago: University of Chicago Press, 1961), chap. 10. 在第四章，我们讨论过在元、明、清三代，福建省广泛存在杀女婴情况。因此，在这一时期，相比中国其他地方，福建也会呈现出一种允许同性恋的态度。田心源注意到："长久缺乏与女性的接触也可以解释同性恋的盛行，这在福建被称为'契兄弟'。……在清朝的法律体系中，犯鸡奸罪……刑罚是重责一百杖。……但在福建，'契兄弟'仍是可以公开夸耀的事，而不是羞耻的事。" T'ien, *Male Anxiety and Female Chastity: A Comparative Study of Chinese Ethical Values in Ming-Ch'ing Times* (New York: E. J. Bill, 1988), p. 31, n. 54. 1850年的一项人口普查显示，在19世纪旧金山的中国城，人口性别比极高，有限的女性中71%都是妓女。参见 Cheng and Bonacich, *Labor Immigration under Capitalism*, p. 421. 在西藏，高性别比传统上导致一妻多夫，而不是对晚出生儿子的剥夺：几个兄弟共有一个妻子。Nancy E. Levine, "Differential Child Care in Three Tibetan Communities: Beyond Son Preference," *Population and Development Review*, Vol. 13, No. 2 (June 1987), pp. 281–304.

⑤ Martin, *The Founding of Australia*, pp. 22–29.

就需要有足够的娼妓。①

把不同文化的女子送到文化单一的地方，像是中国，不一定能解决适婚女性太少的困扰。虽然有很多缅甸、韩鲜及越南的女子被卖到中国去，但她们之中有多少成为新娘、有多少沦为娼妓，就很难说了。② 在这种文化背景下，一个"理性的单身汉"必须通过各种可能的途径在狂乱的婚姻市场中获得可以取胜的资源。③

五、政府的观点

光棍真的会对政府构成威胁吗？如果他们横冲直撞，肆无忌惮，最后倒霉的还是他们自己。虽然光棍会带来治安问题，造成财产损失，但他们也为社区提供了资源。考特莱特描写美国西部的垦荒生活时说："最好的做法就是使用设计好的警察和法院系统加以调控。美国牛仔小镇的正义，就是宽松地应用法律条文，目的是控制、隔离并从牛仔劣行中获利，而不是打击他们。……公开的劣行会让镇上获利，但也带来犯罪，因为饥渴的年轻牛仔渴望开枪，挥霍薪水。但让他们失去金钱的代价就是治安败坏。"④ 在经济蓬勃时，政府任由光棍荒唐下去，让社会支付损失的成本。

但若经济变坏，光棍绝望时，问题就来了。他们不再只是小打小闹，而是打家劫舍，并使用武力。如威尔逊和达利所言："男性和女

---

① Raelene Frances, "The History of Female Prostitution in Australia," in Roberta Perkins, G. Prestage, R. Sharp and F. Lovejoy, eds., *Sex Work and Sex Workers in Australia* (Sydney: University of New South Wales, 1994), pp. 27–52.

② John Pomfret, "Portrait of a Famine," *Washington Post Foreign Service*, February 12, 1999.

③ Mildred Dickemann, "Female Infanticide, Reproductive Strategies, and Social Stratification: A Preliminary Model," in Chagnon and Irons, *Evolutionary Biology and Human Social Behavior*, pp. 321–367.

④ Courtwright, *Violent Land*, pp. 98, 108.

性不同之处,在于男性会去掠取别人的财产,并使用暴力来达到目的。男人之中的长期竞争环境最终可能是造成强烈需要剩余资源——而不只是生存——的重要原因。"① 当人数众多、无家可归,以及在现有的社会秩序中缺乏支撑这几项因素结合起来时,可能会引发光棍们成立强盗集团。

下面提供的历史案例,就是光棍以星星之火燎原的例子。在这些例子中,光棍只是众多充分条件之一。比喻来说,当天气干燥时,光秃的木棍不可能点燃火苗,但当火花飞舞,木棍可以将火花变为熊熊火焰。

(一) 捻乱

捻匪之乱是过度的后代性别选择所带来的灾难之一,它不但威胁到整个地区的安定,清朝还差点为之灭亡。②叛乱发生在 1851 年。捻匪是一个有组织的强盗集团,其成员多来自中国贫穷的淮北地区。他们本来只是为了求生存,但天灾、人祸、政府无能、税赋增加,再加上抢匪领头人的野心,配合了同一时期中国南方的太平天国之乱,最后就演变成清朝最严重的内乱。

19 世纪上半叶,淮北地区平均每 3—4 年就会经历水灾、旱灾及虫灾的肆虐,农作物被毁,大批农民死于饥荒。当时农民的应对方式是杀女婴,保留男孩,因为男孩较有价值,会为家庭带来收入,女孩只会花钱,且在出嫁时还要付出一笔可观的嫁妆。19 世纪时,淮北地区的性别比例高达 129(男):100(女)。③ 但男性的死亡率较高,女性寿命更长,所以实际的出生人口性别比例应该高过这个数字。

根据欧恩比(David Ownby)的观点,当时"穷人的结婚年龄往

---

① Wilson and Daily, "Competitiveness, Risk Taking, and Violence," p. 66.
② 这里叙述引自 Perry, *Rebels and Revolutionaries in North China, 1845–1945*。
③ Perry, *Rebels and Revolutionaries in North China, 1845–1945*. 相比之下,1880 年堪萨斯的 Doclge 城仅是 124(男):100(女)。Courtwright, *Violent Land*, p. 58.

后推了六年，25%的男人根本无法成家"。① 这和清朝末期女婴被杀的数据相符合，据说当时每1000个女婴出生，就有300个被杀。② 李中清（James Lee）和王丰（Wang Feng）说道："在1774年之后的百年里，中国东北的农村家庭中，有五分之一至四分之一的女孩被杀。"③ 多妻制和纳妾制在约占中国10%人口的富人中流行，加重了适婚女性的稀缺性。虽然农村家庭有正当理由养儿不养女，但最后却造成了严重的贫穷的单身男性人口过剩。④ 丹尼尔·利特尔（Daniel Little）写道："父母以为没有女婴，他们的收入和安全性就会增加，但长期来看，反而造成了年轻男性的过剩，徒然为盗匪集团增加新血。"⑤ 他们被称为"光棍"，永远无法成家，因为那些本来要成为他们妻子的女孩都被杀了。一位清朝官员在1827年写道："嫁女不易，所以家庭都不想养女儿。娶妻更难，所以到处都是单身汉。"⑥ 结婚的高成本让许多"无家可归的强盗"只能"去抢、去偷、去骗"。⑦

欧恩比和沃森（Watson）对光棍现象和暴力现象之间的关联作了研究。根据欧恩比的研究："在中国人眼中，未婚男人不算是真正的

---

① Ownby, "Approximations of Chinese Bandits," p. 242 (emphasis in original).

② Ibid.

③ "6.3 Brides for Seven Brothers," *Econmist*, December 19, 1998-January 1, 1999, p. 57. See also James Z. Lee and Wang Feng, *One Quarter of Humanity: Maltb usian My thology and Chinese Realities, 1700 – 2000* (Cambridge, Mass: Harvard University Press, 1999).

④ David Ownby, *Brotherhoods and Secret Societies in Early and Mid-Qing China: The Formation of a Tradition* (Stanford, Calif.: Stanford University, 1996).

⑤ Daniel Little, *Understanding Peasant China: Case Studies in the Philosophy of Social Science* (New Haven, Conn.: Yale University Press, 1989), p. 172.

⑥ Chen Shengshao, Wensulu 1827, as quoted in David Ownby, "Approximations of Chinese Bandits: Perverse Rebels, Romantic Heroes, or Frustrated Bachelors?" in Susan Brownell and Jeffrey N. Wasserstrom, eds., *Chinese Femininities/Chinese Masculinities: A Reader* (Berkeley: University of California Press, 2002), p. 241.

⑦ Chen Shengshao, Wensulu 1827, as quoted in Ownby, "Approximations of Chinese Bandits," p. 245.

成年人。"① 欧恩比认为，一种他所称的"反抗的男性气概"（protest masculinity）在起作用。据这一观点，那些无法满足女子期待的男子只好采取"更激烈的行为来证明自己是个男人"。② 沃森创造"单身汉亚文化"（bachelor subculture）这个词汇来解释反社会行为如何成为这些男人的准则。他这样形容这一关联："光棍有时用来提升他们男性形象的策略就是使公开挑战其他男人面子的行为成为惯例。已婚的男人为了保护家庭，履行义务，必须注重脸面；未婚男人没面子可顾，不被社区尊重。……因而，当然就成为永远长不大的男孩。依据这一观点，可以推论出：未婚青年是不在乎面子的，因而是危险的。……这些'光棍'除了施暴的声誉，没有什么可失去的。"③

欧恩比注意到光棍一词既指暴力的轻罪犯人，也指单身汉。他引用一位19世纪传教士的说法，光棍炫耀自己："胆敢公然反抗官方，并犯下各种罪行。他们在伤人和受伤时，不吭一声，杀人也不眨眼。"④ 欧恩比也认为，中国历史上的强盗皆是光棍。沃森发现，光棍多为家中的第三、第四或第五子，因为家里太穷，无法为他们提供祖产，有些人年纪轻轻的就被父母赶走，只好和其他光棍一起住在收容所。⑤ 成年之后，许多人住到工人宿舍、寺庙等光棍聚集之处，闲暇时则以学武为乐。

19世纪淮北地区的光棍有两个选择：从军或去城市找工作。中国历代的军人多来自淮北。从军中退伍后，许多人因为找不到工作而沦

---

① Ownby, "Approximations of Chinese Bandits," p. 242.

② Ibid.

③ James L. Watson, "Self-Defense Corps, Violence, and the Bachelor Subculture in South China: Two Case Studies," *Proceedings of the Second International Conference on Sinology*, Academia Sinica, Taiwan (Republic of China), June 1989, p. 216.

④ Ownby, "Approximations of Chinese Bandits," p. 244.

⑤ Watson, "Self-Defense Corps, Violence, and the Bachelor Subculture in South China," p. 213.

为乞丐、游民或廉价劳工。这时,做强盗就成为他们唯一的活路。①

这一时期的许多光棍强盗都是从贩私盐起家的。(由于政府对盐征重税,他们从中获利颇丰。)然而地方政府开始注意到这种非法活动。分析形势后,一位地方县令得出结论:制造动乱的男子分为三类:光棍,走私者,强盗——并且这三类人有相当大的重叠。②一位评论者总结了这些年轻男子的态度:他们不遵守朝廷的法律,也不听从父兄的训诫。③

这群强盗原来只是小规模地抢家劫舍,后来开始有了组织。李中清写道:"在1855年,捻匪在雉河集(安徽省的一个小县)结合成一支大军——捻军。他们的目的是推翻清政府。"④其他有相同政治理念的团体如太平军,也与他们互通声气。在捻军最盛时期,其成员包括了10万个光棍,他们活跃于安徽、河南、湖北、江苏及山东省,势力持续增长。1862年安徽巡抚报告朝廷:淮北至少有2000个捻军的碉堡,每处均有1000—3000个居民,控制了200万—600万人。⑤ 1868年,靠着外国武器及西方作战的方式,清朝才得以平息捻乱。

罗伯特·卡普兰(Robert Kaplan)发现19世纪中期的中国与当今中国有许多相似之处。根据卡普兰的说法:"19世纪中期清朝衰弱,引起许多武装叛乱,上百万的中国人被杀……背后的原因是……

---

① See James Tong, "Rational Outlaws: Rebels and Bandits in the Ming Dynasty, 1368 - 1664," in Michael Taylor, ed., *Rationality and Revolution* (Cambridge: Cambridge University Press, 1988), pp. 98 - 128.

② Perry, *Rebels and Revolutionaries in North China, 1845 - 1945*, p. 102.

③ Hsiao Kung-chuan, *Rural China: Imperial Control in the Nineteenth Century* (Seattle: University of Washington Press, 1967), p. 458.

④ Li, "Discussions on the Gender Imbalance in China and the Entailed Social Problems," p. 11.

⑤ Perry, *Rebels and Revolutionaries in North China, 1845 - 1945*, p. 127.

人口的增加无法配合人均耕地的减少。"① 他同时观察到，在20世纪90年代中期发展中国家只有埃及和孟加拉国的人均耕地比中国少。如今，中国正在经历几十年不遇的旱灾，东北部（古代捻军的故乡）受创最重。和19世纪类似的是，国内现在也有大量的年轻单身汉："根据权威部门的报告，中国目前有8000万贫民、8000万流动人口，不久将有8000万单身汉。"② 我们认为，这三个人群的重叠性会非常显著。中国似乎将有一支光棍大军，不逊于19世纪的捻军人数。

（二）中世纪的葡萄牙

中世纪的葡萄牙是一个长子继承制国家。为了完成家族财富的积累和传承，当时的该国各世代将大量资源集中在长子身上，而剩余的光棍们对当时葡国的内政外交产生了巨大的影响。③ 这一时期葡萄牙的成年人口性别比例约为112（男）：100（女），孩童的性别比例还要更高。④ 即便是底层妇女也不愿嫁给底层男人。多种因素导致了极大的政治不稳定，很多底层光棍聚集在一起组成了军队。

葡萄牙上层社会也有光棍，次子以后的贵族子嗣，没有家产可以继承，也找不到妻子。柏恩说道："在青春期过后，男孩会过一段小太保的日子，这被认为是贵族男性成长的必经阶段。小太保们并不孤独，他们集体行动、一起生活、旅行；他们可能武装并叫上和自己同

---

① Robert D. Kaplan, *The Ends of the Earth*: *A Journey at the Dawn of the Twenty-first Century* (New York: Random House, 1996), pp. 299 – 300.

② Ren, "Confronting Three Populations of 80 Million," p. 80.

③ 这一案例研究改编自 Boone, "Noble Family Structure and Expansionist Warfare in the Late Middle Ages"; and Boone, "Parental Investment and Elite family Structure in Preindustrial States".

④ Boone, "Noble Family Structure and Expansionist Warfare in the Late Middle Ages," p. 89.

龄的父亲下属的孩子。"① 一位观察家也提出了对这种行为的解释："家中次子们无法继承父亲的财产,唯有通过参军维护其地位。他们集体行动,除了武力一无所知,他们为非作歹,欺压穷人,令人咬牙切齿。"②

在政治叛乱时期,光棍群体以武力作后盾,支持承诺分配国家财产的叛军,希望新政府成立后,可以分得一杯羹。另一方面,政府也会派遣光棍冒险去征服和殖民。柏恩提到若昂一世的案例,他是葡萄牙国王的私生兄弟,在国王死后靠着他的光棍兄弟夺得政权。若昂一世后来发现光棍兄弟继续掠夺,威胁到他政权的安全,他于是得到罗马教皇的同意,发动了"收复失地运动"(Reconguista)——葡萄牙对北非海岸的军事攻击。柏恩指出,这些无法通过正当途径获取土地和其他资源收入的光棍幼子们,唯有发动战争才能扭转其社会地位和物质条件。③ 正如达比(Georges Duby)注意到的:"显而易见,光棍们被成家男人、族长和屋主等设制的许多社会禁令排除在外,混乱的行为使他们成为社会中不稳定的边缘群体,也是十字军东征的主力。"④

从某种意义上说,葡萄牙的这种扩张战略取得了成功。到了16世纪中期,近25%的成年贵族男性死于战争,有效地减少了光棍人数。值得一提的是,男性在家中的出生顺序越靠后,他死于异域的可能性就愈高。至此可见,在中世纪的葡萄牙,由高性别比例和长子继承制导致了政治动乱、战事和领土扩张。⑤

---

① Boone, "Noble Family Structure and Expansionist Warfare in the Late Middle Ages," p. 89.

② Philip de Mezieres, as cited in ibid. , p. 86.

③ Boone, "Noble Family Structure and Expansionist Warfare in the Late Middle Ages," p. 94 (emphasis in original).

④ Georges Duby, *The Chivalrous Society*, trans, Cynthia Postan (London: Edward Arnold, 1977), p. 120.

⑤ Boone, "Parental Investment and Elite Family Structure in Preindustrial States," p. 871.

(三) 奥德的强盗与叛军

英国在殖民时期发现印度杀女婴后，就采取了一套办法来终止这种恶习。英国观察家注意到杀婴部落与暴力水平的关联。据一位学者观察："许多杀婴的部落，特别是在西北省和奥德，都是较为暴力及反叛的，他们惯于抢劫、骚扰及制造不安。"①

在印度西北部，拉其普特人杀女婴的习俗似乎对当地暴力水平有影响。威廉·克鲁克（William Crooke）写道："由于杀女婴，拉其普特人缺少新娘，年轻人无法享受家庭生活之乐，被迫和野蛮部落——Haburas、Beriyas 的女人媾和。在这种情况下生出的小孩，后来在中部杜布（Central Duab）及罗希尔坎德的暴动中，扮演了主要的角色。"②

杀女婴和暴力之间是有直接关联的。当时许多拉其普特人的家族为儿子找妻子的唯一可行之道，就是绑架。一位观察家注意到："绑架年轻女孩，并把她们卖为妻或卖为娼，令人强烈担忧。西北省的警察长在 1870 年报告，有 28 个年轻女子被卖为娼，121 个被卖为妻，还有更多的案例没被发现——绑架年轻女孩已到了无法无天的地步。"③

与中世纪的葡萄牙一样，女性的稀缺导致了印度部分地区男性之间竞争的加剧。在印度地位越高的家庭越会杀女婴，结果只有长子才能找到妻子，次子以后都得自谋生路，许多人干脆从军。用现代的说法，就是"军队和其他公家机关，成为奥德最重要的安全屏障，年轻男性不必去抢夺土地，他们可以参军或担任公职。……单单奥德的比斯瓦拉（Byswara）区，就有 16000 人参军，而东部的布诺达（Buno-

---

① Lalita Panigrahi, *British Social Policy and Female Infanticide in India* (New Delhi: Munshiram Manoharlal, 1972), p. 12.

② William Crooke, *The North-western Provinces of India: Their History, Ethnology, and Administration* (London: Methuen, 1897), pp. 138–139.

③ Quoted in Panigrahi, *British Social Policy and Female Infanticide in India*, p. 183.

da）参军人数也达到 15000 人"。① 但政府终于无力支付这么大的军饷，因此变相地允许他们去打家劫舍，很多军人在退伍之后，也不愿放弃这种简易的谋生之道。②

还有一批身无分文的年轻男士成为强盗，拥兵自立，谋杀富人，偷窃土地。儿子杀害父亲，兄弟互残，表亲互戕。胆子越大的抢得越多，最残暴的强盗头子反而成为奥德的大地主，他们不加区别地抢占土地。

> 现在大地主们使国家陷入动荡，生命财产变得毫无保障。无论他们是彼此斗争或与地方官争执，有理没理，他们都会在并非与自己同阶层的男人所属土地上乱杀一通，无处幸免，无人幸免。他们滥杀无辜的老人、小孩、妇女，犹如在杀动物一样，眼睛也不眨一下。他们还虐待俘虏，直到拿到赎金为止。③

光棍群建立起碉堡，拥有枪弹，准备和英国政府长期对抗。被派去调查强盗头目财产的人都被谋杀，土地被任意荒弃以避开政府课税。终于在 1815 年一场特别血腥的战役后，英国政府将奥德纳管，以戒严令来镇压叛军。④

史利曼（W. H. Sleeman）是英国殖民时代早期奥德的史学家，他质疑当时英国政府为什么没对强盗头目招降，然后让他们去攻击邻国，这往往是面临内乱时政府的不二选择。结论是英军无所不在，从奥德各地攻入，英国政府强力介入印度和邻国，宁可派出 5 万大军在

---

① Quoted in P. D. Reeves, ed., *Sleeman in Oudh: An Abridgement of W. H. Sleeman's A Journey through the Kingdom of Oude in 1849 – 50* (Cambridge. Cambridge University Press, 1971), pp. 94 – 95.

② 更多案例，参见 ibid.

③ W. H. Sleeman, quoted in ibid., pp. 175 – 176.

④ See ibid.

东印度公司的旗下去攻击所有东方国家,也不愿意结合光棍于其旗帜下共享殊荣。①

由于这段历史,难怪现在的北方邦,曾经的奥德地区,仍有印度最高的性别比例及犯罪率,也依旧荡不安。②

(四) 清朝统治时期台湾的动乱

17—19 世纪末,台湾处于清政府统治之下。在那段时间内,台湾平均每三年就有一次严重的暴动,18 世纪共有 19 次暴动,19 世纪 58 次。从 1787 年至 1862 年,平均每 1.8 年就暴动一次,直到 19 世纪以后才逐渐减少。③

虽然我们不知道台湾地区当时的官方人口数字,但我们知道它有非常扭曲的性别比例。根据许文熊的说法,《台湾日志》的编撰者在 1720 年写道,中国人很难娶到妻子,因为女人很少。在大埔的 257 个居民中,只有 1 个女人。六年后,闽浙总督高其倬说凤山、诸罗及彰化的移民"都没老婆"。当时流行一句话:"一个老婆胜过三个天公老祖。"尽管这一评论有些夸大,但 18 世纪这一地区有着相当明显的非正常性别比例。④

这一时期台湾不断暴动的主因,显然就是台湾的高性别比例,这一现象一直持续到 19 世纪末。从 1684 年至 1788 年,清政府禁止家庭

---

① P. D. Reeves, ed., *Sleeman in Oudh*: *An Abridgement of W. H. Sleeman's A Journey through the Kingdom of Oude in 1849 – 50* (Cambridge. Cambridge University Press, 1971), pp. 298 – 299.

② 在超过 20 年的殖民统治中,杀女婴受到严厉的惩罚。此后,英国 1875 年报告说在奥德的青少年性犯罪率是 118.6%。印度 1991 年的人口普查显示在北方邦的总体人口性别比是 114(男):100(女)。

③ These statistics are from Hsu Wen-hsiung, "Frontier Social Organization and Social Disorder in Ch'ing Taiwan," in Ronald G. Knapp, ed., *China's Island Frontier*: *Studies in the Historical Geography of Taiwan* (Honolulu: University Press of Hawaii, 1980), pp. 87 – 106.

④ Hsu, "Frontier Social Organization and Social Disorder in Ch'ing Taiwan," p. 88.

整家移居台湾，只有单身男子才会获准定居。① 1788年后政府虽然允许家庭移居，但却不鼓励此举。这一家庭移居政策的前后不一致反映了政府的分歧。主张单身男子移居的人认为，政策不鼓励永久移居，可以防止台湾变成反叛基地。主张家庭移居的人认为，只有家庭也一起去，男性移民才不会造反。

当时有不少赞成家庭移居的人发现，台湾的高性别比例造成了清政府最担心的问题。蓝鼎元是1721年清政府派去平乱的最高统帅，他就公开反对单身男性移居的政策。据约翰·谢泼德（John Shepherd）的说法：

> 蓝鼎元指出，广东客家地区的移居劳工是前车之鉴，这些劳工形成了非常团结的小组织，谋杀、打架，甚至大胆到去偷窃有属权标记的牛只。不准妻子及家人移民，必会造成一帮无法无天的暴民。他主张，要移居台湾的，应准许他们带妻小一起过去；已在台湾的，应让他们接家眷过来；没有家庭的不许来，打架生事的一律送回去。他强调，移居者一旦有家庭，就会失去暴动的动因。②

当时的闽浙总督高其倬十分担心台湾的高性别比例会带来的后果，于是给朝廷写了一份奏折，要求改变其禁止携带家属的移民政策。谢泼德写道：

> 高其倬发现，台湾的民俗粗野，喜欢喝酒及沉迷赌博。台南附近老社区的居民有妻有子，但在北部及南部的新社区则多为单

---

① John Robert Shepherd, *Statecraft and Political Economy on the Taiwan Frontier, 1600 - 1800* (Stanford, Calif.: Stanford University Press, 1993), p. 143.

② Shepherd, *Statecraft and Political Economy on the Taiwan Frontier*, p. 149 (emphasis in original).

身汉,"内心毫无情感"。20至40个男性住在一起,没事就喝酒、聚赌,没钱就去抢。如果他们有了老婆,内外生活就会有所不同,就不会有困扰和失序。如果他们要养活老婆,就要戒掉喝酒和赌博的恶习。如果他们要守护各自的家庭,抢劫事件自然会减少。①

早期前去台湾的移民多为年轻男性,"绝大多数未婚。因为中国家庭喜欢儿子,会杀女婴或疏于照顾年幼的女儿,导致适婚年龄的男子多于女子,再加上清廷限制家庭举家移民的政策,未婚男子无法成家,好勇斗狠,造成边界不安"。②

欧恩比称他们为"暴力企业家"。③ 当时的编史者则称他们为"罗汉脚":"罗汉脚是台湾话,形容没有土地、无财产、无妻小、无职业的穷人;他们赌博、偷盗、争斗、叛乱。"那么罗汉脚是什么人?他是单身,四处游荡,形成朋党,衣衫褴褛,一生都打赤脚。在大城市里,他们的人数不下于数百,在乡村中不少于数十人,这也是为什么台湾很难治理的原因。④

华特·陈(Walter Chen)说,光棍组织是台湾动乱的主因,其中

---

① Shepherd, *Statecraft and Political Economy on the Taiwan Frontier*, p. 149.

② Shepherd, *Statecraft and Political Economy on the Taiwan Frontier*, pp. 311 – 312.

③ David Ownby, "The Ethnic Feud in Qing Taiwan: What Is This Violence Business, Anyway? An Interpretation of the 1782 Zhang-Quan Xiedou," *Late Imperial China*, Vol. 11, No. 1 (June 1990), pp. 75 – 98. 种族仇杀或械斗使年轻人有机会从暴力行动中赚钱。事实上,械斗参与者有时候还会雇佣士兵为他们工作。而暴力在其他方面也是合算的:根据一位当时的评论者的话:"家族强人喜欢械斗,因为这能让他们赚大钱。……家族恶棍喜欢械斗,因为他们自己有机会瓜分利益。……讼棍喜欢械斗,因为他们可以通过诡计赚钱。……恶人喜欢械斗,因为他们可以操纵形势,使之有利于己。衙门中人喜欢械斗,因为他们有机会靠自己的关系赚钱。"参见 Ownby, *Brother Hoods Secret Societies in Early and Mid-Qing China*, p. 165。

④ Chen Shengsao, *Wensulu*. Beijing: Shumu wenxian chubanshe, original edition dated 1827, as cited in Ownby, *Brotherhoods and Secret Societies in Early and Mid-Qing China*, p. 20.

最重要的就是天地会。

  天地会是民间团体，目的是反清复明，并帮助其他无助的移民。组织的名称……来自它的口号：天地为父母，入会即兄弟。想加入的人，需"歃血为盟"并宣誓效忠。那时大多数移民都是单身，加入天地会不但可参与反清活动，也可减少寂寞。……在朱一贵起义和林爽文起义时，天地会的动员让他们在很短的时间内，就横扫全台湾。①

  如果不是光棍组织的参与，台湾的状况不至于糟到要清军出动人马的地步。② 清廷设置了一个常驻台湾的新机构来镇暴，新团体的成员也多为来自福建及广东的光棍。换句话说，清廷是以光棍镇压光棍，官军的行为其实和强盗差不多。军队被允许经商，结果腐败及走私盛行，成了清廷当时在台湾留下的典型形象。当时的人认为："台湾的政府是整个朝廷中最腐败的。"③ 直到1787年的一次叛变，清廷终于认识到它送去台湾平乱的军队就是乱源，不得不把名将福康安派去台湾镇压。

  在那之后，禁止携家眷移民的命令解除了，台湾也趋于安定。韩书瑞（Susan Naguin）及罗斯基（Evelyn Rawski）发现，台湾的性别比例在19世纪中期恢复正常，这也正好是岛内暴动减少的时期。④ 1874年清廷派沈葆桢来台，他坚决主张清除一切对家庭移民的障碍。

---

 ① Walter Chen, "The Era of the Ch-ing Dynasty," http://www.leksu.com/mainp4e.htm, p. 8.

 ② 欧恩比注意到，那些在1787—1788年间台湾林爽文起义中因叛乱罪名被抓捕的人中，60%的人中都说他们已结婚。然而这些数据并不真实，首先，这些被抓的人里是无辜的；其次，几乎70%的人未说出或未被问及婚姻状态。参见 Ibid., p. 187。

 ③ Hsu, "Frontier Social Organization and Social Disorder in Ch-ing Taiwan," p. 94.

 ④ Susan Naquin and Evelyn S. Rawski, *Chinese Society in the Eighteenth Century* (New Haven, Conn.: Yale University Press, 1987), p. 210.

总而言之，当时台湾的高性别比例对其暴乱和反叛事件的作用是显著的。将光棍送到岛上去镇乱实非明智之举。

六、其他历史案例

还有其他的案例证明过高的性别比例会扩大、激化并挑起社会内外的冲突。我们在此只作简要介绍，深层分析尚有待进一步研究。

（一）波利尼西亚

根据历史学家的观点，波利尼西亚（Polynesia）过高的性别比例及极有限的领土，造成了次子以降必须出外去闯天下的情况。部落首领也认为如果让这群单身汉留在岛内，势将成为乱源。许多人甚至未曾到达目的地便死去，其余的人也多数就此一去不返。① 狄克曼谈到波利尼西亚的蒂科皮亚人（Tikopia）时写道："在蒂科皮亚人看来，男人出海无异于自杀。……研究家族血统的学者发现，在1929年以前，69个死亡的男子中有23个是死于海上。1929年至1952年，有30次海难，导致81人死亡，20人生还。……他们之中绝大多数未婚，年龄都在30岁以下。"②

（二）中国的太监

古代中国及印度都曾经有太监。但在中国，他们的人数众多，明朝末年有超过10万名太监在朝廷任职。

因为皇帝有太多的妻子及嫔妃，太监被视为皇帝的最佳雇员。穷

---

① James L. Boone, communication with Valerie Hudson, April 11, 1999.
② Mildred Dickemann, "Demographic Consequences of Infanticide in Man," *Annual Review of Ecology and Systematics*, Vol. 6 (1975), p. 124.

人家庭常把次子以后的儿子去势，希望他们有一天可以为皇帝服务，① 但只有十分之一的去势者能成为太监，其他的年轻男性就成为政府的烫手山芋。② 罗宾逊（David Robinson）说："只有少数人能到北京就职，其他的人又残废又穷困潦倒，就变成乞丐或强盗。"他引用沈福（Shen Fu，音译）的话："在河间任丘以北，有一些去势者隐藏在城墙破损之处，当有车马经过时，他们之中较弱的就会去乞讨，强壮的就会握住缰绳要钱，落单的过路人还会被拉下马来。"③

太监的支出严重地耗损国库：每个太监每年发给30石米（一石约400磅）。在明朝末期，太监花了政府成千上万石的米粮。政府如何使这笔巨额花费合理化呢？某种程度上，他们并不想提高这些未被任用的太监的地位。蔡石山叙述道："在1620年，有2万多名去势者涌入首都，向政府讨工作。当他们无法如愿时，就变得愤怒，开始暴动。毫无疑问，来自兵部和礼部的官员在他们开始采取措施对抗可能的叛乱时会表现得极为惊慌。"④

太监也造成了官僚体系的膨胀。许多重要的军职被两类指挥者掌控，一个是太监，另一个则不是；不过，宫廷侍卫则一律是太监，皇帝有时还把最敏感的机密交给太监处理。由于腐败及滥权，不少太监成为当时中国最有钱的人，其他的太监则有人阴谋策反，有人协助叛军登基。⑤ 某种意义上，太监制度让光棍得以进入政府的最高核心，也使政府腐败不堪。

---

① See Mary M. Anderson, *Hidden Power*: *The Palace Eunuchs of Imperial China* (Buffalo. N. Y.: Prometheus, 1990).

② David M. Robinson, "Notes on Eunuchs in Hebei during the Mid-Ming Period," *Ming Studies*, Vol. 34 (July 1995), pp. 1 – 16.

③ Ibid., p. 2.

④ Henry Shih-shan Tsai, *The Eunuchs in the Ming Dynasty* (Albany: State University of New York Press, 1996), p. 25.

⑤ 有关太监在宫廷阴谋中的角色阐述，参见 Anderson, *Hidden Power*。

(三) 中国的僧侣和类宗教的帮会

中国历代常有光棍因出家后来得到荣华富贵的例子。中国历史上和尚深陷于世俗事务，年轻和尚常常参与光棍的行动。① 寺庙和准宗教组织也以武功和财富著称于世。

最著名的和尚是少林寺的武僧。他们曾救过唐太宗的性命，被赐予土地修建庙宇。最盛时，少林寺养了 2500 个武僧。寺庙、尤其是佛教寺庙由于太监的赞助，那些年间迅猛发展，权倾一时。公元 9 世纪末的官方数字显示："100 万名和尚中的五分之一控制了全国 4600 庙宇、4 万宝塔、无数小庙中相当一部分，还包括奴仆和侍从、最好的土地、大量财富，且完全免税。"② 到了 15 世纪末，和尚人数过 50 万人，根据一个官员的计算，供养他们的米可以供应整个首都的人口超过一年以上。③ 根据罗宾逊所说，武僧如佣兵一般，和官军一起并肩平乱。④

大多数和尚来自杀女婴的省份，他们自然也是光棍。在元、明和清代，福建杀女婴行为普遍，田汝康说："人们可能很快想知道这一情形会产生其他什么社会问题。这也是为什么福建与中国其他省份不同。据说，十个行脚僧中有九个来自福建。"⑤

秘密的帮会组织如同宗教团体。环境不利，机会不佳，导致许多年轻人尤其是光棍参与这些秘密帮会组织，至少他们可以混口饭吃。⑥

---

① 事实上，一些修行团体，如道士，并不保持独身，尽管他们也不结婚。

② Anderson, *Hidden Power*, p. 162.

③ Ibid., p. 226.

④ David M. Robinson, "The Management of Violence in the Mid-Ming Capital Region," Colgate University, 1998.

⑤ T'ien, *Male Anxiety and Female Chastity*, p. 31, n. 54.

⑥ Susan Naquin, *Shantung Rebellion: The Wang Lun Uprising of 1774* (New Haven, Conn.: Yale University Press, 1981), p. 48.

沃森谈及产生大量兄弟情义的"单身亚文化"。① 戴维斯（Fei-ling Davis）指出："典型的帮会成员，都是些无土地的农民、无工作的苦力、走卒、解甲的军人、走私犯及天灾的受害者——他们都被称为游民。"②

帮会的活动以习武为主，他们也以拳术表演的方式招募新血。想加入帮会的年轻人得先拜师习武。越穷的地方，加入帮会的人就越多。19世纪末期，有一封地方官员的信中写道："途经茌平。此地极为穷困，村民都在研习义和拳。"③ 学拳的人表现出了光棍的特征："这群流浪汉和无赖汉，常常拔剑来吸引群众，他们创立了'顺刀会、虎尾鞭、义和拳及八卦教'等组织，在村里胡作非为，压迫善良百姓。变化的根源是赌博。他们一到集市就公开架起棚子，收取典当物，开始聚赌。"④

这些秘密帮会组织中的一些成员当了土匪和叛军。1898年山东巡抚报告：今年春雨来得太晚，粮食价格上涨。军队又开始裁员，无业游民成千上万。他们拥有武器枪支，号称借粮，骚扰邻里，抢劫马匹、武器和弹药。⑤ 另一同代人写道：在直隶、河南及山东省，盗匪横行。……一旦发生饥荒，仗着人数众多，他们在光天化日下抢劫，还把这种行为称为劫富济贫。⑥

---

① See Watson, "Self-Defense Corps, Violence, and the Bachelor Subculture in South China", and Ownby, *Brotherhoods and Secret Societies in Early and Mid-Qing China*, p. 20. See Susan Nequin, *Shantung Rebelling: The Wang Lun Uprising of 1774* (New Haven. Conn. : Yale University Press, 1981), p. 48.

② Fei-ling Davis, *Primitive Revolutionaries of China: A Study of Secret Societies in the Late Nineteenth Century* (Honolulu: University of Hawaii Press, 1977), p. 90.

③ Cited in Joseph Esherick, *The Origins of the Boxer Uprising* (Berkeley: University of California Press, 1987), p. 223.

④ Cited in Joseph Esherick, *The Origins of the Boxer Uprising* (Berkeley: University of California Press, 1987), p. 46.

⑤ Quoted in ibid., pp. 176–177.

⑥ Quoted in Hsiao, *Rural China*, p. 447.

光棍在八卦教叛乱、拳匪之乱、黑旗军的叛乱中，扮演着重要的角色。根据拉斐（Ella Laffey）所写，黑旗军的首领刘永福就是光棍。"刘永福的出身是个贫穷的孤儿，也没有妻小。……他曾在河边打零工糊口，在山上捡柴去卖，他精力充沛，是帮会最希望吸收的人才。当刘永福21岁时，他和兄弟及四个同村的人，在钦州加入叛军。"① 最后他当上黑虎头领。刘永福在自传中解释了他加入黑旗军的原因："如果不能有一天光宗耀祖，我会感到耻辱；我总不能一直靠吃米糠来充饥。"②

有些叛乱的光棍及其追随者最后获得成功。明太祖人生的大部分时间曾是"一个流浪汉、乞丐、帮会成员及叛军"。③ 1629年，当明朝裁撤官府职员时，"李自成就是被裁撤的人员之一，他决定加入叛军，最后还成了叛军领袖，把明朝逐出北京"。④ 可以说，明朝始于光棍，也终于光棍。

在中国的历史上，社会边缘人对参与暴动都不会拒绝，偶尔他们也能改朝换代。根据根绍·尼什马拉（Gensho Nishimara）所述，这些人多是些无赖，靠残忍暴力为生。⑤ 上田信（Ueda Makato）称城市无赖的游民以暴力为生，常常形成"强制组织"。⑥ 明朝政府的报告

---

① Ella S. Laffey, "The Making of a Rebel: Liu Yung-fu and the Formation of the Black Flag Army," in Jean Chesnaux, ed. , *Popular Movements and Secret Societies in China, 1840 – 1950* (Stanford, Calif. : Stanford University Press, 1972), pp. 89 – 90.

② Cited in ibid. , p. 90.

③ David M. Robinson, "The Management of Violence in the Mid-Ming Capital Region," Colgate University, 1998, p. 8.

④ David M. Robinson, "Banditry and Rebellion in the Capital Region during the Mid-Ming (1450 – 1525)," Ph. D. dissertation, Princeton University, 1995, p. 490.

⑤ Ueda Makato, "Minmatsu Shinso: Konan no toshino burai o meguru shakui kankei, dako to kyakufu," *Shigaka zasshi* [Journal of historical studies], Vol. 90, No. 12 (1981), pp. 1619 – 1653.

⑥ Gensho Nishimara, "Ryu roku ryu nana no ran ni tsuite," *Toyoshi kenkyu* [Asian historical research], Vol. 32, No. 4 (1974), pp. 44 – 86.

中指出，北京的犯罪都是些"不在册"的人——由光棍组成的帮会干的。但这些罪犯的结局未必都坏。① 用中国民间土话来说："要做官，带根棍子吧！"指的就是政府会以公职来招安盗匪。②

总之，中国的这些类宗教的帮会，不管是正统还是异端，给政府带来了极大的安全隐患。一位17世纪的评论者说，这些组织往往以习武强身始，以叛乱夺政终。③

七、结论

从历史案例中，我们至少可以得到两个结论。第一，光棍用来改善自身命运的策略常常对社会产生负面影响，造成社会暴力，进一步降低女性的地位。第二，政府在了解高性别比例的潜在暴力机制问题之后，得花很大的代价来处理它所造成的问题，包括吸收光棍从军，只是这么做反而会引起更多的不安。在此后章节，我们从现代社会入手分析这个关于性别的理论框架。

---

① Robinson, "Banditry and Rebellion in the Capital Region during the Mid-Ming," pp. 126 – 127.

② Ownby, "Approximations of Chinese Bandits," p. 240.

③ Quoted in Barend J. ter Harr, *The White Lotus Teachings in Chinese Religious History* (Leiden, Netherlands: E. J. Brill, 1992), p. 237.

第六章 21世纪的光棍——政策建议

"缺乏女性的问题已经引起关注。"印度罗赫塔克郊区检查官委米拉（Urmila）说，"年轻未婚男性的犯罪率很高，对女性的暴力也增加了。"① 最近《经济学人》的一篇新闻报道首次指出，年轻男性人口过剩造成了频繁的社会冲突，这也是所有文献中最直接表达未婚和暴力关联的。到了2010年，中国、印度及其他亚洲国家将有更多的年轻男性将要成年，问题会更凸显，所以安全学者应该开始分析：光棍的社会角色为何？如果再不作危机处理的话，这个问题对一国、一地区及国际会造成什么影响？虽然我们没有足够的信息来提供确切的答案，但我们会就所知有所建议，希望政府及学术界可以进一步进行深入研究。

本章中，我们检视现代中国及印度光棍的意识形态和行为特征，并从两国政府的观点来寻找对策。我们分析讨论了一些政策措施，有些政策已开始实施，并对政策的优劣进行了分析。

一、现代光棍的特征与行为分析

从第五章所提出的史料，我们发现当前中国和印度的光棍族群，

---

① "Missing Sisters," *Economist*, April 19, 2003, p. 36.

和他们的前辈相差不大。他们同样来自社会底层，缺乏教育及专长；他们多数是失业游民，混杂在流动人口大军之中，自成帮派，经常聚众生事。他们容易犯罪——抢劫、强暴及谋杀；容易加入犯罪组织、走私军火、敲诈、嫖妓及贩毒；他们之中许多人吸毒、酗酒，进一步提高了其暴力犯罪的几率。总之，中印两国的光棍是一股随时会被引爆的不安定力量，给社会带来了恐惧与不安。

（一）中国的流动人口

中国的光棍多为流动人口，犯罪及吸毒的比例特别高，他们聚集在繁荣的都市，也在西部边疆出没。在1997年，有超过50%的光棍是离乡背井至大都市谋生的乡下人。① 1984年，中央放松对转移劳动力的限制，更助长了流动人口进城的趋势。但直到现在，乡村来的流动人口还是被歧视，他们也被排除在社会福利之外，包括失业救济金及医疗、教育福利等，而这些都是城市居民能够享受到的福利。1998年，中国政府决定对住在中小城市的农民工提供相当的社会福利。他们之中拥有稳定工作及住宅者，还能登记成为城市居民。同时，政府在2003年颁布了一项命令要求停止对农民工的歧视，企业现在可直接雇用他们，不须事先得到地方政府的同意。②

在20世纪80年代中期至末期，中国下列地区的年轻男性中有30%是未婚的：北京、广东、广西、河北、河南、湖南、山东、上海（包括江苏及安徽部分地区）、浙江及四川西部。③ 直至90年代早期，

---

① See Ren Meng, "Confronting Three Populations of 80 Million," *Inside China Mainland*, Vol. 19, No. 1 (January 1997), pp. 78 – 81.

② Feng Jianhua, "Bright Lights, Big City," *Beijing Review*, April 3, 2003, p. 22.

③ Population Census Office of the State Council of the People's Republic of China, and the Institute of Geography of the Chinese Academy of Sciences, *Population Atlas of China* (Oxford: Oxford University Press, 1987).

这些地区人口依然是全中国最多的，也有最高的新生儿性别比。①1990年的数据（2000年的数据尚不可获）证实了在越年轻的族群中，过剩男性越多，性别比例也愈高。例如在28—49岁的未婚者中，97%是男性。② 15—34岁的年龄组中，有13%是过剩男性；在35—55岁年龄组中，有5%的男性。③

虽然中国政府未提供光棍的收入数据，但我们利用其他数据，仍可建立起未婚男性的教育程度和收入之间的关系。在第五章里，我们引用1990年的数据，发现74%的未婚男性高中未读完。④乡村光棍的教育程度更差：97%的年轻男性未受高中教育，40%不识字。⑤有些学者认为中国的光棍和男尊女卑的婚姻制度有关。我们同意这个说法。根据叶文振及林擎国的观点："适婚男性中有大量的光棍，因为社会认为婚姻应该是'男尊女卑'的，而未婚男性的社会地位太低。"⑥

中国把就业数据也列为机密，所以我们无法确定男性光棍失业和

---

① See H. Yuan Tien, Zhang Tianlu, Ping Yu, Li Jingneng, and Lian Zhongtang, "China's Demographic Dilemmas," *Population Bulletin*, Vol. 47, No. 1 (June 1992), pp. 1 – 34; and Terence H. Hull, "Recent Trends in Sex Ratios at Birth in China," *Population and Development Review*, Vol. 16, No. 1 (March 1990), pp. 63 – 83. 正如第三章所指出的，在大都市较高性别比例的一个原因很容易与接近于产前性别检测联系起来。

② Zhang Ping, "Issues and Characteristics of the Unmarried Population," *Chinese Journal of Population Science*, Vol. 2, No. 1 (1990), p. 87. 张萍的94%的数据比例有点低，因为她只考察了28—49岁的人群。她的数据也采集于1987年。基于对我们统计数据的合理调整，我们得出97%的数值。

③ U. S. Bureau of the Census International Data Base, "1998: Population by Marital Status, Age, Sex, and Urban/Rural Residence (China)," http://www.census.gov/ipc/www/idbnew.html/.

④ Zhang, "Issues and Characteristics of the Unmarried Population," p. 88.

⑤ Ibid.

⑥ Ye Wenzhen and Lin Qingguo, "The Reasons and Countermeasures for Demographic Phenomena in China," *Chinese Demography*, Vol. 4 (1998), as quoted in Ren Feng, "Rare Branches among Rural Migrant Laborers in China: Causes, Social Implications, and Policy Proposals," Foreign Affairs College, Beijing, March 1999, p. 6.

不充分就业的比例。但我们认为,这些数据是有意义的。根据 2003 年的统计,失业劳工在乡村劳动人口中占比接近 32%。① 国家发展和改革委员会的研究人员王建说:"我估算中国的总失业率为 12%—15%,这么计算的话,到了 2001 年底,中国就有 7300 万个就业人口及 1 亿个失业人口。"②

高失业率与中国 1990 年间快速的经济转型有关。1994 年时,琳达·王(Linda Wong)说:"连在城市工业开发区里,失业者都越来越多,有 15%—30% 的劳力是过剩的。当国营企业自负盈亏而不得不开除多余的劳工时,连城市人都得去抢工作,当然这又造成更多的游民。"③

1997 年的一份研究报告指出:"有 1500 万的城市劳工失业,占城市劳工的 7.5%,比去年增加一倍。"④ 同年任孟(Ren Meng,音译)估计,有"5% 的城市居民活在贫穷线以下",全国共有 8000 万贫困人口。⑤ 其他人认为这些数字可能偏低。有研究者估算,90 年代后期,"在全国的 2 亿城市人口中,有 1200 万—2200 万绝对贫困人口,连基本的食物、衣物和依据都没有"。⑥ 1998 年中国西北的"生锈区",失业率高于 20%。⑦ 下岗工人(从国营企业解雇的人)当时约

---

① Jian Fa, "China Faces an 'Employment War'," *Beijing Review*, March 20, 2003, p. 26; and Feng Jianhua, "Migrant Workers vs. City Residents," *Beijing Review*, April 3, 2003, p. 21.

② Wang Jian, "Urbanization: A Long-Term Solution to Unemployment," *Beijing Review*, March 20, 2003, p. 28.

③ Linda Wong, "China's Urban Migrants—The Public Policy Challenge," *Pacific Affairs*, Vol. 67, No. 3 (Autumn 1994), p. 354.

④ "Army of Jobless Threatening China," Associated Press, as published in the *Salt Lake Tribune*, December 26, 1997, p. A6.

⑤ Ren, "Confronting Three Populations of 80 Million," p. 79.

⑥ Elisabeth Rosenthal, "Poverty Spreads, and Deepens, in China's Cities," *New York Times*, October 4, 1998, sec. 1, p. 3.

⑦ Erik Eckholm, "Joblessness: A Perilous Curve on China's Capitalist Road," *New York Times*, January 20, 1998, p. A1.

1100万人。① 同年，中央政府宣布将精简400万名公务员，对已恶化的失业情况，无异于雪上加霜。同时，军队宣布裁军50万人，铁道部宣布裁撤超过100万个岗位，纺织系统宣布减员120万。②

乡村的情况也不妙：根据1990年末的统计，共有1.5亿—1.7亿个乡村失业人口③，有研究预测这个数字到21世纪初将达2.5亿。④大量的乡村人口继续流入城市找工作；一份2000年的报告指出，在两周内，就有240万名乡村失业游民从铁路进入广东，170万名从公路进入，10万名以上乘船进入。⑤

中国最大的失业人群就是这群年轻、地位低、未婚的男性游民。他们中有很多乡下人希望有一天赚够了钱，能光荣地返乡结婚。⑥

---

① "Chinese Saw Crime Jump 22% in First Nine Months of 1998, Report Says," Reuters, as published in *Deseret News*, February 10 - 11, 1999, p. A7; and Jian, "China Faces an 'Employment War'," p. 27.

② Eckholm, "Joblessness," Rone Tempest, "China to Close 11 Ministries in Effort to Avoid Fiscal Crisis," *Los Angeles Times*, March 6, 1998, p. 8; Seith Faison, "China Moving to Untie Its Military Industrial Knot," *New York Times*, Jury 28, 1998, p. A1.

③ "Chinese Saw Crime Jump 22% in First Nine Months of 1998"; and Feng, "Migrant Workers vs. City Residents," p. 21.

④ Jeffery R. Taylor and Judith Banister, "China: The Problem of Employing Surplus Rural Labor," CIR Staff Paper No. 49 (Washington, D.C: Center for International Research, U.S. Bureau of the Census, July 1989), pp. viii, 75. 尽管这些数据来自1989年，但在近年的较多研究中得到很大回应。参见 Li Tan, " Population Flow into Big Cities," *Beijing Review*, July 18 – 24, 1994, pp. 15 – 24。另见 Li Jingnen, "Challenge to Chinese Population Theory Research on the Eve of the Twenty-first Century," *Chinese Population Science*, n. s., Vol. 4 (1998), p. 10.

⑤ Wang Rong, "Migrant Labourers to Face Difficulty Finding Work," *China Daily*, February 21, 2000, p. 2.

⑥ 据一位城市流动务工者说："我本来计划这次回家就结婚。但没有一份像样的工作，太不现实了。"见 Elisabeth Rosenthal, " 100 Million Restless Chinese Go Far from Home for Jobs," *New York Times*, February 24, 1999。有意思的是，一项研究计算出这些务工者带回家超过1.6万亿人民币（约2000亿美元），是政府对农村投资的三倍。Cai Fang, "The Regional Character of Labor Flow in the Transitional Period," *Chinese Population Studies*, n. s. 5 (1998), 18 – 24.

1993年的一份抽样调查显示，81.8%的游民是男性。① 更多的研究样本显示80%是35岁以下的年轻人，72%—75%是男性。② 根据2003年美国人口资料局（the Population Reference Bureau）的报告："大多数流动人口都是男性，他们一年有50周离家在外，住在男子单身宿舍中。"③ 这群移民就是中国数量超过2亿的流动人口，至少有一半没有高中学历。④

从乡村到都市之路并不顺畅。有学者说："移民的增加让已经拥挤的城市不堪负荷。在城市外围，计划外的住房如雨后春笋，不但造成治安的问题，也带来仿冒品及色情行业。"⑤ 超过两百万个的游民，住在火车站及仓库里面及周边。⑥

多年来，城市居民与流动人口之间的争执不断。当被问到流动人口对生活的影响时，78%的上海人说很讨厌他们，81%的人担心财物被偷，91%的人抱怨他们造成了公共交通的拥挤。⑦ 为了减少冲突，

---

① As cited in Ji Dangsheng and Shao Qin, *The Tendency and Management of Chinese Population Movement* (Beijing: Beijing Publishing House, 1996), p. 99.

② 年龄数据来自 "HIV/AIDS-What the Chinese Experts Says," http://www.usembassy-china.org.cn/english/sandt/webaids3.htm。性别数据来自 Zhao Yi, *The Population Resources, Environment, Agriculture, and Continuous Development of 21st Century China* (Shanxi: Economic Publishing House, 1997), p. 144; Zhang Xiaohui, Wu Zhigang, and Chen Liangbiao, "Age Difference among the Rural Labor Force in Interregional Migration," *Chinese Journal of Population Science*, Vol. 9, No. 3 (1997), pp. 193 – 202; and Bruce Gilley, "Irresistible Force," *Far Eastern Economic Review*, April 4, 1996, pp. 18 – 22。另一项统计数据是30—44岁的未婚男性中几乎82%的户籍都是在农村地区。China, State Statistical Bureau, *China Population Statistical Yearbook*, 1994 (Beijing: China Statistics Press, 1994), pp. 36 – 53.

③ Http://www.prb.org/Template.cfm?Section = PRB&template =/ContentManagement/ContemtDisplay.cfm&ContentID = 8501.

④ 这一推测根据 Gilley 提供的尚不完整的数字。参见 Gilley, "Irresistible Force," p. 22。

⑤ Ren, "Confronting Three Populations of 80 Million." p. 79.

⑥ Ibid., p. 80.

⑦ Ding Jinhong, "An Analysis in the Extraneous Population Inflow and City Community Integration: Surveys on the Local Shanghaiese's Psychological Acceptance Capacity of Extraneous Population," *Population Survey*, February 1996, p. 48.

政府曾经实行"流动人口"居住登记,并派行政单位加以管理。① 20世纪90年代中期,政府再度要求严格登记移民居住地,拆掉他们无照经营的市场和流动房屋,对合法租房的移民进行登记。一位公安局的领导说:"想让社会长治久安,就必须更为妥善地处理好城市流动人口问题。"②

即使出台了各种社会管理手段,中国社会的犯罪率仍在上升。中国社会科学院法学所的研究指出,流动人口犯下超过50%的城市犯罪,"许多年轻男性甚至无法在建筑工地或工厂找到每天2美元的工作,干脆去偷窃,从下水井盖到钱包,无所不偷"。③ 中国的犯罪记录也是机密,但一些数据还是见报了,根据一份2001—2002年的出版物,枪支炸药犯罪率在这两年内上升了82%,有组织犯罪则上升了6倍。④ 1978年到1998年间,中国的犯罪率增长了三倍。⑤

青少年犯罪和有组织犯罪迅速成为中国社会极大的隐患,帮会从年轻的光棍群中寻找新生力量,危害极大。⑥ 政府已在1998年宣布成年犯罪的法定年龄下降到包括14—18岁的少年。⑦ 为了消灭城市犯罪,1998年政府还推动了"严打"。

《北京周报》(*Beijing Review*)在1996年报道:"外来人口要对首

---

① David M. Robinson, "Banditry and Rebellion in the Capital Region during the Mid-Ming (1450-1525)," Ph. D. dissertation, Princeton University, 1995, see, for example, ibid., p. 16.

② Quoted in Xiao Wang, "Police Keeping Crime Down," *China Daily*, June 8, 2000, p. 3.

③ Quoted in Michael Dorgan, "Growing Rich-Poor Gap. Economic Growth Spur Crime in China," Knight Ridder, March 27, 2002 (from original report, accessed from Proquest, LexisNexis).

④ Ibid.

⑤ Feng Shuliang, "Crime and Crime Control in a Changing China," in Liu Jianhong, Zhang Lening, and Steven F. Messner, eds., *Crime and Social Control in a Changing China* (Westport, Conn.: Greenwood, 2001), p. 123.

⑥ "The Wild East: Guns in China," *Economist*, November 10, 2001, p. 75.

⑦ Damien McElroy, "China Fears Crime Wave of One-Child Generation," May 7, 1998, http://www.future-china.org/fcn/mainland/et980507.htm.

都 80% 的刑事犯罪负责。"此外，在南方的珠江三角洲及其他沿海城市里，80% 的被捕嫌犯是外地人。① 1994 年，铁道部门处理的刑事犯罪及公共治安罪中，有 82% 是流动人口干的。1997 年在上海浦东区金桥地区，流动人口犯下了超过 90% 的罪行，1990 年时这一数据为 30%。②

其他报告也一样惊人。根据段成荣的研究，"在 1994 年，乡村流动劳工的犯罪率为 1.3%，是全国平均值的 4 倍。流动人口犯下了全中国城市三分之一到 70% 的罪行，从偷窃、抢劫、卖淫、贩毒、敲诈及谋杀，无恶不做"。③ 在杭州，20 世纪 90 年代中期 90% 的罪犯是流动人口。④ 张海阳解释了为什么游民容易犯罪："一般来说，乡村劳工较无知，不懂法律。当他们的要求不能被满足时，就会铤而走险。"⑤ 1996 年，两位比较犯罪学专家司徒英宜（Situ Yingyi，音译）及刘伟峥（Liu Weizheng，音译）作出如下分析："尽管一般城市居民实施了一部分犯罪，但新移民成为中国大城市的主要问题所在。游民所犯的暴行，多半毫无道理而且残暴。多说一句话就可能挨揍，小偷一旦感到被看不起便会杀死受害人或证人，高速公路的抢劫、强暴及绑架，往往以受害人的死亡告终；如果抱怨游民的货物不好，还可能会导致肢体伤害。"⑥ 作者所提及游民的行为和光棍几乎一模一样。

在中国，年轻的男性游民似乎也与其他罪行实施者的特征相吻

---

① Li, "Population Flow into Big Cities," p. 17.

② Ren, "Confronting Three Populations of 80 Million," p. 80.

③ Duan Chengrong, "Floating Populations and Their Effects on Rural and Urban Socioeconomic Development," *Population Research*, Vol. 22, No. 4 (1998), pp. 58–63.

④ Wong, "China's Urban Migrants," p. 340.

⑤ Zhang Haiyang, "On Flowing Population in Qiqiha'er: Current Conditions and Management," *Plan Study*, n. s., Vol. 5 (1997), p. 23.

⑥ Situ Yingyi and Liu Weizheng, "Transient Population, Crime, and Solution: The Chinese Experience," *International Journal of Offender Therapy and Comparative Criminology*, Vol. 40, No. 4 (December 1996), p. 295.

合。1996年另一份报告指出:"超过70%的男性流动务工者承认他们经常喝酒及赌博。"① 北京有一半以上的吸毒者不是当地人,他们还会介入贩毒。② 例如1996年在云南省镇康县,有45人因贩毒被捕,其中31人是流动人口。③ 1990年以来,色情场所在都市中不断涌现,主要服务对象仍是流动人口④,结果是,中国大多数的艾滋病患者是流动人口。1997年,北京有130人被报告为艾滋病患者,其中75人是流动人口。⑤ 走私武器成为光棍最重要的收入来源,公安部长陶驷驹在1996年坦承:"非法的武器及弹药,是对法律和公共安全最大的威胁。"⑥

近几年来民间的抗议与日俱增。仅1996年就至少有12000件的罢工及抗议,因为流动务工人员不满工资太微薄。⑦ 罢工的频率、规模及强度,越来越大。辽宁罢工是自从1949年解放以来最大规模的一次⑧,这些抗议有不少是跨省的联合,让政府担心会发生地区性的群体事件。

总体来看,观察家们似乎觉察到中国光棍有参与破坏行为的倾

---

① Yang Ji, "Transient Workers: A Special Social Group," and "Education Transient Workers," both in *Beijing Review*, June 3-9, 1996, p. 21.

② Huang Wei, "Continuing War on Drugs," *Beijing Review*, September 2-8, 1996, pp. 17-19.

③ He Jingwu, "War on Drug Trafficking," *Beijing Review*, September 15-21, 1997, pp. 17-19.

④ See, for example, Vincent E. Gil, Marc Wang, Allen F. Anderson, and Guao Mat thew Lin, "Plum Blossoms and Pheasants: Prostitutes, Prostitution, and Social Control Measures in Contemporary China," *International Journal of Offender Therapy and Comparatiove Criminology*, Vol. 38, No. 4 (December 1994), pp. 319-337.

⑤ "AIDS Day, 1997: China Responds to AIDS," http://www.redfish.com/usembassychina/sandt/aidsdy97.htm.

⑥ Quoted in "Tougher Actions toward Crime," *Beijing Review*, May 20-26, 1996, p. 6.

⑦ Ren, "Confronting Three Populations of 80 Million," p. 78.

⑧ Audra Ang, "Workers in Northeastern China Take to Streets for Back Pay, Better Benefits," Associated Press, March 10, 2003.

向。有人称光棍是"社会暴力的元素",有人认为"中国官方面临的最大挑战"就是如何安定流动务工人员的心,让他们高兴,至少是对现状满意。如果政府失败了,公共秩序就会破产,因为游民是不愿意永远当二等公民的"。①

(二) 光棍与印度的"蛮荒西部"

印度没有类似中国光棍特征的数据,但我们还是确认了印度的性别比例和暴力犯罪成正比。我们也找到证据证明印度的过剩男性逐渐成为社会不稳定的重要因素。

光棍主要住在印度的北部及西北部,如阿萨姆邦、比哈尔邦、旁遮普邦和北方邦、北安查尔邦和西孟加拉邦等。② 这些地区一起构成所谓印度的"蛮荒西部",其毫无法律秩序的情况如同19世纪美国的西部,二者都有奇高的性别比例。③ 印度的西部人口占全国人口近一半,是印度生育率和性别比最高的地区。

印度"蛮荒西部"的政治权力掌握在犯罪组织手上,比哈尔邦及北方邦的情况尤甚,私人军队四处可见,多陷入政治恶斗之中。

印度北部的地方政府以腐败闻名,官员中甚至有流氓当选。在1997年,比哈尔邦有超过10%的国会议员是臭名昭著的罪犯;北方邦的424名国会议员中,有132名是"嫌犯";④ 1998年大选里,一个已被定罪的谋杀犯当选为国会议员。暴力犯罪成了家常便饭,绑架尤其严重。"绑架成为一个朝阳行业,每天平均有两个人被绑以换取

---

① 第一个引用来自 Li, "Population Flow into Big Cities," p. 17; 第二个引用来自 Gilley, "resistible Force," p. 18。1998年前9个月中国的犯罪率升高了22%。

② India, *Census of India*, *1991*, *Series-1*, *part 2-B*（ⅰ）, Vol. 1: *Primary Census Abstract*: *General Population* (New Delhi: India, 1994).

③ David T. Courtwright, *Violent Land*: *Single Men and Social Disorder from the Frontier to the Inner City* (Cambridge, Mass.: Harvard University Press, 1996).

④ Farzand Ahmed and Subhash Mishra, "Stooping to Conquer," *India Today International*, November 10, 1997, p. 22.

赎金。"①

学者曾试着将印度的性别比例和社会不安之间关系作定量分析。在1999年，阿玛蒂亚·森发现二者之间有重要的统计相关性，他在"比较许多区域内的数据后，发现谋杀率与性别比例成正比"。②

引用1981年的犯罪记录，奥登堡（Philip Oldenburg）揭示在印度全国，尤其是北方邦性别比例和谋杀率高度相关（皮尔森相关系数是 -0.72）。正因为性别比奇高，当地被奥登堡称为"女孩的百慕大三角洲"。③ 奥登堡推测，正因为治安不佳，所以当地居民认为儿子越多，"日常生活就越有保障。当然，他们也能保护家庭"。④ 他想确认：是否女儿因为更容易被强暴及绑架，所以被父母视为负担。⑤ 根据第五章提供的理论和历史案例，这样的推测不无道理。然而，看来高性别比例不只是社会不安的果，也可能是因。

2000年让·德瑞茨（Jean Dreze）和里提卡·凯拉（Reetika Khera）重复了奥登堡的研究，把1980—1982年的谋杀率、男女性别比例、城镇化率、贫困人口比例及识字率互相对照，他们发现谋杀率与男女性别比例的相关性最强。⑥

我们引用1991年印度的人口普查及1997年的谋杀率数据，尝试重复奥登堡、德瑞茨和凯拉的分析，来证明印度的总性别比例和谋杀率（表6-1）之间有着显著的统计相关性。我们得到和德瑞茨及凯拉同样的结论："在高性别比例与暴力犯罪之间有某种强烈的联

---

① Samar Halarnkar, Sayantan Chakravarty, and Smruti Koppikar, "Fear in the City," *India Today International*, October 6, 1997, p. 14.

② Amartya Sen, *Development as Freedom* (New York: Alfred A. Knopf, 1999), p. 200.

③ Philip Oldenburg, "Sex Ratio, Son Preference, and Violence in India: A Research Note," *Economic and Political Weekly*, December 5–12, 1992, pp. 2657–2662.

④ Ibid., p. 2659.

⑤ Ibid., p. 2660.

⑥ Jean Dreze and Reetika Khera, "Crime, Gender, and Society in India: Insights from Homicide Data," *Population and Development Review*, Vol. 26, No. 2 (June 2000), p. 342.

系。……这一问题在许多社会中都是理解暴力犯罪的关键。"实证调研证实了这一结论。在 2003 年访问印度哈里亚纳邦时,记者贝蒂(Rahul Bedi)注意到:"在一个农业主导的国家,失业猛增,人们拥有的土地减少,哈利亚纳四处游荡的光棍毫无家庭责任感,靠打牌、酗酒、骚扰当地女子、作贱自己度日。"一位农夫直接评论道:"他们已经成了社会威胁。"①

对妇女的犯罪,特别是绑架、贩卖、强暴,年年增加。② 1999—2000 年,强暴案发生率上升了 6.6%。③ 同时,新娘人数越少,女性出嫁的年龄就越小,新郎的年龄就越大。④ 不少新娘是从孟加拉国买来的,价格是 10000—20000 卢比。⑤ 可以预见的是,印度性别比例在以后的 20 年内会越来越扭曲,社会的不稳定性也会随之加剧。

表 6-1 印度各邦 1991 年的性别比,1997 年的谋杀率整体性别比

邦(地区)	整体性别比^a	谋杀率(每 10000)^b
安得拉邦	102.9	3.9
"阿鲁纳恰尔邦"	116.4	6.3
阿萨姆邦	108.3	5.7
比哈尔邦	109.8	5.6
果阿邦	103.4	2.9
古吉拉特邦	107.1	3.0
哈里亚纳邦	115.6	3.2
喜马偕尔邦	102.5	1.9

---

① Jean Dreze and Reetika Khera, "Crime, Gender, and Society in India: Insights from Homicide Data," *Population and Development Review*, Vol. 26, No. 2 (June 2000), p. 347.

② Rahul Bedi, "Families 'Buying' Girls as Marriage Crisis Deepens," *Irish Times*, March 10, 2003. p. 9.

③ Shefalee Vasudev and Methil Renuka, "Sexual Crimes: Rape!" *India Today*, September 9, 2002, pp. 1, 48.,

④ David Gardner, "Where Have All the Girls Gone?" *Financial Times*, February 9, 2003, p. 1.

⑤ "Missing Sisters," p. 36.

续表

邦（地区）	整体性别比[a]	谋杀率（每10,000）[b]
"查谟和克什米尔"	108.3	8.6
卡纳塔克邦	104.2	3.3
喀拉拉邦	96.5	1.4
中央邦	107.4	4.6
马哈拉施特拉邦	107.1	3.2
曼尼普尔邦	104.4	13.0
梅加拉亚邦	104.7	7.0
米佐拉姆	108.6	3.4
那加兰邦	112.9	12.5
奥里萨邦	103.0	2.9
旁遮普邦	113.4	3.3
拉贾斯坦邦	109.9	3.1
"锡金"	113.9	2.9
泰米尔纳德邦	102.7	3.3
特里普拉邦	105.8	6.8
北方邦	113.8	4.8
西孟加拉邦	109.1	2.3

a. 性别比例数字是由人口总数计算得出。参见 India, Office of the Registrar General, *Census of India*, 1991, Series-1: *Part 2-B (i)*, Vol. 1: *Primary Census Abstract: General Population* (New Delhi: India Office of the Registrar General, 1994), chap. 3. Table2。

b. 数据来源于 National Crime Record, Bureau of India, http://www.ncrbindia.org。

二、政府面对光棍问题的对策

中国和印度政府采取了许多措施来解决超常的大量过剩男性人口给社会造成的威胁。一些措施已经在产生效果。另一些措施会引起法律和伦理层面的关注，而这些关注仅限于提及。我们这里提出只是为了解释为什么这些措施并不成功，即使不考虑伦理因素。

(一) 较可行的措施

中国及印度政府在处理光棍的问题时,至少可以采取以下六种对策,来改善其高性别比例所带来的社会问题:鼓励男性向境外流动、鼓励女性向境内流动、开垦边疆、建全社会保障体系、改善女性社会地位、提供多种激励措施。

1. 鼓励男性向境外流动

鼓励男性到外国工作,对光棍和政府是双赢的。光棍在外打工就有钱寄回家,增加国家的外汇收入,像是19世纪到加州打工的中国移民以及今天到俄罗斯远东地区打工的中国光棍。①

向外流动也有它的问题。第一,其他国家不可能吸收这么多光棍,而且最后他们还是得回家,或娶妻生子,或被解雇,像中国去俄罗斯的农业劳工通常只能在作物生长季待上六个月。② 第二,移民可能成为当地仇外的对象,尤其是在经济不景气时。尽管如此,向境外移民不失为其他政策的有利补充。

2. 鼓励女性向境内流动

另一个选择是鼓励女性向境内流动。贫穷国家或地区的女性,可能会把嫁到境外看成改变命运的机会。中国和印度光棍娶了她们之后可能会安定下来。对于中国大陆而言,观察家想了解台湾女性是否是汉族适婚女性的来源。然而台湾自己也有性别比例过高的情形。更重要的是,埃伯斯塔(Nicholas Eberstadt)计算出,到2020年,"中国大陆过剩的20岁男性人口,将超过台湾所有的女性人口"。③

同时,在印度娶其他种族的女子(或是其他种姓)是被禁止的,

---

① Celestine Bohlen, "In Russian East, Chinese Help for Toiling Farmers," *New York Times*, August 1, 1999, sec. 1, p. 3.

② Ibid.

③ Quoted in "6.3 Brides for Seven Brothers," *Economist*, December 19, 1998, p. 56.

而且就算娶进门后，也会有适应的问题。绑架或买卖女性人口的做法也多受质疑。一位印度议员说，印度男子到印度其他地区及孟加拉国购买的新娘，虽说是新娘身份，"却被视为奴隶，连她们的子女也被歧视"。① 除非政府严控，否则大多数移民入境的女子会被迫为娼，不但对社会治安不利，也对国内女子的地位有负面影响。

3. 开垦边疆

政府也可以决定开放边疆，鼓励移民。在中国，"'汉族青年，到西部去'是北京政府对国内知识青年的期望及五年计划的重点"。② 只是，追随政策者并非知青，而是无一技之长的光棍，他们愿意冒险犯难，以求致富。在过去的几年，中国政府有几项重大的基础建设计划，包括西气东输工程、三峡水坝工程，都需要成千上万的劳工。③ 中国的领导层意识到这些计划不只是出于经济层面的考虑，根据输气管道工程的总工程师陈东升介绍："开发西部是件破天荒的大事，事关国家安全，而且对经济、政治、社会、安全及防御都很重要。"④

北京号召工人移民西部，面临了几个挑战：第一，土地所有权不能私有，影响了移民的意愿。第二，西部边界的外贸伙伴都是中亚贫穷的国家。第三，从历史的经验，开疆辟野只有当女子也同行时，才会成功。没有了女子，许多男子在移民后还会继续光棍的恶行，或宁可回家。尤其当中国适婚的年轻女子越来越少时，男子根本不肯移民。捻军的例子证明了移民边疆不一定会对政府有利。如葛斯东（Jack Goldstone）所言："中国中原地区的悲惨状况，导致大量的人移居西北、西部及南部边界，如此移居不但不会释放社会压力，反而会

---

① "Missing Sisters," p. 36.

② Craig Smith, "Beijing Tries to Lift Economic Standards in Its West," *New York Times*, November 7, 2000, p. C1.

③ "Western China Pining for Prosperity," Associated Press, as Published in *Deseret News*, July 29, 2000, p. D7.

④ Quoted in ibid.

雪上加霜，因为边疆土地贫瘠，而且已有少数民族居住，若是政府管控不周，冲突很快就会发生。"① 类似情况即使在当今中国也同样存在。

政府的另一个基础建设计划是修建大规模的运河系统，其路线由西藏绵延至沿海。完成运河计划要50年，花费超过1000亿元。很难预料中国政府是否会一直有钱来支持这么大的投资，但在所有可能的对策中，这项计划是社会成本最低的。

4. 建全社会保障体系

光棍暴力来自于年轻的未婚男性对社会资源分布不均的愤怒。所以，降低不平等性可以减少社会暴力，但在市场经济的社会中，这个目标很难达成，它似乎也解决不了光棍暴力的主因：找不到老婆。即使收入平等了，过剩男子依然找不到老婆。这种无法成家、生子的痛苦，是不能以平均其他资源的分布来解决的。

政府还是能够采取一些措施来减少社会不平等性，建全社会保障体系就是很好的政策选择，在资本主义社会，政府也作如此选择。北京在过去的五年新增了社会保险系统，以降低穷人及光棍的绝望感。20世纪90年代末期在朱镕基总理的领导下，政府曾考虑把失业保险福利延伸给流动劳工，并提供社会福利保险给老人。② 虽然现在还是只有被解雇的城市工人，可以领取微薄的失业保险金，但政府在这方面的努力，对社会解决光棍问题会大有帮助。

20世纪90年中期，作为试点，浙江省政府开始发放老年津贴，以改善父母重男轻女的心态。《当代中国人口》杂志的编辑谢振明说，该省的新生儿性别比正逐渐正常化。③ 这项试验证明社会保障体

---

① Jack A. Goldstone, *Revolution and Rebellion in the Early Modern World* (Berkeley: University of California Press, 1991), p. 398.

② Li Chunyi, "'Huji' System, Population Flow, and Instability of Cities," Foreign Affairs College, Beijing, 1999, p. 18.

③ "6.3 Brides for Seven Brothers," p. 58.

系的建立，能影响父母对后代性别的选择，改善前者，就会改变后者。

印度学者也发现老年津贴对性别比例的影响。马哈德文（K. Mahadeven）及扎雅斯礼（R. Jayasree）观察到："目前只有子女能提供年老父母社会保障，因此我们需要立刻引进其他社会保障措施。"① 目前为止，印度政府还没有对这项建议作出响应。

5. 改善女性的社会地位

做法有三：（1）奖励选择生女儿的家庭；（2）惩罚选择只生男孩的家庭；（3）提升女性在社会的整体地位。这些做法没有任何害处，但就算这三种做法都付诸实施，也要好几十年之后，年轻男女的比例才会平衡。因此，政府还需要采取其他方法来对付眼前性别比例失常的问题。

中国和印度目前采取的办法包括：两国都禁止杀婴及性别选择性的堕胎（包括用超声波仪器检查胎儿性别）。② 1999 年 1 月 1 日，山东省政府宣布禁止产前超音波检验，但这项禁令是否切实得以贯彻就不得而知了。除此之外，自 1998 年起中国政府公布计划生育官员的惩处名单，如果胁迫堕胎、结扎以达到计划生育指标的官员，都会上榜。国家计划生育委员会国际合作司司长丛军说："国家计生委已向各级计生部门发文，明令禁止各级计生部门强迫妇女接受人工流产和输卵管结扎。"③ 但在同时期的 1999 年 5 月，一位已怀胎 9 个月的中

---

① Mahadevan and R. Jayasree, "Value of Children and Differential Fertility Behavior in Kerala, Andhra Pradesh, and Uttar Pradesh," in Shri Nath Singh, ed., *Population Transition in India* (Delhi: B. R. Publishing Corporation, 1989), p. 131.

② "China Has 20 Percent Male Surplus," Agence France-Presse, January 7, 1999 (accessed from Proquset, LexisNexis).

③ Quoted in "Coercive Tactics Divulged in China's One-Child Policy," Associated Press, as published in Deseret News, June 14, 1998, p. A17; and Vivien Pik-kwan Chan, "Ban Imposed on Forced Abortions," *South China Morning Post*, October 31, 1998, p. 8.

国妇女在澳洲要求政治庇护不得,被迫回中国堕胎。一年前,中国政府就公布了《流动人口计划生育工作管理办法》,要求房屋租赁中介机构、房屋的出租(借)人和物业服务企业等如实提供流动人口的生育情况。夫妻如果违反计划生育政策,就会受到"处置",被迫结扎。①

尽管采取了这些措施,中国和印度的性别比例仍在继续恶化。传统是一股顽固的力量,它若敌视女性,比法律还有效。例如,为了提高女子的社会地位,印度政府在 1956 年通过法律,赋予女性同等的继承权,但这项法律却被所有的人漠视。②

亚洲部分地区仍然继续作后代性别选择。两位观察家说:"东亚社会上升的性别比例,令人触目惊心,更糟的是这些国家的性别比例在升高后就停在高点,父母正在着急地等着最新的控制性别技术的出现……他们也积极地使用这些技术,无视自己的生育水平。"③ 最近,一家美国的公司已研发出分离精子的技术,可以把携带 X 染色体与 Y

---

① Daniel Kwan, "Tougher Laws for Migrant Birth Control," *South China Morning Post*, September 23, 1998, p. 9.

② See, for example, Carol Vlassoff, "The Value of Sons in an Indian Village: How Widows See It," *Population Studies*, Vol. 44, No. 1 (March 1990), pp. 5 – 20.

③ Park Chai Bin and Cho Nam-hoon, "Consequences of Son Preference in a Low-Fertility Society: Imbalance of the Sex Ratio at Birth in Korea," *Population and Development Review*, Vol. 21, No. 1 (March 1995), p. 79. 比较起来,其他国家并不公开主张重男轻女,也不积极作后代性别选择。最近的一项民调中,参与的美国人中75%认为"选择孩子的性别"是"不道德的"。Lois M. Collins, "American Feel Strongly About What Is Ethical," *Desert News*, May 8, 1999, p. E1. 另一项民调中发现,参与调查的美国人中41%愿意选择婴儿的性别;两个人中有一个人愿意选择男孩。"Survey Finds Most Parents Wouldn't Choose Baby's Sex If they Could," Associated Press, March 16, 1999. 因此,整个样本中有25%的人有重男轻女的倾向。一些证据表明,在20世纪上半叶美国重男轻女的倾向较高,并且多为男性的倾向,而实际上17年前的倾向又比现在的低。Lawrence Kilman, "Majority of Americans Wouldn't Choose Baby's Sex If Given a Chance," Associated Press, November 17, 1986. 另见 Stanford Winston, "Birth Control and Sex Ratio at Birth," *American Journal of Sociology*, Vol. 38, No. 2 (September 1932), pp. 225 – 231.

染色体的精子分开①,它把第一家海外分公司设在北京,虽然不被允许把技术卖到印度,但这家公司却把广告的对象锁定美籍及加拿大籍的印度人。②

这些新技术会影响父母对第二、第三胎,甚至第一胎性别的选择。著名的中国人口问题专家巴纳斯特提出警告:"由于中国出生人口一般以上都是第一胎,第一胎要'倒霉了'。"她补充道,性别选择技术已经在扭曲韩国部分地区的头胎儿童的性别比例。③ 但威廉·莱夫利(William Lavely)认为:"这项技术传到中国之后,不但能让父母实现生儿子传宗接代的愿望,也会降低生育率,符合政府的计划生育政策。"④ 换句话说,这些技术的应用不仅是因为它们产生令人满意的结果,更是因为政府不处罚为了要儿子去堕胎的父母,却处罚多生孩子的父母。

印度政府也加强了执行禁止性别选择的法律。在印度 2001 年人口普查中,儿童性别比例的数据受到国际社会的谴责,印度政府无奈之下颁布法令,要求制造超声波仪器的公司削减产量,只能把仪器卖给登记在案的诊所,并要求诊所保存其使用记录。⑤ 这些诊所必须挂出明显的标志:"本诊所不做性别鉴定。"⑥ 政府还建立"摇篮计划",鼓励家庭把不要的女孩寄养在国家领养中心。⑦ 有些地方政府甚至要求怀孕妇女在地区医院注册,并接受性别平等课程的辅导,目的有

---

① Gina Kolata, "Researchers Report Success in Method to Pick Baby's Sex," *New York Times*, September 9, 1998, p. A1.

② Wyndham Murray, communication with Valerie Hudson, October 11, 1998.

③ Quoted in "6.3 Brides for Seven Brothers," p. 57.

④ William Lavely, "Unintended Consequences of China's Birth Planning Policy," University of Washington, July 14, 1997, pp. 18–19.

⑤ "Doctors Should Abide by Sex Selection Act Norms," *Times of India*, April 29, 2003, p. 1.

⑥ Gautam N. Allahbadia, "The 50 Million Missing Women," *Journal of Assisted Reproduction and Genetics*, Vol. 19, No. 9 (September 2002), p. 415.

⑦ Satinder Bindra, "Grim Motives behind Infant Killings," CNN.com, July 7, 2003, http://www.cnn.com/2003/world/asiapcf/south/07/07/india.infanticide.pt1/index.html.

二：(1) 教育妇女不要杀女婴；(2) 提升她们对女儿的珍视程度。① (通常是母亲或婆婆实施杀女婴的行为。)

最近这些年，中国政府也开始教育人民重视女儿。为了阻止后代性别选择，计划生育中心号召"自然生育好"。② 更多的政府官员公开批评中国的高性别比例。十年前，北京大学人口研究所主任曾毅说过："非法的产前性别检查及堕胎、杀女婴，造成女性人数缺乏，终将导致严重的社会问题。"③ 但怀特（Martin King Whyte）提出："中国的分析家似乎更关心这群过多的男士将如何找到老婆，而不是关心这群'消失的女孩'。"④

中国政府采取了几项措施，来提升女儿在父母心中的地位。例如，为了使父母抛弃传统观念中"养儿防老"的想法，政府引用现代西方发达国家案例，说明女儿其实比儿子更能照顾父母。在1996年一个政府设置的路边广告牌上，有两位母亲在谈话，一位衣着褴褛、形单影只的母亲感叹："我有三个儿子，但没人肯照顾我。"一位衣着华丽的母亲，女儿正在给她捶背，她很自豪："我只有一个女儿，但她比你的三个儿子好多了。"⑤ 多年前，伍尔芙（Margery Wolf）曾怀

---

① Satinder Bindra, "State Adopts Infants'Cause," CNN. com, July 7, 2003, http://www.cnn.com/2003/world/asiapcf/south/07/07/india.infanticide.pt2/index.html.

② Celeste McGovern, "Chinese Puzzle: 117 Boys for 100 Girls," *Report*, June 10, 2003, http://report.ca/archive/report/20020610/p56i020610f.html.

③ Quoted in Zeng Yi, Tu Ping, Gu Baochang, Xu Yi, Li Bohua, and Li Yongping, "Causes and Implications of the Recent Increase in the Reported Sex Ratio at Birth in China," *Population and Development Review*, Vol. 19, No. 2 (June 1993), p. 296.

④ Martin King Whyte, "Social Trends and the Human Rights Situation in the PRC," George Washington University, 1998, p. 27.

⑤ 另一个需要考虑的方面是中国未来的预期人口结构。预计人口有明显增长的只有两类人群：(1) 光棍；(2) 超过60岁的老龄人口。世界银行估计到2020年，老龄人口将占中国人口的16%。人们难免会想知道这种前所未有的人口老龄化是否会导致社会更难以应付年轻男性不断制造的不稳定。1982—1995年总体人口的年均增长率大约为1.43%，老龄人口的增长率是3.10%。Li Weidong, "To Keep Economic Prosperity under the Double Pressures of Population Aging and Unemployment," *Economics Selection* (1999), pp. 10 – 11, as cited in Anita Zhong, "China's Aging Population and China's Economy, Foreign Affairs College, Beijing," May 23, 1999, pp. 12 – 13.

疑这种宣传的有效性,她说:"会照顾年迈父母的独生女,似乎只出现在宣传影片或报纸专栏里。"① 但最近观察家发现政府的努力似乎生效了:"许多城里人都说女儿比儿子好,因为她更有可能[在父母年老时]照料父母。"②

政府提升女性地位的努力,也包括说服男性放弃一夫多妻制。因为文化的关系,在印度这项努力几乎无效。但在中国,政府应该继续禁止一夫多妻。女性人数不足已经够糟了,如果有钱有势的男人还去垄断为数不多的女人,像是包二奶,会让情况更加恶化的。2001 年中国《婚姻法》的修订,提出禁止重婚(如一夫多妻),我们希望政府继续严惩违法者。

中国政府从不忌讳公开执行死刑以"教育"群众。最近几年,有一些杀女婴的人被处以死刑。据《新民晚报》报道,浙江省人民法院宣布,一位 63 岁的林姓女子因谋杀了自己的孙女而被处死刑,她有严重的重男轻女观念,孙女的出生让她怒不可遏。林的媳妇生下女婴之后,家中就不停地争吵。在三月份的一次争执中,林姓女子从媳妇怀中抢走了女婴,用力把她丢到地上,打破了孙女的头颅。宁波中级人民法院也判林姓女子的女儿有期徒刑 2 年,缓期执行,因为窝藏罪。③ 在中国,绑架、贩卖男孩,会被处以同样严格的惩罚。④

但尽管处罚则严厉,贩卖女婴的市场依旧大发利市。2003 年 7

---

① Margery Wolf, *Revolution Postponed*: *Women in Contemporary China* (Stanford, Calif.: Stanford University Press, 1985), p. 271.

② Erik Eckholm, "Homes for Elderly Replacing Family Care as China Grays," *New York Times*, May 20, 1998, p. A1.

③ "Death for Killing Granddaughter," Associated Press, as published in South China Morning Post, July 27, 1998, http: //www. scmp. com/ news/template/chinaT…. ina&template = default. htx&maxfieldsize =913.

④ 关于对拐卖人口罪犯的刑罚,参见 "Death for Kidnapper of Twelve Boys," Associated Press, as published in South China Morning Post, May 29, 1998, http: //www. scmp. com/news/templat…ina&template = default. htx&maxfieldsize = 898。

月，有28个2—5个月大的女婴2—4人一组被绑在尼龙口袋中，置放在大巴士的后座。这些女婴原本要被卖到没有女孩子的乡村，与人为妻。此事被揭露后，国家主席胡锦涛要求立即展开调查。①

文化价值观的改变，也会改变重男轻女的心态。据说报道有1100万中国人收看了电视剧《篱笆、女人和狗》、《辘轳、女人和井》、《古船、女人和网》，其剧情讲述了一位订有娃娃亲的农村年轻女子的辛酸命运，以及她不顾丈夫和家庭的反对，决定生下女儿的故事。专栏作家艾伦·古德曼（Ellen Goodman）访问了为该剧情节线索提供意见的国家计划生育委员会官员，该官员说："除了执行政府的政策之外，我们还试着改变人们的观念。"②

为女性提供受更多教育的机会——尤其是在女性文盲特别多的印度，也是有效提升女性地位的办法。但教育不是万灵丹，在中国几乎所有的女性都受过教育，但仍未降低性别比例。而且良好的教育再加上财富似乎也不很管用，如第三章所述，受过教育、经济小康的印度家庭的性别比例，要比最穷、受教育最少的还糟。所以教育和经济还必须和政策互相配合，才能改变家庭对女孩的看法。在中国的南方，经济全球化背景下，女儿（不是儿子）成为家庭的经济支柱。外资及合资企业喜欢雇用年轻女子，使得这些女子成为家庭的主要收入来源。当越多的人了解这个事实后，就会削弱对女性的歧视，虽然她们仍须付出劳力被压榨的代价。③

---

① Elsabeth Rosenthal, "Bias for Boys Leads to Sale of Baby Girls in China," *New York Times*, July 20, 2003, sec. 1, p. 6.

② Ellen Goodman, "Will China's Values Change? Stay Tuned," *Boston Globe*, November 11, 1999, p. A27.

③ 这种认可能够成为一种强有力的文化力量。根据1983年4月2日《人民日报》的报道，自从浙江绍兴戏（指越剧，其中角色都是女性扮演）的诞生，绍兴等地的许多女孩被拯救了。当女婴出生，盛行这样的说法：莫淹死她，让她长大唱戏。引自 T'ien Ju-K'ang, *Male Anxiety and Female Chastity: A Comparative Study of Chinese Ethical Values in Ming-Ch'ing Times* (New York: E. J. Brill, 1998), p. 27, n. 42。

此外，中国及印度政府也应该采取下列的行动：第一，中国政府应该重视年轻女性的自杀问题。第二，把每个被遗弃的女婴视为珍贵的国家资源，好好呵护，并照顾她们长大成人。为了维护这项政策，可以按男孩的人数向其父母征税，这样做似乎是政府承担了养育女孩的角色，但也总比放任年轻男性的人数越来越多好。今天在中国和印度出生的每一个女孩，都会影响这两个国家未来的稳定及生存。如果父母不了解这点，政府就该接手照顾这些女孩的成长。如人类学家芭芭拉·米勒（Barbara Miller）所言，正常的性别比例是"公共物品"，无法提供这项公共物品的政府，无异于自取灭亡。[1]

6. 提供优惠政策

想改变社会对女性的观念，需要上百年时间。较为快捷的途径是改变对后代性别选择行为的激励措施。1997年10月，北京大学人口研究所的主任曾毅表示，中国将放宽独生子女政策。这一断言是基于几个地方成功的政策实验，例如在宜城，"男女若晚婚，结婚三年后才生第一胎的，被允许在30岁之后可生第二胎。使这项政策该地区总生育率到达2.35%（比死亡率高一点点），其人口增长率比邻近的城镇低，孩童的性别比例也较正常"。[2] 一年以后，民政部社会福利与社会进步研究所负责人也预测道："独生子女政策在一定时间。……我期望在五六年后改变。"[3] 现在个别县的地方政府废除了第一胎生育程序。在以前，如果当地人口或工作单位的生育指标用完时，妇女连第一胎的生育资格也无法获得；想生第二胎的，还必须支付一笔可观的"计划生育费"，才可能得到允许（但不能再生）。现在，如果夫

---

[1] Barbara D. Miller, "Female-Selective Abortion in Asia: Patterns, Policies, and Debates," *American Anthropologist*, Vol. 103, No. 4 (December 2001), pp. 1083 – 1095.

[2] "PRC Family Planning: The Market weakens Controls but Encourages Voluntary Limits," http://www.usembassy-china.org.cn/english/sandt/POPMYWB.html.

[3] "hina One-Child Policy Likely to Be Loosened as Birth Rates Drop," Agence France-Presse, February 11, 1998 (accessed from Proquest, LexisNexis)

妻再婚或是婚后五年才生第一胎的，都被允许生第二胎。①

这些变化是中国政府即将改变人口政策的前兆。2003年成立的"国家计划生育及人口委员会"，取代了原来的"国家计划生育委员会"，将起草中国第一个人口发展五年（2006—2010）计划。采取新的人口政策是因为"生育问题之外，还有农民工进城问题、日益加重的性别不平衡问题、人口老龄化问题及日益严重的失业压力"。②

媒体把2002年和2003年中国计划生育政策的变化描述为政府对"一胎化"政策的放宽。然而，这种判断是否准确尚不确定。2002年9月的《人口与计划生育法》，把违反规定生育子女的公民行为定为违法行为。同时，政府也宣布将建立一个育龄妇女信息数据库，以掌握她们的生育情况。另一方面，法律似乎不鼓励处罚超生的父母，而是要求他们支付一笔"社会抚养费"。在一些案例中，这项费用可能达到个人几年的收入。此外，有迹象表明，原本只限于在特定地区执行的独生子女政策的例外情况，可能已在全国范围内出现。这些例外包括再婚夫妻和结婚五年后才要孩子的夫妻。采取更多极端做法是可能的，但它们可能比放宽"一胎化政策"带来更多的社会不稳定因素。③

---

① Quoted in Elisabeth Rosenthal, "For One-Child Policy, China Rethinks Iron hand," *New York Times*, November 1, 1998, sec. 1, p. 1.

② "China to Uaher in Major Changes in Population Policies," People's Daily Online, August 20, 2003, http://english.peopledaliy.com.cn/200308/20/eng20030820-122707.shtml.

③ 更极端的例子恐怕是新中国成立之前在中国历史上的婚姻模式：入赘婚姻。一种是少数民族实行的女娶男嫁。夫妻有时与女方父母同住，有时与男方父母同住。两种情况下，新郎都要负担女方父母的生活。另一种是上门女婿。女婿成为女方家庭的合法继承人，改姓女方的姓。夫妻所生小孩也随女方的姓。如果中国的父母都有50%的机会把他们的姓传给孙辈——不管他们所生的是儿子还是女儿，那可能会发生巨大的社会改变。现行的体系中，有儿子的父母100%能把自己的姓传给后代，而有女儿的父母则无法把姓传给后代。如果机会是平等的，女儿的社会地位可能相应会提高。Arthur P. Wolf and Chieh-shan Huang, *Marriage and Adoption in China*, 1845–1945 (Stanford, Calif.: Stanford University Press, 1980), chap. 7. 有意思的是，中国1980年的《婚姻法》规定，登记婚姻后女方可以成为男方家庭的成员，男方可以成为女方家庭的成员。Information Office of the State Council, *Protection of Chinese Women's Rights and Interests* (Beijing: New Star, 1993), p. 20. 关于当代日本社会中这一婚姻模式的复兴，参见Howard W. French, "New Pressures Alter Japanese Family's Geometry," *New York Times*, July 27, 2000, p. A1.

在印度，社会不平等的种姓制度是后代性别选择的主要原因，所以必须设法改善这种社会不平等。当英国统治印度时，曾经成功地减少杀女婴的陋习，方法是根据各地性别比例的高低来分配行政资源，并对嫁妆的金额规定上限。如果殖民官发现当地还有人在实施后代性别选择行为，则整个地区都得受罚。这种以政策为后来减少后代性别选择的做法，只在一定程度上取得了成效。限制嫁妆的金额，让女儿不再成为父母的负担，鼓励在不同家庭间交换结婚对象，使得父母可以体面地缩减嫁妆的支出。现今这种做法是否仍然有效就不得而知了，印度的新娘越来越少，嫁妆的金额却还在增加，是政府必须介入的时候了。①

（二）较不可行的措施

要应对中国和印度男性过剩的问题，还有两个办法，但两者都有严重的法律及道德瑕疵，较不可行。一是对恶行征税（如嫖娼及贩毒），政府再利用这些收入来处理光棍问题。只是鼓励罪恶像一刀两刃，无法带来社会的长治久安，而且这种政策还会恶化现存的问题，如在亚洲日益泛滥的艾滋病。泰国政府现在后悔当初鼓励卖淫及色情旅游业，因为社会成本太高了。其他负面效果还包括导致更多的犯罪及非法武装组织。

二是征兵，历代统治者常用这个办法来处理光棍问题。从军可让光棍过上体面的生活，提高他们的社会地位。当然，这也让他们受到军事及武力训练，并能运用学来的本事对抗政府。最近中国政府要缩减人民解放军的人数，并遏制军队经商及走私行径，这引起关注，不禁让人担心万一军队真的被解散了，会发生什么后果。② 罗宾逊研究

---

① "Missing Sisters," p. 2.

② Seth Faison, "China's Chief Tells Army to Give Up Its Commerce," *New York Times*, July 23, 1998, p. A3.

明朝中期的历史，发现许多大强盗及叛军领袖都曾经在官军受训。不少人落草时仍身在军营。罗宾逊形容道："管理军人需要微妙的平衡手段，万一失败，代价就太高了。他们对于军官、文官和地方官而言的长处，也正是他们最危险的方面——熟悉武器、身体强壮、好勇斗狠、成群结党。当他们和政权合作时，这些人是一股助力，若他们和政权唱反调，与反动势力结合，就是社会动乱的渊薮。"①

美国历史是前车之鉴，考特莱特说过："军队在美国整个历史中像一块海绵，在动员作战时，他们吸收了社会最危险的成分；在和平时，他们卸下武器，把武力和武器释放回社会。第二次世界大战之后，大多数年轻的退役军人返回家园或另行成家，由退伍军人带来的不安定因素被大大地减缓。但如果像越战之后，退伍军人没能结婚或是离婚，那么他们就会成为社会的心腹大患。"② 中国的性别比例那么高，不可能像第二次世界大战后那样乐观，印度亦然。

中国政府在1999年宣布即将组建14个中国人民武装警察部队支队，约100万人。武警负责维护国内治安，制止包括高失业率、腐败及高税收等在内的因素所导致的国内暴乱。根据约翰·柯柏特（John Corbett）及丹尼斯·布拉斯柯（Dennis Blasko）的分析："中国政府增加了人民武装警察的人数，似乎在暗示对于维护政权的稳定和经济现代化，内忧比外患更值得严加管控。"③

然而，有位专家说一些新加入的武警是"the dregs"（来自社会最底层的男性）。④ 如第五章所讨论，中国历史上以光棍治光棍，常导致反效果。这群穿着制服的光棍，其腐败与暴力有时不下于他们要打

---

① David M. Robinson, "The Management of Violence in the Mid-Ming Capital Region," Colgate University, 1998, p. 35.

② Courtwright, *Violent Land*, p. 46.

③ Quoted in Erik Eckholm, "A Secretive Army Grows to Maintain Order in China," *New York Times*, March 28, 1999, sec. 1, p. 6.

④ Ibid.

击的暴徒,所以让部队驻守在富裕的城市中心,特别不明智。

一些观察家认为,从光棍征兵若想成功,最好把他们外放边防,甚至到国外。这项策略曾为中世纪葡萄牙政府所采用。但有时它也会擦枪走火,因为不管政府把军队送到什么地方,内乱堪忧的边疆或是国外,他们都会面临当地顽强的对抗。这类长期的冲突,会让政府耗尽资源、丧失合法性、失去人民支持,最终在内忧外患夹击下失去政权。

这一方法的另一形式当下正在印度实施。印度的人口由复杂的种姓、种族及宗教所组成。其执政党印度人民党(Bharatiya Janata Party,BJP)毫不掩饰它对宗教及政治的狭猎心理,梦想把印度教国家变成世界大国。他们为了获得支持,公然反对穆斯林,年轻的印度教男性信徒接受大印度的观点,对穆斯林教徒采取了很多暴力行为。我们怀疑印度政府在表面上呈现狭隘的国家主义心态,事实上是想转移越来越多的光棍族群的愤怒焦点,以免他们枪口向内。这是一项危险的政策,它不但会对社会及经济造成大规模的破坏,也会侵蚀政府的权威与正当性。

三、结论

以上所述的各项政策选择致力于解决高性别比例社会中的各种社会问题。然而,有一种变量可能会出人意料地改变中、印两国政府的安全计划:一旦出现经济的长期萎靡,光棍们更难找到维持生计的工作,上述政策措施就都没用了。届时会爆发大规模内乱,威胁政权稳定。中国的高失业率令人忧心,被解雇的城市居民与源源涌入的农民工竞争工作机会,与此同时,犯罪率持续增高。抗议、示威不断[①],其中参与最多的就是光棍兄弟们,套用一位观察家的形容,他们是

---

① Elisabeth Rosenthal, "Factory Closings in China Arouse Workers to Fury," *New York Times*, August 31, 2000, p. A1.

"中国的不满族群"。①

2001年中国加入世界贸易组织（WTO），这有好处也有坏处。一方面，加入WTO将带来长期的繁荣；另一方面，政府必须做的让步也会打击到国内的农业及重工业，而这两个行业都雇有大批的光棍。香港资深的亚洲经济专家罗琦认为，都市就业率将因加入WTO而增加一倍。以目前的趋势来看，的确如此。② 但也有人认为，"上百万的农民……需要离家到都市找工作"。③ 一位不知名的西方经济学家预测，为了加入WTO，中国农民将面临生存的"浴血"战。④ 一些经济学家认为，到了2005年，中国至少会失去3000万个工作机会，潜在的不稳定程度可能比经济学家预期的还要糟。事实上，新闻报道指出"法轮功"的参加者主要是失业族群。⑤

国家的本质将决定它是否能安全度过高性别比例所带来的危机。根据历史记录，高性别比例的社会只能用专制制度来统治。一旦开放，地方主义、军阀政治及社会混乱就会乘机而起。⑥ 虽然我们不支持专制政权，但我们承认这种说法有道理。

近年来，有更多的中国政治人物公开讨论光棍问题。一位地方选

---

① See "Army of Jobless Threatening China."
② Quoted in Paul Eckert, "China's Monumental Leap," Reuters, as published in *Deseret News*, November 21, 1999, p. A1.
③ Ibid.
④ Erik Eckholm, "One Giant Step for Mr. Jiang's China," *New York Times*, November 21, 1999, sec. 4, p. 4.
⑤ Eckert, "China's Monumental Leap."
⑥ Christian G. Mesquida and Neil I. Wiener, "Human Collective Aggression: A Behavior Ecology Perspective," *Ethology and Sociobiology*, Vol. 17, No. 4 (July 1996), pp. 247–262; Laura Betzig, "Despotism and Differential Reproduction: A Cross-Cutural Correlation of Conflict Asymmetry, Hierarchy, and Degree of Polygyny," *Ethology and Sociobiology*, Vol. 3, No. 4 (1982), pp. 209–221.

举的候选人甚至答应:"照顾所有没钱娶妻的单身汉,让大家发财。"① 中央政府应该审慎面对这种直接对光棍的呼吁,以免历史上最糟糕的暴力事件重演。

---

① Quoted in Thomas L. Friedman, "It Takes a Village," *New York Times*, March 10, 1998, p. A19.

第七章　结论：高性别比例社会的安全考虑

如果一个社会因为后代性别选择偏好，导致男性后代数量大幅增加，增加至一个不合理的水平，产生大群光棍，将会产生什么后果呢？中国及印度这两个世界上人口最多的国家需要在21世纪给全世界一个回答。

子女性别选择在开始时，是为了要限制资源的消耗，反而增加了对资源的竞争，结果造成极度的性别失衡和性别歧视，有可能会对环境与人类安全带来严重影响。在第五章中所讨论的捻军、"收复失地运动"，以及19世纪印度奥德和中国台湾的案例，说明了普遍的后代性别选择所带来的严重的不良影响。这些例子也预示着占世界总人口将近40%的中国和印度当前所面临的严峻的性别失衡问题可能会产生的一些不良后果。我们的证据显示高性别比例的社会，尤其是资源缺乏及分配不均的地方，会成为暴力的温床以及会造成持久的社会无序和社会分裂。而光棍在其中的负面影响，要比在低性别比例的社会中大得多。

当15—34岁的人口性别比例接近120（男）：100（女）时，这些问题就会产生。1999年1月，北京的中国社会科学院宣布，中国的出生人口性别比例已达120（男）：100（女）。另外，他们也计算出每6个中国男性中，就会有1个人娶不到妻子。中国的过剩男性数量已经高达 1.11 亿人，比墨西哥全部的人口还要多。① 从最近的趋势来看，中国下一代的性别比例会更高。与此同时印度的性别比例也将达到 120（男）：100（女）。

在有关男女性别比例失衡的历史案例中，执政者最终都会认识到高性别比例对社会所造成的危害。评论家也明白地指出，高性别比例不仅导致社会暴力倾向增加，而且会使政府采取对抗性措施来应对这种暴力趋势。有证据表明，当今北京的领导人也开始察觉光棍的潜在威胁。1996 年，一名中国官员表达了对这种现象的担忧："到本世纪末，我国将有 7000 万名单身大军。"② 2002 年，全国人大代表任玉玲警告，扭曲的性别比例将会裂解中国的社会组织。③ 广东省社会科学院社会与人口学研究所所长郑子珍在 2003 年指出：新生儿性别比的持续不正常，将对中国人口、社会及道德结构形成负面的影响。④ 虽然印度政府官员目前对于扭曲的人口性别比例尚未做出类似的结论，但学者及媒体已经开始关注这个危险的趋势了。观察家认为印度的高性别比例最终会给印度带来负面影响，但是他们并不确定是何种负面影响，在研究的基础上，我们提出了以下几种可能性。⑤

---

① "China Has 20 Percent Male Surplus," Agence France-Press, January 7, 1999.

② Quoted in "Abortion in Asia," *Wall Street Journal*, September 12, 1996, p. A14.

③ Quoted in "Skewed Gender Ratio Endangers Society, Says Delegate," *South China Morning Post*, March 7, 2002, p. 6.

④ Quoted in "Alarming Gender Imbalance," *China Today*, Vol. 52, No. 1（January 2003）, p. 7.

⑤ "Doctors Should Abide by Sex Selection Act Norms," *Times of India*, April 29, 2003, http://web.lexis-nexis.com/universe/documentm? cebe7184a90f2eb7390a4f035fbaddd78 … 6/20/2003; Satinder Bindra, "Grim Motive behind Infant Killings," CNN.com, July, 2003; Satinder Bindra, "India Women in Short Supply," CNN.com, July 19, 2003; Gautam N. Allahbadia, "The 50 Million Missing Women," *Journal of Assisted Reproduction and Genetics*, Vol. 19, No. 9（September 2002）, pp. 410 – 416; Rahul Bedi, "Families' uying Girls as Marriage Crisis Deepens," *Irish Times*, March 10, 2003, p. 10; and Seema Sirohi, "The Vanishing Girls of India," *Christian Science Monitor*, July 30, 2001, p. 9.

一、大预测

到 21 世纪末,处理有关国内为数不少的光棍群体的问题将成为中国、印度以及巴基斯坦政府工作中日益重要和紧迫的工作。领导者们很快会发现,要维持对一个高性别比例的社会的控制需要采取的一些措施和正常性别比的社会是不同的,另外,其他国家的领导者需要明白这些高性别比例国家中的大量过剩男青年对他们国家的潜在威胁以及性别失衡对于政策制定过程产生的影响。这两种类型国家间发生过度反应和误判的可能性是很大的,尤其是当涉及国内、地区以及(很有可能是)国际的安全问题时。

本书从中国和印度过剩的年轻男性人口来考虑,对于中、印两国在 21 世纪可能的发展趋势作出两个大胆的预测。第一,中国要发展西方式民主的可能性不高,印度政府想要维持它现在的民主型态,也会面临很大的挑战。北京和新德里的领导人在处理接下来的几十年里可能会给社会稳定带来潜在威胁的光棍人口数量大幅增加的问题时,会面临日益增大的压力,为了消除这一威胁,他们可能倾向于迈向一种更加威权的道路。印度及巴基斯坦因为宗教及种族引起的暴力事件,也会越来越多。

第二,由于扭曲的性别比例所造成的不稳定联系,印度和巴基斯坦在克什米尔和查谟边界冲突中达成一种永久性解决方案的可能性并不大。高性别比文化中的安全逻辑使这些国家倾向于从国家间冲突中发现好处。除了激发那些容易受到民族自豪感和国家向心力感召的光棍群体的忠诚之外,冲突也常常成为一个国家将其光棍人口转移出去(最好别再回来)的行之有效的方法。

二、结论

21世纪最被忽视的问题之一,就是亚洲人口的男性化。亚洲的性别比例,由于人为选择已经达到了史无前例的地步,这巨大的人口性别冲击会带来怎样的后果呢?现在到了需要环境和人类安全领域,以及政府政策制定圈严肃讨论这一巨大冲击所带来的潜在威胁的时候了。我们认为,一个成年人口男女比例达到120(男):100(女)甚至更高的社会具有内在的不稳定性。

这种现象仅仅是反映社会中女性地位同社会能否迈向民主与和平之间紧密联系的一个例子。在安全研究领域长期被忽略的女性议题将会在21世纪的安全问题研究中成为焦点议题。令弗朗西斯·福山(Francis Fukuyama)[1]感到好奇的是:民主国家相较于非民主国家能更好地保持和平与民主这一现象,是否同民主国家的女性地位比较高而非民主国家的女性地位比较低有关。我们的分析将这一问题向前推进了一步,我们认为在一国国内和国家间全方位的、有实质意义的民主与和平在很大程度上跟女性社会地位的高低有关。通过我们的研究发现,在高性别比例的社会中,女性的社会地位通常都很低,我们不能期望这种高性别比的社会向正常性别比的社会看齐,无论是它们的政府管理方式还是对于和平的追求。在历史上,这样的尝试被证明是短命的和失败的。我们的研究只是一个开端,我们希望其他研究国家安全的学者和分析人士继续就这一议题相关的研究做出努力。[2] 其实,

---

[1] Francis Fukuyama, "Women and the Evolution of World Politics," *Foreign Affairs*, Vol. 77, No. 5 (September/October 1998), pp. 24–40.

[2] 近年来有关高性别比的社会与民主和平之间关系的主题研究,参见 M. Steven Fish, "Islam and Authoritarianism," *World Politics*, Vol. 55, No. 1 (October 2002), pp. 4–37; Rose McDermott and Jonathan A. Cowden, "The Effects of Uncertainty and Sex in a Crisis Simulation Game," *International Interactions*, Vol. 27, No. 4 (October-December 2001), pp. 353–380。

在安全研究领域没有比这更重要的议题了，因为我们认为理解女性社会地位与国家安全之间的关系是非常重要的，而且这将成为21世纪学者和政策制定者所关注的中心议题。

附 表

附表 1 2002 年世界各国（地区）4 岁以下人口性别比例

国家/地区	男女合计	男性	女性	男女人口比例
阿富汗	4464862	2277923	2186939	104.2
阿尔巴尼亚	321236	165969	155267	106.9
阿尔及利亚	3495082	1779964	1715118	103.8
美属萨摩亚	8317	4267	4050	105.4
安道尔共和国	3559	1843	1716	107.4
安哥拉	1816011	916638	899373	101.9
安圭拉岛	941	476	465	102.4
安提瓜和巴布达	6595	3361	3234	103.9
阿根廷	3360940	1720343	1640597	104.9
亚美尼亚	174467	88718	85749	103.5
阿鲁巴岛	4590	2349	2241	104.8
澳大利亚	1267057	649049	618008	105.0
奥地利	406756	208275	198481	104.9
阿塞拜疆	406756	208275	198481	104.9
巴哈马	28192	14232	13960	101.9
巴林	28192	14232	13960	101.9
孟加拉国	14977628	7709590	7268038	106.1
巴巴多斯	18496	9277	9219	100.6

续表

国家/地区	男女合计	男性	女性	男女人口比例
白俄罗斯	483490	247031	236459	104.5
比利时	563346	288347	274999	104.9
伯利兹	38942	19867	19075	104.2
贝宁	1247197	629807	617390	102.0
百慕大群岛	3971	1921	2050	93.7
不丹	310848	160336	150512	106.5
玻利维亚	1073012	547724	525288	104.3
波斯尼亚和黑塞哥维那	248349	127798	120551	106.0
博茨瓦纳	213064	107536	105528	101.9
巴西	15834329	8078742	7755587	104.2
文莱	35225	18005	17220	104.6
保加利亚	301070	154888	146182	106.0
布基纳法索	2307727	1164695	1143032	101.9
缅甸	3938556	2013735	1924821	104.6
布隆迪	1093789	551908	541881	101.9
柬埔寨	1869680	951474	918206	103.6
喀麦隆	2528666	1277982	1250684	102.2
加拿大	1809366	926423	882943	104.9
佛得角	55038	27763	27275	101.8
开曼群岛	2559	1188	1371	86.7
中非共和国	569392	286962	282430	101.6
乍得	1766396	890558	875838	101.7
智利	1301845	666208	635637	104.8
中国	98149545	51358557	46790988	109.8
哥伦比亚	4425244	2240012	2185232	102.5
科摩罗	103418	51951	51467	100.9
刚果（布拉扎维）	473079	238395	234684	101.6
刚果（金沙萨）	10477933	5265765	5212168	101.0

续表

国家/地区	男女合计	男性	女性	男女人口比例
库克群岛	—	—	—	
哥斯达黎加	380652	194783	185869	104.8
科特迪瓦	2872903	1444049	1428854	101.1
克罗地亚	279069	143286	135783	105.5
古巴	702282	360953	341329	105.7
塞浦路斯	50565	25841	24724	104.5
捷克共和国	461455	237095	224360	105.7
丹麦	327481	168098	159383	105.5
吉布提	79481	39938	39543	101.0
多米尼加	6183	3140	3043	103.2
多米尼加共和国	1015944	518886	497058	104.4
厄瓜多尔	1644067	836855	807212	103.7
埃及	8101775	4145316	3956459	104.8
萨尔瓦多	853404	435968	417436	104.4
赤道几内亚	79355	39949	39406	101.4
厄立特里亚	790073	396735	393338	100.9
爱沙尼亚	60607	30975	29632	104.5
埃塞俄比亚	12521590	6307061	6214529	101.5
法罗群岛	3101	1551	1550	100.1
斐济	95335	48715	46620	104.5
芬兰	281470	142938	138532	103.2
法国	3637201	1866248	1770953	105.4
法属圭亚那	19160	9804	9356	104.8
法属玻利尼西亚	23276	11897	11379	104.6
加蓬	146933	73761	73172	100.8
冈比亚	256298	128961	127337	101.3
加沙地带	235037	120228	114809	104.7

续表

国家/地区	男女合计	男性	女性	男女人口比例
格鲁吉亚	263270	133921	129349	103.5
德国	3942338	2023470	1918868	105.5
加纳	2711181	1365887	1345294	101.5
直布罗陀	1566	803	763	105.2
希腊	517474	267282	250192	106.8
格陵兰岛	4610	2337	2273	102.8
格林纳达	10113	5066	5047	100.4
瓜德罗普岛	36372	18595	17777	104.6
关岛	20320	10826	9494	114.0
危地马拉	2070796	1057059	1013737	104.3
根西岛	3241	1648	1593	103.5
几内亚	1256080	628272	627808	100.1
几内亚比绍共和国	217224	108737	108487	100.2
圭亚那	59888	30530	29358	104.0
海地	960024	487315	473810	103.0
洪都拉斯	971746	496697	475049	104.6
中国香港	410148	215493	194655	110.7
匈牙利	472342	243983	228359	106.8
冰岛	20253	10507	9746	107.8
印度	116265706	59663752	56601954	105.4
印度尼西亚	24225742	12336389	11889353	103.8
伊朗	5907671	3020961	2886710	104.7
伊拉克	3674959	1868991	1805968	103.5
爱尔兰	277561	143012	134549	106.3
以色列	560745	286991	273754	104.8
意大利	2630258	1355811	1274447	106.4
牙买加	245492	125542	119950	104.7

续表

国家/地区	男女合计	男性	女性	男女人口比例
日本	6232573	3195490	3037083	105.2
泽西岛	5223	2708	2515	107.7
约旦	655251	335294	319957	104.8
哈萨克斯坦	1310794	667987	642807	103.9
肯尼亚	4246318	2145873	2100445	102.2
基里巴斯	13844	7037	6807	103.4
科威特	219298	111726	107572	103.9
吉尔吉斯斯坦	560233	283156	277077	102.2
老挝	926628	464736	461892	100.6
拉脱维亚	91617	46827	44790	104.5
黎巴嫩	350120	178759	171361	104.3
莱索托	304198	153432	150766	101.8
利比里亚	604122	305451	298671	102.3
利比亚	675580	345179	330401	104.5
列支敦士登	1926	958	968	99.0
立陶宛	177335	90626	86709	104.5
卢森堡	28083	14482	13601	106.5
中国澳门	28166	14496	13670	106.0
前南斯拉夫的马其顿共和国	138927	72132	66795	108.0
马达加斯加	2947528	1480354	1467174	100.9
马拉维	1662744	835998	826746	101.1
马来西亚	2692306	1386589	1305717	106.2
马尔代夫	53806	27623	26183	105.5
马里	2170980	1094144	1076836	101.6
马耳他	24903	12995	11908	109.1
马恩岛	4251	2178	2073	105.1

续表

国家/地区	男女合计	男性	女性	男女人口比例
马绍尔群岛	14382	7347	7035	104.4
马提尼克	33064	16789	16275	103.2
毛里塔尼亚	514757	259441	255316	101.6
毛里求斯	96611	48527	48084	100.9
马约特岛	32139	16170	15969	101.3
墨西哥	11321205	5778654	5542551	104.3
密克罗尼西亚	—	—	—	—
摩尔多瓦	275883	140640	135243	104.0
摩纳哥	1589	814	775	105.0
蒙古	264944	135314	129630	104.4
蒙特内格鲁	49217	25588	23629	108.3
蒙特塞拉特岛	683	349	334	104.5
摩洛哥	3520206	1795105	1725101	104.1
莫桑比克	2995205	1511645	1483560	101.9
纳米比亚	278814	141154	137660	102.5
瑙鲁	1619	827	792	104.4
尼泊尔	3786819	1949068	1837751	106.1
荷兰	966167	492940	473227	104.2
荷属安的列斯	17693	9059	8634	104.9
新喀里多尼亚	20854	10664	10190	104.7
新西兰	278311	142053	136258	104.3
尼加拉瓜	656650	334833	321817	104.0
尼日尔	2084260	1056991	1027269	102.9
尼日利亚	21843255	11026325	10816930	101.9
朝鲜	1929636	987060	942576	104.7
北马里亚纳群岛	6442	3305	3137	105.4
挪威	290413	149946	140467	106.7
阿曼	461717	235661	226056	104.2

续表

国家/地区	男女合计	男性	女性	男女人口比例
巴基斯坦	20457124	10505142	9951982	105.6
帕劳群岛	1818	934	884	105.7
巴拿马	269844	137113	132731	103.3
巴布亚新几内亚	744981	379378	365603	103.8
巴拉圭	836968	426058	410910	103.7
秘鲁	3167937	1610587	1557350	103.4
菲律宾	10873709	5544650	5329059	104.0
波兰	1957618	1004985	952633	105.5
葡萄牙	571135	294648	276487	106.6
波多黎各	299633	153756	145877	105.4
卡塔尔	62650	31946	30704	104.0
留尼旺	78345	40101	38244	104.9
罗马尼亚	1174228	603400	570828	105.7
俄罗斯	6560989	3352909	3208080	104.5
卢旺达	1079634	542377	537257	101.0
圣海伦纳	480	244	236	103.4
圣克里斯托弗和尼维斯岛	3633	1865	1768	105.5
圣卢西亚岛	17031	8794	8237	106.8
圣彼埃尔和密克隆群岛	559	285	274	104.0
圣文森特和格林纳丁斯	10378	5267	5111	103.1
萨摩亚	13690	6967	6723	103.6
圣马力诺	1577	819	758	108.0
圣多美和普林西比	31991	16208	15783	102.7
沙特阿拉伯	3838265	1962142	1876123	104.6
塞内加尔	1725607	871128	854479	101.9
塞尔维亚	609881	316039	293842	107.6

续表

国家/地区	男女合计	男性	女性	男女人口比例
塞舌尔	7021	3545	3476	102.0
塞拉利昂	994362	491669	502693	97.8
新加坡	261767	135687	126080	107.6
斯洛伐克	276164	141538	134626	105.1
斯洛文尼亚	90306	46318	43988	105.3
所罗门群岛	78377	39999	38378	104.2
索马里	1440107	723709	716398	101.0
南非	4324031	2179312	2144719	101.6
韩国	3553559	1869976	1683583	111.1
西班牙	1847695	953454	894241	106.6
斯里兰卡	1600128	818422	781706	104.7
苏丹	6132944	3136054	2996890	104.6
苏里南	44006	22493	21513	104.6
斯威士兰	187915	94000	93915	100.1
瑞典	444614	228385	216229	105.6
瑞士	381200	195571	185629	105.4
叙利亚	2407770	1239392	1168378	106.1
中国台湾	1588251	827060	761191	108.7
塔吉克斯坦	947633	477336	470297	101.5
坦桑尼亚	6313344	3181977	3131367	101.6
泰国	4981367	2544117	2437250	104.4
多哥	856149	430190	425959	101.0
汤加	12781	6532	6249	104.5
特立尼达和多巴哥	77206	39421	37785	104.3
突尼斯	824037	426257	397780	107.2
土耳其	5880127	2998161	2881966	104.0
土库曼斯坦	598613	307349	291264	105.5

续表

国家/地区	男女合计	男性	女性	男女人口比例
特克斯和凯科斯群岛	2231	1137	1094	103.9
图瓦卢	1149	586	563	104.1
乌干达	4897023	2462764	2434259	101.2
乌克兰	2238896	1144825	1094071	104.6
阿拉伯联合酋长国	209462	106949	102513	104.3
英国	3500740	1794466	1706274	105.2
美国	18943886	9677119	9266767	104.4
乌拉圭	285083	146117	138966	105.1
乌兹别克斯坦	2971266	1515542	1455724	104.1
瓦努阿图	22972	11738	11234	103.8
委内瑞拉	2445205	1262008	1183197	106.7
越南	8203860	4248128	3955732	107.4
维尔京群岛	9647	4957	4690	105.7
英属维尔京群岛	1524	773	751	102.9
瓦利斯群岛和富图纳群岛	—	—	—	—
约旦河西岸	262127	185743	176384	105.3
西撒哈拉	—	—	—	—
也门	3441638	1753397	1688241	103.9
赞比亚	1751960	882335	869625	101.5
津巴布韦	1299239	656992	642247	102.3
世界	613926156	314623942	299302214	105.1

来源：U. S. Bureau of the Census, International Data Base.

附表 2　1980 年印度生命表

男性				女性			
年龄 (xtox+n)	死亡概率 (1000nqx)	死亡人数 (ndx)	尚存人数 (lx)	年龄 (xtox+n)	死亡概率 (1000nqx)	死亡人数 (ndx)	尚存人数 (lx)
0—1	113.00	11300	100000	0—1	115.00	11500	100000
1—5	67.83	6017	88700	1—5	80.04	7084	88500
5—10	16.28	1346	82683	5—10	19.57	1593	81416
10—15	8.47	689	81337	10—15	8.27	660	79823
15—20	10.15	819	80648	15—20	14.60	1156	79163
20—25	11.54	921	79830	20—25	18.98	1481	78007
25—30	11.19	883	78909	25—30	19.96	1527	76527
30—35	16.87	1316	78026	30—35	17.70	1327	74999
35—40	23.39	1794	76709	35—40	22.71	1673	73672
40—45	35.46	2656	74915	40—45	27.11	1952	71999
45—50	47.00	3396	72258	45—50	35.99	2521	70047
50—55	70.60	4862	68862	50—55	50.77	3428	67526
55—60	102.29	6547	64001	55—60	8041	5154	64097
60—65	161.48	9278	57454	60—65	128.02	7546	58943
65—70	258.08	12433	48176	65—70	187.55	9640	51397
70—75	412.47	14743	35743	70—75	274.76	11473	41758
75—80	659.21	13844	21000	75—80	402.53	12190	30284
80+	1000.00	7157	7157	80+	1000.00	18094	18094

来源：U. S. Bureau of the Census, International Data Base, Life Table Values by Sex, http://www.census.gov/ipc/www/idbnew.html。

附表3 1990年修订后的印度生命表

男性				女性			
年龄 (xtox+n)	死亡概率 (1000nqx)	死亡人数 (ndx)	尚存人数 (lx)	年龄 (xtox+n)	死亡概率 (1000nqx)	死亡人数 (ndx)	尚存人数 (lx)
0—1	79.50	7950	100000	0—1	80.40	8040	100000
1—5	67.83	6244	92050	1—5	80.04	7360	91960
5—10	16.28	1397	85806	5—10	19.57	1656	84600
10—15	8.47	715	84409	10—15	8.27	686	82944
15—20	10.15	849	83694	15—20	14.60	1201	82258
20—25	11.54	956	82845	20—25	18.98	1538	81057
25—30	11.19	916	81889	25—30	19.96	1587	79519
30—35	16.87	1366	80973	30—35	17.70	1379	77931
35—40	23.39	1862	79607	35—40	22.71	1738	76552
40—45	35.46	2757	77745	40—45	27.11	2028	74813
45—50	47.00	3524	74988	45—50	35.99	2620	72785
50—55	70.60	5045	71463	50—55	50.77	3562	70166
55—60	102.29	6794	66418	55—60	80.41	5356	66603
60—65	161.48	9628	59624	60—65	128.02	7841	61248
65—70	258.08	12903	49996	65—70	187.55	10016	53407
70—75	412.47	15300	37093	70—75	274.76	11922	43390
75—80	659.21	14366	21793	75—80	402.53	12667	31468
80+	1000.00	7427	7427	80+	1000.00	18801	18801

来源：U. S. Bureau of the Census, International Data Base, Life Table Values by Sex, http://www.census.gov/ipc/www/idbnew.html。这一表格是根据美国人口普查局国际数据库1990年婴儿死亡率的数据作出修订的。

附表4　1981年中国生命表

男性				女性			
年龄 (xtox+n)	死亡概率 (1000nqx)	死亡人数 (ndx)	尚存人数 (lx)	年龄 (xtox+n)	死亡概率 (1000nqx)	死亡人数 (ndx)	尚存人数 (lx)
0—1	46.33	4633	100000	0—1	45.33	4533	100000
1—5	17.02	1623	95367	1—5	20.62	1967	95467
5—10	6.84	640	93743	5—10	6.15	573	93498
10—15	4.21	390	93102	10—15	3.84	357	92923
15—20	5.69	527	92710	15—20	5.37	499	92567
20—25	7.59	698	92183	20—25	7.86	724	92069
25—30	7.82	715	91483	25—30	8.67	791	91346
30—35	9.39	854	90768	30—35	9.84	892	90554
35—40	12.98	1166	89916	35—40	12.64	1132	89663
40—45	18.69	1657	88749	40—45	16.95	1501	88530
45—50	28.35	2468	87090	45—50	24.48	2132	87029
50—55	45.87	3882	84621	50—55	38.05	3231	84898
55—60	74.24	5994	80739	55—60	58.15	4750	81668
60—65	123.27	9213	74745	60—65	95.91	7378	76919
65—70	186.71	12236	65531	65—70	146.38	10180	69542
70—75	291.87	15556	53296	70—75	237.54	14101	59362
75—80	411.47	15529	37741	75—80	343.90	15565	45261
80—85	591.41	13136	22211	80—85	524.96	15589	29695
85—90	750.32	6809	9075	85—90	692.52	9769	14107
90+	1000.00	2266	2266	90+	1000.00	4338	4338

来源：U.S. Bureau of the Census, International Data Base, 1998, http://www.census.gov/ipc/www/idbnew.html。

附表5 1990年修订后的中国生命表

男性				女性			
年龄 (xtox+n)	死亡概率 (1000nqx)	死亡人数 (ndx)	尚存人数 (lx)	年龄 (xtox+n)	死亡概率 (1000nqx)	死亡人数 (ndx)	尚存人数 (lx)
0—1	28.20	2820	100000	0—1	32.70	3270	100000
1—5	9.30	904	97180	1—5	9.80	948	96730
5—10	6.84	659	96276	5—10	6.15	589	95782
10—15	4.21	403	95618	10—15	3.84	366	95193
15—20	5.69	542	95215	15—20	5.37	509	94827
20—25	7.59	719	94673	20—25	7.86	741	94318
25—30	7.82	735	93955	25—30	8.67	811	93.577
30—35	9.39	875	93220	30—35	9.84	913	92766
35—40	12.98	1199	92345	35—40	12.64	1161	91853
40—45	18.69	1704	91146	40—45	16.95	1537	90692
45—50	28.35	2536	89443	45—50	24.48	2183	89155
50—55	45.87	3986	86907	50—55	38.05	3309	86972
55—60	74.24	6156	82920	55—60	58.15	4865	83663
60—65	123.27	9463	76764	60—65	95.91	7557	78798
65—70	186.71	12566	67302	65—70	146.38	10428	71240
70—75	291.87	15976	54736	70—75	237.54	14445	60812
75—80	411.47	15949	38760	75—80	343.90	15946	46367
80—85	591.41	13491	22811	80—85	524.96	15970	30421
85—90	750.32	6993	9321	85—90	692.52	10008	14451
90+	1000.00	2327	2327	90+	1000.00	4443	4443

来源：U. S. Bureau of the Census, International Data Base, 1998, Table 014, http://www.census.gov/ipc/www/idbnew.html. Life Table Values, by Sex and Urban/Rural Residence. 这一表格是根据0—1岁与1—5岁年龄段的人口死亡率作出的：1990年婴儿死亡率和1—5岁人口死亡率数据来自Daniel Goodkind, "On Substituting Sex Preference Strategies in East Asia: Does Prenatal Sex Selection Reduce Postnatal Discrimination?" *Population and Development Review*, Vol. 22, No. 1 (March 1996), p. 117。

附表6 1995年后的中国生命表

男性				女性			
年龄 (xtox+n)	死亡概率 (1000nqx)	死亡人数 (ndx)	尚存人数 (lx)	年龄 (xtox+n)	死亡概率 (1000nqx)	死亡人数 (ndx)	尚存人数 (lx)
0—1	30.45	3045	100000	0—1	40.84	4084	100000
1—5	9.30	902	96955	1—5	9.80	940	95916
5—10	6.84	657	96053	5—10	6.15	584	94976
10—15	4.21	402	95396	10—15	3.84	362	94392
15—20	5.69	541	94995	15—20	5.37	505	94029
20—25	7.59	717	94454	20—25	7.86	735	93525
25—30	7.82	733	93737	25—30	8.67	804	92789
30—35	9.39	873	93004	30—35	9.84	905	91985
35—40	12.98	1196	92131	35—40	12.64	1151	91080
40—45	18.69	1700	90935	40—45	16.95	1524	89929
45—50	28.35	2530	89235	45—50	24.48	2164	88404
50—55	45.87	3977	86706	50—55	38.05	3281	86240
55—60	74.24	6142	82728	55—60	58.15	4824	82959
60—65	123.27	9441	76587	60—65	95.91	7494	78135
65—70	186.71	12537	67146	65—70	146.38	10340	70641
70—75	291.87	15939	54609	70—75	237.54	14324	60300
75—80	411.47	15912	38670	75—80	343.90	15811	45977
80—85	591.41	13460	22759	80—85	524.96	15836	30165
85—90	750.32	6977	9299	85—90	692.52	9924	14330
90+	1000.00	2322	2322	90+	1000.00	4406	4406

来源：U.S. Bureau of the Census, International Data Base, 1998, Table 014, http://www.census.gov/ipc/www/idbnew.html. Life Table Values, by Sex and Urban/Rural Residence. 这一表格是根据1995年婴儿死亡率（数据来自中国国家统计局：《中国人口统计年鉴（1996）》，北京：中国统计出版社，1996年，表3-9）和1—5岁人口死亡率（数据来自1990年中国生命表）作出的。

参考文献

"6.3 Brides for Seven Brothers," *Economist*, December 19, 1998–January 1, 1999, pp. 56–58.

Agnihotri, S.B. "Missing Females: A Disaggregated Analysis," *Economic and Political Weekly*, August 19, 1995, pp. 2074–2084.

"AIDS Day, 1997: China Responds to AIDS," http://www.redfish.com/USEmbassy-China/sandt/aidsdy97.htm.

Aird, John S. *Slaughter of the Innocents: Coercive Birth Control in China.* Washington, D.C.: AEI Press, 1990.

"Alarming Gender Imbalance," *China Today*, Vol. 52, No. 1 (January 2003), p. 7.

Alexander, Richard D., and Donald W. Tinkle, eds. *Natural Selection and Social Behavior: Recent Research and New Theory.* New York: Chiron, 1981.

Allahbadia, Gautam N. "The 50 Million Missing Women," *Journal of Assisted Reproduction and Genetics*, Vol. 19, No. 9 (September 2002), pp. 411–416.

Anderson, Mary M. *Hidden Power: The Palace Eunuchs of Imperial China.* Buffalo, New York: Prometheus, 1990.

Anderson, Nels. *The Hobo: The Sociology of the Homeless Man.* Chicago: University of Chicago Press, 1961.

Aptekar, Herbert. *Anjea: Infanticide, Abortion, and Contraception in Savage Society.* New York: William Godwin, 1931.

Arnold, Fred. "Measuring the Effect of Sex Preference on Fertility: The Case of Korea," *Demography*, Vol. 22, No. 2 (May 1985), pp. 280–288.

Arora, Dolly. "The Victimising Discourse: Sex-Determination Technologies and Policy," *Economic and Political Weekly*, February 17, 1996, pp. 420–424.

Ba, P.V. *Socio-economic Renovation in North Vietnam and Its Effect on Fertility and Development in the Rural Plain.* Hanoi: Institute of Sociology, 1992.

Bacon, Margaret K., Irvin L. Child, and Herbert Barry. "A Cross-Cultural Study of Correlates of Crime," *Journal of Abnormal and Social Psychology*, Vol. 66, No. 4 (November 1963), pp. 291–300.

Bae Wha-oak. "Sex Ratio at Birth in Korea," *Journal of Population, Health, and Social Welfare*, Vol. 11, No. 2 (December 1991), p. 120.

Bahr, Howard M., ed. *Disaffiliated Man: Essays and Bibliography on Skid Row, Vagrancy, and Outsiders.* Toronto: University of Toronto Press, 1970.

Bairagi, Radheshyam, Santosh Chandra Sutradhar, and Nurul Alam. "Levels, Trends, and Determinants of Child Mortality in Matlab, Bangladesh, 1966–1994," *Asia-Pacific Population Journal*, Vol. 14, No. 2 (June 1999), pp. 51–68.

Baker, Hugh D.R. *Chinese Family and Kinship.* London: Macmillan, 1979.

Balakrishnan, Radhika. "The Social Context of Sex Selection and the Politics of Abortion in India," in Gita Sen and Rachel C. Snow, eds., *Power and Decision: The Social Control of Reproduction,* Cambridge, Mass.: Harvard University Press, 1994, pp. 267–286.

Balikci, Asen. "Female Infanticide on the Arctic Coast," *Man: The Journal of the Royal Anthropological Institute,* Vol. 2, No. 4 (December 1967), pp. 615–625.

Balikci, Asen. *The Netslik Eskimo.* New York: Natural History Press, 1970.

Bangladesh. Bureau of Statistics. "1991 Population Census," http://www.bbsgov.org/ana_vol1/Projection.htm.

Bangladesh. Bureau of Statistics. "1999 Demographic Data," http://www.bbsgov.org/data-sheet/DEMO_DATA.htm.

Bangladesh. Bureau of Statistics. "Population Census, 2001: Preliminary Report," http://www.bbsgov.org.

Banister, Judith. *China's Changing Population.* Stanford, Calif.: Stanford University Press, 1987.

Banister, Judith. "Implications and Quality of China's 1990 Census Data," paper presented at the International Seminar on China's 1990 Population Census, Beijing, October 1992.

Banister, Judith. "Son Preference in Asia—Report of a Symposium." U.S. Census Bureau, http://www.census.gov/ipc/www/ebspr96a.html.

Barth, Gunter. *Bitter Strength: A History of the Chinese in the United States, 1850–1870.* Cambridge, Mass.: Harvard University Press, 1964.

Bartlett, Thad Q., Robert W. Sussman, and James M. Cheverud. "Infant Killing in Primates: A Review of Observed Cases with Specific Reference to the Sexual Selection Hypothesis," *American Anthropologist,* Vol. 95, No. 4 (December 1993), pp. 958–990.

Basu, Alaka M. "Is Discrimination in Food Really Necessary for Explaining Sex Differentials in Childhood Mortality?" *Population Studies,* Vol. 43, No. 2 (July 1989), pp. 193–210.

Bayliss-Smith, Tim, and Richard G. Feachem, eds. *Subsistence and Survival: Rural Ecology in the Pacific.* San Francisco, Calif.: Academic Press, 1977.

Beach, Frank Ambrose, ed. *Sex and Behavior.* New York: Wiley and Sons, 1965.

Beck, John B. "On Infanticide and Its Relation to Medical Jurisprudence and Medical Police," in John B. Beck, ed., *Researches in Medicine and Medical Jurisprudence.* New York: E. Bliss, 1835.

Beck, John B., ed. *Researches in Medicine and Medical Jurisprudence.* New York: E. Bliss, 1835.

Becker, Jasper. *Hungry Ghosts: Mao's Secret Famine.* New York: Free Press, 1996.

Benton, D. "Do Animal Studies Tell Us Anything about the Relationships between Testosterone and Human Aggression?" in Graham C.L. Davey, ed., *Animal Models of Human Behavior*. Chichester, U.K.: Wiley, 1983, pp. 281–298.

Berndt, Ronald M., and Catherine H. Berndt. *The World of the First Australians: An Introduction to the Traditional Life of the Australian Aborigines*. London: Angus and Robertson, 1964.

Betzig, Laura. "Despotism and Differential Reproduction: A Cross-Cultural Correlation of Conflict Asymmetry, Hierarchy, and Degree of Polygyny," *Ethology and Sociobiology*, Vol. 3, No. 4 (1982), pp. 209–221.

Betzig, Laura. *Despotism and Differential Reproduction: A Darwinian View of History*. New York: Aldine de Gruyter, 1986.

Bhat, P.N. Mari, Samuel H. Preston, and Tim Dyson. *Vital Rates in India, 1961–1981*. Washington, D.C.: National Academy Press, 1984.

Billington, Ray A. *America's Frontier Culture*. College Station: Texas A&M University Press, 1977.

Birdsell, Joseph B. "On Population Structure in Generalized Hunting and Collecting Populations," *Evolution*, Vol. 12, No. 2 (June 1958), pp. 189–205.

Birdsell, Joseph B. "Some Predictions for the Pleistocene Based in Equilibrium Systems among Recent Hunter-Gatherers," in Richard B. Lee and Irven Devore, eds., *Man the Hunter*. Chicago: Aldine de Gruyter, 1968, pp. 229–240.

Blaikie, Piers, and Harold Brookfield, eds. *Land Degradation and Society*. New York: Methuen, 1987.

Blaikie, Piers, Terry Cannon, Ian Davis, and Ben Wisner. *At Risk: Natural Hazards, Peoples' Vulnerability, and Disasters*. London: Routledge, 1994.

Blok, Josine, and Peter Mason, eds. *Sexual Asymmetry: Studies in Ancient Society*. Amsterdam: J.C. Gieben, 1987.

Blundell, Sue. *Women in Ancient Greece*. London: British Museum Press, 1995.

Boal, Barbara M. *The Konds: Human Sacrifice and Religious Change*. Warminster, U.K.: Aris and Phillips, 1982.

Bohle, Hans-Georg, et al., eds. *Famine and Food Security in Africa and Asia*. Bayreuth, Germany: Bayreuth, 1991.

Bohle, Hans-Georg, Thomas E. Downing, and Michael J. Watts. "Climate Change and Social Vulnerability: Towards a Sociology and Geography of Food Insecurity," *Global Environmental Change*, Vol. 4, No. 1 (March 1994), pp. 37–48.

Boone, James L. "Noble Family Structure and Expansionist Warfare in the Late Middle Ages," in Rada Dyson-Hudson and Michael A. Little, eds., *Rethinking Human Adaptation: Biological and Cultural Models*. Boulder, Colo.: Westview, 1983, pp. 79–96.

Boone, James L. "Parental Investment and Elite Family Structure in Preindustrial States: A Case Study of Late Medieval–Early Modern Portuguese Genealogies," *American Anthropologist*, Vol. 88, No. 4 (December 1986), pp. 859–878.

Booth, Beverley E., Manorama Verma, and Rajbir Singh Beri. "Fetal Sex Determination in Infants in Punjab, India: Correlations and Implications," *British Medical Journal*, November 12, 1994, pp. 1259–1261.

Boserup, Ester. *Economic and Demographic Relationships in Development*. Baltimore, Md.: Johns Hopkins University Press, 1990.

Boserup, Ester. *Population and Technological Change*. Chicago: University of Chicago Press, 1981.

Bossen, Laurel. "Women and Development," in Robert E. Gamer, ed., *Understanding Contemporary China*. Boulder, Colo.: Lynne Rienner, 1999, pp. 293–320.

Boswell, John. *The Kindness of Strangers: The Abandonment of Children in Western Europe from Late Antiquity to the Renaissance*. London: Penguin, 1989.

Bouissou, Marie-France. "Androgens, Aggressive Behaviour, and Social Relationships in Higher Mammals," *Hormone Research*, Vol. 18, Nos. 1–3 (1983), pp. 43–61.

Boulding, Elise. *The Underside of History: A View of Women through Time*. Boulder, Colo.: Westview, 1976.

Bourne, Katherine L., and George M. Walker. "The Differential Effect of Mother's Education on Mortality of Boys and Girls in India," *Population Studies*, Vol. 45, No. 2 (July 1991), pp. 203–219.

Boutwell, Jeffrey, and Thomas F. Homer-Dixon. "Environmental Change, Global Security, and U.S. Policy," in Charles F. Hermann, ed., *American Defense Annual*. New York: Lexington, 1994, pp. 201–224.

Boyatzis, Richard E. "Who Should Drink What, When, and Where If Looking for a Fight," in Edward Gottheil et al., eds., *Alcohol, Drug Abuse, and Aggression*. Springfield: Charles C. Thomas, 1983, pp. 314–329.

Bradford, John M.W., and D. McLean. "Sexual Offenders, Violence, and Testosterone: A Clinical Study," *Canadian Journal of Psychiatry*, Vol. 29, No. 4 (June 1984), pp. 335–343.

Bray, Francesca. *Technology and Gender: Fabrics of Power in Late Imperial China*. Berkeley: University of California Press, 1997.

Breen, David H. *The Canadian Prairie West and the Ranching Frontier: 1874–1924*. Toronto: University of Toronto Press, 1983.

Browne, John Cave. *Indian Infanticide: Its Origins, Progress, and Suppression*. London: W.H. Allen, 1857.

Brownell, Susan, and Jeffrey N. Wasserstrom, eds. *Chinese Femininities/Chinese Masculinities: A Reader*. Berkeley: University of California Press, 2002.

Bruns, Roger. *Knights of the Road: A Hobo History*. New York: Methuen, 1980.

Buikstra, Jane E., and Lyle W. Konigsberg. "Paleodemography: Critiques and Controversies," *American Anthropologist*, Vol. 87, No. 2 (June 1985), pp. 316–333.

Bumiller, Elizabeth. *May You Be the Mother of a Hundred Sons: A Journey among the Women of India*. New York: Fawcett Columbine, 1990.

Burnham, John C. *Bad Habits: Drinking, Smoking, Taking Drugs, Gambling, Sexual Misbehavior, and Swearing in American History*. New York: New York University Press, 1993.

Buss, David. *The Evolution of Desire: Strategies of Human Mating*. New York: Basic Books, 1994.

Cai Fang. "The Regional Character of Labor Flow in the Transitional Period," *Chinese Population Studies*, n.s., Vol. 5 (1998), pp. 18–24.

Cameron, Averil, and Amelie Kuhrt, eds. *Images of Women in Antiquity*. Detroit, Mich.: Wayne State University Press, 1993.

Campbell, Bernard, ed. *Sexual Selection and the Descent of Man*. Chicago: Aldine de Gruyter, 1972.

Campbell, Eugene K. "Sex Preferences for Offspring among Men in the Western Area of Sierra Leone," *Journal of Biosocial Science*, Vol. 23, No. 3 (July 1991), pp. 337–342.

Campbell, Eugene K., and Puni G. Campbell. "Family Size and Sex Preferences and Eventual Fertility in Botswana," *Journal of Biosocial Science*, Vol. 29, No. 2 (April 1997), pp. 191–204.

Cantarella, Eve. *Pandora's Daughters: The Role and Status of Women in Greek and Roman Antiquity*, trans. Maureen B. Fant, with a foreword by Mary R. Lefkowitz. Baltimore, Md.: Johns Hopkins University Press, 1987.

Cao Jinqing, *China along the Yellow River: A Scholar's Observations and Reflections on Rural Society*. Shanghai: Shanghai Wenyi Publishing House, 2000.

Carter, C.O. "Sex Differences in the Distribution of Physical Illness in Children," *Social Science and Medicine*, Vol. 12, No. 3B (1978), pp. 163–166.

Castan, Nicole. "Criminals," in Natalie Zemon Davis and Arlette Farge, eds., *A History of Women in the West*, Vol. 3: *Renaissance and Enlightenment Paradoxes*. Cambridge, Mass.: Belknap, 1993, pp. 474–488.

Catton, William R. *Overshoot*. Chicago: University of Illinois Press, 1980.

Chagnon, Napoleon A. "Is Reproductive Success Equal in Egalitarian Societies?" in Napoleon A. Chagnon and William Irons, eds., *Evolutionary Biology and Human Social Behavior: An Anthropological Perspective*. North Scituate, Mass.: Duxbury, 1979, pp. 374–401.

Chagnon, Napoleon A. *Studying the Yanomamo*. New York: Holt, Rinehart, and Winston, 1974.

Chagnon, Napoleon A. *Yanomamo: The Fierce People*, 2d ed. New York: Holt, Rinehart, and Winston, 1977.

Chagnon, Napoleon A., Mark V. Flinn, and Thomas F. Melancon. "Sex-Ratio Variation among the Yanomamo Indians," in Napoleon A. Chagnon and William Irons, eds., *Evolutionary Biology and Human Social Behavior: An Anthropological Perspective*. North Scituate, Mass.: Duxbury, 1979, pp. 290–320.

Chagnon, Napoleon A., and William Irons, eds. *Evolutionary Biology and Human Social Behavior: An Anthropological Perspective*. North Scituate, Mass.: Duxbury, 1979.

Chambers, Robert. "Vulnerability, Coping, and Policy," *IDS Bulletin*, Vol. 20, No. 2 (April 1989), pp. 1–7.

Chang, Kyung-sup. "Birth and Wealth in Peasant China: Surplus Population, Limited Supplies of Family Labor, and Economic Reform," in Alice Goldstein and Wang Feng, eds., *China: The Many Facets of Demographic Change*. Boulder, Colo.: Westview, 1996, pp. 21–45.

Cheatwood, Derral, and Kathleen J. Block. "Youth and Homicide: An Investigation of the Age Factor in Criminal Homicide," *Justice Quarterly*, Vol. 7, No. 2 (June 1990), pp. 265–292.

Chen, Lincoln C., Emdadul Huq, and Stan D'Souza. "Sex Bias in the Family Allocation of Food and Health-Care in Rural Bangladesh," *Population and Development Review*, Vol. 7, No. 1 (March 1981), pp. 55–70.

Chen, Phillip M. *Law and Justice: The Legal System in China, 2400 B.C. to 1960 A.D.* New York: Dunellen, 1961.

Chen, Robert S., and Robert W. Kates. "Special Issue: Climate Change and World Food Security," *Global Environmental Change*, Vol. 4, No. 1 (March 1994), pp. 1–77.

Chen Shengsao. *Wensulu*. Beijing: Shumu wenxian chubanshe, 1827.

Chen, Walter. "The Era of the Ch'ing Dynasty," http://www.leksu.com/mainp4e.htm.

Cheng, Lucie, and Edna Bonacich, eds. *Labor Immigration under Capitalism: Asian Workers in the United States before World War II.* Berkeley: University of California Press, 1984.

Chesnaux, Jean, ed. *Popular Movements and Secret Societies in China, 1840–1950.* Stanford, Calif.: Stanford University Press, 1972.

China. Population Census Office under the State Council and the Department of Population Statistics of the State Statistical Bureau. *The 1982 Population Census of China (Major Figures).* Hong Kong: Economic Information Agency, 1982.

China. State Family Planning Commission of China. *China Birth Planning Yearbook.* Beijing, 1996.

China. State Statistical Bureau. *10 Percent Sampling Tabulation on the 1990 Population Census of the People's Republic of China.* Beijing: China Statistics Press, 1991.

China. State Statistical Bureau. *China Population Statistical Yearbook, 1989.* Beijing: China Statistics Press, 1989.

China. State Statistical Bureau. *China Population Statistical Yearbook, 1990.* Beijing: China Statistics Press, 1990.

China. State Statistical Bureau. *China Population Statistical Yearbook, 1991.* Beijing: China Statistics Press, 1991.

China. State Statistical Bureau. *China Population Statistical Yearbook, 1994.* Beijing: China Statistics Press, 1994.

China. State Statistical Bureau. *China Population Statistical Yearbook, 1995.* Beijing: China Statistics Press, 1995.

China. State Statistical Bureau. *China Population Statistical Yearbook, 1996.* Beijing: China Statistics Press, 1996.

China. State Statistical Bureau. *China Population Statistical Yearbook, 1997.* Beijing: China Statistics Press, 1997.

China. State Statistical Bureau. *Major Figures of the 2000 Population Census.* Beijing: China Statistics Press, March 28, 2001.

China Population Information Center. *Analysis on China's National One-per-Thousand Population Fertility Sampling Survey.* Beijing: China Population Information Center, 1984.

"China's One-Child Policy, Two-Child Reality," a U.S. embassy report, Beijing, October 1997, http://www.usembassy-china.org.cn/english/sandt/fert21.htm.

"China's Population and Development in the 21st Century." Information Office of the State Council of the People's Republic of China, December 18, 2000, http://www.china.org.cn/e-white/21st/.

Chiu, Vermier Y. *Marriage Laws and Customs of China*. Hong Kong: Institute of Advanced Chinese Studies and Research, New Asia College, Chinese University of Hong Kong, 1966.

Chivers, David John, and J. Herbert, eds. *Recent Advances in Primatology*, Vol. 1: *Behavior*. London: Academic Press, 1978.

Choe, Minja Kim. "Sex Differentials in Infant and Child Mortality in Korea," *Social Biology*, Vol. 34 (Spring/Summer 1987), pp. 12–25.

Christiansen, Kerrin, and Rainier Knussmann. "Androgen Levels and Components of Aggressive Behavior in Men," *Hormones and Behavior*, Vol. 21, No. 2 (June 1987), pp. 170–180.

Clark, Alice. "Limitations on Female Life Chances in Rural Central Gujarat," in J. Krishnamurty, ed., *Women in Colonial India: Essays on Survival, Work, and the State*. Delhi: Oxford University Press, 1989.

Clark, Gillian. *Women in Late Antiquity: Pagan and Christian Lifestyles*. Oxford: Clarendon, 1994.

Clark, Shelley. "Son Preference and Sex Composition of Children: Evidence from India," *Demography*, Vol. 37, No. 1 (February 2000), pp. 95–108.

Clark, William C., and R.E. Munn, eds. *Sustainable Development of the Biosphere*. New York: Cambridge University Press, 1986.

Clarke, William Carey. "The Structure of Permanence," in Tim Bayliss-Smith and Richard G. Feachem, eds., *Subsistence and Survival: Rural Ecology in the Pacific*. San Francisco, Calif.: Academic Press, 1977, pp. 363–384.

Cleland, John, Jane Verrall, and Martin Vaessen. "Preferences for the Sex of Children and Their Influence on Reproductive Behavior," World Fertility Survey Comparative Studies No. 27. Voorburg, Netherlands: International Statistical Institute, 1983.

Coale, Ansley J. "Excess Female Mortality and the Balance of the Sexes in the Population: An Estimate of the Number of 'Missing Females,'" *Population and Development Review*, Vol. 17, No. 3 (September 1991), pp. 517–523.

Coale, Ansley J. "Excess Ratio of Males to Females by Birth Cohort in the Census of China, 1953 to 1990, and in the Births Reported in the Fertility Surveys, 1982 and 1988," OPR Working Paper No. 93–6. Princeton, N.J.: Office for Population Research, Princeton University, July 1993.

Coale, Ansley J., and Judith Banister. "Five Decades of Missing Females in China," *Demography*, Vol. 31, No. 3 (August 1994), pp. 459–479.

Cohen, Mark Nathan, and Sharon Bennett. "Skeletal Evidence for Sex Roles and Gender Hierarchies in Prehistory," in Barbara D. Miller, ed., *Sex and Gender Hierarchies*. Cambridge: Cambridge University Press, 1993, pp. 273–296.

Cohen, Mark Nathan, Roy S. Malpass, and Harold G. Klein, eds. *Biosocial Mechanisms of Population Regulation*. New Haven, Conn.: Yale University Press, 1980.

Coleman, Emily. "L'infanticide dans le Haut Moyen Age," *Annales: Economies, sociétés, civilisations*, Vol. 29, No. 2 (March–April 1974), pp. 315–335.

Coleman, Emily R. "Medieval Marriage Characteristics: A Neglected Factor in the History of Medieval Serfdom," in Theodore K. Rabb and Robert I. Rotberg, ed., *The Family in History: Interdisciplinary Essays*. New York: Harper and Row, 1971.

Collins, James J. "Alcohol Use and Expressive Interpersonal Violence," in Edward Gottheil et al., eds., *Alcohol, Drug Abuse, and Aggression*. Springfield: Charles C. Thomas, 1983, pp. 5–25.

Conway, G. "The Properties of Agroecosystems," *Agricultural Systems*, Vol. 24, No. 2 (1987), pp. 95–117.

Courtwright, David T. *Dark Paradise: Opiate Addiction in America before 1940*. Cambridge, Mass.: Harvard University Press, 1982.

Courtwright, David T. *Violent Land: Single Men and Social Disorder from the Frontier to the Inner City*. Cambridge, Mass.: Harvard University Press, 1996.

Cowgill, Ursula M., and G.E. Hutchinson. "Sex-Ratio in Childhood and the Depopulation of the Petén, Guatemala," *Human Biology*, Vol. 35, No. 1 (1963), pp. 90–103.

Croll, Elisabeth J. *Changing Identities of Chinese Women: Rhetoric, Experience, and Self-perception in Twentieth-Century China*. London: Zed, 1995.

Croll, Elisabeth J. *Feminism and Socialism in China*. London: Routledge and Kegan Paul, 1978.

Croll, Elisabeth J. "Introduction: Fertility Norms and Family Size in China," in Elisabeth J. Croll, Delia Davin, and Penny Kane, eds., *China's One-Child Family Policy*. New York: St. Martin's, 1985, pp. 1–36.

Croll, Elisabeth J., Delia Davin, and Penny Kane, eds. *China's One-Child Family Policy*. New York: St. Martin's, 1985.

Crook, John H. "Sexual Selection, Dimorphism, and Social Organization in the Primates," in Bernard Campbell, ed., *Sexual Selection and the Descent of Man*. Chicago: Aldine de Gruyter, 1972, pp. 231–281.

Crooke, William. *The North-Western Provinces of India: Their History, Ethnology, and Administration*. London: Methuen, 1897.

Crumley, Carole L., ed. *Historical Ecology: Cultural Knowledge and Changing Landscapes*. Santa Fe: School of American Research Press, 1994.

Dabbs, James M., Jr., and Robin Morris. "Testosterone, Social Class, and Antisocial Behavior in a Sample of 4,462 Men," *Psychological Science*, Vol. 1 (1990), pp. 209–211.

Daly, Martin, and Margo Wilson. *Homicide*. Hawthorne, N.Y.: Aldine de Gruyter, 1988.

Daly, Martin, and Margo Wilson. "Killing the Competition: Female/Female and Male/Male Homicide," *Human Nature*, Vol. 1, No. 1 (1990), pp. 81–107.

Daly, Martin, and Margo Wilson. *Sex, Evolution, and Behavior: Adaptations for Reproduction*. North Scituate, Mass.: Duxbury, 1978.

Dary, David. *Cowboy Culture: A Saga of Five Centuries*. Lawrence: University Press of Kansas, 1989.

Das, Narayan. "Sex Preference and Fertility Behavior: A Study of Recent Indian Data," *Demography*, Vol. 24, No. 4 (November 1987), pp. 517–530.

Das Gupta, Monica. "Selective Discrimination against Female Children in Rural Punjab, India," *Population and Development Review*, Vol. 13, No. 1 (March 1987), pp. 77–101.

Das Gupta, Monica, and P.N. Mari Bhat. "Fertility Decline and Increased Manifestation of Sex Bias in India," *Population Studies*, Vol. 51, No. 3 (November 1997), pp. 307–315.

Das Gupta, Monica, and P.N. Mari Bhat. "Intensified Gender Bias in India: A Consequence of Fertility Decline," Harvard Center for Population and Development Studies Working Paper Series No. 95.03. Cambridge, Mass.: Harvard University, May 1995.

Davey, Graham C.L., ed. *Animal Models of Human Behavior*. Chichester, U.K.: Wiley, 1983.

Davis, Fei-ling. *Primitive Revolutionaries of China: A Study of Secret Societies in the Late Nineteenth Century*. Honolulu: University of Hawaii Press, 1977.

Davis, Natalie Zemon, and Arlette Farge, eds. *A History of Women in the West*, Vol. 3: *Renaissance and Enlightenment Paradoxes*. Cambridge, Mass.: Belknap, 1993.

de Meer, Kees. "Mortality in Children among the Aymara Indians of Southern Peru," *Social Science and Medicine*, Vol. 26, No. 2 (1988), pp. 253–258.

de Sherbinin, Alex. "Human Security and Fertility: The Case of Haiti," paper presented at the annual meeting of the Association of American Geographers, Chicago, Illinois, March 18, 1995.

de Sherbinin, Alex. "World Population Growth and U.S. National Security," *Environmental Change and Security Project Report*, No. 1 (Spring 1995), pp. 24–39.

deMause, Lloyd. "The Evolution of Childhood," in Lloyd deMause, ed., *The History of Childhood*. New York: Psychohistory Press, 1974, pp. 1–73.

deMause, Lloyd, ed. *The History of Childhood*. New York: Psychohistory Press, 1974.

Devasia, Leelamma, and V.V. Devasia, eds. *Girl Child in India*. New Delhi: Ashish Publishing House, 1989.

deVore, Irven. "Male Dominance and Mating Behavior in Baboons," in Frank Ambrose Beach, ed., *Sex and Behavior*. New York: Wiley and Sons, 1965, pp. 266–289.

Dickemann, Mildred. "Concepts and Classification in the Study of Human Infanticide: Sectional Introduction and Some Cautionary Notes," in Glenn Hausfater and Sarah Blaffer Hrdy, eds., *Infanticide: Comparative and Evolutionary Perspectives*. New York: Aldine de Gruyter, 1984, pp. 427–437.

Dickemann, Mildred. "Demographic Consequences of Infanticide in Man," *Annual Review of Ecology and Systematics*, Vol. 6 (1975), pp. 107–137.

Dickemann, Mildred. "The Ecology of Mating Systems in Hypergynous Dowry Societies," *Social Science Information*, Vol. 18, No. 2 (May 1979), pp. 163–195.

Dickemann, Mildred. "Female Infanticide, Reproductive Strategies, and Social Stratification: A Preliminary Model," in Napoleon A. Chagnon and William Irons, eds., *Evolutionary Biology and Human Social Behavior*. North Scituate, Mass.: Duxbury, 1979, pp. 321–367.

Dickemann, Mildred. "Paternal Confidence and Dowry Competition: A Biocultural Analysis of Purdah," in Richard D. Alexander and Donald W. Tinkle, eds., *Natural Selection and Social Behavior: Recent Research and New Theory*. New York: Chiron, 1981, pp. 417–438.

Ding Jinhong. "An Analysis in the Extraneous Population Inflow and City Community Integration: Surveys on the Local Shanghaiese's Psychological Acceptance Capacity of Extraneous Population," *Population Survey*, February 1996.

Divale, William T., and Marvin Harris. "Population, Warfare and the Male Supremacist Complex," *American Anthropologist*, Vol. 78, No. 3 (September 1976), pp. 521–538.

Dixon-Mueller, Ruth. "Abortion Policy and Women's Health in Developing Countries," *International Journal of Health Services*, Vol. 20, No. 2 (1990), pp. 297–314.

Downing, Thomas. "African Household Food Security: What Are the Limits of Available Coping Mechanisms in Response to Climatic and Economic Variations?" in Hans-Georg Bohle et al., eds., *Famine and Food Security in Africa and Asia*. Bayreuth, Germany: Bayreuth, 1991, pp. 36–68.

Downing, Thomas. "Review of Vulnerability in an African Context," paper presented at the First Open Meeting of the Human Dimensions of Global Change Community, Duke University, Durham, North Carolina, June 1–3, 1995.

Dreze, Jean, and Reetika Khera. "Crime, Gender, and Society in India: Insights from Homicide Data," *Population and Development Review*, Vol. 26, No. 2 (June 2000), pp. 335–352.

Duan Chengrong. "Floating Population and Its Effects on Rural and Urban Socioeconomic Development," *Population Research*, Vol. 22, No. 4 (1998), pp. 58–63.

Duby, Georges. *The Chivalrous Society*, trans. Cynthia Postan. London: Edward Arnold, 1977.

Duffield, Mark. "The Political Economy of Internal War: Asset Transfer, Complex Emergencies, and International Aid," in Joanna Macrae and Anthony Zwi, eds., *War and Hunger: Rethinking International Responses to Complex Emergencies*. London: Zed, 1994, pp. 50–69.

Dunlop, Riley E., and William Michelson, eds. *Handbook of Environmental Sociology*. Greenwich, Conn.: Greenwood, 1991.

Durham, William H. "Resource Competition and Human Aggression," *Quarterly Review of Biology*, Vol. 51, No. 3 (September 1976), pp. 385–415.

Dyson, Tim. "On the Demography of the 1991 Census," *Economic and Political Weekly*, December 17, 1994, pp. 3235–3239.

Dyson, Tim, and Mick Moore. "On Kinship Structure, Female Autonomy, and Demographic Behavior in India," *Population and Development Review*, Vol. 9, No. 1 (March 1983), pp. 35–60.

Dyson-Hudson, Rada, and Michael A. Little, eds. *Rethinking Human Adaptation: Biological and Cultural Models*. Boulder, Colo.: Westview, 1983.

Ebrey, Patricia Buckley. *The Cambridge Illustrated History of China*. Cambridge: Cambridge University Press, 1996.

Ebrey, Patricia Buckley. *The Inner Quarters: Marriage and the Lives of Chinese Women in the Sung Period*. Berkeley: University of California Press, 1993.

Eichhorn, Werner. "Some Notes on Population Control during the Sung Dynasty," in *Etudes d'histoire et de littérature chinoises offertes au Professeur Jarolslav Prusek*, Bibliothèque de l'institut des hautes études chinoises, Vol. 24. Paris: Presses Universitaires de France, 1976.

El Badry, M.A. "Higher Female Than Male Mortality in Some Countries of South Asia: A Digest," *Journal of the American Statistical Association*, Vol. 64, No. 328 (December 1969), pp. 1234–1244.

Elliot, Dorinda. "Trying to Stand on Two Feet," *Newsweek*, June 29, 1998, pp. 48–49.

Ellis, William. *Polynesian Researches, during a Residence of Nearly Eight Years in the Society and Sandwich Islands*, Vol. 1. London: Henry G. Bohn, 1859.

Eng, Robert Y. "Fertility and Infanticide," in Thomas C. Smith, Robert Y. Eng, and Robert T. Lundy, eds., *Nakahara: Family Farming and Population in a Japanese Village, 1717–1830*. Stanford, Calif.: Stanford University Press, 1977, pp. 59–85.

Engels, Donald. "The Problem of Female Infanticide in the Greco-Roman World," *Classical Philology*, Vol. 75, No. 2 (April 1980), pp. 112–120.

Ennen, Edith. *The Medieval Woman*, trans. Edmund Jephcott. Oxford: Basil Blackwell, 1989.

Erikson, Kai T. *Everything in Its Path*. New York: Simon and Schuster, 1978.

Esherick, Joseph. *The Origins of the Boxer Uprising*. Berkeley: University of California Press, 1987.

Fantham, Elaine, Helene Peet Foley, Natalie Boymel Kampen, Sarah B. Pomeroy, and H.A. Shapiro. *Women in the Classical World: Image and Text*. New York: Oxford University Press.

Fei Hsiao-tung. *Peasant Life in China: A Field Study of Country Life in the Yangtze Valley*. 1939, reprint. London: Routledge and Kegan Paul, 1962.

Feng Jianhua. "Bright Lights, Big City," *Beijing Review*, April 3, 2003, pp. 22–24.

Feng Jianhua. "Migrant Workers vs. City Residents," *Beijing Review*, April 3, 2003, pp. 21–22.

Feng Shuliang. "Crime and Crime Control in a Changing China," in Liu Jianhong, Zhang Lening, and Steven F. Messner, eds., *Crime and Social Control in a Changing China*. Westport, Conn.: Greenwood, 2001, pp. 123–130.

Fish, M. Steven. "Islam and Authoritarianism," *World Politics*, Vol. 55, No. 1 (October 2002), pp. 4–37.

Ford, Robert E. "The Population-Environment Nexus and Vulnerability Assessment in Africa." Brigham Young University, 1994.

Forum against Sex Discrimination and Sex Pre-Selection. "Using Technology, Choosing Sex: The Campaign against Sex Determination and the Question of Choice," *Development Dialogue* (Uppsala, Sweden), Nos. 1–2 (1992), pp. 91–102.

Foster, Arnold. *Christian Progress in China: Gleanings from the Writings and Speeches of Many Workers*. London: Religious Tract Society, 1889.

Frances, Raelene. "The History of Female Prostitution in Australia," in Roberta Perkins, G. Prestage, R. Sharp, and F. Lovejoy, eds., *Sex Work and Sex Workers in Australia*. Sydney: University of New South Wales, 1994, pp. 27–52.

Frantz, Joe B., and Julian Ernest Choate Jr. *The American Cowboy*. Norman: University of Oklahoma Press, 1960.

Freedman, Ronald, Ming-cheng Chang, and Te-hsiung Sun. "Taiwan's Transition from High Fertility to Below-Replacement Levels," *Studies in Family Planning*, Vol. 25, No. 6 (November–December 1994), pp. 317–331.

Freeman, Milton M.R. "A Social and Ecologic Analysis of Systematic Female Infanticide among the Netsilik Eskimo," *American Anthropologist*, Vol. 73, No. 5 (October 1971), pp. 1011–1018.

Friedman, Richard C., Ralph M. Richart, and Raymond L. Vande Wiele, eds. *Sex Differences in Behavior*. New York: Wiley, 1974.

Fukuyama, Francis. "Women and the Evolution of World Politics," *Foreign Affairs*, Vol. 77, No. 5 (September/October 1998), pp. 24–40.

Furth, Charlotte. *A Flourishing Yin: Gender in China's Medical History, 960–1665*. Berkeley: University of California Press, 1999.

Gamer, Robert E., ed. *Understanding Contemporary China*. Boulder, Colo.: Lynne Rienner, 1999.

George, Sabu, Rajaratnam Abel, and Barbara D. Miller. "Female Infanticide in Rural South India," *Economic and Political Weekly*, May 30, 1992, pp. 1153–1156.

Ghosh, Srikanta. *Indian Women through the Ages*. New Delhi: Ashish Publishing House, 1989.

Giannini, A. James, Robert H. Loiselle, and Brian H. Graham. "Cocaine-Associated Violence and Relationship to Route of Administration," *Journal of Substance Abuse Treatment*, Vol. 10, No. 1 (January–February 1993), pp. 67–69.

Gibbon, Edward. *The Decline and Fall of the Roman Empire*. Chicago: Encyclopædia Britannica, 1990.

Gibbons, Ann. "Anthropologists Probe Genes, Brains at Annual Meeting," *Science*, April 17, 1998, pp. 380–381.

Gil, Vincent E., Marc Wang, Allen F. Anderson, and Guao Matthew Lin. "Plum Blossoms and Pheasants: Prostitutes, Prostitution, and Social Control Measures in Contemporary China," *International Journal of Offender Therapy and Comparative Criminology*, Vol. 38, No. 4 (December 1994), pp. 319–337.

Giladi, Avner. "Some Observations on Infanticide in Medieval Muslim Society," *International Journal of Middle East Studies*, Vol. 22, No. 2 (May 1990), pp. 185–200.

Gilder, George. *Naked Nomads: Unmarried Men in America*. New York: Quadrangle, 1974.

Gilley, Bruce. "Irresistible Force," *Far Eastern Economic Review*, April 4, 1996, pp. 18–22.

Gleick, Peter H. "Water and Conflict: Fresh Water Resources and International Security," *International Security*, Vol. 18, No. 1 (Summer 1993), pp. 79–112.

Goldstein, Alice, and Wang Feng, eds. *China: The Many Facets of Demographic Change*. Boulder, Colo.: Westview, 1996.

Goldstone, Jack A. *Revolution and Rebellion in the Early Modern World*. Berkeley: University of California Press, 1991.

Goodkind, Daniel. "On Substituting Sex Preference Strategies in East Asia: Does Prenatal Sex Selection Reduce Postnatal Discrimination?" *Population and Development Review*, Vol. 22, No. 1 (March 1996), pp. 111–125.

Goodkind, Daniel. "Vietnam's One-or-Two-Child Policy in Action," *Population and Development Review*, Vol. 21, No. 1 (March 1995), pp. 85–111.

Gordon, Manuel J. "The Control of Sex," *Scientific American*, Vol. 199, No. 5 (November 1958), pp. 87–94.

Gorman-Stapleton, Odesa. "Prohibiting Amniocentesis in India: A Solution to the Problem of Female Infanticide or a Problem to the Solution of Prenatal Diagnosis?" *ILSA Journal of International Law*, Vol. 14, No. 23 (1990), pp. 23–43.

Gottheil, Edward, et al., eds. *Alcohol, Drug Abuse, and Aggression*. Springfield: Charles C. Thomas, 1983.

Granzberg, Gary. "Twin Infanticide: A Cross-Cultural Test of a Materialistic Explanation," *Ethos*, Vol. 1, No. 4 (Winter 1973), pp. 405–412.

Greenhalgh, Susan, and Jiali Li. "Engendering Reproductive Practice in Peasant China: The Political Roots of the Rising Sex Ratios at Birth," Population Council Research Division Working Paper, No. 57. New York: Population Council, 1993.

Gregory, Lisa B. "Examining the Economic Component of China's One-Child Family Policy under International Law: Your Money or Your Life," *Journal of Chinese Law*, Vol. 6, No. 1 (Spring 1992), pp. 45–87.

Grosse, Scott. "The Roots of Conflict and State Failure in Rwanda: The Political Exacerbation of Social Cleavages in a Context of Growing Resource Scarcity," University of Michigan, 1994.

Gu Baochang, and Krishna Roy. "Sex Ratio at Birth in China, with Reference to Other Areas in Asia: What We Know," *Asia-Pacific Population Journal*, Vol. 10, No. 3 (September 1995), pp. 17–42.

Gu Baochang, and Xu Yi. "A Comprehensive Discussion of the Birth Gender Ratio in China," *Chinese Journal of Population Science*, Vol. 6, No. 4 (1994), pp. 417–431.

Guisso, Richard W. "Thunder over the Lake: The Five Classics and the Perception of Woman in Early China," in Richard W. Guisso and Stanley Johannesen, eds., *Women in China: Current Directions in Historical Scholarship*. Youngstown, N.Y.: Philo, 1981, pp. 47–61.

Guisso, Richard W., and Stanley Johannesen, eds. *Women in China: Current Directions in Historical Scholarship*. Youngstown, N.Y.: Philo, 1981.

Gunderson, Lance H., C.S. Holling, and Stephen S. Light, eds. *Barriers and Bridges to the Renewal of Ecosystems and Institutions*. New York: Columbia University Press, 1995.

Gurr, Ted Robert. "On the Political Consequences of Scarcity and Economic Decline," *International Studies Quarterly*, Vol. 29, No. 1 (March 1985), pp. 51–75.

Gurr, Ted Robert. "The State Failure Project: Early Warning Research for International Policy Planning," paper prepared for the annual conference of the International Studies Association, Chicago, Illinois, February 21–25, 1995.

Guttentag, Marcia, and Paul F. Secord. *Too Many Women? The Sex Ratio Question*. Beverly Hills, Calif.: Sage, 1983.

Hallissey, Robert C. *The Rajput Rebellion against Aurangzeb: A Study of the Mughal Empire in Seventeenth-Century India*. Columbia: University of Missouri Press, 1977.

Hammel, E.A., Sheila R. Johansson, and Caren A. Ginsberg. "The Value of Children during Industrialization: Sex Ratios in Childhood in Nineteenth-Century America," *Journal of Family History*, Vol. 8, No. 4 (Winter 1983), pp. 346–366.

Han Lei. "Women's Education in China." Foreign Affairs College, Beijing, 1999.

Hank, Karsten, and Hans-Peter Kohler. "Gender Preferences for Children in Europe: Empirical Results from 17 FFS Countries," *Demographic Research*, Vol. 2 (January 2000), http://www.demographic-research.org/Volumes/Vol2/1.

Harris, William V. "The Theoretical Possibility of Extensive Infanticide in the Graeco-Roman World," *Classical Quarterly*, Vol. 32, No. 1 (1982), pp. 114–116.

Hassan, Shaukat. "Environmental Issues and Security in South Asia," Adelphi Papers No. 262. London: Brassey's, Autumn 1991.

Haughton, Dominique, and Jonathan Haughton. "Using a Mixture Model to Detect Son Preference in Vietnam," *Journal of Biosocial Science*, Vol. 28, No. 3 (July 1996), pp. 355–365.

Hausfater, Glenn, and Sarah Blaffer Hrdy, eds. *Infanticide: Comparative and Evolutionary Perspectives*. New York: Aldine de Gruyter, 1984.

Hayase, Yasuko, and Seiko Kawamata. *Population Policy and Vital Statistics in China*. Tokyo: Institute of Developing Economies, 1991.

Hayes, James. "San Po Tsai (Little Daughters-in-Law) and Child Betrothals in the New Territories of Hong Kong from the 1890s to the 1960s," in Maria Jaschok and Suzanne Miers, eds., *Women and Chinese Patriarchy: Submission, Servitude, and Escape*. London: Zed, 1994, pp. 45–76.

Hazarika, S. "Bangladesh and Assam: Land Pressure, Migration, and Ethnic Conflict," Occasional Paper No. 3. Toronto: Project on Environmental Change and Acute Conflict, University of Toronto and the American Academy of Arts and Sciences, March 1993.

He Jingwu. "War on Drug Trafficking," *Beijing Review*, September 15–21, 1997, pp. 17–19.

Hepner, George. "Vulnerability Assessment Using a Geographic Information Systems Approach on the Mexico/U.S. Border," paper presented at the First Open Meeting of the Human Dimensions of Global Change Community, Duke University, Durham, North Carolina, June 1–3, 1995.

Herlihy, David. "Life Expectancies for Women in Medieval Society," in Rosemarie Thee Morewedge, ed., *The Role of Women in the Middle Ages: Papers of the Sixth Annual Conference of the Center for Medieval and Early Renaissance Studies, State University of New York at Binghamton, 6–8 May 1972*. Albany: State University of New York Press, 1975.

Hermann, Charles F., ed. *American Defense Annual*. New York: Lexington, 1994.

Hewitt, Kenneth, ed. *Interpretations of Calamity from the Viewpoint of Human Ecology*. Winchester, Mass.: Allen and Unwin, 1983.

Hirschi, Travis, and Michael Gottfredson. "Age and the Explanation of Crime," *American Journal of Sociology*, Vol. 89, No. 3 (November 1983), pp. 552–584.

"HIV/AIDS—What the Chinese Experts Say," http://www.usembassychina.org.cn/english/sandt/webaids3.htm.

Ho Ping-ti. *Studies on the Population of China, 1368–1953*. Cambridge, Mass.: Harvard University Press, 1959.

Holliday, J.S. *The World Rushed In: The California Gold Rush Experience*. New York: Simon and Schuster, 1981.

Holling, Crawford S. "The Resilience of Terrestrial Ecosystems: Local Surprise and Global Change," in William C. Clark and R.E. Munn, eds., *Sustainable De-*

velopment of the Biosphere. New York: Cambridge University Press, 1986, pp. 292–317.

Hom, Sharon K. "Female Infanticide in China: The Human Rights Specter and Thoughts towards (An)other Vision," *Columbian Human Rights Law Review*, Vol. 23, No. 2 (Summer 1992), pp. 249–314.

Homer-Dixon, Thomas F. "Environmental Scarcities and Violent Conflict: Evidence from Cases," *International Security*, Vol. 19, No. 1 (Summer 1994), pp. 5–40.

Homer-Dixon, Thomas F. *Environmental Scarcity and Global Security*. New York: Foreign Policy Association, 1993.

Homer-Dixon, Thomas F. "Strategies for Studying Causation in Complex Ecological-Political Systems." Toronto: Environment, Population, and Security Project, University of Toronto, June 1995.

Hsiao Kung-ch'uan. *Rural China: Imperial Control in the Nineteenth Century*. Seattle: University of Washington Press, 1967.

Hsu Wen-hsiung. "Frontier Social Organization and Social Disorder in Ch'ing Taiwan," in Ronald G. Knapp, ed., *China's Island Frontier: Studies in the Historical Geography of Taiwan*. Honolulu: University Press of Hawaii, 1980, pp. 87–106.

Huang Wei. "Continuing War on Drugs," *Beijing Review*, September 2–8, 1996, pp. 17–19.

Hull, Terence H. "Recent Trends in Sex Ratios at Birth in China," *Population and Development Review*, Vol. 16, No. 1 (March 1990), pp. 63–83.

Hutchinson, Charles F. "Early Warning and Vulnerability Assessment for Famine Mitigation," Famine Mitigation Strategy Paper. Washington, D.C.: Office of U.S. Foreign Disaster Assistance, 1992.

Hyde, Janet Shibley. "Gender Differences in Aggression," in Janet Shibley Hyde and Marcia C. Linn, eds., *The Psychology of Gender: Advances through Meta-Analysis*. Baltimore, Md.: Johns Hopkins University Press, 1986.

Hyde, Janet Shibley, and Marcia C. Linn, eds. *The Psychology of Gender: Advances through Meta-Analysis*. Baltimore, Md.: Johns Hopkins University Press, 1986.

India. National Crime Records, Bureau of India, 1997.

India. Office of the Registrar General. *Census of India, 1991, Census Data Online*, http://www.censusindia.net/cendat/datatable23.html.

India. Office of the Registrar General. *Census of India, 1991, Series-1: India, Paper 2 of 1992: Final Population Totals: Brief Analysis of Primary Census Abstract*. New Delhi: India, 1992.

India. Office of the Registrar General. *Census of India, 1991, Series-1, Part 2-B(i)*, Vol. 1: *Primary Census Abstract: General Population*, New Delhi: India, 1994.

India. Office of the Registrar General. *Census of India, 1991, Series-1: India, Part 4 A-C Series: Socio-Cultural Tables*, Vols. 1 and 2. New Delhi: India, 1998.

India. Office of the Registrar General. *Census of India, 2001, Series 1: India, Paper 1 of 2001: Provisional Population Totals*. New Delhi: India, 2001, http://www.censusindia.net/results.

India. Office of the Registrar General. *Compendium of India's Fertility and Mortality Indicators Based on the SRS*. Delhi: Controller of Publications, 1991.

"Infanticide," in Maria Leach, ed., *Dictionary of Folklore, Mythology, and Legend*, Vol. 1. New York: Funk and Wagnalls, 1949, pp. 522–524.

Ingerson, Alice E. "Tracking and Testing the Nature-Culture Dichotomy," in Carole L. Crumley, ed., *Historical Ecology: Cultural Knowledge and Changing Landscapes*. Santa Fe: School of American Research Press, 1994, pp. 43–66.

Ishii, Ryoichi. *Population Pressure and Economic Life in Japan*. London: P.S. King and Son, 1937.

James, William H. "The Sex Ratio of Oriental Births," *Annals of Human Biology*, Vol. 12, No. 5 (September–October 1985), pp. 485–487.

Janis, Irving Lester. *Groupthink: Psychological Studies of Policy Decisions and Fiascoes*. Boston: Houghton Mifflin, 1982.

Jasanoff, Sheila. *Risk Management and Political Culture*. New York: Russell Sage Foundation, 1986.

Jaschok, Maria, and Suzanne Miers, eds. *Women and Chinese Patriarchy: Submission, Servitude, and Escape*. London: Zed, 1994.

Jeffery, Roger, and Patricia Jeffery. "Female Infanticide and Amniocentesis," *Economic and Political Weekly*, April 16, 1983, pp. 655–656.

Jeffery, Roger, Patricia Jeffery, and Andrew Lyon. "Research Note: Female Infanticide and Amniocentesis," *Social Science and Medicine*, Vol. 19, No. 11 (1984), pp. 1207–1212.

Jhunjhunwala, Bharat. "Sex Ratio Riddles," *Statesman* (India), June 2, 2001, http://web.lexis-nexis.com/universe/docu . . . A1&_md5?f11fe824a367b3b589 54ba7cdd5c72c5.

Ji Dangsheng and Shao Qin. *The Tendency and Management of Chinese Population Movement*. Beijing: Beijing Publishing House, 1996.

Jian Fa. "China Faces an 'Employment War,'" *Beijing Review*, March 20, 2003, pp. 26–27.

Jimmerson, Julie. "Female Infanticide in China: An Examination of Cultural and Legal Norms," *Pacific Basin Law Journal*, Vol. 8, No. 1 (Spring 1990), pp. 47–79.

Johansson, Sten, and Ola Nygren. "The Missing Girls of China: A New Demographic Account," *Population and Development Review*, Vol. 17, No. 1 (March 1991), pp. 35–51.

Johansson, Sten, Zhao Xuan, and Ola Nygren. "On Intriguing Sex Ratios among Live Births in China in the 1980s," *Journal of Official Statistics*, Vol. 7, No. 1 (1991), http://www.jos.nu/Articles/abstract.asp?article=7125.

Johnson, Kay, Huang Banghan, and Wang Liyao. "Infant Abandonment and Adoption in China," *Population and Development Review*, Vol. 24, No. 3 (September 1998), pp. 469–510.

Johnson, Kay Ann. *Women, the Family, and Peasant Revolution in China*. Chicago: University of Chicago Press, 1983.

Johnson, Norris R., James G. Stemler, and Deborah Hunter. "Crowd Behavior as 'Risky Shift': A Laboratory Experiment," *Sociometry*, Vol. 40, No. 2 (June 1977), pp. 183–187.

Johnson, S., and Zhao Xuan. "Live Birth Sex Ratio for China in the 1980s," collected theses of the Beijing International Symposium for China Fertility and Contraception Sample.

Kabir, M., Ruhul Amin, Ashraf Uddin Ahmen, and Jamir Chowdhury. "Factors Affecting Desired Family Size in Bangladesh," *Journal of Biosocial Science*, Vol. 26, No. 3 (July 1994), pp. 369–375.

Kakonen, Jyrki. *Perspectives on Environmental Conflict and International Politics.* New York: Pinter, 1992.

Kanazawa, Satoshi. "Why Productivity Fades with Age: The Crime-Genius Connection," *Journal of Research in Personality*, Vol. 37, No. 4 (August 2003), pp. 257–272.

Kanazawa, Satoshi, and Mary C. Still. "Why Men Commit Crimes (and Why They Desist)," *Sociological Theory*, Vol. 18, No. 3 (November 2000), pp. 434–447.

Kaplan, Robert D. "The Coming Anarchy," *Atlantic Monthly*, Vol. 272, No. 2 (February 1994), pp. 44–81.

Kaplan, Robert D. *The Ends of the Earth: A Journey at the Dawn of the Twenty-first Century.* New York: Random House, 1996.

Karlekar, Malavika. "The Girl Child in India: Does She Have Any Rights?" *Canadian Woman Studies*, Vol. 15, Nos. 2–3 (Spring/Summer 1995), pp. 55–57.

Kates, Robert W. "Drought in the Sahel," *Mazingira*, Vol. 5, No. 2 (1981), pp. 72–83.

Kates, Robert W. "Natural Hazards in Human Ecological Perspective: Hypotheses and Models," *Economic Geography*, Vol. 47, No. 3 (July 1971), pp. 438–451.

Kaur, Manmohan. *Role of Women in the Freedom Movement (1857–1947).* Delhi: Sterling, 1968.

Kellum, Barbara A. "Infanticide in England in the Later Middle Ages," *History of Childhood Quarterly: The Journal of Psychohistory*, Vol. 1, No. 3 (Winter 1974), pp. 367–388.

Kemper, Theodore D. *Social Structure and Testosterone: Explorations of the Socio-Bio-Social Chain.* New Brunswick, N.J.: Rutgers University Press, 1990.

Kennedy, Robert Emmet. *The Irish: Emigration, Marriage, and Fertility.* Berkeley: University of California Press, 1973.

Kertzer, David. "Gender Ideology and Infant Abandonment in Nineteenth-Century Italy," *Journal of Interdisciplinary Studies*, Vol. 4 (Summer 1991), pp. 1–25.

Khan, M.E., Sandya Barge, and George Philip. "Abortion in India: An Overview," *Social Change*, Vol. 26, Nos. 3–4 (September–December 1996), pp. 208–225.

Kinney, Anne Behnke, ed. *Chinese Views of Childhood.* Honolulu: University of Hawaii Press, 1995.

Kinney, Anne Behnke. "Dyed Silk: Han Notions of the Moral Development of Children," in Anne Behnke Kinney, ed., *Chinese Views of Childhood.* Honolulu: University of Hawaii Press, 1995, pp. 17–56.

Klapisch-Zuber, Christiane, ed. *A History of Women in the West*, Vol. 2: *Silences of the Middle Ages.* Cambridge, Mass.: Belknap, 1992.

Klasen, Stephan. "'Missing Women' Reconsidered," *World Development*, Vol. 22, No. 7 (July 1994), pp. 1061–1071.

Klasen, Stephan, and Claudia Wink. "'Missing Women': Revisiting the Debate," *Feminist Economics*, Vol. 9, Nos. 2–3 (July–November 2003).

Knapp, Ronald G. *China's Island Frontier: Studies in the Historical Geography of Taiwan.* Honolulu: University Press of Hawaii, 1980.

Knight, Olive. *Life and Manners in the Frontier Army.* Norman: University of Oklahoma Press, 1978.

Ko, Dorothy. *Teachers of the Inner Chambers: Women and Culture in Seventeenth-Century China.* Stanford, Calif.: Stanford University Press, 1994.

Kogan, Nathan, and Michael Wallach. *Risk Taking: A Study in Cognition and Personality.* New York: Holt, Rinehart, and Winston, 1964.

Kohl, Marvin, ed. *Infanticide and the Value of Human Life.* New York: Prometheus, 1978.

Krishnaji, N. "Poverty and Sex Ratio: Some Data and Speculations," *Economic and Political Weekly,* June 6, 1987, pp. 892–897.

Krishnamurty, J., ed. *Women in Colonial India: Essays on Survival, Work, and the State.* Delhi: Oxford University Press, 1989.

Krishnan, Vijaya. "Gender of Children and Contraceptive Use," *Journal of Biosocial Science,* Vol. 25, No. 2 (April 1993), pp. 213–221.

Krishnan, Vijaya. "Preferences for Sex of Children: A Multivariate Analysis," *Journal of Biosocial Science,* Vol. 19, No. 3 (July 1987), pp. 367–376.

Kristof, Nicholas D., and Sheryl WuDunn. *China Wakes: The Struggle for the Soul of a Rising Power.* New York: Vintage, 1994.

Krzywicki, Ludwik. *Primitive Society and Its Vital Statistics.* London: Macmillan, 1934.

Kundu, Amitabh, and Mahesk K. Sahu. "Variation in Sex Ratio: Development Implications," *Economic and Political Weekly,* October 12, 1991, pp. 2341–2342.

Kunreuther, Howard C., and Joanne Linnerooth, eds. *Risk Analysis and Decision Processes: The Siting of Liquified Energy Gas Facilities in Four Countries.* Berlin: Springer-Verlag, 1983.

Laffey, Ella S. "The Making of a Rebel: Liu Yung-fu and the Formation of the Black Flag Army," in Jean Chesnaux, ed., *Popular Movements and Secret Societies in China, 1840–1950.* Stanford, Calif.: Stanford University Press, 1972, pp. 85–96.

Lang, Alan R. "Alcohol-Related Violence: Psychological Perspectives," in Susan E. Martin, ed., *Alcohol and Interpersonal Violence: Fostering Multidisciplinary Perspectives,* NIAAA Research Monograph No. 24. Rockville, Md.: National Institutes of Health, 1993, pp. 121–147.

Langer, William L. "Checks on Population Growth, 1750–1850," *Scientific American,* Vol. 226, No. 2 (February 1972), pp. 92–99.

Langer, William L. "Further Notes on the History of Infanticide," *History of Childhood Quarterly: The Journal of Psychohistory,* Vol. 2, No. 1 (Summer 1974), pp. 129–134.

Langer, William L. "Infanticide: A Historical Survey," *History of Childhood Quarterly: The Journal of Psychohistory,* Vol. 1, No. 3 (Winter 1974), pp. 353–365.

Langness, L.L. "Sexual Antagonism in the New Guinea Highlands: A Bena Bena Example," *Oceania,* Vol. 38, No. 3 (March 1967), pp. 161–177.

Lannoy, Richard. *The Speaking Tree: A Study of Indian Culture and Society.* Oxford: Oxford University Press, 1971.

Laub, John H., Daniel S. Nagin, and Robert J. Sampson. "Trajectories of Change in Criminal Offending: Good Marriages and the Desistance Process," *American Sociological Review,* Vol. 63, No. 2 (April 1998), pp. 225–238.

Lavely, William. "Unintended Consequences of China's Birth Planning Policy." University of Washington, July 14, 1997.

Lavely, William, and R. Bin Wong. "Revising the Malthusian Narrative: The Comparative Study of Population Dynamics in Late Imperial China," *Journal of Asian Studies*, Vol. 57, No. 3 (August 1998), pp. 714–748.

Leach, Maria, ed. *Dictionary of Folklore, Mythology, and Legend*, Vol. 1: New York: Funk and Wagnalls, 1949.

Lecky, William Edward Hartpole. *History of European Morals from Augustus to Charlemagne*, Vol. 2. London: Longmans, Greens, 1869.

Lee, Bernice J. "Female Infanticide in China," in Richard W. Guisso and Stanley Johannesen, eds., *Women in China: Current Directions in Historical Scholarship*. Youngstown, N.Y.: Philo, 1981.

Lee, James, Cameron Campbell, and Guofu Tan. "Infanticide and Family Planning in Late Imperial China: The Price and Population History of Rural Liaoning, 1774–1873," in Thomas G. Rawski and Lillian M. Li, eds., *Chinese History in Economic Perspective*. Berkeley: University of California Press, 1992, pp. 145–176.

Lee, James, Wang Feng, and Cameron Campbell. "Infant and Child Mortality among Qing Nobility: Implications for Two Types of Positive Checks," *Population Studies*, Vol. 48, No. 3 (November 1994), pp. 395–411.

Lee, James Z., and Wang Feng. *One Quarter of Humanity: Malthusian Mythology and Chinese Realities, 1700–2000*. Cambridge, Mass.: Harvard University Press, 1999.

Lee, Richard B. "Lactation, Ovulation, Infanticide, and Woman's Work: A Study of Hunter-Gatherer Population Regulation," in Mark Nathan Cohen, Roy S. Malpass, and Harold G. Klein, eds., *Biosocial Mechanisms of Population Regulation*. New Haven, Conn.: Yale University Press, 1980, pp. 321–348.

Lee, Richard B., and Irven deVore, eds. *Man the Hunter*. Chicago: Aldine de Gruyter, 1968.

Lefkowitz, Mary R., and Maureen B. Fant. *Women's Life in Greece and Rome*. Baltimore, Md.: Johns Hopkins University Press, 1992.

Levine, Nancy E. "Differential Child Care in Three Tibetan Communities: Beyond Son Preference," *Population and Development Review*, Vol. 13, No. 2 (June 1987), pp. 281–304.

Levinson, David. "Social Setting, Cultural Factors, and Alcohol-Related Aggression," in Edward Gottheil et al., eds., *Alcohol, Drug Abuse, and Aggression*. Springfield: Charles C. Thomas, 1983, pp. 1–58.

Levy, Mark. "Global Environmental Degradation: National Security and U.S. Foreign Policy," Working Paper No. 9. Cambridge, Mass.: Project on the Changing Security Environment and American National Interests, John M. Olin Institute for Strategic Studies, Harvard University, November 1994.

Li Chunyi. "'Huji' System, Population Flow, and Instability of Cities." Foreign Affairs College, Beijing, May 26, 1999.

Li, Eva B.C. "Modernization: Its Impacts on Families in China," in Phylis Lan Lin, Ko-wang Mei, and Huai-chen Peng, eds., *Marriage and the Family in Chinese Societies: Selected Readings*. Indianapolis: University of Indianapolis Press, 1994, pp. 39–52.

Li Ji. "Discussions on the Gender Imbalance in China and the Entailed Social Problems." Foreign Affairs College, Beijing, 1999.

Li Jieping, and Shao Wei. "Single Children and Their Mothers," in China Population Information Center, *Analysis on China's National One-per-Thousand Population Fertility Sampling Survey.* Beijing: China Population Information Center, 1984, pp. 144–148.

Li Jingnen. "Challenge to Chinese Population Theory Research on the Eve of the Twenty-first Century," *Chinese Population Science,* n.s., Vol. 4 (1998).

Li Li. "Gender Imbalance and Family Planning in China." Foreign Affairs College, Beijing, March 1999.

Li, Lillian M. "Life and Death in a Chinese Famine: Infanticide as a Demographic Consequence of the 1935 Yellow River Flood," *Comparative Studies in Society and History,* Vol. 33, No. 3 (July 1991), pp. 466–510.

Li Tan. "Population Flow into Big Cities," *Beijing Review,* July 18–24, 1994, pp. 15–19.

Li Weidong. "To Keep Economic Prosperity under the Pressures of Population Aging and Unemployment," *Economics Selection* (1999), pp. 10–11.

Li Xiaorong. "License to Coerce: Violence against Women, State Responsibility, and Legal Failures in China's Family-Planning Program," *Yale Journal of Law and Feminism,* Vol. 8, No. 1 (Summer 1996), pp. 145–191.

Lin, Phylis Lan, Ko-wang Mei, and Huai-chen Peng, eds. *Marriage and the Family in Chinese Societies: Selected Readings.* Indianapolis: University of Indianapolis Press, 1994.

Lin Yutang. *My Country and My People.* New York: Reynal and Hitchcock, 1935

Lindert, Peter. *Fertility and Scarcity in America.* Princeton, N.J.: Princeton University Press, 1978.

Lindsay, Jack. *The Ancient World: Manners and Morals.* New York: G.P. Putnam's Sons, 1968.

Little, Daniel. *Understanding Peasant China: Case Studies in the Philosophy of Social Science.* New Haven, Conn.: Yale University Press, 1989.

Liu Hui-chen Wang. *The Traditional Chinese Clan Rules.* Locust Valley, N.Y.: J.J. Augustin, 1959.

Liu Jianhong, Zhang Lening, and Steven F. Messner, eds. *Crime and Social Control in a Changing China.* Westport, Conn.: Greenwood, 2001.

"The Lost Girls," *Economist,* September 18, 1993, pp. 38–41.

Lutz, Elaine. "When the Women Cry, Who Will Listen?" *International Relations Journal* (San Francisco State University), Vol. 14, No. 2 (Spring 1993), pp. 29–32.

Maccoby, Eleanor Emmons, and Carol Nagy Jacklin. *The Psychology of Sex Differences.* Stanford, Calif.: Stanford University Press, 1974.

MacCormack, Carol P. "Health and the Social Power of Women," *Social Science and Medicine,* Vol. 26, No. 7 (1988), pp. 677–683.

Mack, Andrew. "The Security Report Project Background Paper." Human Security Centre, University of British Columbia, Vancouver, Canada, 2003, http://www.humansecuritybulletin.info/archive/en_v1i2.

Macrae, Joanna, and Anthony Zwi, eds. *War and Hunger: Rethinking International Responses to Complex Emergencies*. London: Zed, 1994.

Mahadevan, K., and R. Jayasree. "Value of Children and Differential Fertility Behaviour in Kerala, Andhra Pradesh, and Uttar Pradesh," in Shri Nath Singh, ed., *Population Transition in India*. Delhi: B.R. Publishing, 1989, pp. 123–131.

Makato, Ueda. "Minmatsu Shinso: Konan no toshino burai o meguru shakui kankei, dako to kyakufu," *Shigaku zasshi* [Journal of historical studies], Vol. 90, No. 12 (1981), pp. 1619–1653.

Mandelbaum, David G. "Family, *Jati*, Village," in Milton Singer and Bernard S. Cohn, eds., *Structure and Change in Indian Society*. Chicago: Aldine de Gruyter, 1968.

Martin, Ged, ed. *The Founding of Australia: The Argument About Australia's Origins*. Sydney: Hale and Iremonger, 1978.

Martin, Susan E., ed. *Alcohol and Interpersonal Violence: Fostering Multidisciplinary Perspectives*, NIAAA Research Monograph No. 24. Rockville, Md.: National Institutes of Health, 1993.

Marzuk, P.M., K. Tardiff, D. Smyth, M. Stajic, and A.C. Leon. "Cocaine Use, Risk Taking, and Fatal Russian Roulette," *JAMA*, May 20, 1992, pp. 2635–2637.

Mazur, Allan, and Alan Booth. "Testosterone and Dominance in Men," *Behavioral and Brain Science*, Vol. 21, No. 3 (June 1998), pp. 353–397.

Mazur, Allan, and Joel Michalek. "Marriage, Divorce, and Male Testosterone," *Social Forces*, Vol. 77, No. 1 (September 1998), pp. 315–330.

McCague, James. *Moguls and Iron Men: The Story of the First Transcontinental Railroad*. New York: Harper and Row, 1964.

McDermott, Rose, and J. Cowden. "The Effects of Uncertainty and Sex in a Crisis Simulation Game," *International Interactions*, Vol. 27 (2001), pp. 353–380.

McDonald, Hamish. "Unwelcome Sex," *Far Eastern Economic Review*, December 26, 1991–January 2, 1992, pp. 18–19.

McElroy, Damien. "China Fears Crime Wave of One-Child Generation." May 7, 1998, http://www.future-china.org/fcn/mainland/et980507.htm.

McGovern, Celeste. "Chinese Puzzle: 117 Boys for 100 Girls," *Report*, June 10, 2002, http://report.ca/archive/report/20020610/p56i020610f.html.

McKee, Lauris. "Sex Differentials in Survivorship and the Customary Treatment of Infants and Children," *Medical Anthropology: Cross-Cultural Studies in Health and Illness*, Vol. 8, No. 2 (Spring 1984), pp. 91–108.

McLaren, E.C. *The Story of Our Manchurian Mission*. Edinburgh: Offices of United Presbyterian Church, 1896.

Medhurst, Walter Henry. *The Foreigner in Far Cathay*. London: Edward Stanford, 1872.

Meindl, Richard S., and Katherine F. Russell. "Recent Advances in Method and Theory in Paleodemography," *Annual Review of Anthropology*, Vol. 27 (1998), pp. 375–399.

Melbin, Murray. "Night as Frontier," *American Sociological Review*, Vol. 43, No. 1 (February 1978), pp. 3–22.

Melbin, Murray. *Night as Frontier: Colonizing the World after Dark*. New York: Free Press, 1987.

Menon, Nivedita. "Abortion and the Law: Questions for Feminism," *Canadian Journal of Women and Law*, Vol. 6, No. 1 (1993), pp. 103–118.

Mesquida, Christian G., and Neil I. Wiener. "Human Collective Aggression: A Behavioral Ecology Perspective," *Ethology and Sociobiology*, Vol. 17, No. 4 (July 1996), pp. 247–262.

Messner, Steven F., and Robert J. Sampson. "The Sex Ratio, Family Disruption, and Rates of Violent Crime: The Paradox of Demographic Structure," *Social Forces*, Vol. 69, No. 3 (March 1991), pp. 693–713.

Miczek, Klaus A., Elise M. Weerts, and Joseph F. DeBold. "Alcohol, Aggression, and Violence: Biobehavioral Determinants," in Susan E. Martin, ed., *Alcohol and Interpersonal Violence: Fostering Multidisciplinary Perspectives*, NIAAA Research Monograph No. 24. Rockville, Md.: National Institutes of Health, 1993, pp. 83–119.

Miller, Barbara D. "Daughter Neglect, Women's Work, and Marriage: Pakistan and Bangladesh Compared," *Medical Anthropology: Cross-Cultural Studies in Health and Illness*, Vol. 8, No. 2 (Spring 1984), pp. 109–126.

Miller, Barbara D. *The Endangered Sex: Neglect of Female Children in Rural North India*. Ithaca, N.Y.: Cornell University Press, 1981.

Miller, Barbara D. "Female-Selective Abortion in Asia: Patterns, Policies, and Debates," *American Anthropologist*, Vol. 103, No. 4 (December 2001), pp. 1083–1095.

Miller, Barbara D., ed. *Sex and Gender Hierarchies*. Cambridge: Cambridge University Press, 1993.

Miller, Norman S., Mark S. Gold, and John C. Mahler. "Violent Behaviors Associated with Cocaine Use: Possible Pharmacological Mechanisms," *International Journal of the Addictions*, Vol. 26, No. 10 (1991), pp. 1077–1088.

Mirsky, Jonathan. "Return of the Baby Killers," *New Statesman*, March 21, 1986, p. 19.

"Missing Sisters," *Economist*, April 19, 2003, p. 36

Mitra, Ashok. *Implications of the Declining Sex Ratio in India's Population*. Bombay: Allied Publishers, 1979.

Mohnot, S.M. "Peripheralization of Weaned Male Juveniles in Presbytis entellus," in David John Chivers and J. Herbert, eds., *Recent Advances in Primatology*, Vol. 1: *Behavior*. London: Academic Press, 1978, pp. 87–91.

Monkkonen, Eric H. *Walking to Work: Tramps in America, 1790–1935*. Lincoln: University of Nebraska Press, 1984.

Moore, Trent Wade. "Fertility in China, 1982–1990: Gender Equality as a Complement to Wealth Flows Theory," *Population Research and Policy Review*, Vol. 17, No. 2 (April 1998), pp. 197–222.

Morewedge, Rosemarie Thee, ed. *The Role of Women in the Middle Ages: Papers of the Sixth Annual Conference of the Center for Medieval and Early Renaissance Studies, State University of New York at Binghamton, 6–8 May 1972*. Albany: State University of New York Press, 1975.

Moseley, Kathryn L. "The History of Infanticide in Western Society," *Issues in Law and Medicine*, Vol. 1, No. 5 (March 1986), pp. 345–362.

Moyer, Kenneth E. "Sex Differences in Aggression," in Richard C. Friedman,

Ralph M. Richart, and Raymond L. Vande Wiele, ed., *Sex Differences in Behavior.* New York: Wiley, 1974, pp. 335–372.

Muhuri, Pradip K., and Samuel H. Preston. "Effects of Family Composition on Mortality Differentials by Sex among Children in Matlab, Bangladesh," *Population and Development Review,* Vol. 17, No. 3 (September 1991), pp. 415–434.

Murray, Christopher J.L., and Alan D. Lopez, eds. *The Global Burden of Disease: A Comprehensive Assessment of Mortality and Disability from Diseases, Injuries, and Risk Factors in 1990 and Projected to 2020.* Cambridge, Mass.: Harvard University Press, 1996.

Murray, Christopher J.L., and Alan D. Lopez. *Summary of the Report: The Global Burden of Disease: A Comprehensive Assessment of Mortality and Disability from Diseases, Injuries, and Risk Factors in 1990 and Projected to 2020.* Geneva: World Health Organization, 1996.

Murthi, Mamta, Anne-Catherine Guio, and Jean Dreze. "Mortality, Fertility, and Gender Bias in India: A District-Level Analysis," *Population and Development Review,* Vol. 21, No. 4 (December 1995), pp. 745–782.

Mutharayappa, Rangamuthia, Minja Kim Choe, Fred Arnold, and T.K. Roy. "Son Preference and Its Effect on Fertility in India," National Family Health Survey Subject Reports No. 3 (March 1997).

Muthulakshmi, R. *Female Infanticide: Its Causes and Solutions.* New Delhi: Discovery Publishing House, 1997.

Nan Li, Shripad Tuljapurkar, and Marcus Feldman. "High Sex Ratio at Birth and Its Consequences," *Chinese Journal of Population Science,* Vol. 7, No. 3 (1995), pp. 213–221.

Naquin, Susan. *Shantung Rebellion: The Wang Lun Uprising of 1774.* New Haven, Conn.: Yale University Press, 1981.

Naquin, Susan, and Evelyn S. Rawski. *Chinese Society in the Eighteenth Century.* New Haven, Conn.: Yale University Press, 1987.

Neel, James V., and Napoleon A. Chagnon. "The Demography of Two Tribes of Primitive, Relatively Unacculturated American Indians," *Proceedings of the National Academy of Sciences,* Vol. 59, No. 3 (March 1968), pp. 680–689.

Nelson, Joan M. *Migrants, Urban Poverty, and Instability in Developing Nations,* Occasional Papers in International Affairs No. 22. Cambridge, Mass.: Center for International Affairs, Harvard University, September 1969.

Nichols, R.H., and F.A. Wray. *The History of the Foundling Hospital.* London: Oxford University Press, 1935.

Nigg, Joanne M., and Dennis S. Mileti. "Natural Hazards and Disasters," in Riley E. Dunlop and William Michelson, eds., *Handbook of Environmental Sociology.* Greenwich, Conn.: Greenwood, 1991.

Nishimara, Gensho. "Ryu roku ryu nana no ran ni tsuite," *Toyoshi kenkyu* [Asian historical research], Vol. 32, No. 4 (1974), pp. 44–86.

Nyrop, Richard F., ed. *India: A Country Study,* Foreign Area Studies, the American University. Washington, D.C.: For sale by the Superintendent of Documents, U.S. Government Printing Office, 1985.

Oberai, A.S. *Population Growth, Employment, and Poverty in Third-World Mega-Cities.* New York: St. Martin's, 1993.

O'Donnell, Lynne. "Sex Imbalance Fuels China's Flesh Trade." January 4, 1999, http://www.freerepublic.com/forum/aa36904a553c75.htm.

Oldenburg, Philip. "Sex Ratio, Son Preference, and Violence in India: A Research Note," *Economic and Political Weekly*, December 5, 1992, pp. 2657–2662.

Oldenziel, Ruth. "The Historiography of Infanticide in Antiquity: A Literature Stillborn," in Josine Blok and Peter Mason, eds., *Sexual Asymmetry: Studies in Ancient Society*. Amsterdam: J.C. Gieben, 1987, pp. 87–107.

Olweus, Dan, Ake Mattsson, Daisy Schalling, and Hans Loew. "Circulating Testosterone Levels and Aggression in Adolescent Males: A Causal Analysis," *Psychosomatic Medicine*, Vol. 50, No. 3 (May–June 1988), pp. 261–272.

Ono, Kazuko. *Chinese Women in a Century of Revolution: 1850–1950*. Stanford, Calif.: Stanford University Press, 1989.

Opitz, Claudia. "Life in the Middle Ages," in Christiane Klapisch-Zuber, ed., *A History of Women in the West*, Vol. 2: *Silences of the Middle Ages*. Cambridge, Mass.: Belknap, 1992, pp. 267–317.

Ownby, David. "Approximations of Chinese Bandits: Perverse Rebels, Romantic Heroes, or Frustrated Bachelors?" in Susan Brownell and Jeffrey N. Wasserstrom, eds., *Chinese Femininities/Chinese Masculinities: A Reader*. Berkeley: University of California Press, 2002, pp. 226–253.

Ownby, David. *Brotherhoods and Secret Societies in Early and Mid-Qing China: The Formation of a Tradition*. Stanford, Calif.: Stanford University Press, 1996.

Ownby, David. "The Ethnic Feud in Qing Taiwan: What Is This Violence Business, Anyway? An Interpretation of the 1782 Zhang-Quan Xiedou," *Late Imperial China*, Vol. 11, No. 1 (June 1990), pp. 75–98.

Pakistan. Population Census Organization. "Table-1: Area, Population By Sex, Sex Ratio, Population Density, Urban Proportion, Household Size, and Annual Growth Rate," http://www.statpak.gov.pk/depts/pco/statistics/pop_table1/pop_table1.html.

Pakrasi, Kanti B. *Female Infanticide in India*. Calcutta: Editions India, 1970.

Panigrahi, Lalita. *British Social Policy and Female Infanticide in India*. New Delhi: Munshiram Manoharlal, 1972.

Pantel, Pauline Schmitt, ed. *A History of Women in the West*, Vol. 1: *From Ancient Goddesses to Christian Saints*. Cambridge, Mass.: Belknap, 1992.

Parikh, Manju. "Sex-Selective Abortions in India: Parental Choice or Sexist Discrimination?" *Feminist Issues* (Fall 1990), pp. 19–32.

Park Chai Bin. "Preference for Sons, Family Size, and Sex Ratio: An Empirical Study in Korea," *Demography*, Vol. 20, No. 3 (August 1983), pp. 332–352.

Park Chai Bin, and Cho Nam-hoon. "Consequences of Son Preference in a Low-Fertility Society: Imbalance of the Sex Ratio at Birth in Korea," *Population and Development Review*, Vol. 21, No. 1 (March 1995), pp. 59–84.

Parke, Charles Ross. *Dreams to Dust: A Diary of the California Gold Rush, 1849–1850*, ed. James E. Davis. Lincoln: University of Nebraska Press, 1989.

Parson, Edward A., and William Clark. "Sustainable Development as Social Learning: Theoretical Perspectives and Practical Challenges for the Design of a Research Program," in Lance H. Gunderson, C.S. Holling, and Stephen S. Light, eds., *Barriers and Bridges to the Renewal of Ecosystems and Institutions*. New York: Columbia University Press, 1995, pp. 428–460.

Patel, Vibhuti. "Sex Determination and Sex Preselection Tests in India: Modern Techniques for Femicide," *Bulletin of Concerned Asian Scholars*, Vol. 21, No. 1 (January–March 1989), pp. 2–11.

Pedersen, Frank A. "Secular Trends in Human Sex Ratios: Their Influence on Individual and Family Behavior," *Human Nature*, Vol. 2, No. 3 (1991), pp. 271–291.

Peggs, James. *Cries of Agony: An Historical Account of Suttee, Infanticide, Ghat Murders, and Slavery in India*. Originally published as *India's Cries to British Humanity*, 1830; reprint, Delhi: Discovery Publishing House, 1984.

Perkins, Roberta, G. Prestage, R. Sharp, and F. Lovejoy, eds. *Sex Work and Sex Workers in Australia*. Sydney: University of New South Wales, 1994.

Pernanen, Kai. "Alcohol-Related Violence: Conceptual Models," in Susan E. Martin, ed., *Alcohol and Interpersonal Violence: Fostering Multidisciplinary Perspectives*, NIAAA Research Monograph No. 24. Rockville, Md.: National Institutes of Health, 1993, pp. 37–69.

Perry, Elizabeth. *Rebels and Revolutionaries in North China, 1845–1945*. Stanford, Calif.: Stanford University Press, 1980.

Pomeroy, Sarah B. "Infanticide in Hellenistic Greece," in Averil Cameron and Amelie Kuhrt, eds., *Images of Women in Antiquity*. Detroit, Mich.: Wayne State University Press, 1993, pp. 207–222.

Population Census Office of the State Council of the People's Republic of China, and the Institute of Geography of the Chinese Academy of Sciences. *Population Atlas of China*. Oxford: Oxford University Press, 1987.

Poston, Dudley L., Jr., and David Yaukey, eds. *The Population of Modern China*. New York: Plenum, 1992.

Potter, Sulamith Heins. "Birth Planning in Rural China: A Cultural Account," in Nancy Scheper-Hughes, ed., *Child Survival: Anthropological Perspectives on the Treatment and Maltreatment of Children*. Dordrecht, Netherlands: D. Reidel, 1987.

Power, Eileen. *Medieval Women*, ed. Michael Moissey Postan. Cambridge: Cambridge University Press, 1975.

Prakash, Padma. "Decline in Sex Ratio," *Economic and Political Weekly*, December 19, 1992, p. 2670.

"PRC Family Planning: The Market Weakens Controls but Encourages Voluntary Limits," http://www.usembassy-china.org.cn/english/sandt/POPMYWB.html.

Premi, Mahendra K. "The Missing Girl Child," *Economic and Political Weekly*, May 26, 2001, pp. 1875–1880.

Premi, Mahendra K., and Saraswati Raju. "Born to Die: Female Infanticide in Madhya Pradesh," *Search Bulletin*, Vol. 13, No. 3 (July–September 1998), pp. 94–105.

Preston, Samuel H. *Mortality Patterns in National Populations with Special Reference to Recorded Causes of Death*. New York: Academic Press, 1976.

Prigogine, Ilya, and Isabelle Stengers. *Order Out of Chaos: Man's New Dialogue with Nature*. Boulder, Colo.: Shambala/New Science Library, 1984.

Protection of Chinese Women's Rights and Interests. Beijing: New Star, 1993.

Rabb, Theodore K., and Robert I. Rotberg, eds. *The Family in History: Interdisciplinary Essays.* New York: Harper and Row, 1971.

Rajan, S. Irudaya. "Decline in Sex Ratio: An Alternative Explanation?" *Economic and Political Weekly,* December 21, 1991, pp. 2963–2964.

Rajan, S. Irudaya. "Heading towards a Billion," *Economic and Political Weekly,* December 17, 1994, pp. 3201–3205.

Rajan, S. Irudaya, U.S. Mishra, and K. Navaneetham. "Decline in Sex Ratio: Alternative Explanation Revisited," *Economic and Political Weekly,* November 14, 1992, pp. 2505–2508.

Raju, Saraswati, and Mahendra K. Premi. "Decline in Sex Ratio: An Alternative Explanation Re-examined," *Economic and Political Weekly,* April 25, 1992, pp. 911–912.

Rawski, Thomas G., and Lillian M. Li, eds. *Chinese History in Economic Perspective.* Berkeley: University of California Press, 1992.

Redclift, Michael. *Development and the Environmental Crisis.* New York: Methuen, 1984.

Rees, Sian. *The Floating Brothel: The Extraordinary True Story of an Eighteenth-Century Ship and Its Cargo of Female Convicts.* New York: Theia/Hyperion, 2002.

Reeves, P.D., ed. *Sleeman in Oudh: An Abridgement of W.H. Sleeman's* A Journey through the Kingdom of Oude in 1849–50. Cambridge: Cambridge University Press, 1971.

Ren Feng. "Bare Branches among Rural Migrant Laborers in China: Causes, Social Implications, and Policy Proposal." Foreign Affairs College, Beijing, March 1999.

Ren Meng. "Confronting Three Populations of 80 Million," *Inside China Mainland,* Vol. 19, No. 1 (January 1997), pp. 78–81.

Ren, Xinhua Steve. "Sex Differences in Infant and Child Mortality in Three Provinces in China," *Social Science and Medicine,* Vol. 40, No. 9 (May 1995), pp. 1263–1264.

Renner, Michael. *National Security: The Economic and Environmental Dimensions,* Worldwatch Paper No. 89. Washington, D.C.: Worldwatch Institute, 1989.

Renteln, Alison Dundes. "Sex Selection and Reproductive Freedom," *Women's Studies International Forum,* Vol. 15, No. 3 (May–June 1992), pp. 405–426.

Riches, David. "The Netsilik Eskimo: A Special Case of Selective Female Infanticide," *Ethnology: An International Journal of Cultural and Social Anthropology,* Vol. 13, No. 4 (October 1974), pp. 351–361.

Riddle, John M. *Contraception and Abortion from the Ancient World to the Renaissance.* Cambridge, Mass.: Harvard University Press, 1992.

Risley, Herbert Hope. *The People of India,* ed. William Crooke. Delhi: Oriental Books Reprint Corporation, 1969.

Robinson, David M. "Banditry and Rebellion in the Capital Region during the Mid-Ming (1450–1525)," Ph.D. dissertation. Princeton University, 1995.

Robinson, David M. "The Management of Violence in the Mid-Ming Capital Region," Colgate University, 1998.

Robinson, David M. "Notes on Eunuchs in Hebei during the Mid-Ming Period," *Ming Studies,* Vol. 34 (July 1995), pp. 1–16.

Roizen, Judith. "Issues in the Epidemiology of Alcohol and Violence," in Susan E. Martin, ed., *Alcohol and Interpersonal Violence: Fostering Multidisciplinary Perspectives*, NIAAA Research Monograph No. 24. Rockville, Md.: National Institutes of Health, 1993, p. 3036.

Rooney, James F. "Societal Forces and the Unattached Male," in Howard M. Bahr, ed., *Disaffiliated Man: Essays and Bibliography on Skid Row, Vagrancy, and Outsiders*. Toronto: University of Toronto Press, 1970, pp. 13–38.

Roosevelt, Anna, ed. *Amazonian Indians from Prehistory to the Present: Anthropological Perspectives*. Tucson: University of Arizona Press, 1994.

Root-Bernstein, Robert. "How Scientists Really Think," *Perspectives in Biology and Medicine*, Vol. 32, No. 4 (Summer 1989), pp. 472–490.

Rose, Lionel. *The Massacre of the Innocents: Infanticide in Britain, 1800–1939*. London: Routledge and Kegan Paul, 1986.

Rouselle, Aline. "Body Politics in Ancient Rome," in Pauline Schmitt Pantel, ed., *A History of Women in the West*, Vol. 1: *From Ancient Goddesses to Christian Saints*. Cambridge, Mass.: Belknap, 1992, pp. 296–336.

Rozman, Gilbert. *Population and Marketing Settlements in Ch'ing China*. Cambridge, Mass.: Cambridge University Press, 1982.

Russell, J.K. "Exclusion of Adult Male Coatis from Social Groups: Protection from Predation," *Journal of Mammalogy*, Vol. 62, No. 1 (February 1981), pp. 206–208.

Sachar, R.K., J. Verma, V. Prakash, A. Chopra, R. Adlaka, and R. Sofat. "Sex-Selective Fertility Control—An Outrage," *Journal of Family Welfare*, Vol. 36, No. 2 (June 1991), pp. 30–35.

Sampson, Robert J., and John H. Laub. *Crime in the Making: Pathways and Turning Points through Life*. Cambridge, Mass.: Harvard University Press, 1993.

Sanchez, Roberto. "Vulnerability of Urban Areas in Latin America to Climate Change," paper presented at the First Open Meeting of the Human Dimensions of Global Change Community, Duke University, Durham, North Carolina, June 1–3, 1995.

Sarda, Har Bilas. *History of Ancient Hindu Society: An Attempt to Determine the Position of the Hindu Race in the Scale of Nations*. Delhi: Anmol, 1985.

Scheper-Hughes, Nancy, ed. *Child Survival: Anthropological Perspectives on the Treatment and Maltreatment of Children*. Dordrecht, Netherlands: D. Reidel, 1987.

Schran, Peter. "China's Demographic Evolution 1850–1953 Reconsidered," *China Quarterly*, No. 75 (September 1978), pp. 639–646.

Scrimshaw, Susan. "Infanticide in Human Populations: Societal and Individual Concerns," in Glenn Hausfater and Sarah Blaffer Hrdy, eds., *Infanticide: Comparative and Evolutionary Perspectives*. New York: Aldine de Gruyter, 1984, pp. 439–462.

Sen, Amartya. *Development as Freedom*. New York: Alfred A. Knopf, 1999.

Sen, Amartya. "Missing Women," *British Medical Journal*, March 7, 1992, pp. 587–588.

Sen, Amartya. "More Than 100 Million Women Are Missing," *New York Review of Books*, December 20, 1990, pp. 61–66.

Sen, Amartya. *Poverty and Famines*. Oxford: Clarendon, 1981.

Sen, Gita, and Rachel C. Snow, eds. *Power and Decision: The Social Control of Reproduction.* Cambridge, Mass.: Harvard University Press, 1994.

Seth, Swapan. "Two-Way Movement of Sex Ratio," *Economic and Political Weekly,* October 5, 1996, pp. 2730–2733.

Seymour, James D., and Richard Anderson. *New Ghosts, Old Ghosts: Prisons and Labor Reform Camps in China.* London: M.E. Sharpe, 1998.

Shah, A.M., B.S. Baviskar, and E.A. Ramaswampy, eds. *Social Structure and Change,* Vol. 2: *Women in Indian Society.* New Delhi: Sage, 1996.

Shahidullah, M. "Breast-Feeding and Child Survival in Matlab, Bangladesh," *Journal of Biosocial Science,* Vol. 26, No. 2 (1994), pp. 143–154.

Shakur, Sanyika. *Monster: The Autobiography of an L.A. Gang Member.* New York: Atlantic Monthly Press, 1993.

Sharma, Brij Narain. *Social Life in Northern India [A.D. 600–1000],* foreword by A.L. Basham. Delhi: Munshiram Manoharlal, 1966.

Shepherd, John Robert. *Statecraft and Political Economy on the Taiwan Frontier, 1600–1800.* Stanford, Calif.: Stanford University Press, 1993.

Shiva, Vandana. *Staying Alive: Women, Ecology, and Development.* London: Zed, 1989.

Simmons, George B., Celeste Smucker, Stan Bernstein, and Eric Jensen. "Post-Neonatal Mortality in Rural North India: Implications of an Economic Model," *Demography,* Vol. 19, No. 3 (August 1982), pp. 371–390.

Singer, Milton, and Bernard S. Cohn, eds. *Structure and Change in Indian Society.* Chicago: Aldine de Gruyter, 1968.

Singh, Shri Nath, ed. *Population Transition in India.* Delhi: B.R. Publishing Corporation, 1989.

Situ, Yingyi, and Liu Weizheng. "Transient Population, Crime, and Solution: The Chinese Experience," *International Journal of Offender Therapy and Comparative Criminology,* Vol. 40, No. 4 (December 1996), pp. 293–299.

Smith, Arthur Henderson. *Village Life in China: A Study in Sociology.* New York: F.H. Revell, 1899.

Smith, Eric Alden, and S. Abigail Smith. "Inuit Sex-Ratio Variation: Population Control, Ethnographic Error, or Parental Manipulation?" *Current Anthropology,* Vol. 35, No. 5 (December 1994), pp. 595–624.

Smith, George. *A Narrative of an Exploratory Visit to Each of the Consular Cities of China and to the Islands of Hong Kong and Chusan on Behalf of the Church Missionary Society in the Years 1844, 1845, 1846.* London: Seeley, Burnside, and Seeley, 1847.

Smith, Herbert L. "Nonreporting of Births or Nonreporting of Pregnancies? Some Evidence from Four Rural Counties in North China," *Demography,* Vol. 31, No. 3 (August 1994), pp. 481–486.

Smith, Herbert L., Tu Ping, M. Giovanna Merli, and Mark Hereward. "Implementation of a Demographic and Contraceptive Surveillance System in Four Counties in North China," *Population Research and Policy Review,* Vol. 16, No. 4 (August 1997), pp. 289–314.

Smith, Richard J. *China's Cultural Heritage: The Ch'ing Dynasty, 1644–1912.* Boulder, Colo.: Westview, 1983.

Smith, Thomas C., ed., with Robert Y. Eng and Robert T. Lundy. *Nakahara: Family Farming and Population in a Japanese Village, 1717–1830*. Stanford, Calif.: Stanford University Press, 1977.

Sommerfelt, Elisabeth, and Fred Arnold. "Sex Differentials in the Nutritional Status of Young Children," in United Nations, Population Division of the Department of Social and Economic Affairs, *Too Young to Die: Genes or Gender?* New York: United Nations, 1998, pp. 133–153.

South, Scott J., and Katherine Trent. "Sex Ratios and Women's Roles: A Cross-National Analysis," *American Journal of Sociology*, Vol. 93, No. 5 (March 1988), pp. 1096–1115.

South Korea (Republic of Korea). *2001 Report of the National Statistical Office of South Korea*. Seoul: National Statistical Office, July 2001.

South Korea (Republic of Korea). "Census Population 2000." Seoul: National Statistical Office, 2000, http://www.nso.go.kr.

Srikumar, K.P. "Amniocentesis and the Future of the Girl Child," in Leelamma Devasia and V.V. Devasia, eds., *Girl Child in India*. New Delhi: Ashish Publishing House, 1989, pp. 51–65.

Stacey, Judith. *Patriarchy and Socialist Revolution in China*. Berkeley: University of California Press, 1983.

Stern, Paul, Oran Young, and Daniel Druckman, eds. *Global Environmental Change: Understanding the Human Dimensions*. Washington, D.C.: National Academy Press, 1992.

Suhrke, Astri. "Pressure Points: Environmental Degradation, Migration, and Conflict," Occasional Paper No. 3. Toronto: Project on Environmental Change and Acute Conflict, University of Toronto and the American Academy of Arts and Sciences, March 1993.

Sumner, William Graham. *Folkways*. New York: Dover, 1959.

Svare, Bruce B., ed. *Hormones and Aggressive Behavior*. New York: Plenum, 1983.

Taiwan (Republic of China). *The Republic of China Yearbook—Taiwan, 2002*. Taipei: Ministry of the Interior, 2002, http://www.gio.gov.tw/taiwan-website/5-gp/yearbook/chpt02–1.htm#1.

Tao Chun fung, ed. *General View of the Social Status of Women*. Beijing: Chinese Women's Publishing House, 1991.

Taylor, Jeffrey R., and Judith Banister. "China: The Problem of Employing Surplus Rural Labor," CIR Staff Paper No. 49. Washington, D.C.: Center for International Research, U.S. Bureau of the Census, July 1989.

Taylor, Michael, ed. *Rationality and Revolution*. Cambridge: Cambridge University Press, 1988.

ter Harr, Barend J. *The White Lotus Teachings in Chinese Religious History*. Leiden, Netherlands: E.J. Brill, 1992.

Tern, Warren M. "Health and Demography of Native Amazonians: Historical Perspective and Current Status," in Anna Roosevelt, ed., *Amazonian Indians from Prehistory to the Present: Anthropological Perspectives*. Tucson: University of Arizona Press, 1994, pp. 123–149.

Thomas, Keith. "Fateful Exposure," *Times Literary Supplement*, August 25–31, 1989, pp. 913–914.

Thompson, Drew. "HIV/AIDS Epidemic in China Spreads into the General Population." Population Reference Bureau, http://www.prb.org/Template.cfm?Section=PRB&template=/ContentManagement/ContentDisplay.cfm&ContentID=8501.

Thompson, M. "Postscript: A Cultural Basis for Comparison," in Howard C. Kunreuther and Joanne Linnerooth, eds., *Risk Analysis and Decision Processes: The Siting of Liquified Energy Gas Facilities in Four Countries*. Berlin: Springer-Verlag, 1983, pp. 232–262.

Thornhill, Randy, and Nancy Thornhill. "Human Rape: An Evolutionary Analysis," *Ethology and Sociobiology*, Vol. 4, No. 3 (1983), pp. 137–173.

Tien, H. Yuan. "Abortion in China: Incidence and Implications," in Dudley L. Poston Jr. and David Yaukey, eds., *The Population of Modern China*. New York: Plenum, 1992, pp. 287–310.

Tien, H. Yuan. *China's Strategic Demographic Initiative*. New York: Praeger, 1991.

Tien, H. Yuan. "Provincial Fertility Trends and Patterns," in Elisabeth J. Croll, Delia Davin, and Penny Kane, eds., *China's One-Child Family Policy*. New York: St. Martin's, 1985, pp. 114–134.

Tien, H. Yuan, Zhang Tianlu, Ping Yu, Li Jingneng, and Lian Zhongtang. "China's Demographic Dilemmas," *Population Bulletin*, Vol. 47, No. 1 (June 1992), pp. 1–34.

T'ien Ju-k'ang. *Male Anxiety and Female Chastity: A Comparative Study of Chinese Ethical Values in Ming-Ch'ing Times*. New York: E.J. Brill, 1988.

Tiger, Lionel. *Men in Groups*. London: Marion Boyars, 1984.

Timœus, Ian, Katie Harris, and Francesca Fairbairn. "Can Use of Health Care Explain Sex Differentials in Child Mortality in the Developing World?" in United Nations, Population Division of the Department of Economic and Social Affairs, *Too Young to Die: Genes or Gender?* New York: United Nations, 1998, p. 156.

Tong, James. "Rational Outlaws: Rebels and Bandits in the Ming Dynasty, 1368–1644," in Michael Taylor, ed., *Rationality and Revolution*. Cambridge: Cambridge University Press, 1988, pp. 98–128.

Torry, W. "Anthropological Studies in Hazardous Environments: Past Trends and New Horizons," *Current Anthropology*, Vol. 20 (1979), pp. 517–540.

"Tougher Actions toward Crime," *Beijing Review*, May 20–26, 1996, p. 6.

Trexler, Richard C. "The Foundlings of Florence, 1395–1455," *History of Childhood Quarterly: The Journal of Psychohistory*, Vol. 1, No. 2 (Fall 1973), pp. 259–284.

Trexler, Richard C. "Infanticide in Florence: New Sources and First Results," *History of Childhood Quarterly: The Journal of Psychohistory*, Vol. 1, No. 1 (Summer 1973), pp. 98–116.

Tsai, Henry Shih-shan. *The Eunuchs in the Ming Dynasty*. Albany: State University of New York Press, 1996.

UNICEF (United Nations Children's Fund). *Statistical Review of the Situation of Children in the World*. New York: UNICEF, 1986.

United Nations. *The World's Women, 1995: Trends and Statistics*. New York: United Nations, 1995.

United Nations. *The World's Women, 2000: Trends and Statistics*, http://unstats.un.org/unsd/demographic/ww2000/.

United Nations. Department for Economic and Social Information and Policy Analysis. Population Division. *The Sex and Age Distribution of the World Populations: The 1994 Revision*. New York: United Nations, 1994.

United Nations. Department of International and Economic Social Affairs. *Consequences of Mortality Trends and Differentials*. Population Studies No. 95. New York: United Nations, 1986.

United Nations. Department of International and Economic Social Affairs. *World Population Prospects, 1990*. Population Studies No. 120. New York: United Nations, 1991.

United Nations. Department of Social Affairs. Population Division. *Foetal, Infant, and Early Childhood Mortality*, Vol. 1: *The Statistics*. Populations Studies No. 13. New York: United Nations, 1954.

United Nations. Population Division of the Department of Economic and Social Affairs. "The 1998 Revision of the United Nations Population Projections," *Population and Development Review*, Vol. 24, No. 4 (December 1998), pp. 891–895.

United Nations. Population Division of the Department of Economic and Social Affairs. *Too Young to Die: Genes or Gender?* New York: United Nations, 1998.

United Nations. Population Division of the Department of Economic and Social Affairs. *World Population Prospects: The 2002 Revision* and *World Urbanization Prospects: The 2001 Revision*, http://esa.un.org/unpp.

United Nations Development Programme. *India: The Road to Human Development*. India Development Forum, Paris, June 23–25, 1997, document of the United Nations Development Programme, New Delhi, http://www.undp.org.in/REPORT/IDF97/default.htm.

"Urbanization: A Long-Term Solution to Unemployment," *Beijing Review*, March 20, 2003, pp. 28–29.

U.S. Bureau of the Census. International Data Base, 1998, http://www.census.gov/ipc/www/idbnew.html/.

Vallois, Henri V. "The Social Life of Early Man: The Evidence of Skeletons," in Sherwood L. Washburn, ed., *Social Life of Early Man*. New York: Wenner-Gren Foundation for Anthropological Research, 1961, pp. 214–235.

van Gulik, Robert Hans. *Sexual Life in Ancient China: A Preliminary Survey of Chinese Sex and Society from ca. 1500 B.C. till 1644 A.D.* Leiden, Netherlands: E.J. Brill, 1974.

Vasudev, Shefalee, and Methil Renuka. "Sexual Crimes: Rape!" *India Today*, September 9, 2002, pp. 1, 48.

Visaria, Leela, and Pravin Visaria. "India's Population in Transition, *Population Bulletin*, Vol. 50, No. 3 (October 1995), pp. 2–49.

Visaria, Pravin M. "Indian Population Problem: Emerging Perspective after the 1991 Census, *Demography India*, Vol. 20, No. 2 (July–December 1991), pp. 273–295.

Vishwanath, L.S., "Female Infanticide and the Position of Women in India," in A.M. Shah, B.S. Baviskar, and E.A. Ramaswampy, eds., *Social Structure and Change*, Vol. 2: *Women in Indian Society*. New Delhi: Sage, 1996, pp. 179–205.

Vlassoff, Carol. "The Value of Sons in an Indian Village: How Widows See It," *Population Studies*, Vol. 44, No. 1 (March 1990), pp. 5–20.

Wadley, Susan S. "Family Composition Strategies in Rural North India," *Social Science and Medicine*, Vol. 37, No. 11 (December 1993), pp. 1367–1376.

Walker, B.H., and A.R.E. Sinclair. "Problems of Development Aid," *Nature*, February 15, 1990, p. 587.

Walter, Ann. *Getting an Heir: Adoption and the Construction of Kinship in Late Imperial China*. Honolulu: University of Hawaii Press, 1990.

Walter, Ann. "Infanticide and Dowry in Ming and Early Qing China," in Anne Behnke Kinney, ed., *Chinese Views of Childhood*. Honolulu: University of Hawaii Press, 1995.

Walton, John, and David Seddon. *Free Markets and Food Riots: The Politics of Global Adjustment*. Cambridge, Mass.: Blackwell, 1994.

Ware, Helen R. "Differential Mortality Decline and Its Consequences for the Status and Roles of Women," in *Consequences of Mortality Trends and Differentials*, Population Studies No. 95. New York: Department of International Economic and Social Affairs, United Nations, 1986, pp. 113–125.

Warren, Mary Anne. *Gendercide: The Implication of Sex Selection*. Totowa, N.J.: Rowman and Allanheld, 1985.

Washburn, Sherwood L., ed. *Social Life of Early Man*. New York: Wenner-Gren Foundation for Anthropological Research, 1961.

Watson, James L. "Self-Defense Corps, Violence, and the Bachelor Subculture in South China: Two Case Studies." *Proceedings of the Second International Conference on Sinology*. Taiwan (Republic of China): Academia Sinica, June 1989.

Watson, Rubie S. "Afterword: Marriage and Gender Inequality," in Rubie S. Watson and Patricia Buckley Ebrey, eds., *Marriage and Inequality in Chinese Society*. Berkeley: University of California Press, 1991, pp. 347–368.

Watson, Rubie S., and Patricia Buckley Ebrey, eds. *Marriage and Inequality in Chinese Society*. Berkeley: University of California Press, 1991.

Watts, Michael. "Entitlements or Empowerments? Famine and Starvation in Africa," *Review of African Political Economy*, Vol. 19, No. 51 (July 1991), pp. 9–26.

Watts, Michael. *Silent Violence: Food, Famine, and Peasantry in Northern Nigeria*. Berkeley: University of California Press, 1983.

Watts, Michael J., and Hans-Georg Bohle. "The Space of Vulnerability: The Causal Structure of Hunger and Famine," *Progress in Human Geography*, Vol. 17, No. 1 (March 1993), pp. 43–67.

Wen Xingyan. "Effect of Son Preference and Population Policy on Sex Ratios at Birth in Two Provinces of China," *Journal of Biosocial Science*, Vol. 25, No. 4 (October 1993), pp. 509–521.

Westermarck, Edward. *The Origin and Development of the Moral Ideas*. London: Macmillan, 1924.

Westing, Arthur H., ed. *Global Resources and International Conflict: Environmental Factors in Strategic Policy and Action*. Oxford: Oxford University Press, 1986.

"Where Have All the Daughters Gone?" *Sinorama Magazine*, http://www.taiwaninfo.org/info/sinorama/8502/502006e1.html.

White, Gilbert F., ed. *Natural Hazards: Local, National, Global*. New York: Oxford, 1974.

White, Gilbert F., and John Eugene Haas. *Assessment of Research on Natural Hazards*. Cambridge, Mass.: MIT Press, 1975.

Whyte, Martin King. "Social Trends and the Human Rights Situation in the PRC." George Washington University, 1998.

"The Wild East: Guns in China," *Economist*, November 10, 2001, p. 75.

Wildavsky, Aaron B., and Mary Douglas. *Risk and Culture: An Essay on the Selection of Technical and Environmental Dangers*. Berkeley: University of California Press, 1982.

Wiley, Bell I. *The Life of Billy Yank: The Common Soldier of the Union*. Baton Rouge: Louisiana State University Press, 1978.

Williams, Christopher. "Environmental Victims," paper presented at the First Open Meeting of the Human Dimensions of Global Change Community, Duke University, Durham, North Carolina, June 1–3, 1995.

Williamson, Laila. "Infanticide: An Anthropological Analysis," in Marvin Kohl, ed., *Infanticide and the Value of Human Life*. New York: Prometheus, 1978, pp. 61–75.

Williamson, Nancy E. *Sons or Daughters: A Cross-Cultural Survey of Parental Preferences*. London: Sage, 1976.

Wilson, Margo, and Martin Daly. "Competitiveness, Risk Taking, and Violence: The Young Male Syndrome," *Ethology and Sociobiology*, Vol. 6, No. 1 (1985), pp. 59–73.

Winston, Sanford. "Birth Control and Sex Ratio at Birth," *American Journal of Sociology*, Vol. 38, No. 2 (September 1932), pp. 225–231.

Woirol, Gregory R. *In the Floating Army*. Chicago: University of Illinois Press, 1992.

Wolf, Arthur P., and Chieh-shan Huang. *Marriage and Adoption in China, 1845–1945*. Stanford, Calif.: Stanford University Press, 1980.

Wolf, Margery. *Revolution Postponed: Women in Contemporary China*. Stanford, Calif.: Stanford University Press, 1985.

Wolpert, Stanley. *India*. Berkeley: University of California Press, 1991.

Wolpert, Stanley. *A New History of India*, 4th ed. New York: Oxford University Press, 1993.

Wong, Linda. "China's Urban Migrants—The Public Policy Challenge," *Pacific Affairs*, Vol. 67, No. 3 (Autumn 1994), pp. 335–355.

Wooster, Robert. *Soldiers, Sutlers, and Settlers: Garrison Life on the Texas Frontier*. College Station: Texas A&M University Press, 1987.

World Bank. *World Population Projections, 1994–95 Edition: Estimates and Projections with Related Demographic Statistics*. Washington, D.C.: World Bank, 1994.

World Health Organization. *Women's Health in South-East Asia*, http://w3.whosea.org/women/index.htm.

World Vision International. "The Girl Child: Female He Created Them," *World Vision Today* (Spring 1998), p. 2.

Worster, Donald. "The Ecology of Order and Chaos," *Environmental History Review*, Vol. 14, Nos. 1–2 (Spring/Summer 1990), pp. 1–18.

Wrangham, Richard, and Dale Peterson. *Demonic Males: Apes and the Origins of Human Violence*. New York: Houghton Mifflin, 1996.

Wright, David. "Rebellion on the Chinese Frontier: The Lin Shuang-wen Uprising in Taiwan, 1787–1788," *Thetean* (April 1987), pp. 54–84.

Wright, Robert. *The Moral Animal*. New York: Pantheon, 1994.

Xu Song. "A Quest on the Causes of Gender Imbalance in China." Foreign Affairs College, Beijing, May 1999.

Yang Ji. "Transient Workers: A Special Social Group" and "Educating Transient Workers," *Beijing Review*, June 3–9, 1996, pp. 20–21.

Yao, Esther S. Lee. *Chinese Women: Past and Present*. Mesquite, Tex.: Ide House, 1983.

Ye Wenzhen and Lin Qingguo. "The Reasons and Countermeasures for Demographic Phenomena in China," *Chinese Demography*, Vol. 4 (1998).

Yen Chih-t'ui. *Family Instructions for the Yen Clan: Yen-Shih Chia-Hsun*, trans. Teng Ssu-yu. Leiden, Netherlands: E.J. Brill, 1968.

Yu Xie. "Measuring Regional Variation in Sex Preference in China: A Cautionary Note," *Social Science Research*, Vol. 18, No. 3 (September 1989), pp. 291–305.

Yulman, Nur. "On the Purity of Women in the Castes of Ceylon and Malabar," *Journal of the Royal Anthropological Society*, Vol. 93, Pt. 1 (January–June 1963), pp. 42–43.

Yutang, Lin. *My Country and My People*. New York: Reynal and Hitchcock, 1935.

Zeng Yi, Tu Ping, Gu Baochang, Xu Yi, Li Bohua, and Li Yongping. "Causes and Implications of the Recent Increase in the Reported Sex Ratio at Birth in China," *Population and Development Review*, Vol. 19, No. 2 (June 1993), pp. 283–302.

Zerner-Chardavoine, Monique. "Enfants et jeunes au IXe siècle : La démographie du polyptype de Marseille, 813–814," *Provence historique*, No. 126 (1981), pp. 335–384.

Zhang Haiyang. "On Flowing Population in Qiqiha'er: Current Conditions and Management," *Plan Study*, n.s., Vol. 5 (1997).

Zhang Ping. "Issues and Characteristics of the Unmarried Population," *Chinese Journal of Population Science*, Vol. 2, No. 1 (1990), pp. 87–97.

Zhang Xiaohui, Wu Zhigang, and Chen Liangbiao. "Age Difference among the Rural Labor Force in Interrregional Migration," *Chinese Journal of Population Science*, Vol. 9, No. 3 (1997), pp. 193–202.

Zhao Yi. *The Population, Resources, Environment, Agriculture, and Continuous Development of 21st Century China*. Shan Xi: Economic Publishing House, 1997.

Zhong, Anita. "China's Aging Population and China's Economy." Foreign Affairs College, Beijing, May 23, 1999.

Zillmann, Dolf. *Connections between Sex and Aggression*. Hillsdale, N.J.: Lawrence Erlbaum, 1984.

Zimmerer, Karl S. "Human Geography and the 'New Ecology': The Prospect and Promise of Integration," *Annals of the Association of American Geographers*, Vol. 84, No. 1 (March 1994), pp. 108–125.

Bare Branches: The Security Implication of Asia's Surplus Male Population
By Valerie M. Hudson and Andrea M. den Boer
Copyright © 2004 by the Belfer Center for Science and International Affairs
John F. Kennedy School of Government, Harvard University
Published by The MIT Press
Simplified Chinese Translation Copyright © 2016 by Central Compilation & Translation Press
All Rights Reserved

图书在版编目（CIP）数据

光棍危机：亚洲男性人口过剩的安全启示／（美）瓦莱丽·M. 赫德森，（英）安德莉亚·M. 邓波尔著；邱彰译. —北京：中央编译出版社，2016.8
书名原文：Bare Branches: The Security Implication of Asia's Surplus Male Population
ISBN 978-7-5117-3058-9

Ⅰ. ①光…
Ⅱ. ①瓦… ②安… ③邱…
Ⅲ. ①男性－人口过剩－影响－国家安全－研究－亚洲
Ⅳ. ①C924.3 ②D730.35

中国版本图书馆 CIP 数据核字（2016）第 165647 号

光棍危机：亚洲男性人口过剩的安全启示

出 版 人：	葛海彦
出版统筹：	贾宇琰
责任编辑：	贾宇琰
责任印制：	尹 珺
出版发行：	中央编译出版社
地　　址：	北京西城区车公庄大街乙5号鸿儒大厦B座（100044）
电　　话：	（010）52612345（总编室）　（010）52612375（编辑室）
	（010）52612316（发行部）　（010）52612317（网络销售）
	（010）52612346（馆配部）　（010）55626985（读者服务部）
传　　真：	（010）66515838
经　　销：	全国新华书店
印　　刷：	北京紫瑞利印刷有限公司
开　　本：	787 毫米×1092 毫米　1/16
字　　数：	306 千字
印　　张：	19
版　　次：	2016 年 8 月第 1 版第 1 次印刷
定　　价：	59.00 元
网　　址：	www.cctphome.com　　邮　箱：cctp@cctphome.com
新浪微博：	@中央编译出版社　　　　微　信：中央编译出版社(ID: cctphome)
淘宝店铺：	中央编译出版社直销店(http://shop108367160.taobao.com)
	（010）52612349

本社常年法律顾问：北京嘉润律师事务所律师　李敬伟　问小牛
凡有印装质量问题，本社负责调换，电话：（010）55626985